BIOVIOLENCE: PREVENTING BIOLOGICAL TERROR AND CRIME

Bioviolence is the hostile infliction of disease. Terrorists or criminals could use disease to cause catastrophic consequences and panic, making everyone vulnerable. Too little is being done to prevent bioviolence, and accelerating advances of bioscience open new threat potential. While bio-offenders are becoming more focused and organized, prevention policies are vague, gap-ridden, and unsupervised. No other threat presents such severe danger yet such a failure of leadership to reduce risks. This book explores how global governance should evolve to address bioviolence challenges. Law enforcers, scientists, and public health officials should coordinate their prevention efforts. Nations and international organizations, especially the United Nations, need to cooperatively improve humanity's security. Altogether, the strategy for preventing bioviolence requires a global covenant to promote bioscience while understanding its inherent and unavoidable dangers.

Barry Kellman is professor of international law and Director of the International Weapons Control Center at DePaul University College of Law. He is Special Advisor to the Interpol Program on Prevention of Bio-Crimes and senior chair of the American Bar Association Committee on International Law and Security. Professor Kellman served on the National Academies of Sciences Committee on Research Standards and Practices to Prevent the Destructive Application of Biotechnology (2003). He was Legal Advisor to the National Commission on Terrorism and was later commissioned by the Memorial Institute for the Prevention of Terrorism (MIPT) to draft *Managing Terrorism's Consequences*, which reviews legal authorities for responding to terrorism in the United States. He has published widely on weapons proliferation and smuggling, the laws of armed conflict, Middle East arms control, and nuclear nonproliferation.

BIOVIOLENCE

Preventing Biological Terror and Crime

BARRY KELLMAN

DePaul University College of Law

CAMBRIDGE
UNIVERSITY PRESS

CAMBRIDGE UNIVERSITY PRESS
Cambridge, New York, Melbourne, Madrid, Cape Town, Singapore, São Paulo,
Delhi

Cambridge University Press
32 Avenue of the Americas, New York, NY 10013-2473, USA

www.cambridge.org
Information on this title: www.cambridge.org/9780521883252

First published 2007

Printed in the United States of America

A catalog record for this publication is available from the British Library.

Library of Congress Cataloging in Publication Data

Kellman, Barry. Bioviolence : preventing biological terror and crime / Barry
Kellman.
      p. ; cm.
Includes bibliographical references and index.
ISBN 978-0-521-88325-2 (hardback) – ISBN 978-0-521-70969-9 (pbk.)
1. Bioterrorism.   2. Bioterrorism – Prevention.   I. Title.
[DNLM: 1.   Bioterrorism – prevention & control.   2. Biomedical Research.
3. Bioterrorism – legislation & jurisprudence.   4. International Cooperation.
5. Public Health.   6. Public Policy. WA 295 K29b 2007]
HV6433.3.K45   2007
363.325'37–dc22   2007016153

ISBN   978-0-521-88325-2 hardback
ISBN   978-0-521-70969-9 paperback

For

Aly, Bobby, and Shannon
and Theirs and Theirs and Theirs

May This Book's Fears Prove Illusory

Contents

Prologue   *page* xiii

Foreword, by Ronald K. Noble, Interpol Secretary General   xvii

Acknowledgments   xxvii

Introduction 1

     The Bioviolence Policy Failure   2

     Thematic Foundations   3

         Three Crossroads   3

         Law for Humanity   4

     Terminology   5

     Presentation of the Argument   7

PART I. THE BIOVIOLENCE CONDITION AND HOW IT CAME TO BE

1   **Why Worry?** 11

     Why Bioviolence Is Different   11

         Delayed Anonymity   12

         Concealable Devastation   15

         Contagious Panic!!!   17

     Evaluating Risks   18

2   **Methods of Bioviolence** 20

     Interwoven Choices   21

     Smallpox   24

         Eradication?   24

         The Challenge: Getting the Virus   25

Influenza and Hemorrhagic Fevers 28
  Influenza 28
    Reasons for Concern 28
    Limits of Protection 29
  Hemorrhagic Fever Viruses 31
    Acquiring the Agent: Initiating the Attack 31
    Disseminating the Virus 32
Anthrax 33
  Getting and Cultivating Seed Stock 35
  Disseminating the Agent 36
Botulinum in Food 38
Agroviolence 40
  Motivations and Feasibility 41
  Attacks of Grave Concern 42
    Livestock Diseases 42
    Crop Diseases 43
  International Prevention Systems 44
Agents Historically Used as Bioweapons 45
  Plague 45
  Tularemia 46
  Q Fever 47
  Ricin 47
Emerging Micro-Sciences and Bioviolence 47
  Molecular Biology's Emerging Risk 49
    Modification of Weapons Agents 49
    Improving Target Specificity 51
  Synthetic Genomics 51
    Re-Creation of Diseases 51
    Synthetic Viruses 52
    RNA Inhibitors and Bioregulators 52
  Nanotechnologies 53

3 **Who Did Bioviolence? Who Wants to Do It?** **55**

The Biological Weapons Experience 55
  The Road to Geneva 56
  Mid-20th-Century Bioweapons Programs 56
    Unit 731 57
    The U.S. Offensive Bioweapons Program 57
    The Soviet Biological Weapons Program 59
    Iraq's Biological Weapons Program 61

South Africa's Project Coast   63

Egypt   64

Israel   65

Current (Alleged) State Biological Weapons Programs   66

Questions about Military Efficacy   67

Suspected State Bioweapons Programs   68

North Korea   69

Iran   70

Syria   71

Terrorist and Fanatic Interest in Bioviolence   71

Islamic Fundamentalist Interest in Bioviolence   72

Al Qaeda's Intentions   73

Religious and "Legal" Justification   74

Acquisition of Agents and Expertise   77

Production   78

Concluding Observations   82

PART II. THE GLOBAL STRATEGY FOR PREVENTING BIOVIOLENCE

4   Strategic Foundations **87**

The Indictment   88

Obstacles to Policy Progress   92

Bioviolence Is a Crime!   94

Overview of the Prevention Strategy   95

Complication   96

Resistance   96

Preparedness   97

Nonproliferation   98

Guiding Principles   98

5   Complication: What Law Enforcers Should Stop **101**

Irresponsible Gaps   102

The Logic of Complication   103

Denial + Interdiction   104

Bioscience's Anxieties   105

Registration and Census   108

Denial Tactics   109

Denying Access to Pathogens   109

Pathogen Census   111

Pathogen Marking   111
Denying Access to Laboratories   112
Denying Access to Equipment   114
Interdiction   116
Legislating the Crime   117
The Dilemma of Pre-Attack Interdiction   118
Clues of Bioviolence   119
Pattern Recognition   121
Transport Security and Counter-Smuggling   124
Packaging and Labeling   126
Shipping Security   127
Intrusive Counter-Smuggling   129

6   **Improving Resistance through Science** **132**

Dual-Implication Research   133
The Challenge of Overseeing Bioresearch   134
Constraining Science?   137
Virtues and Limitations of Codes of Ethics and
     Self-Regulation   139
The Need for Translucency   142
Bioscientists as the First Line of Defense   144
Bioresearch Education and Training   144
Professional Certification   145
Whistleblowers   146
Development of Vaccines and Medicines   147
Financial Barriers   149
Liability Barriers   152
Patent Barriers   155

7   **Public Health Preparedness** **160**

Preparedness vs. Complication – The False Debate   161
Hardening Targets   164
Protecting Air Circulation Systems   165
Protecting Water Supplies   165
Sensors   166
Response Interventions   168
Detecting and Analyzing a Bioviolence Attack   169
Law Enforcement – Public Health Cooperation   171
Biosurveillance   171
Microbial Forensics   172

Containing Contagion   173
  Compulsory Vaccination for First Responders   175
  Placement of Victims   178
  Stockpiling and Distribution of Medical Resources   179
  Compulsory Medical Interventions   181
Maintaining Public Confidence   184
Quarantines   185
Considerations of a Quarantine's Efficacy   186
Quarantines and the World Health Organization's
  Authority   188

8   International Nonproliferation **192**

Defining Biological Weapons   196
The General Purpose Criterion   196
"Nonlethal" Bioagents   197
  Arguments For and Against Nonlethal Bioagents   198
  Types of NLBAs   200
  U.S. Military Nonlethal Programs   202
  Implications for the Biological Weapons Convention   204
Compliance, Verification, and Confidence Building   205
The Biodefense Dilemma   207
  The Problem of Secrecy Reprised   209
  Biodefense Projects of Concern   211
Strengthening Confidence   213
Disarming Soviet Bioweapons Stockpiles   215
Two Issues for Removal   219
Protecting the Free Trade in Bioscience   220
A Global BWC Organization   221

9   The Challenge of Global Governance **222**

Governance Mission: The Global Covenant   222
Governance Agencies   226
The United Nations Commission on Bioscience and
  Security (Commission)   228
  Promote Bioscience Research   228
  Define Standards for Bioscience   230
  Promote Capacity Building and Resource Mobilization   231
The Bioviolence Prevention Office (Office)   233
  Information Gathering and Analysis   234
  Impelling Implementation   235

United Nations Bioviolence Committee (Security Council
    Committee)   238
   Predecessors   239
   A New Inspectorate   240
   A Final Note on Governance   241

Conclusion **242**

Notes   247
Bibliography   285
Index   355

Prologue

As this book is written, civil war and insurgency inflame Iraq; Palestinians and Israelis unrelentingly clash; and genocide perpetuates in Darfur. With time, other and perhaps worse conflicts will come to the fore. Eventually, some combatant or fanatic will choose to raise the stakes by using a weapon that altogether multiplies casualties. Just as planes flying into towers on 9/11 instantly became an historical marker dividing strategic perspectives before from after, that day will herald the onslaught of disease as an instrument of malevolence, profoundly changing everything.

Today, leaders proclaim that they are doing everything possible to meet this threat. Following a truly catastrophic act of bioviolence, they will likely tell the public that they had no idea where, when, or how a bioattack would occur – if they had known, they would of course have dedicated all their prodigious powers to thwart it. And the evil perpetrators of this horrible crime surely will be caught and punished.

These proclamations are disingenuous and these avowals will be half-truths, deluding all of us about where security may be found and how to get there – not so much a deliberate lie but a mirage grounded on little more than a wish and a prayer. The more complete truth is that little is being done to prevent bioviolence; if catastrophe occurs, leaders must be held responsible for willful disregard of the well-being of countless victims who entrust them to prevent unspeakable horrors. There is no way to know where, when, or how a bioattack will occur, but much can be learned if we gather information more effectively. A promise to hold the attackers to account is a small gesture: most likely they will be dead or very hard to find; in any event, punishing them will scarcely compensate for the massive injuries inflicted.

This book is in small part an indictment, in larger part a policy map. More broadly, it is a discussion of how international law should cope with

the planetary implications of advancing bioscience. It is born of seven years
of traversing five continents and participating in hundreds of workshops,
meetings, and briefings with officials of governments and international
organizations, scientists, diplomats, and advocates of peace and development. Emerging from this experience is a strong belief that humanity is
more vulnerable than it should be and that the dangers are speedily and
unnecessarily accelerating.

The central reality of bioviolence is that it is an immense threat, but a
massive catastrophe has not yet happened. Few informed policy makers
are sanguine about this threat, but it is at the periphery of their vision,
superseded by more urgent crises. Without a bioattack that reveals the
failure of current policies, support for progressive initiatives is difficult to
rouse. Truth is, we are likely to take appropriate steps to prevent a second
bioattack, but we seem fated to suffer the wounds of one disease disaster
before this conjectural threat becomes real enough to embrace complex
policies. Frustrating as this realization might be, it exposes the dilemma
of how to make tough choices in uncharted policy arenas at the frontiers
of science and law.

Ultimately, placing blame would be pointless. It is important to know
why decisions have been unwise, and readers are entitled to be discouraged by our leaders' disarray in addressing bioviolence. Yet, the analytical
challenges associated with preventing bioviolence are difficult to resolve.
The threat is a multifaceted phenomenon; each facet reflects angles and
depths that intersect with ever more far-reaching implications. At the heart
of this difficulty is how to grapple with a problem that necessarily demands
humanity-wide cooperation in the context of fragmented and anarchic
political systems.

A pervasive question is whether the sweeping changes called for in
this book are "worth it." Does the level of risk justify the cost of globally implementing expensive intrusions into scientific freedom, national
sovereignty, and personal privacy? Many policies must be pursued with
potentially adverse ramifications for professional and scientific communities that are key to addressing bioviolence. And underlying this question
is the wish that anxiety about bioviolence turns out to be a false alarm –
hopefully much ado about something that never occurs.

What is certain is that trend lines are pointing the wrong way. Technological progress increasingly enables a mere handful of maniacs to commit
a monstrous level of violence. Until recently, only a powerful nation-state
could threaten such devastation. Whatever their motives – greed, distorted
sense of political grievance, nihilism – a nano-fraction of humanity can

now inflict a species-wide catastrophe that breaches the progression of history. At the beginning of the third millennium, bioviolence scenarios that crack the foundations of modern civilization's stability are the most likely deliberate threat to humanity's survival and progress.

How these risks should be measured, what they justify in terms of commitment of resources and insistence on change – these are questions that deserve serious discussion. Currently, that discussion is impaired by inadequate systematic analyses of relevant issues. Absent breadth of perspective, threats of bioviolence are met with planetary silence. This book is a refusal to perpetuate that silence.

We can make the world a lot safer, save some children from dying whether by hand of nature or man, and, most intriguing, we can appreciate the role of law in shaping human affairs at this time.

Barry Kellman
Chicago, USA

Foreword

Ronald K. Noble

Secretary General, Interpol

Throughout the centuries, diseases unleashed by nature have savaged humankind on a horrific scale, inflicting wide-scale death, as well as social, political, and economic upheaval. In the 20th Century alone, more people died of smallpox (over three hundred million) than in both world wars combined, and an influenza epidemic claimed over forty million lives. Even a disease that afflicts only animals can have devastating consequences. The outbreak of foot and mouth disease in the United Kingdom in 2001 took months to control, required the slaughter of millions of animals, and caused billions of dollars in losses.

These are the risks posed by nature. Now, added to these risks, we face the threat of bioterrorism.

We know from recent events that terrorists remain committed to perpetrating large-scale violence. And we also know that there is much evidence that terrorists have a strong interest in the use of biological weapons and are planning to use them. The eleventh volume of Al Qaeda's *Encyclopedia of Jihad* is devoted to chemical and biological weapons. Captured terrorist suspects have admitted that their organizations are plotting potential biological attacks. Authorities have seized documents, computer hard drives, and terrorist training materials that discuss the acquisition, production, and use of bioweapons.

We also know that, as biotechnology industries continue to expand throughout the world, new pathogens and pathogen-making technologies are rapidly proliferating, increasing the risk that terrorists could get their hands on deadly pathogens or on the means of producing them. And many experts believe that advances in biotechnology could produce genetically engineered pathogens more lethal than any currently known to man.

There are many ways for terrorists to obtain deadly pathogens. They can buy or steal them from universities, research labs, pharmaceutical companies, military stockpiles, or commercial supply houses; acquire them from "friendly states" or other sympathizers; buy them on the black market; or produce the agents on their own.

It is also becoming ever more possible for terrorists to themselves produce the pathogens, as the volume and sophistication of the necessary information becomes increasingly accessible through publications, the internet, and other sources.

Once terrorists get their hands on the pathogens, they can all too easily determine how to use them in a biological attack. The information and materials for creating biological weapons – both crude and sophisticated – are publicly available. They could even cause a so-called "martyr" to become infected and act as a suicide bioweapon. Or they could simply adopt the approach used by the anthrax terrorists in 2001 in the United States, who disrupted the world's economy by targeting and murdering nearly ten U.S. citizens merely by placing powder laced with anthrax in envelopes mailed to just a handful of people.

In my view, Al Qaeda's global network, its proven capabilities, its deadly history, its desire to do the unthinkable, and the evidence collected about its bioterrorist ambitions and plans ominously portend a clear and present danger of the highest order that Al Qaeda (or another terrorist group) will someday perpetrate a biological terrorist attack.

As was made clear in a letter dated December 1, 2003, addressed to the president of the United Nations Security Council from the chairman of the United Nations Security Council Committee established pursuant to Resolution 1267 concerning Al Qaeda and the Taliban and associated individuals and entities, "Undoubtedly Al Qaeda is still considering the use of chemical or biological weapons to perpetrate its terrorist actions. When might this happen? Nobody really knows. It is just a matter of time before the terrorists believe they are ready. They have already taken the decision to use such chemical and biological weapons in their forthcoming attacks. The only restraint they are facing is the technical complexity of operating them properly and effectively."

To be sure, there are some technical and other obstacles involved in obtaining pathogens and effectively deploying them on a mass scale in the real world, but as we learned on September 11, 2001, where there's a will there's a way.

Now, I realize that my statement that the bioterrorist threat is real goes against the natural human tendency to operate under the assumption that terrorists will not use biological weapons in the future on a large scale because they have not done so in the past. But this assumption is dangerous.

Some would prefer not to think about the possibility of such deadly terrorist acts. Yet, we cannot avoid the danger by ignoring it. Both the assumption that it won't happen because it hasn't happened and the tendency to want to avoid a danger by not thinking about it are irresponsible.

Moreover, whatever the history, the current threat is real. Indeed, no one ever crashed commercial airplanes into buildings before September 11, 2001, and, yet, as we learned, that threat was nevertheless all too real.

Given the magnitude of the harm that would be caused by a bioterrorist attack – hundreds, thousands, and even millions of deaths are possible – it is clear to me that this alone mandates that we take this threat seriously. Even if hundreds or thousands do not die, the panic and the social and economic upheaval that could follow such an attack represent another set of reasons why we should take this threat seriously. Unfortunately, however, the world is not taking this threat seriously, and this represents a very grave situation.

There is a lack of awareness and understanding of the threat, lack of the required specialized training, lack of required specialized resources, lack of the required legal and regulatory framework, and lack of the required coordination mechanisms for the most effective prevention and response.

Because governments and their law enforcement agencies have limited experience dealing with bioterrorism, it remains a remote and esoteric topic understood by few officials, given little attention by policy makers, and perceived by the political leadership as having little domestic impact. Political support and funding for security programs tend to be oriented toward the traditional and concrete areas of crime that affect citizens on a daily basis, such as robbery, rape, murder, and so on. There is a natural tendency for governments to neglect threats of future harm in favor of the seemingly more pressing matters of the day with which they are more comfortable in dealing, but this is putting the world's citizens at great risk. The world must start paying much more attention to the threat of bioterrorism. Pretending that this threat does not exist is a recipe for disaster.

THE ACTIONS REQUIRED TO MEET THIS THREAT

Meeting the threat of bioterrorism requires capabilities in the following four areas: 1) threat assessment, 2) attack prevention, 3) attack detection, and 4) attack response (mitigating the damage, apprehending the perpetrators, and gaining knowledge and expertise to enhance future capabilities in these four areas).

Threat assessment is required to shape and guide the other three areas. Attack prevention includes tactical intelligence, interdiction, disruption, facilities protection, pathogen control, etc. Attack detection means being able to detect a biological attack as early as possible (many pathogens have incubation periods ranging up to a week or more before symptoms appear, and even then it can take time to realize that they are the product of an attack). Early detection is critical to save the injured, contain the disease, and apprehend the perpetrators before they can attack again. Attack response includes medical services, containment, security, environmental remediation, investigation, apprehension, intelligence gathering, and learning.

To accomplish these things, the relevant constituencies must develop or acquire the requisite skilled personnel, tools, and equipment. They must also establish and implement protocols and procedures to share information and cooperate in prevention and detection efforts, to mobilize response resources in the event of an attack, and to coordinate all of these efforts and resources (within and across functions, agencies, levels of government, and internationally).

Written plans should be created covering the conceivable potentialities (e.g., mass decontamination, medical supply distribution, isolation, evacuation, quarantine, compulsory medical exams and vaccinations, security for health care sites and shipments, etc.). Personnel should be trained and equipped to execute the plans, and the plans should be exercised through periodic drills.

Benchmarking and best practices should be developed and shared to guide the design, exercise, implementation, and revision of plans, protocols, and procedures. Measurable standards and metrics must be developed to promote and determine accountability, performance, and progress.

The relevant constituencies include police, customs, immigration, intelligence, bioscientists, health care professionals, emergency management, military/security organizations, environmental management, agriculture, and other relevant private and public resources (local, regional, national, and international).

Broadly speaking, however, the principal relevant constituencies are the law enforcement, bioscience, and public health communities. These three communities must work together nationally and internationally to analyze the relevant threats that each sees in order to help society enhance the likelihood of preventing a bioterrorist attack and of minimizing the damage if such an attack occurs. Unfortunately, the law enforcement, bioscience, and public health communities have very limited history of working together nationally in most countries, even less so internationally.

These three communities must forge partnerships in order to ensure an integrated approach. This is required to maximize the synergies of their complementary skills, methodologies, perspectives, and resources, and to minimize their conflicts (e.g., in the collection, transport, and analysis of evidence so as to best serve medical, epidemiological, intelligence, and law enforcement purposes). This means overcoming many formidable obstacles (security clearance, patient privacy, cultural divides, etc.), but it is essential to do so.

Each agency has its own deeply embedded culture, and, generally speaking, is highly resistant to change, even in times of crisis. Each agency responds with its own routines, its own distinctive view of "the threat," and its own understanding of its particular mission. Although it is beneficial for each agency to pursue its own mission, and with the methods that are uniquely suited to that mission, it is also important to integrate these missions and methods across agencies. This type of coordination is difficult even among agencies that are all within the law enforcement community. It is dramatically more so when the agencies are in different professional communities. This is why it is so challenging to achieve effective collaboration between law enforcement, bioscience, and public health agencies.

Undergirding all of the above is the need to modify legal and regulatory frameworks to support the necessary activities. This means 1) the frameworks for controlling the manufacture, possession, storage, transportation, use, trafficking, and deployment of pathogens, and their means of production, weaponization, and delivery; 2) the frameworks for thwarting attacks before they occur (e.g., intelligence, investigation, interdiction, and disruption); 3) the frameworks relating to the protection of the points of possible pathogen intrusion (e.g., those relating to water supplies and the food chain); 4) the frameworks relating to activities aimed at early detection of attacks that do occur (e.g., so-called medical surveillance systems); and 5) the frameworks governing the activities required for attack response (isolation, quarantine, forced medical exams, forced vaccinations, investigation, etc.).

All of the above-described required actions should be done on the local, national, regional, and international levels. The inherent nature of this threat is global. International coordination is therefore essential. For example, national and international Incident Response Teams specialized in bioterrorism should be assembled for rapid deployment whenever and wherever a major incident occurs. Ultimately, to address the threat of bioterrorism, international cooperation must be strengthened. Achieving this is a central part of Interpol's mission.

WHAT INTERPOL IS DOING

In order to understand Interpol's role in the international effort to prevent and respond to bioterrorism, one must understand what Interpol is today. Interpol is the world's largest international law enforcement organization, linking together essentially all of the world's law enforcement agencies (covering 186 member countries). It has been around since 1923, but it is virtually all new.

Interpol has reorganized itself around three core functions. The first core function is to maintain the world's first secure global law enforcement communication system. This system, called I-24/7, was created by Interpol in 2001, and it now allows law enforcement agencies around the world to exchange information in real time, and to have instant access to Interpol databases and notices.

The second core function is to further develop Interpol databases (such as our database of wanted and suspected terrorists and other international criminals, stolen passports, fingerprints, and DNA) and international notices (which serve to alert global law enforcement of fugitives, suspected terrorists, dangerous criminals, missing persons, weapons threats, and unidentified dead bodies, and, in the case of the Red Notice, to request the arrest of a wanted person anywhere in the world). These databases and notices represent powerful tools in the fight against terrorism and other serious international crime, and their contents, usage, and results have been soaring in recent years.

The third core function is to provide operational police support services to Interpol's National Central Bureaus and member countries' law enforcement agencies wherever and whenever it is needed. This means access to Interpol experts who are available to aid police agencies in specific investigations. It also means access to Interpol's Command and Coordination Centre, which operates around the clock in all of Interpol's four official languages (English, French, Spanish, and Arabic) and serves as the first point of contact for any member country faced with a crisis situation. Incident Response Teams are also available and can be dispatched to the scene within hours of an attack. Major Event Support Teams are available to help secure major international events.

These types of communication, coordination, access to information, and expert assistance are crucial in the fight against terrorism and other serious international crime.

Together with its 186 National Central Bureaus in its 186 Member Countries, Interpol has in recent years implemented major changes in response to the threat of terrorism. In 2004, we began moving into the area of bioterrorism prevention and response in particular.

We sought and received funding from the Alfred P. Sloan Foundation to create a Bioterrorism Prevention Program to be delivered to law enforcement in collaboration with the bioscience and public health communities, as well as the other relevant professional communities. The Sloan Foundation has since committed $2.5 million and the Canadian Department of Foreign Affairs and International Trade has since committed $300,000, which will support Interpol's Bioterrorism Prevention Program in its current form through 2007.

We identified the former Director General of the UK National Criminal Intelligence Service, John Abbott, to chair a steering committee to guide the program. We recruited a small but talented staff to develop and implement the program. We have regularly drawn on the expertise of experts from various related fields. In fact, it was Professor Barry Kellman who first inspired me to make this a priority for Interpol and the international law enforcement community.

To kick off the program in a way that would bring together all of the professional communities under one roof at one time, Interpol hosted the Global Conference on Preventing Bioterrorism in March 2005 at Interpol Headquarters in Lyon, France. That event was attended by over 500 law enforcement officials and other professionals from 155 countries, as well as representatives of 16 international organizations. It was the largest gathering of international law enforcement in history.

The results of that conference have been positive and far-reaching, but they have also highlighted the tremendous amount of work needed to be done in this area.

Through the Interpol Bioterrorism Prevention Program, we provide an awareness campaign, capacity-building measures, expertise, training, and knowledge to law enforcement – to help them develop effective plans to meet the threat of bioterrorism. And we help them form bridges to the bioscience and public health communities. We encourage them to enhance interagency cooperation at the national and international levels. And we urge policy makers to enact laws and regulations that provide law enforcement with the tools they need to prevent attacks and to respond to them.

Relevant information and training are provided to law enforcement worldwide through workshops and other training modalities. We have conducted regional workshops in Africa, South America, Europe, and Asia, attended by law enforcement officials and other professionals from a total of 115 countries. This knowledge transfer and training improve capabilities to prevent attacks and to respond to them. It also forges partnerships among the relevant communities. And it encourages national police forces to become advocates for resources to augment their capabilities and for improvements in the legal and regulatory frameworks within which they operate.

We have created a "Bioterrorism Prevention Resource Center" on our website that is now at the disposal of the entire law enforcement community. This site helps police find training materials, online tests, scientific documents, planning guidelines, response and crisis management materials, and other useful resources.

We are developing another part of our website that will be dedicated to training materials that have been provided to us by our National Central Bureaus and governments, to show what is being done at national levels in terms of bioterrorism preparedness and response.

We have designed "Table-Top" exercises that are conducted with great effect at our workshops. We will be conducting various "Train-the-Trainer" programs and international interagency exercises. We have created the "Interpol Bioterrorism Incident Pre-Planning and Response Guide" to be used by police around the world.

We convened a board of experts comprised of professionals from the health and bioscience fields, the police, and the specialized bodies of the United Nations to help us network with these diverse communities, and to identify emerging developments and opportunities that might enhance our program.

In the future, we hope to find financing for a police officer rotation program in which police can rotate through our Bioterrorism Prevention Program, bringing their added expertise to the program, and then returning home with still greater expertise to share with their national colleagues in building their own programs.

With the help of the U.S. State Department, which provided a grant of $554,000, we launched a new project that focuses on biocriminalization. The project's goal is to assess the relevant criminal and administrative laws around the world, and to assist countries in drafting, enacting, and enforcing such laws.

We are studying the possibility of making available to global law enforcement a database of information relating to all known cases of bioterrorism.

There is a great need for the development of other global databases relating to bioterrorism – databases relating to the manufacture, possession, storage, transportation, and use of pathogens, and their means of production, weaponization, and delivery. Unfortunately, such development is costly, and Interpol would require external funding for any such new initiatives.

As the world's largest international law enforcement organization, embracing 186 member countries and their National Central Bureaus, Interpol can play a critical role in helping the world confront the threat of bioterrorism. But the world must begin taking this threat much more seriously. This means devoting greater focus and greater resources, which are always in limited supply, but never more precious than the life itself that hangs in the balance.

Acknowledgments

Here, I can inadequately offer a few words to recognize the enormous debts owed to colleagues and friends. If there is a *fun* aspect to working on a subject as inherently dismaying as bioviolence, it is the opportunity to engage and be engaged by these people and many others who, due to limited space and failing memory, are regrettably omitted.

First, to the DePaul University College of Law. DePaul University is dedicated to the Vincentian Mission, which propounds community service. Viewing global bioviolence prevention as community service might have seemed questionable, yet the institution's support for my work has never wavered. I am most grateful to Dean Glen Weissenberger, the law school's tireless administrators and staff, and my colleagues, all of whom have provided a working environment that nurtures development and exercise of both scholarship and active participation in the global community.

Over the years, I have benefited immensely from the research assistance offered by many law students and other student associates. In particular, this book would be much less thorough and far later had it not been for the contributions of Peter Zube, Gabriel Sanchez, Andrea Garcia, and Shannon Kellman.

I am very proud of the network of scholars and friends who have generously offered advice and education. Of these, three deserve special gratitude for their intellectual stimulation and outright help. Special appreciation to Cherif Bassiouni, who teaches me that international law is an edifice with ever-strengthening architecture and that we can contribute to humanity by devoting intellectual effort to amplifying that legal architecture. To Elizabeth Rindskopf Parker, who teaches me to elevate the tactics of my lawyer craft and who demonstrates that a powerful mind wielded gracefully can move the world. To Interpol Secretary General Ronald Noble, who, on the strength of his personal reputation and that of Interpol, has actually taken my ideas into the arena of international governance.

I would also like to gratefully acknowledge the wisdom offered by the colleagues who have read and commented upon portions of this book: Barbara Kelly, Gigi Kwik, Jeanne Guilleman, Kay Mereish, Nancy Connell, and Rocco Casagrande. There would be many more errors but for their advice; remaining errors are entirely of my own making.

This book is very much the product of active engagement in policy communities. That activity has been intensely stimulating because the following individuals and others unmentioned but appreciated have generously opened opportunities to participate and learn: Adrian Baciu, Alexander Custaud, David Franz, David Hamon, David Heyman, David Koplow, Eden Forsythe, Edward Tanzman, Eileen Choffnes, Guy Roberts, Iain Gillespie, James Leonard, Jenny Gromoll, Jo Husbands, John Parker, John Steinbruner, Jonathan Granoff, Lela Bakanidze, Malcolm Dando, Marc Ostfield, Maurizio Barbeschi, Michael Allswede, Michael Moodie, Mihnea Motoc, Orley Lindgren, Ottorino Cosivi, Robert Mikulak, Ronald Atlas, Samuel Manteaw, Seth Carus, Sevim Garibayli, Suzanne Spaulding, Swithin Munyantwali, Thomas Graham, and Tibor Toth. My work is so much the better for your confidence and for the wisdom you have imparted. To those whom I've neglected, please know that I regret any unintentional slight.

Deserving special mention are the foundations and particular persons who provide the resources that enable ideas to be pursued and spread: Paula Olsiewski at The Sloan Foundation, Lukas Haynes and Kennette Benedict and now Amy Gordon at The MacArthur Foundation, Patricia Nicholas at the Carnegie Corporation, and Charles Curtis at the Nuclear Threat Initiative. I am grateful for your personal and institutional trust.

And for everything else, my love and more: Hope.

Introduction

This book is about species treason – giving aid to the enemy in the per-petual war between humanity and microbes. Using disease, traitors to humanity could inflict death tolls beyond the great historical scourges and unleash panic of biblical proportions. These traitors crucially impart the one quality that microbes lack: they think. The microbes, operating through remarkable processes of trial and error, have never designed a strategic battle plan to resist the onslaught of modern medicine. But their new ally can strategize and find people's most sensitive vulnerabilities. This ally of disease is as dastardly as can be imagined for this ally is human.

Bioviolence is the infliction of harm by the intentional manipulation of living micro-organisms or their natural products for hostile purposes. It is the ultimate act of terror, making everyone potentially vulnerable. It's a crime that must be prevented. It should be a crime whether the inflic-tor is a State or a person, a terrorist or a criminal, or just a lunatic. Broad prophylactic measures to heighten security against biothreats should be implemented in every nation. Law enforcers worldwide should be pre-pared to interdict this crime. These are complex challenges with many intricate details requiring elaborate twists and turns through policies that implicate science, diplomacy, health care, and law enforcement. Yet, noth-ing here is so abstruse or beyond human intellect as to impair policy progress.

This book is a brief – an argument – that: 1) bioviolence is a threat that merits serious attention; 2) there are wise strategies that can reduce bioviolence threats; and 3) those strategies have serious ramifications that demand important changes in global governance. This argument is pro-voked by the realization that no other problem facing humanity is so poten-tially cataclysmic and has been so inadequately addressed.

THE BIOVIOLENCE POLICY FAILURE

In recent years, vast monetary and scientific resources have been devoted to developing vaccines and antidotes against the most feared bioagents. Efforts to combat disease have dramatically improved, motivated in part by escalating concerns for natural pandemics. Some threats have been mitigated, and we are gaining a better understanding of lethal microbes and how to stop them. Many developed nations have prepared rapid response capabilities for a bioviolence event; in some regions, sophisticated exercises have been conducted to improve coordination and identify unanticipated difficulties.[1] Various international and regional organizations have taken modest steps to become more vigilant in addressing bioviolence threats. Interpol has initiated an entire program for bioterrorism prevention to train police and coordinate relevant information. Most important, national and multilateral intelligence communities that are broadly attentive to terror and criminal threats are certainly alert to risks associated with intentionally inflicted disease.

Nevertheless, it is striking how little has been done to make it hard to be a bioweaponeer and shocking that all these resources have been expended without anything like a global approach that might actually make us safer. Across a broad panoply of policy arenas, readily adaptable initiatives to prevent bioviolence are stalled. Throughout the vast majority of the world, outside of perhaps two dozen developed States, bioviolence preparations could proceed without substantial chance of detection and could inflict unimaginable damage against unprotected populations. A handful of threats receive substantial attention, but many easily accomplishable attack modes are virtually ignored.

In short, advancing policies to prevent bioviolence is what the international community does worst. It must be asked why bioviolence has not already been addressed, why international and national leaders have done such a remarkably poor job in diminishing bioviolence risks leaving us all virtually naked to a bio-attack from a powerful military, group, or single person. No other threat presents such a stark contrast between, on one hand, severity of harm along with global denunciation but, on the other hand, a failure of leadership to reduce risks.

Although many disciplines – science, history, politics etc. – have relevant responsibilities, this is fundamentally a book about international law. The thesis here is that humanity is vulnerable to bioviolence because, at this time, international law is unable to devise, implement, and enforce preventive policies. Such policies are potentially available and effective, but they demand progressive changes in prevailing legal concepts.

It is only because bioviolence has not yet taken a truly catastrophic toll that humanity tolerates international law's infirmity. That bioviolence perpetrators have not yet capitalized upon this failure is grounds for solace but not confidence. How long our luck will continue will be decided by the wrong people for entirely the wrong reasons. We can take preventive measures now, or we can hope that bioviolence continues forever to be only a hypothetical threat. The former option is complicated and has costs; the latter option is irresponsible.

THEMATIC FOUNDATIONS

Three Crossroads

Bioviolence stands at the intersection of three transformative phenomena. First is the changing condition of strife. State-to-State warfare with explicit battlefield confrontations is, for the most part, a thing of the past. In place of warfare, however, are three types of strife: slaughter of defenseless groups (Cambodia, Bosnia, Rwanda, Darfur, etc.); terrorism; and proliferation of weapons of mass destruction. Significantly, bioviolence is ideal for today's forms of strife and could magnify their already horrific implications. Using bioviolence, a handful of culprits can ever more easily cause profound harm to enormous numbers of people.

Second is the globalization of pandemic disease. For decades, infectious calamities have only peripherally affected geopolitics. There have been stunning successes against smallpox and polio; measles, rubella, diphtheria, and other maladies persist in sharply confined domains. But initially HIV/AIDS, then SARS, and more recently the Avian Flu have undermined the perception that modern medicine can altogether abate infectious disease. Today, disease threatens international peace and security and has the potential to unhinge global order.[2] Bioviolence can initiate, propel, or ride upon disease's potential for devastation. Disease and strife are the Achilles' heels of our age; bioviolence is where they intersect.

The third phenomenon here is the radical pace of change in the biological sciences. Bioscience is a dynamic phenomenon that stretches from inquiries about humanity's most existential search – what is the architecture of life? – to the development of medicines for improving health. If eras can be labeled according to the technology that is most transformative of humanity (Stone Age, Industrial Age, Nuclear Age), then ours is indisputably the Genomic Age. The cracking of the human genome symbolized a seismic shift not only of technology and pharmaceuticals but, more fundamentally, of how we perceive "humanness." Our commonality as a species has never been so tangible, and never before have we so had to face possibilities of altering the essence of what we are. Capabilities that might emerge in a decade are almost beyond estimation. Indeed, the advance of bioscience is a major theme of this book. And, unfortunately, these advances can endow perpetrators of bioviolence with previously unimagined abilities.

Law for Humanity

Bioviolence is a threat without borders to the human species. Like other challenges facing humanity – for example, global warming – it simply makes no sense to try to insulate any particular country or region from the threat. To prevent bioviolence requires policies that focus on humanity as a *biological species entity*.[3] These policies must be implemented everywhere with centralized governance.

A sizeable bioattack will have transnational implications, exposing our human commonality and demanding new modes of cooperation. The opportunities for bioviolence are everywhere, and perpetrators might emerge from virtually anywhere. They can prepare their attack through easy networks of communication and transport lethal devices in defiance of traditional notions of sovereign jurisdiction. Moreover, the effects of igniting a severe bioviolence pandemic will not respect borders or distinguish among victims according to their race, religion, or nationality; the effects will quickly bind humanity into a suffering collectivity. Said Gro Harlem Brundtland, "Today, in an interconnected world, bacteria and viruses travel almost as fast as e-mail and financial flows. Globalization has connected Bujumbura to Bombay and Bangkok to Boston. There are no health sanctuaries."[4]

The challenge is how to confront these threats in a flattening world where accelerating circulation abets the ready movement of science and technology and makes each of us targets of unnamed perpetrators of catastrophe. A prevention strategy must be global. Every State and many international institutions must make a serious commitment in concert.

Looking forward, it is striking how little attention has been devoted to the changes in governance that will be necessary in a world of rapidly mutating bioscience and associated technologies. Yet, discussion of such policies makes it instantly apparent that the world is very awkwardly organized. Today, efforts to initiate global policies rapidly crash on the shoals of an anarchic division of the world into almost two hundred sovereign fortresses with separate claims to independent and unfettered decisional power. This is not the place to call for a radical restructuring of the Westphalian system and centuries-old concepts of national sovereignty, but it is imperative to see that this global threat inherently shrinks the planet into an interdependent neighborhood. Nations must realize that adamant proclamations about the inviolability of State sovereignty are, in this context, a recipe for disaster.

There is another sense in which bioviolence prevention must be expansive: policies must be sustainably effective for a species-community that is prospectively multigenerational. Prevention is not something that will be done once, then humanity can move on. Prevention must be a process of decisions that reconfigure our approaches to science, law enforcement, and public health; these reconfigured approaches will carry forward in perpetuity. Whatever decisions are made now, whatever actions are taken now, must withstand the test of time. Action is needed now because the threat is on our doorstep, yet what we do to thwart bioviolence will entail changes that our successors will inherit. Their interests must be considered as we make our decisions.

To consider how to prevent bioviolence is to open peepholes into the near-term future of international law and to ask what institutions and rules our grandchildren will want us to have created. Ultimately therefore, this book is something more than a policy manifesto about current threats of biological weapons in an era of non-State terrorism; it is an exploration of how global governance should evolve to address challenges of advancing science and technology.

TERMINOLOGY

Bioviolence is used here instead of the far more common term *bioterrorism* because of the many disputes and ambiguities about the meaning of *terrorism*. There is no globally accepted definition of *terrorism* despite years of United Nations negotiations, yet the term suggests conduct of: 1) a non-State actor that is 2) motivated by a political or religious agenda. A State can support terrorists, but *terrorism* is not a term that typically applies to deployment of military capabilities. Nor does the term apply to criminals motivated exclusively by financial gain or lunatics motivated by idiosyncratic alienation or revenge. Another ambiguity attends how to distinguish a terrorist from someone seeking to overthrow a repressive regime.

Where to draw precise lines that separate terrorism from other categories of wrongdoing or use of armed force is, from this book's perspective, an irrelevant exercise. The objective here is more generic. There are real differences among the many potential perpetrators of intentionally inflicted disease, but those differences are secondary to the challenge of preventing any and all hostile plots to make people ill. The term *violence* captures the phenomenon without regard to the actor or the motivation so long as it is deliberately malevolent.

Notably, there are other risks associated with advancing bioscience, such as use of genetically modified organisms with unpredicted consequences, but this book advocates policies against violence – that is, wrongful activity that is intended to cause injury. Also important to note is that the focus of this book is mass catastrophe, not biohomicide or biovandalism. Although there is no specific demarcation between murder and mass murder, the reality is that little in this book will prevent someone from lacing salmonella on his or her spouse's pasta. The term *bioviolence* here implies an act that has far more extensive consequences.

Used to similarly generic effect here is the term *bioweapon* and the verb to *weaponize*. Among some diplomats, a *weapon* is something possessed or procured by a State military; by definition, a non-State actor cannot make a bioweapon, only a biodevice. Besides being semantically clumsy, this distinction is artificial. What is a State's *bioweapon* that has been handed to a non-State actor; is it suddenly no longer a *weapon*? It is nonsensical to use different terms to describe the same thing on the basis of who has it. In this book, a *bioweapon* is simply what someone uses to commit bioviolence, and *weaponization* is any process that is designed to make a pathogen into a bioweapon. Correspondingly, *bio-offender* refers to someone who would commit bioviolence whether a State actor, terrorist, lunatic, criminal, or anyone else.

The word *pathogen* here refers to any live agent or poison created by a live agent (a toxin) that causes disease, whether in humans or other living beings. The scientifically sophisticated reader knows that the outer boundaries of what might be referred to as a pathogen – distinct from a pollutant or even a mechanism (nanotechnology) – are increasingly fuzzy. Once again, this term is used broadly and flexibly to refer to any disease agent that has a living source.

Critically, the term *prevention* deserves clarification. It does not refer to eliminating risk. The policies recommended here will not confer an ironclad shield from bioviolence. *Prevention* is used here in the same way that "seatbelts prevent car accident fatalities" or "a low-calorie diet prevents diabetes" – of course, some seatbelt wearers will die in accidents, and some careful dieters will get diabetes. *Prevention* is not an absolute term. Yet, compared to the prevailing situation that in many respects is heedless of palpable risks, adoption of proposed policies can make us safer even if not totally safe. Absent a prevention strategy, the threats will grow larger and more unmanageable.

PRESENTATION OF THE ARGUMENT

This book is comprised of two parts. Part I's three chapters describe the problem of bioviolence and explain how it evolved to its current intractable condition. Chapter 1 is a brief essay about why bioviolence should be a matter of pressing concern. There are easily understood plots that could have debilitating consequences. Chapter 2 explains bioviolence: what is it, how is it done, and how technological advance is changing the phenomenon. There are many bioviolence options; science is opening new opportunities and making existing methods easier. Chapter 3 addresses the question of who has perpetrated bioviolence and who might perpetrate it today. Whether viewed from historical experience or from today's news, it is clear that many people are not inhibited about inflicting disease.

Part II recommends the global strategy for preventing bioviolence. Chapter 4 explains the foundations of that strategy based on criminalization of wrongful conduct. Chapter 5 focuses on complicating bioviolence by making it difficult to get needed pathogens and capabilities and by strengthening law enforcement's authority to detect and interdict bioviolence preparations. We need to know far more about the capabilities for committing bioviolence, and we need to raise hurdles to their wrongful applications. Chapter 6 considers how the potential for harm inherent in bioscience research should be understood and how science can develop resistance against bioviolence by creating vaccines and medicines. Globalizing policies to promote bioscience presents critical financial challenges as well as potential conflicts with intellectual property protections.

Chapter 7 discusses public health preparedness to deal with bio-attacks by hardening targets, planning response interventions, and establishing quarantines if necessary. Although preparedness measures can be useful in mitigating the consequences of a bioattack, excessive reliance on public health is false security. Chapter 8 considers the unique problems of State bioweapons programs and today's challenges for the Biological Weapons

Convention, including nonlethal bioagents and national biodefense programs. Also relevant here are measures to ensure dismantlement of the former Soviet Union's bioweapons stockpiles. Chapter 9 discusses how relevant policies should be progressively governed under the rule of law and supervised by three United Nations entities. In all, the book is intended to provide a multidimensional blueprint for today's decision makers and concerned citizens to improve humanity's security.

PART I

The Bioviolence Condition and How It Came to Be

1. Why Worry?

If someone really despises 21st Century civilization, what can be done? For the truly diehard nihilist, passionate terrorist, or zealous lunatic, there are frustratingly few options. At some point, they have to realize that conventional attacks just are not doing the trick. The 9/11 attacks, the bombing of the Madrid and London subways, and numerous smaller attacks have all put civilization on edge, but history marches inexorably forward more or less as it was before. The United States and its allies are resolute, continuing to assert materialistic values and using their force of arms and media to propound those values to everyone else. A few thousand people can be killed, yet western armies still traverse the world. The sun never sets on a U.S. military base.

There is, however, one way to shred the predominant social fabric. It is how the deity has done it since the days of pharaoh: inflict a scourge. The Bible is replete with lessons of how the infidels were beset by pestilence – the holy wrath of the righteous. What more symbolically justifiable way to provoke an apocalyptic confrontation between the forces of good and evil? Causing collective death and misery may be seen as performing a sacramental reckoning that morally justifies mass murder.

The threat of bioviolence is unique among perils facing humanity, and those who would perpetrate bioviolence are villains in a class of their own.

WHY BIOVIOLENCE IS DIFFERENT

Bioviolence is ultimately about destruction of living organisms, not buildings or equipment. In operation, bioweapons – the devices of bioviolence – kill or impair people (or animals or vegetation) within range, then dissipate leaving victims as the only evidence of their use. Bioweapons are very quiet.

They most closely resemble chemical weapons. Some bioweapons are, in fact, chemical weapons. Toxins such as ricin are inanimate poisons that happen to be made by living organisms. They are bioweapons because their source is biological, yet they interrupt key life functions in ways similar to sarin or mustard gas. Toxins aside, all other bioweapons share the common attribute of engaging a live agent to infect the victim.

Delayed Anonymity

Bioweapons are distinguishable by their *naturalness*. Most other weapons, including chemical weapons, have uniquely unnatural effects, but bioweapons resemble and can be mistaken for a natural disease outbreak. Many pathogens generate flu-like symptoms, and it might appear at first that victims are suffering from an acute flu outbreak. Although some diseases, notably smallpox, have unmistakably distinctive symptoms that could be readily observed, this is more the exception than the rule. For most types of pathogen attacks, identification would be difficult until long after the bio-offenders have fled.

Another distinction is the length of time between the attack and its consequences. Chemical or explosive weapons kill virtually immediately, but a victim of a bioattack might not have even the slightest indication of a problem for a few days. Detonation of a bioweapon need not draw an iota of attention. The attack could unfold in a prolonged process involving exposure, incubation, and eventually illness, even death. In time, mounting numbers of the sick and dying could lead to a diagnosis that patients are suffering from a disease that is not a natural outbreak. This diagnosis might convince authorities that a bioviolence attack has been committed, but that could easily be a week after the attack occurs.

From the perspective of a bio-offender, these two characteristics of using bioweapons – its symptoms similar to those of natural disease and its lengthy incubation time for effects to become manifest – are very desirable. He could commit the attack and then have all the time he needs to blissfully move away unimpeded by police or officials who would have no reason to suspect that a horrible crime has been committed. He could release anthrax in a sports stadium and leave at will; the game would be yesterday's news well before a single victim shows up at an emergency room or doctor's office.

Far more ominous, bioviolence's delayed effects could enable a sophisticated bio-offender (or team) to wage a strategic series of attacks. He can release pathogens in one location; as the toll of sick victims multiplies, he moves to another location perhaps thousands of miles away. After a few days as victims appear and authorities begin to respond, attention and treatment resources will flood the target site. Now it is time for a second attack. This pattern could go on repeatedly as the bio-offender is always a few days ahead of the law enforcers and public health officials who are trying to stop him. Importantly, by moving around, he could strain response resources and transportation networks as his first attack draws those resources to one corner of the nation then in a few days must hurriedly scramble to a distant corner and so on.

In a highly developed country such as the United States, for example, an attack in Miami would draw vast quantities of antidotes and responders into southern Florida. The attack's consequences might be contained if authorities respond quickly and with massive resources. Getting more resources to Seattle to cope with the second attack might not be a problem for a country as rich and prepared as the United States. But getting them to Boston to deal with the third attack might provoke some confusion: moving medical supplies and trained personnel back and forth across a continent takes substantial logistical execution, any aspect of which could stumble in the stress of a series of bioattacks. When Dallas gets hit a few days later, exhaustion and disarray might be taking a real toll on the response community. A clever bio-offender could save his *coup de grâce* – a massive attack in Chicago – until the end. However, citizens of hundreds of other cities would not know that he has finished; their levels of panic would be elevated for months. No one would know where the next attack might happen. Remember that the primary motivation for committing bioviolence is to create panic, and multiple attacks with ceaseless nightmares about where and when the next attack might occur are most fearsome. No other weapon offers a comparable capacity to inflict catastrophe anonymously.

Moreover, a bio-offender who is sophisticated enough to execute multiple-site bioviolence could likely prepare more than one agent. Attacks with different agents could radically compound the challenges for containing consequences. For example, it is difficult to ignite an epidemic in the face of medical counter-measures even if one has a highly contagious agent. If medical counter-measures are absorbed with the effects of an anthrax attack, however, a different epidemic might have the opportunity to spread. Indeed, one of the great fears associated with anthrax is that it might be used to "cover" a contagious outbreak, the delayed effects of which might be initially ignored in the face of hundreds (or more) anthrax casualties.

A close look at most nations' response strategy for a terrorist attack reveals that security officials shortsightedly neglect the delayed effects of a bioattack as well as the potential for repeated attacks. Even more significantly, they tend to neglect the consequences of fatigue, chaos, and the sheer challenge of coping across large distances. Most important, they tend to assume that the response will proceed in an ordered environment where authority is clear and the media is accurate. But this is palpable nonsense.

The anthrax attacks of late 2001 were by any measure of violence very small scale. Only a few people were infected by anthrax, but the entire nation was infected with panic for weeks. American law enforcers have still not identified the bio-offenders. Not much imagination is needed to envision the chaos that would follow a relentless series of attacks in one city after another. Nor should it be ignored that even a natural disaster for which there was massive warning with effects concentrated in a single region – Hurricane Katrina – provoked governmental responses that were, to say the least, not optimal. Imagine those same officials responding to multiple outbreaks of disease not knowing where the next one will occur or when the last one will be over.

Most ominously, an attack need not happen in the United States or a comparably sophisticated nation. Whatever confidence that American officials might have about their ability to confine a catastrophe is obviously vapid if the threat scenario entails sites in developing nations. Indeed, these officials manifest a remarkable conceit by claiming that they can contain a bioattack's consequences as if offenders will attack only once, using a readily detectable agent at a locale where defenses are strongest, and as if only North Americans or Western Europeans might be targets.

In the vast majority of cities in the world, detection capabilities are essentially nonexistent, and available medical response capacities are already overburdened with a host of natural epidemics. The bioviolence tactics that might be devastating in the United States – multiple attacks at geographically distant locations involving different agents – could be many orders of magnitude more catastrophic where populations are crowded and public health capabilities are already strained and ineffective. An attack could readily spread among victims infected with HIV/AIDS and tuberculosis leaving innumerable fatalities and masses of ungoverned survivors. It is hard to predict what would be the implications for stable governance.

A bioviolence attack could ride on the coattails of a natural epidemic. For example, a natural flu pandemic could provide perfect conditions for bioviolence. Even if the flu is ultimately contained, it would so absorb resources and attention as to make it exponentially more difficult to cope with the intentionally inflicted disease. As mentioned, many bioviolence agents cause flu-like symptoms; during a natural flu pandemic, they likely would be misdiagnosed. Only when many patients who should be responsive to countermeasures against flu fail to regain health might it become clear that something else is causing the symptoms – something that has been deliberately spread.

Consider all this from the perspective of a bio-offender deeply hostile to the United States and its western allies. He could, of course, initiate an attack in mid-Manhattan, Chicago, or London. But there is some risk that the world's most sophisticated police will find out about him and the world's most sophisticated public health and medical communities will devote their expertise and resources to an effective response. What's a bio-offender to do? It is easy to name dozens of capital cities around the globe that:

1. are teemingly overcrowded,
2. have woefully deficient public health systems,
3. are major international transport hubs, and
4. are in States that have close diplomatic linkages with the United States.

Envision a series of attacks against these capitals of developing States, perhaps timed to follow local officials' expressions of friendship to visiting U.S. dignitaries. The attacks could carry a well-publicized yet simple warning: "If you are a friend of the United States, receive its officials, or support its policies, thousands of your people will get sick." How many attacks in how many such cities would it take before international diplomacy, to say nothing of international transit, comes to a crashing halt? How many attacks that cause how many victims would it take before panic and interruptions of international trade provoke officials to close stock markets? At some point, even if not a single American is actually sickened, the nation's economy and political leadership would be near collapse.

Concealable Devastation

Bioviolence is distinctive by yet another attribute: in comparison to using chemical weapons (or indeed any other type of weapon but one), the potential death toll could be huge. A well-planned attack using chemicals or explosives could be devastating, but it is hard to conceive an attack with casualties exceeding ten thousand victims. By contrast, it has been estimated that release of 250 pounds of highly refined anthrax spores over a major American city could infect up to three million people.[1] In truth, the potential number of victims is unknowable – it depends on where it happens, the type of pathogen, and the sophistication of the weapon maker. Yet, there is widespread consensus among experts that a high end bioattack would inflict casualties exponentially greater than any chemical or conventional attack.

In this respect, bioweapons should be compared to nuclear weapons. Just in terms of potential casualties these weapons stand out from all other tools of catastrophe, and for this reason alone they deserve special attention. One big difference, of course, is that bioweapons leave buildings standing and infrastructure intact. There are other more important differences. Biotechnology is far more forgiving, and bioweapons are far easier to manufacture than nuclear weapons where even a miniscule error could produce a dud. Bioweapons are not as easy to make as the media might suggest; there are far more obstacles than with making and using a conventional explosive. Indeed, the difficulties of making an effective bioweapon are keys to detecting and interdicting bioviolence. Yet, making a lethal bioweapon is well within many people's capabilities. In terms of difficulty, making a bioweapon is more comparable to making a dirty bomb that disperses radioactive material without detonating a nuclear reaction. But a bioweapon can kill many more people than can a dirty bomb.

Preparing and effectively weaponizing pathogens might require sophisticated equipment and scientific expertise but far less than what would be required to produce even a rudimentary nuclear weapon. Pathogens are naturally available, and refined seed stocks of potentially weaponizeable agents are found widely in laboratories around the world. Getting weapons-grade nuclear material is, by contrast, extraordinarily difficult and far more expensive. Handling nuclear material requires radiation protective gear that is harder to get and use properly than the biological protective gear one would use to prevent self-infection. Furthermore, the equipment necessary to produce nuclear weapons is far more tightly regulated than what biological weapons would require.[2] And the risks of a covert laboratory being detected are slim.

The "footprint" of making and transporting a nuclear weapon is, by orders of magnitude, larger and more detectable than comparable activities related to bioweapons. If a nuclear weapon has to be moved from its place of preparation to its place of use, the chances of detecting a heavy metal item that emits radioactivity and is surrounded by precision explosives is incomparable to the chances of detecting a tiny vial full of an innocuous-looking gas or liquid. A single individual can transport bioweapons across borders by land, sea, or air and through airports and customs checks. A common perfume bottle can deliver plenty of agent that can, of course, multiply on its own to meet the bio-offender's requirements.

Contagious Panic!!!

The truly unique characteristic of some bioweapons – the characteristic that distinguishes them from nuclear weapons or indeed from all other types of weapons – is contagion. No other type of weapon can replicate itself and spread. Any other type of attack, regardless of its horror, is confineable in time and space; the harm is inflicted at the point of attack. It is awful for the victims, but if you aren't there, its effects are emotional – grief, empathy, rage; it does not harm you physically. But a contagious bioattack somewhere puts everyone at risk everywhere.

The Spanish Flu outbreak of 1918 killed more than forty million people in a world with one-third of today's population and without modern transportation networks. With today's modes of circulation, an effective biological attack could be far more strategic than nature in spreading a highly contagious disease that could run amok and expose vulnerabilities around the planet. No other attack offers similar capabilities to spread itself.

A bio-offender could infect himself with a disease, cross through customs or border control before symptoms are obvious, and then spread it to unsuspecting victims who would themselves become extended bioweapons carrying the disease indiscriminately. There are challenges in timing one's entry to precede the onset of symptoms and yet be in a crowded area before one succumbs to the overwhelming agony of a horrible disease. Taking a stroll through Grand Central Station or Heathrow Airport while contagious with ebola would require true dedication. Yet, a well-executed "invasion" of purposely infected carriers could be effective. It bears mentioning here that fanatical terrorist organizations seem to have an endless supply of suicide attackers.

All this leads to the final distinguishing characteristic: mass panic. All weapons are frightening, but the insidiousness and omnipresence of disease raises incomparable fears. Use of contagion means hiding our children. It is about planes flying empty or perhaps not flying at all. It is about people refusing to interact with each other for fear of unseen and horrible affliction. It is about canceling public entertainment and tourism – even going to a movie would be too dangerous. It is about seismic disruption of investment markets, perhaps for months. A biological attack makes everyone in a society potentially vulnerable to our most fundamental terror: the fear of disease.

Ultimately, if your ambition is to rattle the pillars of modern civilization and perhaps cause it to collapse, there are only two options: nuclear or biological weapons. Use of either would set in motion political, economic, and health consequences so incomparably severe as to call into question the ability of existing governments to maintain their citizens' security. Bioweapons are far more available, cheaper, easier to use, undetectable, and could have more widespread and long-lasting effects. If you want to stop modern civilization in its tracks, bioviolence is the way to go.

EVALUATING RISKS

How likely is it that rogue States, terrorists, or criminal organizations will get and perhaps use bioweapons to commit a catastrophic attack? Any definitive answer here must be suspect; in truth, no one can say with any confidence. Most experts concur that a small attack (for example, murder of a spouse) is virtually inevitable, but it is not a simple matter to leap to an attack that far exceeds what can be done with a knife or gun. Another unanswerable issue has to do with the risks posed by lone attackers or small groups of persons who are tragically disaffected. The Unabomber, Ted Kaczynski, was a sophisticated mathematician capable of making ingenious letter bombs in his covert cabin in the woods – a similar loner with bioscience sophistication could produce far more lethal devices. Perpetrators of the Columbine and Virginia Tech massacres did not share an ideological commitment with Al Qaeda or anyone else; assessing the risk that similarly alienated teenagers will turn to disease instead of guns would be mere speculation.

Consider the recent warnings from Interpol Secretary General Ronald K. Noble:

> We know from recent events that terrorists remain committed to perpetrating large-scale violence.
>
> We also know that as biotechnology industries continue to expand throughout the world, new pathogens and pathogen-making technologies are rapidly proliferating, increasing the risk that terrorists could get their hands on deadly pathogens or their means of production. This is the so-called dual-use dilemma, and it is not going away anytime soon.

It is also becoming ever more possible for terrorists themselves to produce the weapons, as the volume and sophistication of the necessary information becomes increasingly accessible through publications, the Internet, and other sources. . . . And there is much evidence that terrorists have a strong interest in the use of biological weapons and are planning to use them.

Yet, in the face of all of this, some people still question whether the danger is real. They question whether it is truly necessary to prepare for it. I have no doubt that the threat is real. Moreover, given the magnitude of the harm that would be caused by a bioterrorism attack – hundreds, thousands, and even millions of deaths are possible – it is clear to me that this alone mandates that we take this threat seriously. Even if thousands or millions did not die, the panic and the subsequent harm that would follow such an attack would represent yet another set of reasons why we should care about this potential harm and do all in our power to fight against it.

Unfortunately, the progression of bioscience is raising risks. This progression is both vertical and horizontal. Vertically, escalating biological research offers the potential to uncover elemental principles of pathogenicity that could enable cultivation of a disease of such devastation that civilization itself could be fundamentally maimed with attendant risks of economic collapse and political upheaval. Horizontally, the bioscience sectors (academic research, pharmaceutical, and governmental) are proliferating rapidly across the planet, with a concomitant multiplying of the diversity of persons trained and engaged in that sector.

In short, there is opportunity and there is motive, and anyone concerned with crime and violence will attest to the danger of passivity in such circumstances.

2 Methods of Bioviolence

There are countless ways to commit bioviolence. Bioweapons are not a single, undifferentiated set of devices all used to common effect. Choices can be made from a lengthy menu of pathogens and a longer menu of dissemination methods to create many combinations; each faces different obstacles and has different consequences. Decades ago, there were only a few ways to commit a biocatastrophe, but bioscience progress is reconfiguring and rapidly expanding options.

How hard is it to commit bioviolence and how much specialized knowledge is needed? Much depends on the perpetrator's objective, the available pathogens and equipment, his organization's technical skill and sophistication, the risks of detection, and how those risks could be avoided. His choices in turn affect our tactics to defeat him. The essence of bioviolence prevention strategies is to make the hurdles of committing bioviolence more arduous; the bio-offender's challenge is to surmount or outwit those hurdles. This perpetual threat-response dynamic is one reason why bioviolence poses unique threats.

It is widely reported that bioviolence is easy, but even well-funded State programs have stumbled trying to make effective bioweapons. If it is that easy, why has there not yet been a successful catastrophic attack? Perhaps because it is actually more complicated. Many pathogens are ubiquitous and easily propagated; critical challenges tend to be about how to disseminate them either by physically spreading them amidst the target or by contagion. Yet, modern genomics is opening gateways for novel pathogens, and innovative engineering makes them easier to disseminate. There are premier scientists who certainly know how to make awesome bioweapons with minimal resources and pedestrian equipment, but it is unclear whether anyone so skillful wants to inflict a mass catastrophe.

For policy makers trying to prevent bioviolence, these back-and-forth assertions are frustrating. Where should limited resources be most effectively allocated? What risks are more serious and therefore deserve more attention? What risks are far-fetched and therefore might be deferred in view of more immediate threats? Answering these questions requires understanding how a catastrophic bioattack might proceed and what technical hurdles must be overcome.

This chapter discusses only catastrophic attacks having extensive and severe casualties or causing immense costs or long-term panic. There are virtually limitless ways to use bioagents for murder or vandalism; little purpose would be served in cataloguing the many ways to do what guns and explosives can already do more simply. This discussion is limited to what makes bioviolence unique – its potential to inflict truly vast harm – and focuses on how that high-end catastrophe can be accomplished.

INTERWOVEN CHOICES

Choices about which pathogen to use, how to obtain and prepare it for dissemination, and what device to use against which targets are all interwoven. Obstacles in one aspect affect choices in other aspects. No single pathogen is perfect for all objectives. Some are harmful to humans; some attack livestock or crops. A few are contagious. Some are easy to get but need to be highly refined to be used as weapons; some are difficult to get but, if obtained, can be readily put to malevolent use. For some there are vaccines; some are susceptible to environmental stress; some have a long incubation period; some cause diseases that are difficult to distinguish from a natural outbreak.

This chapter highlights some of the more realistic and often-discussed methods of bioviolence but does not try to present an encyclopedic description of diseases. Attention focuses on 1) smallpox, 2) influenza and hemorrhagic fevers, 3) anthrax, 4) toxin contamination of food, 5) attacks against agriculture, and 6) various agents historically used as bioweapons. Following discussion of these types of bioviolence, attention turns to emerging scientific advances and how they might contribute to bioviolence.

Table 2-1. briefly describes the more notable bioviolence agents.

Readers might notice this discussion's vagueness. Specifications that might be misused are intentionally omitted. Experts who focus on bioviolence have an ongoing debate about what information and ideas should be

Table 2-1. PRINCIPAL BIOVIOLENCE AGENTS

Pathogen	Lethality	Incubation; Symptoms	Contagiousness	Special Attack Attributes
Anthrax *Bacillus Anthracis* (spore–bacteria)	Inhalational = near 100% if untreated; gastroenteric = 25–65% if untreated; cutaneous = 2% if untreated	0.5–60 days; Organs swell and fail, bleeding of brain and nervous system	Cutaneous lesions are slightly contagious; not contagious via respiratory sputum	Natural agent needs to be refined; very stable; easy to store for long periods; extremely lethal; can be disseminated by air with proper equipment
Botulinum Toxin from *Clostridium botulinum*	6% if treated; nearly 100% if untreated	2–72 hours; respiratory paralysis and collapse	Not contagious	Extremely poisonous; easy to cultivate and transport
Brucellosis *Brucella* (Bacterium)	1–3%	7–21 days; Long-term fever	Not readily contagious	Can be transmitted through dairy products; used as an incapacitating agent
Cholera *Vibrio cholerae* (Bacterium)	1% if treated (depending on the type of strain; 50–90% if untreated	0.5–5 days; Diarrhea leading to dehydration	Low: primarily via contaminated water	Could be used to contaminate food and water supplies in developing countries
Ebola *Filoviridae* family (Virus)	50–90%	2–21 days; Fever leading to bleeding from bodily orifices	Moderate: through direct human-to-human contact; recovered patients may still be infectious	No approved vaccine; high mortality rate; victim is infectious after recovery; exists naturally in primates
Glanders *Burkholderia mallei* (Bacterium)	50% if treated	1–14 days; Fever, organ and circulatory system dysfunction	Low: via direct human-to-human contact; possible animal-to-human via aerosol	Common in the developing world; historical use in World War I; high mortality rate in humans; highly infectious
Influenza *Orthomyxoviridae* family (Virus)	Normal =.008% 1918 = 1% H5N1 = 50%	1–4 days; Fever, aches	Always, but rates vary greatly. 1918 = High; Avian flu = Low	Readily available; hard to eradicate; fast incubation; slow vaccine production; highly contagious
Marburg *Filoviridae* family (Virus)	25–100%	3–9 days; Vomiting, rash, bleeding, organ failure hypovolemic shock	Moderate: spread only through close human-to-human contact	No cure or vaccine; extremely infectious; spreads and multiplies in the host quickly

22

Agent	Fatality rate	Incubation period; Symptoms	Contagiousness / Transmission	Notes
Mad Cow *Bovine spongiform encephalopathy*	100% plus euthanasia of animals in contact	2–8 years	Through feed made with infected tissue	Huge economic effects; long incubation period leads to mass euthanasia of infected herds
Plague *Yersinia pestis* (Bacterium)	Septicemic = 30–75% if untreated; 4–15% if treated; pneumonic = 95% if untreated	pneumonic = 3 hours–4 days; Fever, coughing up blood, lymph node inflammation, septic shock	High: Infected vector; aerosol/person-to-person contact	Rapidly fatal if untreated; possible aerosolized delivery; highly sensitive to weather conditions; rapid incubation requires prompt response
Q fever (*Coxiella burnetii*) (Bacterium)	1%	10–20 days; Fever, pulmonary edema, heart inflammation	Low (rare): spread via food or airborne dust particles	Disseminated by water or aerosol; stable in environment; can survive for long periods outside host
Ricin Toxin produced from *Ricinus communis*	100% with 0.2 milligrams	8 hours	Not contagious	Easily produced from castor beans; highly lethal; useful for assassination
Salmonella (Bacterium)	0.5%	12–72 hours; diarrhea, severe dehydration	Not contagious	Easy to acquire; useful for food contamination to incapacitate
Smallpox *Variola major* (Virus)	20–40%	10–12 days; Rash, internal bleeding, organ failure	Moderately high: Person-to-person via respiratory sputum; contact with bodily fluids or contaminated objects	Thought to be unavailable; if obtained would spread rapidly through unvaccinated populations
Tularemia	2% if treated; 30–60% if untreated	1–14 days; Fever, diarrhea, can lead to meningitis	Not contagious; only spreads via aerosol or arthropod bites	Highly infectious; can be aerosolized (slow progression; low case fatality rate)
Typhus *Rickettsia prowazekii* Bacterium	10–60%	6–12 days; Fever, delirium	Not contagious; spreads by infected vectors	Thrives in regions infested by fleas, lice, mites, and rats; readily preventable
Venezuelan Equine Encephalitis (Virus)	1–20%	1–5 days	No reported human-to-human transfer; infection by vectors	Difficult to distinguish from influenza; no specific therapy; experimental vaccines not licensed for distribution

put in writing. Undeniably, information about how to conduct bioviolence is widely available. Yet, unlikely as it might be that this book would be a reference for a bio-offender, I am hesitant to put such information in print.

SMALLPOX

Smallpox, *Variola major*, is perhaps the most feared bioviolence agent. It is exceptionally lethal (up to 30 percent of its victims die). Smallpox is unique to humans; there is no other animal or insect vector. Except for specialized laboratory conditions, it can survive only briefly outside the human body – six to twenty-four hours depending on temperature and humidity.

Smallpox is contagious through inhalation of droplets exhaled by victims but only after a rash appears about ten days after exposure. Victims remain contagious but less so in the disease's later stages as scabs form and separate; during this period, most patients are incapacitated. Death usually occurs during the second week. It has a high incidence of second-generation cases. A single carrier can infect on average three but as many as twenty people.[1]

Eradication?

An effective vaccine was discovered centuries ago that led to the eradication of naturally occurring smallpox. After World War II, in humanity's greatest victory against disease, 120,000 doctors and health care personnel affiliated with the World Health Organization (WHO) initiated the *ring vaccination* campaign to identify smallpox victims and vaccinate everyone around them. If the disease would have nowhere to go, it would eventually die out for lack of a host. Identifying victims was horrifyingly easy due to the disease's unique red blisters; immune survivors could be identified by the disease's permanent scars. Key to the campaign's success was that WHO encouraged people in villages to report smallpox carriers – perhaps history's most successful global health reporting system. The campaign worked; the last reported case of naturally occurring smallpox occurred in the late 1970s. During the campaign, few unvaccinated people from smallpox-infected areas moved transnationally which helped contain outbreaks. This type of strategy might be less effective today especially if an outbreak occurs in global transport hubs.

Mass vaccination has serious consequences. For every million persons, 14 to 52 will experience life-threatening adverse reactions; one or two may die.[2] For people who are immune-compromised (e.g., carriers of HIV/AIDS or chemotherapy patients), the vaccine's lethality skyrockets. Therefore, following eradication, the WHO recommended that all nations cease vaccinations. In the United States, vaccinations stopped around 1972. Anyone born since then lacks immunity; older people's residual immunity has certainly faded over the years. Likely less than 15 percent of Americans are immune, but the percentages are even lower in less developed nations. Among children and young adults, only a handful of emergency responders and military personnel in advanced countries are vaccinated. Everyone else is susceptible. Ironically, vaccination led to eradication, which in turn has led to vulnerability should the disease reappear.

Today, a smallpox pandemic would run rampant through unvaccinated populations until health authorities could immunize enough people to once again enclose its spread. Speed is essential; vaccination can be administered within four days of first exposure, but it has limited effect thereafter.[3] In regions heavily impacted by HIV/AIDS, emergency vaccination administrators would have to carefully select who should be vaccinated. Safer and more effective vaccines are being developed, but their availability and consequences cannot now be accurately assessed. Moreover, while natural smallpox cannot easily leap over a ring of vaccinated persons, a human attacker could readily outwit tactics for containing the disease's spread.

The Challenge: Getting the Virus

Smallpox is not available in nature and may not be available anywhere else. If so, smallpox should not be a big worry. When the WHO declared the world free of smallpox, it recommended that every seed stock of the virus be destroyed. Only two viral stocks are known to exist, and they are tightly secured in the Centers for Disease Control and Prevention (CDC) in Atlanta and VEKTOR, a research laboratory outside of Novosibirsk, Russia. An attack on these sites is unlikely as it would set off worldwide alarms. Of greater concern is the risk that samples have been diverted. For example, after the Russians moved their strains from the Institute for Viral Preparations in Moscow, three samples of a specific strain were discovered missing and never seen again.[4] The WHO, which does not conduct on-site verification of either CDC or VEKTOR, was not informed of the move.

Whether to destroy the two remaining stockpiles has been controversial. During the 1980s and 1990s, the WHO Executive Committee on Orthopox unanimously decided (under U.S. pressure) to destroy the world's last strains of smallpox; each time, scientists and medical providers questioned the prudence of the virus's destruction. In the late 1990s, President Clinton reluctantly changed course and promoted a delay in destruction. Several types of research to develop an improved vaccine and antiviral medications (needed if there is ever a smallpox outbreak) require a viable virus sample. The WHO agreed to allow two to three additional years of research to combat the threat of smallpox's re-emergence. Clinton's spokesman Joe Lockhart said, "The decision reflects our concern that we cannot be entirely certain that after we destroy the declared stocks in Atlanta and Koltsovo, we will eliminate all the smallpox virus in existence."[5]

In December 2002, President Bush initiated the U.S. smallpox vaccination program; over 350 million doses of vaccine have been stockpiled, and health care response professionals are prepared to provide assistance if there is an outbreak. The U.S. military must vaccinate some service people, but mandatory vaccination for everyone was ruled out.

Why retain samples and vaccinate health care workers if the disease is unavailable? Maybe reports of its eradication are premature. A great fear is that the virus might exist outside the two designated high-security storage labs, perhaps at the former Soviet Union's bioweapons facilities. Former senior VEKTOR official, Ken Alibek, has testified that the Soviet Union produced dozens of tonnes of smallpox and other diseases during the Cold War until 1992, as will be discussed in Chapter 3. According to Alibek, VEKTOR scientists, starting with a strain obtained from India in 1959, genetically altered at least fifty strains of smallpox. They might have spliced smallpox with ebola thereby combining the two diseases' symptoms in order to create a "battle strain" that would be impervious to vaccine and incurable. Alibek said, "It is important to note that, in the Soviet's view, the best biological agents were those for which there was no prevention and no cure."[6] Most frightening is that the Soviets might have isolated a specific strain that causes hemorrhagic smallpox; instead of a mortality rate of about one in three, this virus could have a mortality rate of virtually 100 percent. These allegations are not currently verifiable, and some experts question them. Unquestionably, the Soviets figured out how to grow large quantities of smallpox, and they accomplished what some scientists believed was impossible: aerosolization.[7]

Former Soviet scientists might have sold virus samples or hidden them for later sale. If the virus exists in an undisclosed site, a bio-offender might overcome lax security or gain access via an insider's malfeasance. Russian scientists are known to have taught genetic engineering and molecular biology to scientists from Eastern Europe, Cuba, Libya, India, Iran, and Iraq. A recent intelligence assessment posits that Iraq and North Korea might have weaponized smallpox.[8] Iraq at one time had camelpox, although reports that Iraq created a smallpox-like disease have not been substantiated. North Korea continues to vaccinate its troops against small-pox to this day – an ominous sign in view of its research on bioweapons including propagation of germs for weaponization.

Even more frightening than the possibility of smallpox existing out-side WHO-approved sites is that scientists might re-create the virus using modern genetic engineering techniques. Scientists posit that this is beyond current capabilities: the smallpox genome has been deciphered, but it is among nature's most complex viruses. Yet, many scientists agree that it is only a matter of time – perhaps within a decade – before the virus might be re-engineered "from scratch."

What is beyond doubt is that if the virus were to fall into the wrong hands, a global pandemic could be ignited with innumerable casualties. No intricate steps are needed to start its spread. Ring vaccination would be complicated by the disease's long incubation period (over a week) that would allow carriers to move around the world without anyone (including themselves) knowing that they are an infectious timebomb. In some coun-tries, widespread vaccination would be rapidly initiated upon discovery of an outbreak – as the disease does not exist in nature, a victim would be proof that there has been an attack. If there is enough vaccine and it can be rapidly distributed into target communities where trained personnel can apply it and separate the immune-deficient from carriers, then the death toll could be limited.

The United States is far better prepared to meet a smallpox attack than it was a few years ago; likely the same can be said about other highly developed countries where response preparation is ongoing. The WHO's rapid response capabilities are commendably being enhanced. However, upwards of 75 percent of the world's population lacks emergency access to smallpox vaccine. A deliberately ignited epidemic in over-crowded cities in developing nations would horrifyingly meet few public health systems that are remotely capable of containing its spread. Outside perhaps two dozen States, a smallpox attack could kill three in ten unvaccinated healthy persons and many more who are weakened by HIV, malaria, tuberculosis, or other widespread afflictions. Conservatively stated, millions of people could die from a well-planned attack. [9] Short of thermonuclear holocaust, it is hard to envision any worse human-inflicted cataclysm.

INFLUENZA AND HEMORRHAGIC FEVERS

Today, the direst biothreats are contagious viruses that are much more available than smallpox. These viral agents can be weaponzied in moderately equipped laboratories and disseminated by human carriers. There are obstacles to using viruses, and some of these viral threats exceed current capabilities. Yet, there are techniques for circumventing those obstacles readily within tomorrow's grasp.

Influenza

Influenza is ubiquitous and remarkably contagious after a short one to two day incubation period.[10] Its common variants have low lethality rates but are so widespread that flu causes more deaths than any of the 1,500 human disease microbes: over one million people worldwide in an average year.[11] Scientists estimate that an influenza pandemic could spread across the globe in eight to twelve months infecting 40 percent of humanity.[12] It bears remembering that the worst global pandemic in modern times was the 1918–19 Spanish Flu that killed more than forty million people. The 1957 Asian Flu and the 1968 Hong Kong Flu each accounted for millions of casualties.

Reasons for Concern

A key to flu's dangers is its mutability. It is among nature's simplest and most mutation-prone RNA viruses, with an eight-segment genome encoding ten proteins.[13] Its segments break up in the host and absorb different genetic material in a process called reassortment. As the virus moves from migratory birds to domesticated foul and swine and then to humans, its genetic code "shifts" creating new strains. This natural process is random, but it is a trivial matter to induce changes with rudimentary equipment, a stockpile of eggs, and pedestrian understanding of its well-mapped gene sequence. Legitimate scientists extensively study the influenza virus and regularly mix and match flu genes; modifying its genome requires common knowledge and equipment.[14] It is more difficult to direct that process to make flu effective for bioviolence.

The lethality of a particular strain of flu depends in part on how rapidly the virus replicates within the host. Most human strains replicate slowly enough so that healthy persons' immune systems can defeat the invasion albeit after a few days of fever and discomfort. People with compromised immune systems or elderly persons succumb more readily because even a slowly replicating virus meets little resistance. By contrast, the 1918 virus (an H_5N_1 variant) replicated thousands of times faster than common strains; young healthy adults died disproportionately, often within a day of contracting the disease. Midlife healthy persons' stronger immune systems might have been their death sentence as the wildly multiplying virus caused shock due to immune system overload.

Recently, scientists took RNA fragments of the 1918 influenza from the lungs of victims preserved in pathology museums or frozen permafrost[15] and reconstituted the disease using commonly available reverse genetics techniques.[16] Researchers learned which genes were responsible for making the virus so harmful[17] and, in 2005, published the virus's genetic code on the internet and in *Science* magazine.[18] Experts are concerned that hostile perpetrators could abuse these widely understood techniques to reproduce the 1918 influenza.[19]

At this time, the Avian Flu (another H_5N_1 variant) is threatening to ignite a new pandemic. Remarkably lethal, it has killed upward of 50 percent of those who contracted it from infected birds or very close contact with infected persons. Fortunately, it is not now readily contagious human-to-human via casual aerosol delivery. Could the virus, through natural mutation, stumble upon a genetic combination that is equally lethal but far more contagious? How difficult would it be for a malevolent bioscientist to manipulate the natural virus to augment its contagiousness?[20] Some experts predict that a readily contagious Avian Flu pandemic could generate more than 180 million casualties worldwide.[21] What might that number be if human malevolence operates to transmit the virus throughout diverse population centers? What if suicide carriers deliberately outwit health care responders trying to contain the disease, thwarting efforts to curtail the disease's spread by harassing medical supplies and disrupting quarantines?[22]

Limits of Protection

On April 1, 2005, President Bush authorized the use of quarantines and other isolation measures against international travelers suspected of carrying influenza.[23] Yet, because influenza naturally occurs, medical personnel would have a difficult time identifying a bioviolence flu attack early on.[24] An attack might initially be mistaken for a natural outbreak. Moreover, it is unlikely that isolation measures would be successful given influenza's high level of contagiousness. These measures might be marginally effective in the United States, but it is unrealistic to believe that comparable measures could have a discernible impact in developing nations.

Vaccines are the best line of defense for seasonal influenza outbreaks but would have doubtful efficacy in controlling an intentional flu pandemic.[25] Influenza vaccines are produced each year after the WHO identifies the likely disease strain. For vaccines to work, people must be vaccinated before exposure to the virus; once a person has contracted the disease, it is dangerous to administer a vaccine made from viral strains because it might re-assort with the actual virus. After an outbreak of an unexpected strain, it would take approximately six months to develop and distribute influenza vaccines and additional months to deliver them, just about the same time it would take for the virus to spread around the world.[26] In view of influenza's very short incubation period, masses could already be exposed before health officials could administer the vaccine. Vaccines would therefore play only a limited role within the first twelve to eighteen months of the pandemic.

Moreover, there are barriers to vaccine preparation. Producers complain that they could not manufacture sufficient doses of vaccine in such haste without special liability protection.[27] (Liability protections for vaccine producers are discussed in Chapter 6.) Vaccines are produced now by companies in nine developed nations: Australia, Canada, France, Germany, Italy, Japan, the Netherlands, the United Kingdom, and the United States.[28] Likely, during a flu pandemic, these nations will nationalize vaccine production facilities and reserve supplies for domestic populations. If so, perhaps fewer than 500 million people (7 percent of the world's population) would be vaccinated.[29]

Antiviral medications and inhibitor drugs could be an effective countermeasure to an influenza attack, but these medications are in short supply. Moreover, because of flu's short incubation period, administering these drugs quickly enough would be a grave challenge, and they cannot repair damage already done to the host.[30] Yet, it is noteworthy that in April 2007, the World Health Organization brought experts together to discuss the creation, maintenance, and funding of a global stockpile of H_5N_1 vaccine and medications. These experts agreed that the stockpile was feasible and consistent with International Health Regulations that are the overarching framework to ensure global health security.[31]

Even if a super-lethal influenza outbreak could be contained and the number of casualties limited, the devastating economic impact throughout the world could have dire international security implications. The WHO estimates as much as $200 billion in losses worldwide with a modest avian influenza pandemic.[32] Also worth remembering here is that social interaction stopped during the 1918 epidemic; people were afraid to embrace, shake hands, or even stand next to one another. Group

stereotypes were exaggerated, and doctors, nurses, and healthcare workers were accused of deliberately infecting patients. A modern influenza
attack could have similar disruptive consequences.

Hemorrhagic Fever Viruses

The hemorrhagic fever viruses including ebola, marburg, lassa virus, rift
valley fever, yellow fever, omsk hemorrhagic fever, and kyasanur forest
disease are widely considered to be bioviolence agents. Indeed, both the
former Soviet Union and the United States weaponized these viruses; the
Soviets allegedly stockpiled large quantities of the ebola and marburg
viruses until 1992. These viruses can be exceptionally lethal – marburg
has a death rate of 25–70 percent; ebola has a much higher case fatality
of 50–90 percent. No cure and no vaccine are available for these viruses.
Treatment is limited to supportive therapy requiring continual attentive
care. A widespread outbreak would put enormous strain on public health
personnel who would have to monitor everyone in a major city that exhibits
symptoms as well as take radical measures to protect themselves and the
public from contagion.

These viruses have substantial disadvantages for use as weapons. An
offender would have to avoid the substantial risk of unintentional self-
infection. Also, carriers are contagious only after the two to twenty-one
day period of incubation when symptoms of fever, chills, headache, and
body ache are horribly manifest. Yet, these viruses are regularly cited as
topics of potential research that could alter key attributes so as to make
them more favorable terror weapons.[33] With advancing knowledge about
how to manipulate viruses, the traits that make these agents difficult to
weaponize might be a diminishing barrier.

Acquiring the Agent: Initiating the Attack

The first challenge is acquiring the agent. One option would be to obtain
the virus from a naturally occurring outbreak. Indeed, in 1992, the Japanese
cult Aum Shinrikyo (now known as Aleph) sent a "medical mission" to
Zaire to purportedly help care for the victims of an ebola outbreak; it really
sought to collect and cultivate ebola samples to bring back to Japan.[34] Its
efforts, however, did not give rise to a successful attack.

A more covert way to acquire these viruses would be from animal carriers. The offender would have to travel to the rainforests of Africa or to
areas in the Western Pacific where the virus is indigenous.[35] He would
have to canvass numerous bats (the disease's natural reservoir)[36] and collect several field samples in order to isolate the virus. Even if he finds an

infected animal, it would be difficult to carry it undiscovered through customs. He could, of course, self-infect by coming into direct contact with the animal's feces, urine, or saliva or by handling an infected carcass. But if he self-infects prematurely, he will be dead or obviously ill before arriving at population centers. An attack of this type would, therefore, require substantial logistical planning.

Alternatively, a bio-offender might try to acquire agent strains from a laboratory. It is unlikely, however, that an offender would purchase or steal agents from a guarded laboratory lest he raise alarms and expose the criminal plot to authorities. Experiments with viral strains are performed in Biosafety Level (BSL) 4 labs (the highest level requiring the utmost protection and security), although specimens can be stored in BSL-2 facilities.[37] A less-guarded laboratory or clinic, especially near locations where these viruses are endemic, might pose considerably fewer obstacles.

Disseminating the Virus

Although these viruses are contagious, transmission among humans is not as easy as transmitting the flu. Natural aerosol transmission is not considered effective for these viruses,[38] although it has been documented.[39] Certainly, direct contact with infected body fluids or contaminated bed sheets and clothing would suffice, but this is not an efficient dissemination method for a mass attack. To ensure transmission, offenders would have to aggressively yet undetectably expose people to a patient's blood, saliva, or feces by coughing up sputum, contaminating door knobs or hand rails with mucus or blood, bumping into people to expose their skin to sweat, or even pricking them with a contaminated needle. There is a window of at most a few days before being severely debilitated during which time offenders would have to come into close contact with as many people as possible to transmit the disease. Soon, the rash, jaundice, and massive hemorrhaging would likely lead to their detection and isolation; health authorities would be put on alert and could institute preemptive precautionary measures to curb the outbreak. Anyone exhibiting symptoms would be advised to seek medical attention.

With a modified virus or many attackers (or both), the best dissemination system is via the enclosed cabin of a crowded passenger jet where constantly recirculating air and the close proximity of passengers could expose many people on board. At the destination, the attackers could walk around the airport, sneeze and cough in crowds, and board another flight to a new destination. At the same time, unknowing victims would board other flights to yet other destinations. Even this method of infecting many people is haphazard. Because death is so quick and so horrifying, victims would be incapacitated then dead before having much opportunity to infect others. Yet, if a well-designed attack could infect a critical mass of people, the contagion could spread as the victims would unknowingly become attackers and continue to spread the virus on their own to an unlimited number of people.

Aerosol release of a weaponized virus would require isolation, cultivation, and stabilization of large quantities of the virus. This would require a thorough knowledge of the virus and sophisticated laboratory as well as safety equipment for avoiding accidental infection. Moreover, the theory that humans can contract the ebola or marburg viruses via aerosol delivery has been based upon reported laboratory experiments on monkeys; even if perpetrators have the knowledge and capacity to obtain aerosolized viruses, it is uncertain if an aerosol attack would be effective against humans.

Another dissemination method for contagious viruses would be to use living *vectors* – typically insects – to transmit infectious agents. Conceivably, large quantities of mosquitoes could be infected with a disease that they carry in nature. However, the insect species must be compatible with the chosen pathogen; many mosquitoes have limited geographic and climatic range; and they are notoriously unreliable. The Soviet Union researched this dissemination method, and the U.S. Army Chemical Corps in 1956 released uninfected mosquitoes in the southeast United States to test the feasibility of insects as dissemination vectors. Although there is scant evidence that terrorists have mastered techniques for insect dissemination, experts have noted that even developed nations such as the United States are ill-prepared to address this type of attack:

> Tools for responding to bioterrorism involving insect agents are lacking. Effective traps or other detection methods, federal and state action plans, eradication plans tested in the region of the insects' origins, pesticides registered for use against insect agents, educational plans for the agricultural community and general public, and legal understanding and enforcement to institute control measures are needed.[40]

ANTHRAX

Anthrax is atop everyone's list of bioviolence agents. U.S., Soviet, and Iraqi bioweaponeers valued anthrax as one of the best agents for offensive military purposes. It is remarkably lethal. Inhaled anthrax spores rapidly multiply and release powerful toxins; the fatality rate for untreated inhalational anthrax approaches 100 percent. Prompt treatment with powerful antibiotics can save lives, but the larger the quantity of inhaled anthrax, the more quickly those antibiotics must be administered.[41] If administered too late, victims face agonizing death regardless of modern medicine's best efforts. Fortunately, anthrax is not contagious person-to-person. Igniting a global anthrax epidemic is impossible, but multiple separate attacks throughout the world present a hugely potent threat.

The WHO estimates that fifty kilograms of anthrax disseminated over an urban population of five million would result in 250,000 casualties. The United States Congressional Office of Technology Assessment estimates that at least 130,000 deaths could result from the aerosolized dissemination of one hundred kilograms of anthrax spores upwind from the Washington, DC, area. According to a CDC economic model, an anthrax attack would cost $26.2 billion for every 100,000 persons exposed.[42]

In late 2001, only weeks after the World Trade Center bombings, highly refined anthrax powder was laced on envelopes mailed to senators and media figures. Twenty-two cases (eleven cutaneous – through skin – and eleven inhalational) were identified; five people died. The genetic fingerprint of the anthrax proved it was a version of the Ames strain that was used in U.S. and other bioweapons programs, although experts contend that the anthrax was not of weapons-quality. The spores were highly refined, enabling them to float for optimal dispersion and easy inhalation.[43] When asked of the potential origin of the Ames strain of anthrax mailed to the Senate office buildings, Dr. Alibek answered, " . . . to get this type of product [anthrax], there is no necessity to have any sophisticated equipment. . . . It could be done if this person knows how to do this by using very simple techniques, very simple equipment, and this product could be obtained in any amount."[44] Elaborating on who could obtain this particular type of anthrax, Dr. Alibek added:

> I am talking about the lowest level of expertise. It could be a lab technician. It could be a technician working at one of the companies or even somebody who worked before, many years before, in this field. . . . Recently, there was a publication in the *New York Times* that one individual from Utah was selling some manuals on how to make anthrax. . . . In this case, if somebody bought this manual and has some knowledge, has some time and training, this person would be able to develop this product.[45]

There is an anthrax vaccine. Although its effectiveness and side effects are disputed in connection with its use during the first Gulf War, it is now available to military personnel, first responders, and other officials. This vaccine could enable a bio-offender to handle anthrax with less risk of self-infection. A State contemplating use of bioweapons could inoculate its troops so as to diminish risks of blowback (changes in wind direction that blow the aerosol in unanticipated directions).

Getting and Cultivating Seed Stock

Anthrax is widely endemic to grazing animals such as sheep, cattle, and goats; cutaneous infection is an occupational hazard for people who work with such animals or their hides. Eating undercooked meat from infected animals can lead to gastrointestinal anthrax. These types of natural anthrax infections occur, not surprisingly, most in countries with low health safety standards but are rare in developed nations. Neither cutaneous nor gastrointestinal anthrax pose a risk of a biocatastrophe that is comparable to inhalational anthrax.

Unlike smallpox, which requires scant if any weaponization, preparation of anthrax for a mass catastrophe is challenging. Anthrax is a spore; in its natural condition, it falls to the ground where it is unlikely to be inhaled. An attacker would have to suspend spores in the air at nose-height, heavy enough to not be blown away and small enough to penetrate into the lungs. Although growing it is easy, it is difficult to separate and aerosolize large amounts with requisite size, weight, and viscosity for a widespread attack. Moreover, there are myriad strains, most of which are not particularly useful from a weapons perspective. The attacker would have to choose a particular strain that satisfies technical requirements for weaponization.

Starting with a natural seed stock, even one of a usable strain, would entail refining, which requires know-how and equipment that could be very expensive and could risk detection.[46] Most bio-offenders would probably prefer to divert an already refined strain cleansed of impurities that might impede its lethality or complicate handling. In most developed States, purchase of refined anthrax stocks is limited to authorized persons, and these purchases are well-recorded and traceable. (This legal requirement is more fully discussed in Chapter 5.) Breaking into a laboratory to steal pathogens would alert law enforcers and leave clues of who is preparing a bioattack. A better alternative would be to divert agents from an insecure facility either by sneaking in or using someone already inside. Or, refined pathogens might be diverted during transport from one legitimate user to another, especially if the carrier fails to observe basic antitheft measures. Unfortunately, in too many places, transport of lethal pathogens and bio-equipment is inadequately supervised.

A large quantity of agent will likely be needed for a catastrophic attack. Reports that anthrax spores can be cultured in nothing more sophisticated than a beer fermenter are half-true; certainly cultivating spores is trivial, but sustaining optimal growth conditions to produce highly refined, near-weapons-quality anthrax for effective dissemination to a large target is challenging. Slight changes in prevailing conditions might allow undesirable microorganisms to grow and perhaps kill the desired cells. These obstacles might be easier to overcome with sophisticated cultivation equipment that is more forgiving of minor mistakes.[47] For someone who is technically knowledgeable, researching growth and media requirements and techniques to propagate anthrax is easy. There is a correlation, therefore, between the offender's expertise, the pathogen strain, and whether the offender has sophisticated equipment.

The agent must be separated from its growth medium, formulated, and loaded in the chosen dissemination device. These steps can vary enormously. It might be appropriate to mill the agent into a very fine powder, but milling requires considerable sophistication in order to preserve the agents' viability. Milling is not required; it appears that the anthrax used in 2001 was not milled.[48] Containment and safety are always top priorities lest agent release sicken the bio-offender and his team as well as reveal covert preparations. Protective equipment including glove boxes, air filtration systems, respirators, high-efficiency particulate filter masks, and encapsulated suits can reduce risks. These items are commercially available, but purchasing them might be traced.

Disseminating the Agent

The hardest technical challenge of anthrax bioviolence is to match the agent's characteristics with appropriate dissemination technology so that it has the intended effect. Aerosol delivery is the most commonly discussed dissemination method, but it is challenging to produce a cloud of particles that are light enough to not instantly drop to the ground and small enough to be inhaled deep into the lung.

Aerosols can be sprayed either as a dry powder or liquid suspension. It is easier to produce a liquid spray, but processing it to a desired particle size is harder. Dry powders are more stable – an important consideration for storing and shipping – but the drying process can destroy many organisms. Significantly, drying creates a dangerous work environment. Most drying equipment (drum pelletizers, pan dryers, and spray or freeze-drying equipment, etc.) is commercially available, but an astute tracking system might recognize systematic high-end purchases as suggesting covert bioweapons preparations.

Pressurized sprayers mounted on a vehicle can spread agent evenly over the chosen area, but they must be adapted to disperse the agent in a fine mist. Such sprayers can be as simple as an insect fogger or as complex as a specialized cluster warhead carried on a ballistic missile. Sprayers suitable for insecticides would need to be altered to work; achieving proper flow for widespread dissemination of precise particles faces serious obstacles. The Aum Shunrikyo cult in Japan planned to disseminate pathogens from a modified briefcase consisting of a small tank to contain the agent, a small fan, a vent, and a battery. With a modified sprayer, a crop duster could be an ideal attack vehicle. This explains why so much concern has been expressed over discovery that some terrorist cells tried to acquire crop dusters, and why work on drone aircraft, unsuitable for carrying for explosives but very effective for carrying biological or chemical agents, raises anxiety.[49]

An alternative to spraying is to use explosives. However, much of the agent would be destroyed, and a lot of what remains would be too big to get into the lungs. Moreover, an explosion would deposit the agent in thick concentrations where detonated without evenly spreading it over a large area; military programs developed cluster munitions to address this concern. Yet, the difficulties of using munitions to spread an even carpet of agent might be irrelevant to a terrorist or criminal who is already planning to bomb a target and is considering adding pathogens for extra effect.

Because anthrax is noncontagious and difficult to get into the air for mass inhalation, it is most likely to be used in a confined space under controlled conditions. Large stadiums are logical places to attack – crowds of 50–100,000 spectators are easy to find. Outdoor stadiums would mean exposure to sunlight, wind, and rain, which diminishes the chances for a successful attack; if weather conditions permit, however, an anthrax attack on an outdoor stadium can be catastrophic. Indoor arenas provide a more controlled environment; modern ventilation technology could douse large sections.[50] Air conditioning and circulation units at arenas could be manipulated to blow anthrax throughout an entire stadium. Domed arenas with negative air pressure could take advantage of powerful fans that circulate air and thereby the anthrax powder.[51]

There are even simpler dissemination techniques. A strategically placed team could wave banners, towels, or pompoms that are saturated with anthrax powder and resaturated from a cooler or large bag. Fans at music and other entertainment venues often wave items in the dark. Only slightly more complex would be to use rudimentary pumps that can be purchased for less than $50; modifying such devices to discretely spread anthrax is trivial. More complex would be to use foggers; in a rock concert using pyrotechnics, such devices and the resulting cloud might be seen as "special effects."

Densely populated office buildings could also be an anthrax target. If the offender can deposit the anthrax into a building's air circulation system, it could circulate throughout the building. Security personnel could be an obstacle, but many of the world's huge office buildings are unguarded; in some instances, guards might be bribable. Better would be to have a team member in the target building employed as a guard or janitor with essentially unlimited access to these systems. Electronic locks and alarms on these systems could be effective safeguards; even more effective are HEPA filters.[52] However, few buildings are so equipped. Elevator shafts are also effective means of distributing clouds of powder. It is not very difficult to use the shaft's vertical movement to pump a lot of agent throughout a modern skyscraper.

Subway systems are another enclosed venue for launching an anthrax attack. In New York City, subways carry nearly one million people per day in tunnels with fans to circulate air. With enough anthrax and enough people to distribute it, the trains and the fans could circulate the powder.

All of these attack modes face impediments that could make them more complicated than portrayed here. Many experts believe that, today, an attack causing tens of thousands of casualties would probably be beyond the capabilities of a lunatic or sole fanatic but not impossible for a terrorist organization with access to laboratory seed stocks. It is worth remembering that the 2001 attacks that killed five people effectively shut down Congress and, according to the EPA, cost hundreds of millions of dollars in clean-up fees and detection expenses.[53] An attack that kills 500 people would generate incalculable panic and need for remediation. Repetition of comparable attacks would have unquantifiable consequences.

BOTULINUM IN FOOD

Botulinum toxin, produced by the bacterium *Clostridium botulinum*, is one of the most poisonous substances known. In a single gram is enough toxin to kill over one million people. It is lethal if inhaled, injected into the bloodstream, or ingested through contaminated food products. Botulinum is unsuitable for aerosol delivery against a widely dispersed target and therefore considered not to be an effective battlefield agent, but it could be effective against persons in a highly confined space. Symptoms first appear as stomach cramps, vomiting, and diarrhea (if ingested), leading to complete muscle paralysis in a matter of hours. If untreated, botulism can have a mortality rate of 100 percent; but only a 6 percent mortality rate in intestinal botulism cases if promptly diagnosed and treated.[54]

According to a Senate Report on the Alleged Assassination Plots Involving Foreign Leaders, the United States developed various schemes to use botulinum toxin to assassinate Fidel Castro. In 1961, the CIA saturated a box of Castro's favorite cigars with concentrations of the toxin so potent that a person would die simply after putting one of the cigars in his mouth. The cigars were delivered to an unidentified person but did not actually get to Castro. Later, the CIA tried to poison Castro's food with botulinum toxin. This was seen as "something 'nice and clean, without getting into any kind of out and out ambushing' preferably a poison that would disappear without a trace."[55] Pills containing the toxin were delivered to two persons with access to Castro, but in each case the recipient returned the pills unused.

After the 1991 Persian Gulf War, Iraq admitted to have stockpiled 19,000 liters of concentrated botulinum toxin (10,000 liters had been loaded into 13 ballistic missiles and 100 bombs). Nearly 20,000 liters of toxin are not accounted for.[56]

Disseminating botulinum is challenging. Released into the air, the toxin degrades quickly due to temperature and humidity. Released into water, the toxin is readily inactivated by purification systems.[57] To commit a catastrophic attack, botulinum would likely be aimed at the food industry. The toxin is colorless, odorless, and tasteless making it undetectable in food. Because the toxin is inactivated when exposed to temperatures over 85 degrees Celsius for five minutes, it would be most effective if laced on food products that are eaten raw. Getting access to fruit or vegetables is trivial, and toxins can be spread by hand; contaminating salad bars or other unguarded food supplies could sicken a few people. An infamous example involving not botulinum but salmonella was when the Rajanishee cult in Oregon spread it on salad bars. Escalating from a local disturbance to a mass catastrophe, however, multiplies the difficulties of circulating enough agent to many people without being noticed.

Recently, two Stanford researchers published an article in the Proceedings of The National Academies of Sciences suggesting that terrorists could easily kill or injure hundreds of thousands of people by putting botulinum toxin in the milk supply.[58] Twenty billion gallons of milk distributed yearly in the United States are stored in unprotected tanks prior to processing. It would be a relatively simple matter, they alleged, to release botulinum toxin into these tanks. Although the pasteurization process will inactivate 68.4 percent of the toxin, over a half million people would consume contaminated milk resulting in 100,000 casualties, perhaps more. Notably, most victims would be children who are preponderant drinkers of milk.

After publication, other scientists disputed the ease of such an attack, claiming that it would take an enormous amount of toxin to spread throughout the milk supply. Moreover, advanced pasteurization processes can eliminate over 99 percent of the toxin. Nevertheless, the article's specificity about how to execute a successful attack has fueled debate about whether to constrain publication of scientific articles lest potential bio-offenders gain access to dangerous information.[59] Accompanying the article's publication was an editorial by NAS President Bruce Alberts explaining that the article did not contain any technical information that is not readily available and that it is useful for other scientists to think of solutions to the problem.

AGROVIOLENCE

The modern era of biological weapons began in World War I when German agents infected horses with glanders. The Soviets took agroviolence the farthest. Its *Ecology* program weaponized variants of foot and mouth disease (FMD), rinderpest, African swine fever, various poultry diseases, and diseases to be sprayed from low-flying airplanes against economically important crops. More recently, the Iraqi bioweapons program included anti-crop agents such as wheat smut.

Today, agroviolence is a way to trigger widespread disruption that has crippling economic effects without necessarily causing mass human casualties. The 2001 natural outbreak of foot and mouth disease (FMD) in the United Kingdom inflicted costs at $6–30 billion. A single case of mad cow disease in the United States caused a $2.4 billion drop in beef exports.[60] Agro-attacks will have a disproportionate effect on farmers, ranchers, and food processors and will be most devastating against countries that produce nearly all of their population's diet. Countries where food exports are a substantial component of the economy would also suffer substantially. An attack against United States agriculture, for example, would not mean starvation because of advanced international trade systems, but there would be untold damage to a $50 billion per year export market in food.

Motivations and Feasibility

Some bio-offenders might be disinclined to commit mass murder whether for moral reasons or lest the attack blow back against them or their allies. For bio-offenders especially concerned with self-preservation, it is safer to work with agents that uniquely threaten crops and livestock than with human pathogens. Bio-offenders who are fretful of capture might use pests to resemble a natural blight. Or, agroviolence perpetrators might be motivated by simple greed: "Profit could be made by manipulation of futures markets, selling short the stock of major agrochemical companies, or intentionally sabotaging overseas competitors to capture lost import markets."[61]

One unique group of potential bio-offenders opposes the use of animals in research and treatment of livestock. An anti-crop attack might highlight their fury by striking a heavy economic loss while not hurting animals (including humans). Some opponents of genetically modified (GM) crops and animals could use pathogens to destroy GM organisms. Radical animal rights groups might attack livestock to prevent businesses from profiting from animal suffering. Ingrid Newkirk, president of the People for the Ethical Treatment of Animals, stated her hope "that FMD comes to the United States. It will bring economic harm only for those who profit from giving people heart attacks and giving animals a concentration camp-like existence. It would be good for animals, good for human health, and good for the environment."[62]

Agro-pathogens are abundant. Numerous diseases could be used against livestock. The Animal Health Organization (Office Internationale des Epizooties [OIE]) lists seventeen readily transmissible animal diseases that can seriously disrupt internationally traded animals and animal products.[63] It is easy to locate disease outbreaks; various internet sites post veterinarians' reports. Getting a pathogen sample could be as easy as wiping an animal's infected area with a cloth; disease could be spread by rubbing other animals' faces or injecting a slurry from infected tissue. As the pathogen multiplies in the host animal's system, the perpetrators increase their arsenal. A few milligrams of pathogenic material could initiate multiple outbreaks in widely dispersed locales. Refined seed stock of harmful agro-agents could also be obtained from any of 450 repositories in 67 nations. It is easy to transport agro-pathogens with scant risk of detection; they can be cultured without expensive or specialized laboratory equipment. "For instance, a few hundred micro-liters of scrapings from the blistered mucosa of an FMD-infected animal, or blood from an animal hemorrhaging from ASF, or a handful of wheat tillers heavily infected by the stem rust pathogen can provide more than enough agent to initiate an epidemic."[64]

Attacks of Grave Concern

Livestock Diseases

Attacks against livestock could take advantage of farm animals' living conditions to accelerate the spread of disease. Feedlots commonly hold up to 100,000 head of cattle, and poultry production units can house a million birds. In the United States, thirty feedlots fatten over five million head of cattle, and the thirty-two largest packing plants process over 80 percent of all beef.

Some diseases are essentially untreatable; at least twenty-two livestock diseases have no vaccine.[65] Infected carriers must be isolated and destroyed. If one animal in a herd is identified as infected, usually an entire herd must be destroyed. Worst are diseases that vaccines have long eradicated from a region. Because vaccinations have ceased, deliberate re-introduction of the disease would face no existing immunity or responsive veterinary infrastructure. Foot and mouth disease can become airborne and travel as far as 60 kilometers over land and 300 kilometers over sea; it can also be spread by animate vectors and through direct contact with an infected animal. Bio-offenders could use multiple agents, attack many sites simultaneously, or use drug-resistant organisms.[66] Igniting an extensive pandemic is challenging, yet smaller attacks could entail merely spraying viral preparations with a simple atomizer, perhaps where animals are densely penned (as in chicken houses or piggeries). Even if each attack is eventually contained, the threat of new attacks could arouse economically ruinous quarantines and trade sanctions.

In 2003, two U.S. government expert panels assessed the threat from animal pathogens that could be used for bioviolence and established research and development priorities to reduce these threats: The Interagency Weapons of Mass Destruction (WMD) Counter Measures Working Group – Animal Pathogens Research and Development Subgroup (2003), and a White House Office of Science and Technology Policy (OSTP)

Agroterrorism Countermeasures Blue Ribbon Panel (December 2003).[67] Ten animal diseases were identified for urgent vaccine and antiviral research and development; significant investments were recommended.

Perhaps the livestock disease of greatest concern involves prions – particles of protein that alter normal proteins in the body and can cause incurable neurological ailments (bovine spongiform encephalopathy or mad cow disease in cattle; Creutzfeldt-Jakob disease or CJD in humans). It is infectious through consumption of infected meat regardless of cooking; an attack against animals could be transmitted to humans. It was once common practice to feed cattle ground-up bits of other animals; if the disease was in this feed, it could readily spread to other animals. In the 1990s in the United Kingdom, an outbreak of mad cow disease and the subsequent discovery that CJD had caused over a hundred human fatalities ultimately caused as much as $50 billion in losses.[68] Most developed nations now prohibit feeding livestock the ground brains or skeletal remains of other animals, but there is dispute about whether the disease can be transmitted via consumption of still-allowed muscle tissue.

Crop Diseases

Attacks against crops are easy to execute. Pathogens can be obtained virtually anywhere; methods for preparing the seed stock are widely understood; and large quantities of the agent can be produced with little more than a backyard garden. A perpetrator could mix the spores into fertilizer and hand-spread it in an unprotected field. Spores could be loaded into a crop duster and sprayed over a large area without special preparation; natural weather conditions would continue to spread the pathogen. All this activity could be performed with scant risk of detection by law enforcement.

From an offender's perspective, the problem in using crop diseases is that, at least in developed nations, effective mitigation and response measures could limit the harm. Large agri-business has ready access to response tools such as antifungal crop sprays, soil treatments, and alternative seed grain cultivars specifically bred to be disease-resistant. Reversing crop damage is impossible, but these techniques can stop the spread of disease quickly and prevent soil contamination from threatening future crops. However, in less developed nations where sophisticated farming techniques are not widely practiced, the financial costs of combating a crop disease outbreak could be prohibitive for impoverished farmers. The high concentration of monocultures (single species) limits genetic diversity thereby reducing resistance to contagious diseases. An epidemic could spread throughout the region, threaten the entire crop for the year, and contaminate the soil with fungal spores that could threaten future crops as well.

A quandary of agroviolence against crops is distinguishing wrongful from legitimate activity. Drug control efforts of the United States and the United Nations have supported use of virulent strains of fungi, notably *Fusarium*, against crops of opium, poppy, coca, and cannabis. The work is alarmingly analogous to the Soviet Union's anti-crop bioweapons programs and raises concerns about dual use pathogen research: the difference between anti-drug-crop programs and agroviolence programs is that the targeted crop is designated as "illegal." But that can be an inconsistent justification for inflicting widespread agro-disease. Moreover, deliberately releasing plant pathogens to destroy drug crops could provoke drug criminals to retaliate by attacking food crops thereby initiating a sustained exchange of bioweapons.

International Prevention Systems

The good news about agroviolence is that the international system to prevent the spread of crop and livestock diseases is quite sophisticated. The OIE has robustly risen to the challenge. It informs governments about diseases and how to control them, assists States in implementing consistent regulatory systems, and helps coordinate resources and information efficiently in the event of disease.

The international system to control crop diseases is supervised by the International Plant Protection Convention[69] (IPPC, under the auspices of the United Nations Food and Agriculture Organization [FAO]) which promotes standards to prevent the spread of harmful plant pests and pathogens. Also noteworthy is that the international system to prevent traffic of diseased animals and plants (whether unintentionally or deliberately smuggled) is among the world's most sophisticated regulatory systems, jointly supervised by the FAO and the World Customs Organization (WCO). Yet, there is widespread concern that more action is needed. According to the United States National Research Council,

> The United States should investigate the global eradication of those animal diseases posing significant threats and cooperate with international agricultural and wildlife experts in doing so. A continuing international mechanism to identify measures needed for global eradication of particular diseases should be established. Through such a mechanism, a global

vaccination and eradication strategy could be developed with the participation of diverse experts and stakeholders.[70]

AGENTS HISTORICALLY USED AS BIOWEAPONS

A handful of agents are widely cited for their previous development or
use as bioweapons. Today, these agents might seem less threatening; there
are difficult obstacles to using them for mass catastrophe. A sophisticated
weapons program, however, could develop very dangerous strains. Four
of the most prominent agents are briefly mentioned here.

Plague

Japan, the United States, and the former Soviet Union developed plague
as a biological weapon.[71] Plague is infamous because of the Black Death
pandemic that swept through Europe killing up to one-third of the continent's population. A more recent pandemic began in 1855 in China, spread
worldwide, and killed over twelve million people.

The bacterium, *Yersinia pestis*, is naturally available in infected rodents.
In its most dangerous pneumonic form, it is a highly contagious disease
that can spread by respiratory droplet to people within two meters. It
can cause death within days if not treated; because its clinical symptoms
resemble progressive pneumonia, rapid diagnosis and treatment is difficult. In 1970, the World Health Organization reported that 50 kilograms
(111 pounds) of aerosol plague disseminated over a city of five million
could infect up to 150,000 inhabitants with pneumonic plague and could
cause as many as 36,000 fatalities. The aerosol would remain viable for a
period up to an hour after dispersal and could spread up to 10 kilometers
(6.2 miles). This amount of aerosol disseminated over New York City could
infect more than 243,000 people.[72]

A plague vaccine was discontinued in 1999. The disease is treated by
administering prophylactic antibiotic drugs within twenty-four hours after
the onset of symptoms.[73] In the event of a plague epidemic, health officials would likely administer these drugs to people with a fever or a cough
without awaiting definitive proof that they have the disease. Although
most public health systems throughout the developed world have ample
antibiotics to limit the disease's impact, a widespread attack in developing nations could exhaust drug stockpiles rendering health care systems
impotent.

These numbers should not disguise plague's significant drawbacks for use as a weapon. *Yersinia pestis* is sensitive to sunlight and heat and does not survive long outside a host. It is difficult to handle and aerosolize. If there are a limited number of victims, it is relatively easy to prevent plague's spread. To become an epidemic, plague requires a critical mass to develop the cycle of transmission whether via direct contagion or indirectly via fleas. A highly contagious strain of plague would have to be widely disseminated in order to infect many people simultaneously so that the number of infected persons would overwhelm a health system's ability to distribute antibiotics. That said, a large plague attack using vectors (fleas or mosquitoes deliberately infected and released) in the developing world could be regionally devastating. Moreover, the Soviet bioweapons program is reported to have modified plague for easier dissemination. Whether today's bio-offenders have comparable capabilities is unknown.

Tularemia

The Japanese, the Soviet Union, and the United States extensively researched tularemia during World War II. The Soviet Union is widely believed to have intentionally caused tularemia outbreaks among German soldiers in Eastern Europe during World War II to slow their advance. During the Cold War, both the United States and the Soviet Union weaponized the disease; the Soviets weaponized it for use in a specially devised bomblet.

Tularemia is contracted through the skin, mucous membranes, gastrointestinal tract, and lungs. It is transmitted either by insect bites or by inhaling the bacteria. Tularemia is a threat because it is highly infectious. On average, ten organisms of *F. tularensis* can cause illness if inhaled. Virulent strains of the bacteria have been reported to cause 30–60 percent mortality if left untreated, but the overall fatality rate for tularemia is around 7 percent, dropping to 2 percent if treated with antibiotics. It is considered more as an incapacitating agent. Microbiologists can transform *F. tularensis* with plasmids to enhance its virulence and make it resistant to certain antibiotic drugs.[74]

The WHO estimated in 1969 that an aerosol dissemination of 50 kilograms of tularemia over a city of five million people could incapacitate 250,000 and kill more than 19,000.[75] However, the disease is difficult to propagate and is subject to environment stresses. A military bioweapons attack using tularemia might inflict catastrophic damage, but dissemination problems could inhibit its use as a terrorist weapon.

Q Fever

Q fever, short for Queensland Fever, is a zoonotic disease caused by one of the world's most infectious bacterium, *Coxiella burnetii*–a single organism can generate infection. The bacterium itself can be acquired from cattle, sheep, goats, and other herd animals. Culturing the bacteria using routine laboratory techniques is difficult, but dissemination is not arduous. The bacterium is highly resistant to heat, drying, disinfectants, and other environmental factors.[76]

The most common acute form of the disease has a very low death rate, only 1–2 percent. The chronic form of the disease, however, has a much higher death rate of 65 percent but can take from one to twenty years to kill the victim. A vaccine for Q fever has been developed but is not commercially available in the United States. Also, people who have previously been exposed to the bacteria are strongly advised against receiving the vaccination because of potentially severe complications. A population would have to be preemptively vaccinated before an actual terrorist attack.[77] Antibiotic treatment is available but would be effective only if administered soon after infection.

Ricin

Ricin, a toxic protein extracted from castor beans, is extremely lethal if inhaled, ingested, or injected directly into the bloodstream. No antidote exists. It is highly stable and less affected by meteorological conditions than most bacteria. Ricin toxin is most reknowned as a means of assassination. The Soviets used it to assassinate Bulgarian dissident Georgi Markov in 1978 by injecting a 1.7 millimeter-wide ricin pellet underneath his skin with a modified umbrella tip.[78] The ease of obtaining the poison and lethality of infection make ricin a credible biomurder threat, but disseminating lethal doses to many people is challenging – more challenging even than disseminating other toxins. If the objective is to cause mass casualties, enormous amounts of the agent would have to be released into the air in hopes of infecting people inhalationally.

EMERGING MICRO-SCIENCES AND BIOVIOLENCE

Bioscience is racing forward into directions that science fiction writers could barely have imagined only a short time ago. Simultaneously, other technologies such as micro-engineering (nanotechnology) and information technology are eroding the line that separates the life sciences from other disciplines. It is now possible to create viruses from chemicals – the "creators" of the polio virus referred to it as an *animate chemical compound*.[79] The day is not far off when more complex life forms can be similarly re-created. Easier than creating altogether new living organisms is manipulating existing life with new attributes. Altogether, emerging sciences offer radical transformations in medicine, agriculture, and technology. Where they will lead us, even in the span of a few decades, is virtually unforeseeable.

A major note of caution is in order. Much is *possible*, but it is not altogether certain which discoveries offer serious potential for bioviolence. Scientific advances certainly thicken the fog of bioviolence prevention, but less certain is whether we should fear Frankensteins lurking in the shadows. Even if the threat of nightmares erupting from bioscience is real, how imminent is the peril? Scientists agree that genetically engineering a new species that can be effectively weaponized is extremely tricky with many obstacles. Dangerous possibilities should be recognized, but possibilities do not necessarily become reality.[80]

Bioscientists can awe nonexperts by describing emerging capabilities even as other bioscientists, no less awe-inspiring, describe why those capabilities will not work effectively. For anyone trying to grapple with the policy implications of emerging bioscience, these debates seem part of the problem: scientific vacillation complicates assessment of risks and the efficacy of safeguards. The level of scientific discourse far exceeds most policy makers' knowledge or patience. Further obscuring how to identify advancing science's risks – as well as identifying policies to reduce those risks – is the rush of scientific change that opens corridors to new processes and insights that, in turn, open exponentially more corridors. Even if scientific possibilities are not realistic today, they may be realistic by the time a policy to address them is in place.

This section can only sketch the potentially dangerous applications of emerging bioscience. Two concerns deserve emphasis. First, one reason States have refrained from developing bioweapons is that military leaders have not enthusiastically championed the prospect of deploying them: pathogens are hard to use and unreliable for strictly military applications. Yet, emerging techniques could enable development of weapons uniquely and precisely tailored to modern and highly specific military objectives.[81] Second, enormous resources are being devoted to developing vaccines and antidotes (discussed in Chapter 6); rapid and effective use of medications will hopefully mitigate the harm of a bioattack.

A sophisticated offender will likely try to circumvent them, and new techniques will make it increasingly easy to do so.

Molecular Biology's Emerging Risks

Molecular biology refers to the science of transferring, inserting, or deleting individual genes, perhaps from a different species, into a species' genetic code thereby altering its properties. It is a commentary on the pace of bioscience to say that molecular biological techniques are now pedestrian. Less pedestrian is knowing how to control the outcome: moving genes is trivial, but being assured of the outcome of a particular movement can be trickier.

Modification of Weapons Agents

Perhaps the most urgent concern here is the potential to modify lethal microbes to increase their lethality or physiological impact, make them resistant to antibiotic treatments, enable them to evade existing vaccines, or enhance their environmental stability and survivability. For example, anthrax's already high standing as a bioviolence agent would escalate if it could be modified to be less vulnerable to current immunizations or antibiotic treatments. Some known anthrax strains are resistant to conventional antibiotic treatment – extending that resistance would produce a remarkably frightening agent. More speculative would be transferring genes from highly contagious yet otherwise innocuous pathogens into the anthrax genome thereby producing an anthrax that more readily spreads among victims.

Scientists are currently able to generate antibiotic-resistant bacteria to determine, for example, how readily those bacteria might become resistant to a new treatment. Various bacterial agents such as plague or tularemia could be altered to increase their lethality or to evade antibiotic treatment. Another "defect" of plague is that its especially lethal pneumonic form is short-lived as an aerosol, and it is transmissible only over short distances. Designing a plague bacterium that lives longer in the air would increase its contagiousness. Until now, the development of such pathogens has been limited because changing one characteristic of a pathogen, for example contagiousness, could adversely affect another characteristic, for example lethality. The genetic engineering that is required for antibiotic resistance might undercut the agent's pathogenicity; a genetically engineered agent that meets both of these requirements might be unstable. Yet, it is becoming ever more realistic to manipulate a specific agent characteristic without affecting other attributes.

Immunologically altered pathogens could defeat standard identification, detection, and diagnostic methods.[82] Indeed, there is some precedent: State bioweapons programs, primarily of the former Soviet Union, created truly frightening organisms decades before the genetic engineering revolution. Both anthrax and plague were made immune to several forms of antibiotics; anthrax was altered to disguise its presence with enhanced ability to bypass the immune system; and genes causing unusual symptoms were inserted in the bacteria causing tularemia. An interesting innovation was the insertion of "sun-tanning" genes that enable pathogens to survive exposure to sunlight, which heightens their effectiveness for midday attacks.[83]

The effects of natural diseases could be modified. Most natural diseases have evolved to kill ineffectively lest they die out for lack of hosts, but a laboratory-altered pathogen would have no such constraints. Even if lethality is not the objective, pathogens could be designed to have devastating consequences. Some diseases that cause only high fevers could be induced to inflict more incapacitating neural damage. Viruses could be engineered to produce pharmaceutically active compounds causing a wide range of disabling effects from mild disorientation to severe psychosis. Such viruses could be contagious and could persist for years in the body (like herpes viruses and retroviruses) causing permanent, contagious, mental or physical disability.[84] An example of unintended results occurred when British scientists created a hybrid pathogen by combining the viruses causing dengue fever and hepatitis C for the objective of reducing the number of laboratory animals needed for testing a hepatitis C vaccine. If the resulting pathogen had escaped through accidental or intentional release, a new disease could have emerged with unique symptoms and unknown virulence.

Perhaps the single most important question today is whether the Avian Flu virus could be genetically modified so that it is far more readily transmissible person-to-person. This issue was recently (and ominously) addressed by a panel of the National Academies of Science

[A]dvances in technology have led to the possibility that, even if a new lethal influenza A virus does not emerge in nature within the near future, one could be artificially generated through reverse genetic engineering. . . . Although the knowledge, facilities, and ingenuity to carry out this sort of experiment are beyond the abilities of most non-experts at this time, this situation is likely to change over the next 5 to 10 years.[85]

Improving Target Specificity

A most disturbing and increasingly realistic possibility is creation of an ethnic-specific bioweapon: a virus or bacteria that targets genetic markers belonging to a particular ethnic population.[86] Until recently, it was believed that there were no particular genetic sequences in a given ethnic population or race that could be targeted to affect a particular biological activity. That belief is unraveling as genetic sequencing becomes more sophisticated and the human genome is better understood. In the opinion of some experts, it will be possible in the near future to create a virus or bacteria that targets only persons of specific ancestry. An ethnic-specific bioweapon would ideally target certain genetic markers that are present in close to 0 percent of the user's population and anywhere over 10 percent of the target population. Even if such a bioweapon affects only 10–20 percent of a targeted population, the effects could be devastating.[87]

Synthetic Genomics

"Synthetic genomics" refers to an array of emerging technologies for constructing novel bioengineered microbial genomes from standardized, chemically produced short strands of synthetic DNA.[88] Synthetic genomics is part of a larger set of technologies that involve construction of new proteins by assembling gene networks for specifically designed tasks. Scientists will someday build segments of desired genetic components with their associated function that could then be programmed to execute particular processes. Although offering enormous potential for good, these capabilities have some frightful implications.

Re-creation of Diseases

In the near future, synthetic genomics technology could enable re-creation of an existing or eradicated virus having a completely known DNA sequence. As mentioned, the polio virus was created in a laboratory using its genetic sequence – available on the internet – and a series of commercially available DNA sequences. As more pathogens are fully sequenced and that information is made available, it will become increasingly possible to synthetically replicate any pathogen from scratch without going through all the bother of painstaking collection from the environment or infiltration of a secure laboratory. This would enable scientists to circumvent the control measures that limit access to agents that pose a uniquely high risk of bioviolence.[89]

Moreover, re-creation of eradicated or highly confined diseases would enable their spread in regions where there is no natural immunity. For example, ebola could be released outside Africa. Through effective vaccination programs and worldwide cooperation, some of the great killer viruses have been eradicated from the planet or at least substantially confined. Current advances in biotechnology, however, have made the potential for resurrecting these historic killers a reality. Of course, if smallpox were synthetically created, it would find humans unvaccinated and with little residual immunity. Less spectacular but certainly devastating would be re-creation of long-eradicated plant and livestock diseases which would now find a susceptible population that is severely lacking in genetic diversity.

According to experts, the assembly of entire genomes is not a simple undertaking. Said Dr. Craig Venter: "The number of pathogens that can be synthesized today is small and limited to those with sequenced genomes. And for many of these the DNA is not infective on its own and poses little actual threat. Our concern is what the technology might enable decades from now."[90] A particularly grave threat is the re-creation of the Spanish Flu influenza strain that killed over forty million people in 1918–19. Through reverse genetic engineering techniques, the virus has been fully re-created. Although the availability of the genome is tightly controlled, there is nothing to say that malevolent persons could not copy the process.

Synthetic Viruses

One of the most dramatic developments of genomics is the impending capability to create synthetic living systems – living in terms of being able to replicate themselves using known life processes involving nucleic acids and proteins. Scientists are actively working on the synthetic creation of cellular life. Such agents could be useful to control pests such as weeds, rodents, or insects; the lessons, however, could be transferable to construction of weapons. Somewhat farther in the distance is the specter of creating altogether new pathogens, most likely viruses. Scientists are now able to change parts of a virus' genetic material so that it can perform specific functions. Although complicated, scientists can delete genes from a cell line and thereby "precisely map which parts of the virus allow it to get into cells, which are responsible for virulence, and what parts might become a component of a vaccine."[91]

RNA Inhibitors and Bioregulators

Technologies involving active molecules could also lead to potential weapons capabilities. RNA interference (RNAi) involves destroying sequence-specific RNA with small molecules. These emerging technologies hold enormous promise for treatments that impede the pathway of disease but might also open potential for new malevolent applications.[92] Bioregulators are small organic compounds that modify body systems and could enhance targeted delivery technologies. Some experts are concerned that new weapons could be aimed at the immune, neurological, and neuroendocrine systems. Again, according to the National Academies of Science,

> The threat spectrum is broad and evolving – in some ways predictably, in other ways unexpectedly. The viruses, microbes, and toxins listed as "select agents" are just one aspect of the continually changing, complex threat landscape. In the future, genetic engineering and other technologies may lead to the development of pathogenic organisms with unique, unpredictable characteristics ... [93]

Nanotechnologies

Nanotechnology, the science of building things in a size range from 1 to 100 billionths of a meter, enables constructing objects from their most basic materials thereby offering an unprecedented degree of precision and control over the final product. Nanotechnology is not a life science and is not limited to existing natural systems. Yet, biotechnology can be viewed as a subset of nanotechnology; biotechnology is "nature's nanotechnology."

Some experts warn that misuse of nanotechnology could lead to horrifically effective weapons, most of which have nothing to do with bioviolence. Yet, the potential combination of nanotechnology with emerging bioscience raises new potential for inflicting harm – albeit a potential that is still somewhat on the horizon. Nanotechnology designed to deliver medicines in a more effective and targeted fashion could also be used to deliver disease agents into a person's system. As an example, a nanotech-built antipersonnel weapon capable of seeking and injecting toxins into unprotected humans could carry lethal doses of botulinum. As many as fifty billion toxin-carrying devices – theoretically enough to kill every human on earth many times over – could be packed into a single suitcase. Moreover, although far on the scientific horizon, nanotechnology research is exploring processes of self-replication.

This is most certainly not the place to explore the social and strategic implications of nanotechnology, yet it is worth contemplating the implications of "merging" advances in nanotechnology with advances in more traditional biosciences. Consider the warning offered by Bill Joy, cofounder and chief scientist of Sun Microsystems in an often cited article in *Wired* magazine:

> Nanotechnology has clear military and terrorist uses . . . – such devices can be built to be selectively destructive, affecting, for example, only a certain geographical area or a group of people who are genetically distinct. . . . The 21st-century technologies – genetics, nanotechnology, and robotics – are so powerful that they spawn whole new classes of accidents and abuses. Most dangerously, for the first time, these accidents and abuses are widely within the reach of individuals or small groups. They will not require large facilities or rare raw materials. Knowledge alone will enable the use of them. Thus we have the possibility not just of weapons of mass destruction but of knowledge-enabled mass destruction (KMD), this destructiveness hugely amplified by the power of self-replication.[94]

3 Who Did Bioviolence? Who Wants To Do It?

The subject of bioviolence inevitably leads to the question: who would do such a repulsive thing? Some experts argue that terrorists and rogue States are not interested in bioviolence – the threat might therefore be overblown. Hopefully, they are correct. An enormous amount of evidence, however, suggests they are wrong.

Here's the dirty truth: from the dawn of biology's ability to isolate pathogens, people have pursued hostile applications of disease. To ignore this extensive history and presume that today's villains are not fervent about weaponizing disease is very dangerous. As bioviolence becomes easier and more lethal, we ignore this penchant for making people sick at our peril.

The first section of this chapter portrays the historical experience with biological weapons. The second section focuses on existing State bioweapon programs. The final section turns to terrorist and fanatic bioviolence – today's most critical threats.

THE BIOLOGICAL WEAPONS EXPERIENCE

Disease has been entwined with war and violence for millennia. Plagues inflicted on Egyptians compelled the Exodus. Greek swordsmen coated their blades with feces. Tartar besiegers of Caffa – a port city on the Black Sea – hurled plague-ridden corpses over city walls possibly beginning the Black Death that killed almost one in three Europeans.[1] Centuries later in the American colonies, General Jeffrey Amherst, commander of British forces at Fort Pitt, responsible for "the Total Extirpation of those Indian Nations,"[2] gave blankets previously worn by smallpox patients at nearby hospitals to Native Americans.

With the onset of gunpowder weapons in the late 1400s, disease receded from overt military use. It was too slow and incapable of direction to have much battlefield relevance. Yet, with the ability to isolate and classify micro-organisms in the late 19th Century came the possibility that disease could be harnessed for weapons purposes.

The Road to Geneva

By World War I, a few pathogens could be cultured, but bioweapons were not substantially used. German secret agents infected Allied forces' horses and cattle with bacteria and attempted to spread plague in St. Petersburg. They are also alleged to have poisoned wells with corpses and dropped bacteria-infected fruits and chocolates over civilian areas. Yet, moral constraints might have curbed use of disease against humans. German scientists who recommended use of antipersonnel bioweapons received negative instructions: "All respects to your courage and patriotism, but if we undertake this step we will no longer be worthy to exist as a nation."[3]

Into the 1920s, bioweapons were not viewed as militarily credible. The U.S. Chemical Warfare Service asserted that bioweapons "would have little effect on the actual issue of a contest in view of the protective methods which are available for circumscribing its effects."[4] It was Auguste Trillat, director of the French Naval Chemical Research Laboratory, who initiated research on anthrax and other diseases as potential weapons, seeing them as effective against enemy reserves, civilians, livestock, and water supplies. Thereafter, concerned that the Nazis were pursuing bioweapons, the French military actively pursued bioweapons production but met substantial technical difficulties that precluded success before the Germans invaded.[5]

In 1925, international diplomats agreed to prohibit bioweapons as well as chemical weapons. However, their agreement, the Geneva Protocol, did not address research, production, development, or stockpiling of banned weapons; neither did it ban their use in internal or civil conflicts. Many States reserved the right to retaliate in kind for an adversary's use of chemical or bioweapons. These shortcomings notwithstanding, the Geneva Protocol expressed a widely shared repugnance for chemical and bioweapons.

Mid-20th Century Bioweapons Programs

The proliferation of bioweapons programs during the mid-20th Century was not the fault of the Geneva Protocol's limitations. Likely, more proliferation would have occurred had there been no internationally recognized prohibition. The Protocol's humanitarian norms deserve credit for convincing some States to shun bioviolence, but the profusion of bioweapons programs undercut confidence that a norm can be effective by itself.

Unit 731

Japan used bioweapons (plague, cholera, epidemic hemorrhagic fever, and even some sexually transmitted diseases) in China, causing perhaps a quarter of a million casualties. The infamous Unit 731 laboratory complex employed over three thousand scientists and technicians to develop and disseminate diseases including typhoid and cholera. Plague-infected fleas were dropped over Manchuria from high altitude aircraft. As their war fortunes soured, the Japanese contaminated water sources and food to slow down advancing Chinese troops.

Near the war's end, plague was unsuccessfully deployed against American forces in the Pacific. Rather than exacting retribution, U.S. military planners were intrigued. Upon armistice, they granted immunity from prosecution to Japanese scientists associated with Unit 731 in exchange for their research data. As one official noted, these valuable first-hand accounts of human experiments "could not be obtained in our own laboratories because of scruples attached to human experimentation."[6] Secrecy shrouded both Japanese criminality and the burgeoning U.S. bioweapons program. "Professional deference was accorded the Japanese scientists, with whom the Americans from Detrick and G-2 had tea and dined. Japan was no longer the enemy; the enemy was the Soviet Union."[7] National security took precedence over criminal prosecution.

The U.S. Offensive Bioweapons Program

Soon after Pearl Harbor, Secretary of State Henry L. Stimson recommended pursuit of bioweapons research. The U.S. program, run jointly by the War Research Service and the Chemical Warfare Service, prepared various anti-personnel, anti-animal, and anti-crop agents primarily at Camp Detrick, Maryland. Two open-air testing facilities were established near Dugway Proving Grounds (Utah) and at Horn Island (Pascagoula, Mississippi). Secretary of War, George Merck, proudly pointed to the program's successes: pilot and large-scale production facilities for human and agro pathogens; mass production of anthrax and virulent brucellosis for filling bombs; and field testing new cluster bombs for biological munitions. Near the end of the war, production of anthrax munitions began with plans to drop over four million four-pound anthrax bombs on six major German cities to inflict three million civilian deaths. These weapons were not supplied to Allied forces and thus never used.

Created in 1948, the Committee on Biological Warfare found that the United States was highly vulnerable to attack and recommended that the U.S. Research and Development Program be enhanced in order to: 1) detect and identify biological agents; 2) decontaminate, protect, and treat exposed victims; and 3) test dissemination of innocuous organisms in ventilation systems, subway systems, and public water supplies as well as "stamps, envelopes, money, biologicals, and cosmetics . . . contamination of food and beverages" as a primary means of spreading biological agents.[8] For twenty years, pathogens such as brucellosis, tularemia, Q fever, Venezuelan equine encephalitis, anthrax, and botulinum, along with anti-personnel and anti-crop cluster bombs were produced without much public attention.

Most distressingly, humans and animals were exposed to aerosolized agents to test the effectiveness of experimental munitions. In 1950, the first open-air sea tests released an anthrax simulant (*Bacillus globigii*) from naval vessels near Norfolk, Virginia. Near San Francisco, a U.S. Navy minesweeper dispersed aerosolized bacteria to see what would happen in a possible bioweapons attack; several people reported urinary tract infections which the military claimed were coincidental. After the experiments and testing were declassified, family members of a victim who died allegedly as a result of the experiments filed a wrongful-death suit against the U.S. government. The case was dismissed because the experiments were part of national defense planning.[9]

In other experiments, human volunteers were injected with harmful anthrax simulants or exposed to fungal agents. In 1955, Army Operation CD-22 ("Operation Whitecoat") released Q fever a half-mile upwind from animals and people to test dissemination techniques. In 1956 throughout Georgia and Florida, uninfected mosquitoes were released over fifty times to test the feasibility of using them as dissemination vectors; residents were later canvassed to determine how many people were bitten. In 1966, the Army conducted an open air test at Washington D.C.'s National Airport: "Traps were placed throughout the facility to capture the bacterium as it flowed in the air. Laboratory personnel, dressed as travelers carrying brief cases, walked the corridors and without detection sprayed the bacterium into the atmosphere."[10] In a Manhattan subway, light bulbs filled with bacteria were dropped onto tracks to measure the bacteria's spread. Thus, to prepare biological agents to use against an enemy, they were aimed at Americans.

In November 1969, however, President Nixon, concerned that biological weapons offered little value to the American arsenal, but their proliferation might undermine nuclear deterrence, unilaterally cancelled the U.S. offensive program. He declared that the United States would destroy its entire bioweapons stockpile. Shortly thereafter, the U.S. Army Medical Unit ceased developing bioweapons and began developing vaccines. The U.S. Army Medical Unit was renamed the U.S. Army Medical Research Institute of Infectious Diseases (USAMRIID).[11] The decision quickly led to negotiations for the Biological Weapons Convention.

It must be noted that the United States has the world's largest and most advanced biodefense programs. There is a very fine line that distinguishes biodefense from bio-offense. Whether the United States has crossed that line is discussed thoroughly in Chapter 8.

The Soviet Biological Weapons Program

The Soviet Union's program began in 1928 by weaponizing typhus. By World War II, the Soviets could produce and disseminate typhus, tularemia, and Q fever via insects. In 1946, with data from the Japanese Unit 731, the Soviet Ministry of Defense began research, development, testing, production, and delivery of numerous agents. Bioweapons facilities, officially known as *Scientific Field Testing Laboratories*, were built around Moscow and on the Aral Sea. By the late 1960s, the Soviet bioweapons arsenal included smallpox (with a strain received from India), ebola, lassa fever, and monkey pox.

Shortly after the Soviet Union ratified the Biological Weapons Convention in the early 1970s, Biopreparat (the Chief Directorate for Biological Preparations) was formed. Altogether, fifty-two biotechnology sites employing over fifty thousand scientists and technicians were concealed as civilian biotechnological and pharmaceutical research laboratories. Its offensive objectives were: 1) to develop pathogen strains that could resist vaccines and antibiotics and could degrade victims' natural defenses, and 2) to discover methods of weaponization. A high priority was to mass produce exceptionally viable agents with short incubation periods. Soviet scientists spliced ebola and Venezuelan equine encephalomyelitis (VEE) genes into smallpox to create a so-called chimera virus that would have synergistic effects and be resistant to vaccines or antiviral treatments. In the late 1980s, the Soviets combined a strain of mousepox (a close relative of smallpox) and VEE genes to cause symptoms of both diseases. If a victim were to seek antibiotic treatment for the symptoms of one agent, the other agent in the "cocktail" could still finish him off.

Biopreparat produced and stockpiled hundreds of tons of plague, tularemia, glanders, anthrax, smallpox, and VEE. Within two decades, nearly sixty pathogens had been genetically modified into more potent diseases. To deploy these agents, the Soviet Army had twenty specially equipped crop duster planes, medium-range bombers, intercontinental ballistic missiles, and cruise missiles capable of delivering agents to multiple cities. Tularemia and VEE were the principal agents designated for battlefield use; anthrax and marburg virus were nominated for attacking rear areas.

Smallpox was produced in liquid form and loaded into submunitions that SS-18 intercontinental ballistic missiles could deliver against enemy population centers. The Soviet program also explored very sophisticated dissemination methods including modified ICBM warheads with refrigeration equipment and special heat-venting fins enabling the warhead to re-enter the atmosphere without broiling its pathogenic cargo. Near the target, the warhead was programmed to release numerous aerosol bomblets that would gently descend by parachute until reaching a preset altitude where they would release their contents in a fine mist.

There are no officially confirmed reports of the Soviet Union deliberately testing bioweapons on its own people. Yet, in Kazakhstan in 1971, accidental civilian exposure to smallpox killed two children and a young woman; nearly fifty thousand residents received emergency vaccinations, and hundreds of civilians were quarantined. A small explosion at a military laboratory on an island in the Aral Sea released 400 grams of smallpox; a few passengers on a ship that sailed impermissibly close to the island became infected and died. Outbreaks of plague in Central Asia also have been attributed to bioweapons testing on the Aral Sea. The most infamous incident occurred in 1979 in Sverdlovsk (now Yekaterinburg) where a plume of anthrax escaped from a testing facility killing from sixty-eight to one hundred people as well as animals in a 30 mile radius.[12]

In 1992, President Boris Yeltsin officially announced that Biopreparat's offensive weapons program had ended with the Soviet Union's demise. Yet, the quantity and condition of pathogen stockpiles remains highly worrisome. Conversion of bioweapons facilities to peaceful uses and employment of former bioweapons scientists has progressed, but there are reports of at least four former Soviet military facilities that have not opened their doors to inspection.[13] Other reports suggest that former Biopreparat-trained scientists and technicians are now working abroad, possibly for Iran and North Korea.

The Soviet program, in retrospect, defies strategic justification. It may be that Soviet bioweapons were intended to cause casualties among American survivors of a nuclear war. In the event of the final conflict with the United States, however, the Soviet Union's nuclear weapons carried more than enough destructive power to obliterate American war-fighting capabilities. Moreover, as Biopreparat was kept secret, it had no deterrent effect – an adversary cannot be deterred by something it does not know about. Perhaps the weapons were designed for use in a conflict with China. Disease agents could annihilate the numerical superiority of Chinese forces without crossing the nuclear threshold that might provoke a U.S. nuclear response. More likely, the Soviet bioweapons program was self-justifying – as the program's infrastructure grew and proved that it could construct awesome weapons, it became a juggernaut that had to fulfill unbounded demands for more experimentation and production regardless of the product's military utility. The pursuit of new and more destructive bioweapons evolved into its own justification.

The imperial disintegration of the Soviet Union denuded control of its bioweapons program leaving a horrifying legacy of environmental contamination, thousands of highly trained bioscientists, and thousands of weapons to destroy before they become a reservoir for any madman capable of gaining access. According to Dr. Gerald Poste:

> The fate of the personnel and pathogens from the FSU [Former Soviet Union] bioweapons programme is of particular concern. The Biopreparat effort in the civilian sector employed at least 70,000 people in its illicit bioweapons programme. Concern persists that elements of the military programme may not have stopped. There are also reports of FSU scientists working in Iraq, Iran, and North Korea. Security at FSU bioweapons facilities is lax and economic pressures have increased the risk that both personnel and biological specimens are available at a price.[14]

The problems associated with preventing terrorists and proliferators from gaining access to these stockpiles and expertise are discussed in Chapter 8.

Iraq's Biological Weapons Program
The scale of the Iraqi biological weapons program repudiated any faith that regional powers would voluntarily eschew weaponization of pathogens.

The Iraqi offensive biological weapons program dates back to the mid-1970s when Nassir al Hindawi and other western-trained scientists began a program under the aegis of the State Organization for Trade and Industry, later subsumed by the Military Industrial Commission. In 1984, biologists at the Al-Muthanna chemical weapons complex were tasked to discover how to weaponize pathogens – anthrax and botulinum in particular. In 1987, this research group moved to the Al-Salman facility where they developed fungal and antiplant agents. A notable expansion of the program in 1988 was the establishment of the Al-Hakam facility, codename "Project 324," to mass produce weapons-grade anthrax and botulinum toxin. Later, Iraqi officials would assert that Al-Hakam was a single cell protein (SCP) production plant used to produce animal feed and "biopesticides," but in fact SCP was only produced in insignificant quantities as a camouflage. Only later did Iraq disclose that the Al-Hakam facility had produced thousands of gallons of anthrax and botulinum.

Throughout this period, Iraq purchased various strains of anthrax from the American Type Culture Collection (ATCC) for research purposes. In 1986, Baghdad University purchased three strains of anthrax, five types of botulinum, and three kinds of brucella. In 1988, the Iraqi Ministry of Trade's Technical and Scientific Materials Import Division received licenses from the U.S. Commerce Department to purchase additional agents (four anthrax strains in particular) from ATCC, purportedly for legitimate scientific research.[15] Iraq eventually disclosed that it had produced aerosolizable particles of these strains through its spray drying procedure, making it easier and faster to achieve weapons-quality anthrax and other deadly agents. Iraq also disclosed that it produced nearly 20,000 liters of concentrated botulinum toxin, nearly 10,000 liters of concentrated anthrax, and lesser quantities of aflatoxin, *Clostridium perfringens* spores, ricin, wheat rust, and corn smut. Tularemia, plague, brucellosis, and camelpox had also been researched and developed.

Despite producing such a stockpile of biological agents, Iraqi officials later denied having a parallel weapons delivery effort and claimed that it had destroyed or deactivated all of its biological weapons and bulk biological agents in 1991. Iraq admitted to the program's weaponization objectives only after the defection of the head of Iraq's intelligence agency, General Hussein Kamal, Saddam Hussein's brother-in-law who had supervised the bioweapons program. Indeed, Iraq produced twenty-five Al-Hussein missile warheads and two hundred R-400 aerial bombs filled with bioweapons agents (one hundred with botulinum toxin, fifty with anthrax spores, and seven with aflatoxin). Iraq also manufactured four aircraft drop tanks and twelve aerosol generators to modify helicopter-borne insecticide disseminators and worked on developing a pilotless L-29 trainer aircraft that could carry the tanks and release the toxins. Even after the United Nations adopted resolutions specifically requiring destruction of Iraqi bioweapons, Saddam Hussein was alleged to have built and equipped major bioweapons production, storage, and research and development facilities.

Later, United Nations inspectors asserted that Iraq made inconsistent claims concerning the location of remnant biological weapons found by UNSCOM. For example, R-400A bombs carrying biological weapons were discovered in an airfield where no biological weapons had previously been declared. Documentary evidence of the purported destruction and deactivation of these weapons was incomplete, and subsequent inspections discovered significant undisclosed dual-use equipment that "could readily be used in a BW programme."[16] The inspectors determined that substantial bacterial growth media imported into Iraq could not be accounted for. The fermenting capacity of the Iraqi biological weapons program also suggested that the amount of anthrax and botulinum toxin reported by Iraq actually accounted for only a fraction of the total Iraqi stockpile of these agents.

After nearly seven years of hindering weapons inspections, Iraq formally discontinued compliance. By early 2003, the United Nations inspectors concluded that Iraq had taken "active steps" to conceal its biological weapons program through "inadequate disclosures, unilateral destruction, and concealment activities," and as a result, the nature and extent of Iraq's biological weapons program has "not been possible to verify."[17] The inspectors left Iraq soon thereafter in anticipation of the U.S. invasion.

South Africa's Project Coast

South Africa's Project Coast was an apartheid-era, top-secret chemical and bioweapons program with roots back to World War I research. During the 1970s, anxious that Soviet-backed Cuban troops fighting in Angola might use battlefield bioweapons, it initiated defensive vaccine research and response procedures. Offensive bioweapons followed thereafter.

In 1983, Project Coast, headed by Dr. Wouter Basson (nicknamed "Dr. Death"), was formed to conduct highly secretive research into chemical and biological warfare. Front companies were established to provide covert support. Project Coast produced plague, salmonella, and botulinum as well as genetically modified anthrax that allegedly was incurable by conventional treatments. It also spliced a toxin-producing gene from *Clostridium perfringens* into *E. coli*, which, had it escaped into human populations, could have ignited a gas gangrene epidemic. A high priority was designing assassination devices to look like everyday objects such as umbrellas, walking sticks, beer cans, and envelopes. Other apparently unexecuted ideas included drugs to render black women infertile and a slow-acting poison for Nelson Mandela while he was imprisoned.[18]

Project Coast was dismantled in 1993 just before the transfer of power in South Africa. The front companies were privatized and materials were reportedly dumped at sea. Dr. Basson was tried and subsequently acquitted of charges of murder, drug trafficking, fraud, and theft because prosecutors had failed to prove the allegations, although the High Court of South Africa has called for a new trial alleging conspiracy to commit offenses outside South Africa. Libya is reported to have tried to hire Basson in 1994 for his germ warfare expertise.[19]

Pathogens remain missing and, along with the secrets of Project Coast, might have fallen into the hands of terrorists. In 2002, a former Project Coast researcher offered to sell some biological weapons to the U.S. government. He freeze-dried and packaged a sample inside a tube of toothpaste that he mailed to a CIA officer who carried the weapon to the FBI. After delivering this one vial of a genetically altered pathogen, he promised delivery of an entire collection of vials containing genetically altered anthrax, plague, salmonella, and botulinum. His asking price was $5 million plus immigration permits to the United States for nineteen of his associates and family members. The United States, appalled at the thought of buying this "product," balked at the offer and the deal fell through.[20]

Readers should know that the remaining material in this section discussing bioweapons development in the past by Egypt and Israel as well as currently by North Korea, Iran, and Syria is the product of extensive open-source research, but no classified information was available or could have been used. It is impossible, therefore, to verify this material much less to suggest that these are the only suspected bioweapons development programs. Certainly, the U.S. government alleges that there are more ongoing programs than those discussed here. The section's remaining material summarizes as accurately as possible the publicly available information about the predominant State threats but cannot claim independent confirmation of that information.

Egypt

In the 1960s, Egypt, assisted by the Soviet Union, is alleged to have embarked on a secretive bioweapons program (known as "Izlis"). The Ministry of Defense experimented with various pathogens at the El-Nasr Company for Pharmaceutical Chemicals and Antibiotics near its chemical weapons facility, "Military Plant 801." By 1972, Egyptian President Anwar Sadat allegedly announced that "Egypt has biological weapons stored in refrigerators and could use them against Israel's crowded population."[21] Two months later, in April 1972, Egypt signed the Biological Weapons Convention (BWC) but has yet to ratify it 35 years hence.

In 1993, the Russian Foreign Intelligence Service reported that Egypt was studying various toxins and that "[t]here is information on cooperation between Egypt's research centers in areas of biological research related to biological weapons and certain civilian and military laboratories of the United States, particularly in the field of highly pathogenic microorganisms and dangerous vectors." Yet, "no data [has] been obtained to indicate the creation of biological agents in support of military offensive programs."[22] Shortly thereafter, the U.S. Arms Control and Disarmament Agency alleged that Egypt had an active biological weapons program: "There is no evidence to indicate that Egypt has eliminated this capability and it remains likely that the Egyptian capability to conduct biological warfare continues to exist."[23] Notably, in the late 1980s, Egypt assisted Iraq in developing "defensive" measures against chemical and biological warfare and might have acquired some of the Iraqi bioweapons delivery systems such as aerial bombs, cluster warheads, and aerosolization systems.[24] However, Egyptian authorities have consistently denied having an offensive bioweapons program or that it ever developed, produced, or stockpiled bioweapons.

Israel

Israel's interest in acquiring a bioweapons program began in 1948 when Prime Minister David Ben-Gurion asked Ehud Avriel to recruit Jewish scientists in Eastern Europe who could "either increase the capacity to kill masses or to cure masses; both things are important."[25] General Yigal Yadin, the *Haganah* operations chief, approved creation of a bioweapons program, Hemed Beit, to be established by Alexander Keynan in Jaffa. The program was later relocated to Abu Kabir and kept wholly isolated from the rest of the Israeli bureaucracy.

Disputed allegations abound concerning Israel's alleged use of bioweapons. In the Arab town of Acre, a typhoid epidemic spread just days before Israeli forces attacked in May 1948. Some reports suggest that Israeli forces contaminated Acre's water supply to soften resistance. At the time, Egyptian soldiers in the Gaza Strip captured four Israeli soldiers near water wells reportedly carrying a liquid containing typhoid and dysentery. Israel has denied these accusations as "wicked libel."[26]

It has been alleged that, upon learning of Iraq's bioweapons program during the late 1980s through the mid-1990s, Israel secretly expanded its own bioweapons program.[27] However, relevant information is highly classified. In 2002, Dr. Amy Sands testified before the Senate Foreign Relations Committee that "Israel is conducting a wide array of biological weapons-related research, with a possible production of numerous types of agents."[28] However, an unclassified 2003 CIA report on WMD did not name Israel as a State with an active bioweapons program despite purportedly retaining bioweapons.[29]

CURRENT (ALLEGED) STATE BIOLOGICAL WEAPONS PROGRAMS

Today, not a single State admits to having a bioweapons program, and there is no proof that any State is, in fact, preparing to commit bioviolence. Diplomats have not recently argued that bioweapons are legitimate; the claim that they are *the poor nation's nuclear weapons* has fallen into disuse. Of course, virtually any State with a reasonably sophisticated bioscience sector has the wherewithal to make bioweapons. It might be inferred that these assets are being wrongfully operationalized as part of a bioweapons program, but capability does not unequivocally lead to a program. There is a huge difference between *what could be* and *what is*.

What purpose would such weapons achieve? Just because a weapon can be easily, safely, and cheaply built does not answer whether it is worthwhile to do so. This is especially true for bioweapons that are universally condemned. For a State (unlike a terrorist organization), an offensive bioweapons program could jeopardize its diplomatic status. It is unlikely that any State would make that decision lightly.

Yet, State programs are potentially worrisome. Some States are thought to support terror organizations – a military program could do the hard work of preparing a bioweapon and then pass it to terrorists for dissemination. Moreover, a State program necessarily trains scientists and technicians in the subtleties of bioweapons production; materials or personnel might contribute to criminal activity even if the State is not planning to deploy weapons. Most importantly, State consensus is essential to implement bioviolence prevention policies; if some States have bioweapons programs, that consensus is unachievable.

Questions about Military Efficacy

In the past, one reason for bioweapons' low profile was that military planners did not regard them as especially useful. As stated earlier, President Nixon abandoned the U.S. offensive bioweapons program partly because military strategists resisted assimilating bioweapons into operational planning.[30] In recent years, Iraq's bioweapons program is the only certain effort to focus explicitly on battlefield use. Bioweapons did not do much good for Hussein; anxiety over bioweapons arguably contributed to his downfall.

In the context of traditional warfare, bioweapons have some exceptional disadvantages. Most have no impact against an adversary's armaments (although they can impair personnel from operating them). The weapon would have to overcome the adversary's immunizations, but one's own troops and nearby noncombatants would have to sustain resistance to the spreading disease lest disastrous results befall them. If the agent is not contagious (e.g., anthrax), the attack would have to kill or disable enough personnel to affect the battle, but it might be difficult to create a large yet stable cloud that dissipates precisely over the adversary's alignment. If the agent is contagious, there is an inherent risk of igniting an epidemic that would affect one's own citizens.

Most military planners want a weapon that works quickly; bioweapons' delayed impact, while a virtue perhaps for terrorists, is problematic for a military leader who wants to stop an adversary force at a specific place at a definable moment. Military planners want a weapon that can be accurately controlled, but changing winds could blow a cloud of pathogens in unplanned directions. Also, sunlight adversely affects some agents. For example, ultraviolet radiation renders most strains of plague inactive which makes it hard to use during the day. Rain will push most of the agent to the ground. The best conditions are cloudy evenings with little wind, but battle exigencies might not cooperate. The challenge of making a bioweapon with predictably controllable effects is even greater if testing is foreclosed. Field testing might alert the international community and provoke substantial denunciation. For a commander with limited carrying capacity and supply lines, an untested weapon that might be usable only on rare occasions is not logistically practical.

For a superpower with arrays of nuclear weapons, bioweapons have incidental deterrent effect. Perhaps for countries unable to produce nuclear weapons, a bio-arsenal might be seen as a deterrence substitute, yet using (or threatening to use) bioweapons to deter a nuclear armed adversary does not make much sense. Bioweapons might be called weapons of mass destruction and are no doubt horrifying, but they are more appropriate for stealth attack than head-to-head conflict. Perhaps States view bioweapons as an effective "doomsday" deterrent that signals an adversary to watch its steps lest a catastrophe be unleashed: even if your attack against us is successful, you will pay an unimaginable price. The flaw in this logic is that no State is pursuing a bioweapons program overtly; any active program is under a shroud of secrecy. In contrast to nuclear weapons programs, bioweapons' deterrent effect derives from innuendo and suspicion, not from brandishing armaments. It is unclear, therefore, whether even non-nuclear States are seriously interested in proliferating bioweapons in defiance of international norms.

Most likely, State bioweaponeers are nations caught in regional conflicts. Bioweapons can be cheaply produced, especially compared to the cost of developing defensive capabilities against them. Getting the requisite equipment and disguising an offensive bioweapons program would not be very difficult. Ready access to a diverse array of pathogen seed stocks with assorted effects could enable a State to prepare a flexible and credible arsenal for various military purposes. For example, military operations to squelch guerilla resistance could use bioweapons to "soften" entrenched pockets of resistance without destroying physical infrastructure.

Bioweapons have long been seen as effective against poor, segregated populations lacking resistance to the onslaught of disease. Since the 16th Century, the lessons of the early conquistadors of the Americas were obvious: disease can swiftly slice through the numerical superiority of indigenous populations denuding vast territories and simplifying military subjugation. Indeed, some of the bioweapons programs of the 20th Century were explicitly designed for use against helpless civilians. Both the Japanese Unit 731 during World War II and the South African Project Coast produced weapons that were not designed for use against an adversary with comparable military power but for use against the indigenous majority. Today, where ethnic conflict is rife, State bioweapons programs might be resurging as modern bioscience increasingly enables precise targeting against specific populations.

Suspected State Bioweapons Programs

The following claims concerning suspected State bioweapons programs reflect the pronouncements of declassified intelligence and diplomatic sources. It is impossible to verify these assertions without access to classified intelligence. Perhaps as many as ten States might have active bioweapons programs. The three leading suspects are North Korea, Iran, and Syria.

North Korea[31]

North Korea tops the U.S. list of likely suspects with bioweapons programs. In May 2002, John Bolton, then-Under Secretary of State for Arms Control and International Security, stated:

> Despite the fact that its citizens are starving, the leadership in Pyongyang has spent large sums of money to acquire the resources, including a biotechnology infrastructure, capable of producing infectious agents, toxins, and other crude biological weapons. It likely has the capability to produce sufficient quantities of biological agents for military purposes within weeks of deciding to do so, and has a variety of means at its disposal for delivering these deadly weapons.[32]

In February 2005, then-CIA Director Porter Goss testified, "We believe North Korea has active CW and BW programs and probably has chemical and possibly biological weapons ready for use."[33]

North Korea is believed to have begun development of a bioweapons program in the 1960s. In 1980, North Korean Leader Kim Il Sung recognized the efficacy of using poisonous gas and bacteria during war and ordered the "concentrated development of biological weapons."[34] The North Korean Academy of National Defense organized biological laboratories, recruited foreign scientists and microbiologists (mainly from the Soviet Union), and imported bacteria cultures for producing anthrax, cholera, and plague from Japan.

North Korea has experimented with nearly a dozen different types of pathogens, weaponizing anthrax, cholera, tuberculosis, and typhus. Reportedly, North Korea has developed a strain of anthrax similar to the former Soviet Union's anthrax weapon that was specially treated to withstand environmental stress. Half of North Korea's long-range missiles and a third of its artillery shells are capable of delivering bioweapons.[35] More troubling is the possibility that small groups of North Korean special operatives might infiltrate a South Korean or U.S. base to disseminate lethal agents. One expert testifies, "Such operations may be set into motion if the North decides to conduct full-scale military operations against South Korea."[36] As an indication of North Korea's plans for biological warfare, North Korea continues to immunize members of its armed forces against smallpox.

Iran[37]

Iran has been openly accused of offering training, weaponry, and safe haven to a number of terrorist organizations such as Hezbollah, Islamic Jihad, and Hamas. It has also been accused of seeking to develop bioweapons capabilities.[38] The U.S. government has long suspected that Iran has acquired biological weaponry and could launch a biological warhead.[39] According to a 1996 CIA report, "Iran has had a biological warfare program since the early 1980s. Currently the program is in its research and development stages, but we believe Iran holds some stocks of BW agents and weapons."[40] These accusations are consistent with the 1988 statement of Hashemi Rafsanjani, then Speaker of the Iranian Parliament: ". . . we should fully equip ourselves in defensive and offensive use of chemical, bacteriological, and radiological weapons."[41]

More recently, Lieutenant General Michael D. Maples, the Director of the U.S. Defense Intelligence Agency testified, "We believe that Iran maintains offensive chemical and biological weapons capabilities in various stages of development."[42] The U.S. Department of State's *2005 Report on Adherence and Compliance with Arms Control, Nonproliferation, and Disarmament Agreements and Commitments* asserts, "The Iranian BW program has been embedded within Iran's extensive biotechnology and pharmaceutical industries so as to obscure its activities. The Iranian military has used medical, education, and scientific research organizations for many aspects of BW-related agent procurement, research, and development."[43]

Iran could support an independent bioweapons program with little foreign assistance in view of its advanced biotechnology facilities, its pharmaceutical and military infrastructure, and its highly trained personnel. Various countries have exported sensitive biotechnologies to Iran. In 1989, Canadian and Dutch officials were approached by personnel from the Iranian Research Organization for Science and Technology and the Iranian Imam Reza Medical Center seeking to acquire mycotoxin-producing fungi. Iran has also sought to acquire castor beans that could be used for producing ricin and has several anthrax cultures. Iran allegedly hired former Soviet bioweapons scientists to work on pathogens that cause diseases such as marburg, plague, smallpox, and tularemia.[44]

According to U.S. officials, Iran certainly has the capability to segregate and cultivate lethal pathogens as well as the capability to weaponize them for dispersal by artillery and aerial bombs.[45] Moreover, Iran has conducted chemical and biological defense military exercises with helicopter sprayers and has worked with ballistic, cruise, and scud missiles. The Iranian Shahab missile is capable of carrying biological warheads up to twelve hundred miles, but no definitive evidence shows that Iran has actually developed a warhead for that purpose.

Syria[46]

Syria has long been suspected of having an elementary biotechnology industry capable of making offensive biological weapons. A 1997 Pentagon report asserts, "Syria probably has an adequate biotechnical infrastructure to support a small biological warfare program, although the Syrians are not believed to have begun any major weaponization or testing related to biological warfare." The report concludes that "[w]ithout significant foreign assistance, it is unlikely that Syria could advance to the manufacture of significant amounts of biological weapons for several years."[47]

In the early 1970s, Syria received a limited biodefense capability including biological protective equipment from the Soviet Union. This equipment is now obsolete, and it is questionable if Syria has developed its protective capability any further. In the late 1980s, Syria invested significant resources in its pharmaceutical and biotechnology sectors by establishing over twelve pharmaceutical factories. Although its biotechnology sector likely has the resources to develop weapons, there is no confirmed proof that Syria has stockpiled bioweapons.

In February 2006, the Director of the U.S. Defense Intelligence Agency testified, "We believe Syria already has a stockpile of the nerve agent sarin and apparently has tried to develop a more toxic and persistent nerve agent. We also believe the Syrian government maintains an offensive biological weapons research and development program."[48] Although Syria signed the Biological Weapons Convention in 1972, it has yet to ratify the agreement.

TERRORIST AND FANATIC INTEREST IN BIOVIOLENCE

We should be no less worried about bioviolence by non-State terrorists and fanatics than by States. Intelligence reports reveal that many terrorist organizations have expressed interest in acquiring biological weapons.[49] This worry is not new. In 1995, the Director of the CIA's Nonproliferation Center, Dr. Gordon C. Oehler, testified, "Extremist groups worldwide are increasingly learning how to manufacture chemical and biological agents, and the potential for additional chemical and biological attacks by such groups continues to grow."[50] Then-FBI Director Louis Freeh declared, "A growing number – while still small – of 'lone offender' and extremist splinter elements of right-wing groups have been identified as possessing, or attempting to develop or use [weapons of mass destruction]."[51]

Some experts assert that the biothreat has been grossly exaggerated. That there have been no catastrophic bioviolence attacks as of this writing is evidence, goes the argument, that terrorists lack the intention and capability to make bioweapons that can reach a western target.[52] Asserting that they lack intention seems baseless as the following discussion reveals. Asserting that they lack capability might be well-founded for the moment but offers absolutely no security for tomorrow. Indisputably, bioviolence is getting easier to do so with every passing day.

A terrorist or criminal has scant need for a military-styled weapon with precision control and therefore does not face stringent requirements in developing a lethal device. Information about how to make biological weapons is widely available on terror and hate websites.[53] Targets include just about anyone in an urban area as well as food and water supplies. Even failure can be followed up with other attempts. Whatever significance the taboo against inflicting disease might have for States, it is obviously irrelevant to terrorists, criminals, and lunatics. Of course, deterrence by threat of retaliation is essentially meaningless for groups with suicidal inclinations who likely intermingle with innocent civilians.

Readers should know that, as indicated above concerning State programs, it is impossible without highly classified information to confirm allegations about terrorists' interest in bioviolence. The following material distills the publicly available information about terrorists, focusing on Al Qaeda and associated international terror networks because there is so much information available. However, there have been many bioviolence hoaxes, and it is far easier to talk about doing bioviolence than actually carrying out an attack.

Islamic Fundamentalist Interest in Bioviolence

The chief fear is about Al Qaeda and affiliated Islamic Fundamentalist organizations in roughly sixty-five countries.[54] Manifesting antipathy to the United States and western allies, these groups have overtly proclaimed their intention to develop and use bioweapons. If they are duplicitously exaggerating their plans in order to spark unfounded anxiety, they are very good at it.

As early as 1994, Osama bin Laden professed an interest in acquiring weapons of mass destruction. The eleventh volume of Al Qaeda's *Encyclopedia of Jihad* is devoted to chemical and biological weapons.[55] According to the 9/11 Commission, Al Qaeda had long been planning to eliminate the Jews in Iran by using air conditioning systems to pump poisons into the buildings where they work.[56] Al Qaeda has acknowledged that "biological weapons are considered the least complicated and the easiest to manufacture of all weapons of mass destruction."[57] In a 1999 interview with a *Time Magazine* reporter, bin Laden proclaimed:

> Acquiring weapons for the defense of Muslims is a religious duty. If I have indeed acquired these weapons [of mass destruction] then I thank God for enabling me to do so. And if I seek to acquire these weapons, I am carrying out a duty. It would be a sin for Muslims not to try to possess the weapons that would prevent the infidels from inflicting harm on Muslims.[58]

Moreover, an Al Qaeda website proclaimed that "these [biological] weapons are also considered to be the most affordable. With $50,000 a group of amateurs can possess a biological weapon sufficient to threaten a superpower."[59] A memo perhaps written by Ayman al-Zawahri after the African Embassy bombings in April 1999 declared, "The destructive power of these [biological] weapons is no less than that of nuclear weapons."[60] Because disseminating biological agents to cause mass casualties is difficult, low-scale attacks and assassinations should be undertaken:

> Go to the supermarket where the American pigs shop. Observe him well and make sure that you are close to him especially to his shopping cart . . . if this pig puts some uncovered vegetables or fruit in his cart you should spray this material (poison) on them when he is not paying attention . . . if you can, it is preferable to stick the needle in the fruit.[61]

Al Qaeda's Intentions

Al Qaeda leadership has not always favored use of WMD. According to a bin Laden confidant, Abu Walid al-Misri, the Al Qaeda leadership before 9/11 debated whether to acquire weapons of mass destruction.[62] Objections focused on whether acquisition of such weapons might be strategically unwise. The process of acquiring the weapons risked exposing operatives, and delivery or dissemination of the weapon would be too challenging for the group.

By 1998, rising concerns about a United States or Israeli strike against Muslim nations evoked reconsideration of biological and other weapons of mass destruction. At a meeting of the Majlis al-Shura's, Al Qaeda's governing council, the decision was made to acquire weapons of mass destruction as a potential deterrent against the United States and allied aggression. A biological attack against the United States was planned as a "second wave" to be unleashed by Al Qaeda after the 9/11 attacks.[63] After the U.S.-led invasion into Afghanistan and Iraq, Al Qaeda proclaimed that WMD would be used as a first-strike option in retaliation for mass casualties of Muslims. Osama bin Laden proclaimed, "The time has come for us to be equal . . . Just as you kill, you are killed. Just as you bombard, you are bombarded. Rejoice at the harm coming to you."[64]

Even in recent years as the war on terrorism has been chasing Al Qaeda members, postings on the internet have included an article by 'Abd al-'Aziz al-Muqrin (Abu Hajir), an Al Qaeda fugitive in Saudi Arabia, calling for supporters to attack the Saudi government with nuclear and biological weapons.[65] This view has been championed by the group's strategists. According to a videotape declaration from June 2002 by Abu Graith, an Al Qaeda representative, Al Qaeda is morally justified in killing over four million Americans, including one million children, with biological weapons.[66]

The same perspective was voiced by Mustafa Setmariam Nasar (a.k.a. Abu Musab al-Suri), Al Qaeda's lead strategist for developing WMD capabilities. Setmariam proclaimed that the 9/11 attacks on the World Trade Center and Pentagon did not do enough damage: "I feel sorry that there were no weapons of mass destruction in the planes that attacked New York and Washington on 9/11."[67] Setmariam, a veteran Syrian Jihadi, has been a staunch advocate of incorporating WMD into conventional terrorist attacks; using conventional means to attack the United States would take "many years and enormous sacrifices." Therefore, "an attack on the United States with WMD has become necessary . . . by means of decisive strategic operations with weapons of mass destruction including nuclear, chemical, or biological weapons."[68] He is known to have helped the Al Qaeda chief of WMD, Abu Khabab al-Misri, train terrorists on how to use WMD. He assembled a sixteen-hundred-page collection of his lectures, entitled *Call for Global Resistance*, that urges terrorists to break the structure and hierarchy of the current Al Qaeda organization in order to branch off into their own lone commando operations to more effectively inflict terror. Although Setmariam was captured in Pakistan in 2005, his manuscript *The International Islamic Resistance Call* and his *Letter Reply to the U.S. State Department*, as well as various lectures, are reportedly widely available.[69] More important, his analysis is reprehensibly logical.

Religious and "Legal" Justification
Manifesting a remarkable combination of concern for law while planning mass murder, bin Laden sought legalistic endorsement for using weapons of mass destruction from a Saudi Arabian cleric Sheikh Nasir bin Hamd

Al-Fahd.[70] In May 2003, bin Hamd wrote a twenty-five-page fatwa entitled, *A Treatise on the Legal Status of Using Weapons of Mass Destruction Against Infidels.*[71] It provides a religious and legal justification for Muslims to use all means at their disposal, including biological warfare if necessary, to pursue and repel the enemy infidels – America. As a purported albeit specious dissertation on international law, it deserves substantial attention here.

Under the *principle of reciprocity,* Muslims are entitled to use weapons of mass destruction against the infidels, even if it means innocent women, children, and Muslims are killed. Citing scholars' writings and the sayings of the Prophet Mohammad concerning the nature of jihad, bin Hamd asserts: "If the infidels can be repelled from the Muslims only by using such weapons, their use is permissible, even if you kill them without exception and destroy their tillage and stock." Using weapons of mass destruction is justified in order to break the strength and disrupt the unity of the enemy: "God commanded that the polytheists should be killed. He did not specify the manner in which it should be done, nor did he obligate us to do it in a certain manner. Therefore, there is nothing to prevent their being killed by every cause of death; shooting, piercing, drowning, razing, casting from a cliff, and so forth."

Pay no heed, says Bin Hamd, to "what they pretend to call 'the rights of man,' or talk about 'the peace-loving peoples.'" Weapons of mass destruction have been "internationally banned" by the infidels' laws in order to "frighten others." The infidels "do not wish to protect humanity by these terms, as they assert; rather, they want to protect themselves and monopolize such weapons on the pretext of 'banning them internationally.'" "[T]hese terms have no legal standing in Islamic law, only God Almighty has reserved judgment and legislation to himself." The very term "weapon of mass destruction" misleadingly refers only to nuclear, chemical, and biological weapons; it should include "internationally permissible" conventional weapons:

> If anyone should use any of those weapons [weapons of mass destruction] and kill a thousand people, they would launch accusations and media wars against him saying that he had used "internationally banned weapons." If he had used high explosive bombs weighing seven tons a piece and killed three thousand or more because of them, he would have used internationally permitted weapons.

It does not matter that weapons of mass destruction cannot be specifically targeted or calculated. Says bin Hamd, "[T]he effect of several kilograms of TNT can be considered mass destruction if you compare it to the effect of a catapult stone of old. An RPG or mortar projectile can be considered mass destruction if you compare it to the shooting of arrows of old." "[A] catapult stone does not distinguish between woman, children, and others; it destroys anything that it hits, buildings or otherwise." There is nothing wrong with "putting blood, dung, or poison in their water to befoul it for them. Muslims have been commanded to subdue them and break their strength. All these things are military tactics that will cause their strength to break; they derive from obedience, not disobedience to what has been commanded." If the enemy is so fortified and entrenched that the Muslims are powerless, then the enemy "may be bombarded with catapults, siege engines, fire, scorpions, snakes, and anything hateful to them."

Bin Hamd distinguishes the "jihad of pursuit" – an offensive military campaign against infidels in the theatre of the infidels – from the "jihad of repulsion" – a defensive struggle to expel the infidels from Muslim territory. During a jihad of repulsion, the use of such weapons is imperative and obligatory: "[N]othing is a greater duty, after faith itself, than repelling an enemy attacker who sows corruption to religion and the world. No conditions limit this: one repels the enemy however one can." In a jihad of pursuit, the use of weapons of mass destruction against the infidels must be proportional: "whoso commits aggression against you, do you commit aggression against him like as he has committed against you." Because America has killed ten million Muslims during the past decades, Muslims are justified in killing just as many Americans.

There are three situations where using weapons of mass destruction is beneficial: 1) taking the enemy by surprise; 2) subduing and weakening the enemy's strongholds; and 3) bombarding the enemy until they are conquered. Although one should kill in a good manner when one can, "If those engaged in jihad cannot do so, for example when they are forced to bomb, destroy, burn, or flood, it is permissible." For Muslims employed in jihad, "burning and devastating are permissible in enemy territory" in order to "sap their polytheist enemy's strength, weaken their cunning, and facilitate victory over them. They may cut down their crops, divert their water, and besiege them."

Bin Hamd similarly dismisses Islam's prohibition on the killing of women and children. This applies, he says, only to the *intentional* killing of women and children; if women and children are killed unintentionally, such as when the attacker cannot or does not distinguish between the enemy, then they are mere collateral damage of a justified attack. "One avoids killing women and children only when one can distinguish them. If one cannot do so, as when the infidels make a night attack or invade, they may be killed as collateral to the fighters." It is imperative to prevent the enemy from using the killing of civilians, especially women and children, to undermine Al Qaeda's cause and techniques. Thus, weapons of mass destruction may be used even though women and children may be killed because "they are of them" and "they do not have the legal factor of faith, which spares one's blood, nor do they live in abode of faith, which prevents an attack on that abode."

Another strictly held Islamic prohibition is against the killing of fellow Muslims. However, asserts bin Hamd, "if those engaged in jihad are forced to kill him because they cannot repel the infidels or fight them otherwise, it is permitted, as when the Muslim is being used as a living shield." "There is no way to avoid striking them while still obeying the commandment to subdue the polytheists. What cannot be avoided must be pardoned."

The justification for killing fellow Muslims is about intention. If there is no intention of killing fellow Muslims, although there might be the knowledge that fellow Muslims might die in the crossfire, the legal status of the Muslim bystander is that of the infidels. No fault rests with the Muslim who besieges the enemy with weapons of mass destruction and happens to kill an innocent Muslim because the defense of the Muslim community far outweighs the individual loss suffered by the innocent bystander. The enemy cannot force Muslims to abandon the jihad by simply using other Muslims as shields.

Acquisition of Agents and Expertise

Al Qaeda is widely reported to have acquired lethal pathogens via publicly available scientific sources. In April 1999, bin Laden sought to acquire agents such as anthrax, ebola, botulinum toxin, plague, and salmonella through the mail from sources in the former Soviet Union, East Asia, Sudan, Afghanistan, and the Czech Republic.[72] A senior bin Laden associate on trial in Egypt, Al Qaeda military commander Ahmad Salama Mabruk, claimed his group had acquired biological weapons from Europe and the former Soviet Union from 1996–1998.[73] In July 1999, an Islamist attorney, Muntasir al-Zayyat, who defended some of the 107 suspected jihadists tried with Mabruk in Egypt, affirmed that Al Qaeda had acquired biological weapons and will likely use them against the United States.[74] In 2001, bin Laden visited with two Pakistani scientists, Sultan Bashir ul Din Mehmood and Abdul Majid, to share information relating to the production of biological weapons.[75]

In 2000, Al Qaeda operatives are believed to have purchased anthrax and plague from arms dealers in Kazakhstan.[76] In December 2001, Malaysian authorities arrested Yazid Sufaat, a member of the Al Qaeda affiliate Jemaah Islamiyah. Intelligence reports linked Sufaat to a plan to obtain and produce biological warfare agents.[77] Some Russian scientists allegedly provided technical and scientific expertise to assist in weaponizing anthrax as well.[78] According to Dame Eliza Manningham-Buller, Director General of the British intelligence service MI5, "We know that renegade scientists have cooperated with Al Qaeda and provided them with some of the knowledge they need to develop these [chemical, biological, radiological, and nuclear – CBRN] weapons."[79] Egyptian and Israeli intelligence have revealed that Al Qaeda has sought to acquire and use small-scale, easy-to-produce, toxic materials.[80]

Al Qaeda urged followers to recruit microbiology and biotechnology experts in the "fastest, safest, and cheapest" manner possible. Al Qaeda leaders also encouraged militants to enroll in educational institutions in order to research the American history of germ warfare providing them "easy access to specialists, which will greatly benefit us in the first stage [of the program], God willing."[81] On September 28, 2006, in a twenty-minute audio file posted on an Al Qaeda website, Al Qaeda terror chief in Iraq identifying himself as Abu Hamza al-Muhajir, also known as Abu Ayyub al-Masri, called upon scientists to join the jihad against Americans in Iraq. Addressing scientists, the terror leader proclaimed, "We are in dire need of you," adding "The field of jihad can satisfy your scientific ambitions, and the large American bases (in Iraq) are good places to test your unconventional weapons, whether biological or dirty, as they call them."[82]

The story of Ali al Timimi is illustrative. American-born, he received religious education in Saudi Arabia and was active in the Islamic Assembly of North America (IANA). Known as a spiritual leader among radical Islamists,[83] he lectured at the Center for Islamic Information and Education in Falls Church, Virginia.[84] By spring 2002, as a computational biology doctoral student at George Mason University, he worked in a program designed to coordinate bioresearch at several universities. He thus had ready access to various facilities involved in current research.[85] He was discovered by the FBI, convicted on charges of incitement to wage war against the United States, and sentenced to life in prison in 2005.[86]

Production

Al Qaeda had facilities potentially capable of producing biological and chemical weapons. In a June 1999 memo, Zawahiri instructed Al Qaeda members to build laboratories in a particular manner to "facilitate cleaning" of the laboratories where the biological and chemical agents would later be produced.[87] Notably, investigations of the medical history of Ahmet Al-Haznawi, one of the 9/11 hijackers, revealed that he might have been suffering from cutaneous anthrax. Also, Mohammad Atta (leader of the 9/11 attacks) had irritated, red hands purportedly from using too much bleach to clean up anthrax labs.

With the capture of Khalid Shaykh Muhammad in Pakistan, investigators uncovered detailed production plans for chemical and biological weapons as well as indications that Al Qaeda had material capabilities for producing cyanide and was close to producing weapons-quality anthrax.[88] Al Qaeda was also working on a pesticide and nerve-agent cocktail combined with a chemical compound in order to increase absorption. One discovered document provided detailed tables illustrating the recommended lethal doses of various poisons.[89]

A recently declassified CIA report asserts that Al Qaeda conducted significant research on bioagents, particularly anthrax.[90] A computer found in an abandoned Al Qaeda office in Kabul, Afghanistan, purportedly belonging to Dr. Ayman al-Zawahiri, contained a file describing plans for a bioweapon program code-named "al Zabadi," or "curdled milk."[91] Documents were also found revealing that Al Qaeda was researching how to use botulinum toxin to kill two thousand people.[92]

Al Qaeda organizations including the World Islamic Front Against Jews and Crusaders purchased three chemical and biological agent production facilities in Zenica, Bosnia, and built another factory for producing anthrax near Kandahar, Afghanistan, that U.S. forces discovered in early 2002.[93] No biological agents were found in the facility,[94] but the lab equipment suggested that Al Qaeda had acquired items for a "very limited production of biological and chemical agents."[95] Al Qaeda took steps to ensure that their covert bioweapons program would go undetected. One memo advised, "[p]eriodically (for example about every three months) one of the locations is to be canceled and replaced by another."[96]

Following the U.S.-led invasion in Afghanistan, five Al Qaeda biological weapons labs tested positive for traces of anthrax, including al-Zawahiri's residence in Kabul.[97] U.S. officials also announced that Al Qaeda members including Zarqawi established a weapons lab in Kirma, Iraq, to produce ricin and cyanide.[98] With the capture of Khalid Shaykh Muhammad in Pakistan, investigators uncovered detailed production plans for other chemical and bioweapons facilities. In 2002, Ansar al-Islam allegedly tested ricin and experimented with cyanide-based toxins and aflatoxin on live animals and at least one human, but the group's representative Muhammad Hasan Muhammad denied this report.[99]

Al Qaeda seems to have stumbled on the last step of bioviolence preparation: testing a dissemination device. Zacharias Moussaoui and Mohammad Atta sought to acquire crop dusters to disseminate bacteriological weapons.[100] Later, a captured operative reaffirmed bin Laden's interest in acquiring aircraft to commit bioviolence.[101] Documents calculating aerial dispersal methods of anthrax via balloon were discovered in Kabul along with anthrax spore concentrate at a nearby vaccine laboratory.[102]

Concluding Observations

There is no convincing explanation for why catastrophic bioviolence has not yet occurred. Experts speculate at length, and perhaps there have been plots that covert intelligence has foiled. It has been suggested that the failed attempts to prepare for and commit bioviolence are evidence that bioviolence is beyond the capabilities of terrorists and cults; certainly, making a lethal device is not a pedestrian matter. Most of the experience with bioviolence involves small cults and lunatics whose capabilities have fallen short of what would be necessary to conduct a global biocatastrophe. Noted bioviolence incidents, plans, and hoaxes are listed in Box 3-1.

However, it might be quite wrong to conclude that terrorist groups and cults pose no cause for concern. Even more worrisome is the bio-offender that we do not know about or do not associate with widespread malevolence. Perhaps our greatest concern should not be Al Qaeda or its associates but the possibility that a handful of deeply alienated people would inflict a biological catastrophe. This threat is far more difficult to penetrate than is Al Qaeda. In due time, hindsight will enable accurate measures of risk. If the past is predictive of the future, then the danger of bioviolence is worth taking seriously.

BOX 3-1. NOTED BIOVIOLENCE INCIDENTS, PLANS, AND HOAXES

- In January 2003, London police dismantled the *Poison Cells*, a part of the France-based Benchellali network, arresting six Algerians in a flat where the police thought, incorrectly, were trace amounts of ricin.[a] The cell was allegedly plotting to attack a British military base by poisoning the food. Discovered documents indicated that they sought to produce several poisons.[b] In the men's apartment in Manchester, police discovered equipment to process castor beans. Similar documents relating to the production and dissemination of bioweapons were found when seven members of the Benchellali network were later arrested in Lyon, France. When Benchellali was arrested for producing ricin for an attack in France, authorities discovered that he had been storing the agents in *Nivea Cream* cosmetic containers.[c]

- In September 1984, the Rajneeshee religious cult contaminated self-service restaurants and grocery stores in Oregon with salmonella in order to disable hundreds of Oregonians from voting against their candidates in local elections. Nearly 1,000 people reported symptoms and 751 cases were confirmed; no one died. The outbreak was quickly recognized and investigated. The U.S. Centers for Disease Control and Prevention found salmonella in milk and coffee creamers of some restaurants and in salad dressings of another but did not conclude that there had been an attack until a year later when the cult's leader revealed that the outbreak was deliberately caused. Subsequent investigation revealed that the Rajneeshee Medical Corporation and pharmacy were legally able to acquire bio-agents from medical supply companies. The cult also purchased a quick-freeze dryer to stabilize agents for effective weaponization.[d]

- The Japanese cult Aum Shinrikyo (now known as Aleph) was comprised fifty thousand members including biochemists, doctors, and policemen from Russia and Japan and had a net worth of over $1 billion. Aum spent considerable sums to build modern high-tech laboratories for producing bioweapons such as anthrax, botulinum, and Q fever. During the 1990s, Aum tried to perpetrate over a dozen germ attacks in Japan but disseminated them too amateurishly to have detectable consequences. In one attempt, the cult sprayed aerosolized anthrax from atop an eight-story building in downtown Tokyo; no harm resulted. The group also tried disseminating botulinum toxin and anthrax spores by driving a truck with an aerosol mechanism loaded in the back; intended targets included the Imperial Palace,

---

[a] John Steele & Sandra Laville, *Six Arrested in Poison Terror Alert*, DAILY TELEGRAPH (January 8, 2003); *See also*, Roland Jacquard & Atmane Tazaghart, BENLADEN, LA DESTRUCTION PROGRAMMÉE DE L'OCCIDENT (December 2004); Warren Hoge, *British Officer Slain, 4 Hurt as Terror Suspects are Seized*, NEW YORK TIMES (January 15, 2003).

[b] Jeffrey Bale, Anjali Bhattacharjee, Eric Croddy, & Richard Pilch, M.D., *Ricin Found in London: An al-Qa'ida Connection*, CENTER FOR NONPROLIFERATION STUDIES (January 23, 2002).

[c] Joby Warrick, *An Al Qaeda 'Chemist' and the Quest for Ricin*, WASHINGTON POST (May 5, 2004).

[d] Judith Miller et al., GERMS: BIOLOGICAL WEAPONS AND AMERICA'S SECRET WAR, Simon & Schuster, p. 28 (2001).

BOX 3-1. CONTINUED

the Parliament building, and American navy bases. Having spent enormous sums to develop bioweapons without success, they turned to chemical weapons.[e] On March 19, 1995, the group attacked the Tokyo subway system with sarin nerve gas killing twelve people and hospitalizing thousands more. Six months later, during U.S. Senate hearings, Senator Nunn declared, "The scenario of a terrorist group either obtaining or manufacturing and using a weapon of mass destruction is no longer the stuff of science fiction or even adventure movies."[f]

- In 1993, Thomas Lavy was stopped by Canadian Customs Officials near the Alaskan-Canadian border. He had racist literature, a stockpile of weapons, and ammunition as well as 130 grams of ricin (enough to kill over 130,000 people). Police later found castor beans and instructions explaining how to produce ricin in Lavy's apartment. Lavy committed suicide in his jail cell days after his arrest; his intentions are unknown.[g]

- In 1998, members of a right-wing extremist faction the "Republic of Texas" purportedly discussed plans to weaponize rabies and anthrax and to use them against families of government employees. Reports allege that members wanted to modify cigarette lighters to inject a cactus needle coated with HIV, rabies, botulinum, or anthrax. Two members were convicted of sending threatening e-mails to assassinate President Clinton, Attorney General Janet Reno, and other officials using bioweapons.[h] They were sentenced to twenty-four years in prison. They were acquitted, however, of charges of planning to produce weapons of mass destruction.[i]

- Larry Wayne Harris, a member of the neo-Nazi Aryan Nations, wrote a book on how to protect against a bioattack: *Bacteriological Warfare: A Major Threat to North America*. He experimented with bubonic plague-causing bacteria, three vials of which he purchased from the American Type Culture Collection for $300.[j] At the time, no law prohibited possession of such agents. His attempt to order other agents including anthrax led to his highly publicized arrest in 1998 on charges of conspiracy to possess a bioweapons agent. However, lab results on Harris's anthrax samples revealed that it was a harmless vaccine and not the weaponized agent as feared. Therefore, these charges were dropped.

- In 1992, the Minnesota Patriots Council produced ricin to be used against a U.S. deputy marshal and deputy sheriff. The group never used it against those persons,

---

[e] See generally, Miller, pp. 151–154, 159–164; See also, Jeremy Manier & Jeff Long, *State Tackles Readiness for Biochemical Attack*, CHICAGO TRIBUNE (October 7, 2001).

[f] (Miller, p. 191).

[g] *Beyond Anthrax: Extremism and the Bioterrorism Threat*, ANTI-DEFAMATION LEAGUE, p. 5 (2001).

[h] Jessica Stern, *Domestic Terrorists Constitute a Potentially Serious Biological Warfare Threat*, in BIOLOGICAL WARFARE: OPPOSING VIEWPOINTS, William Dudley (ed.), p. 80 (2004).

[i] *Beyond Anthrax: Extremism and the Bioterrorism Threat*, p. 4.

[j] Miller, p. 197 .

but group members were convicted for possessing 0.7 grams of ricin for use as a weapon (enough to kill over 100 people).[k]

- In 1981, an environmental extremist group known as the "Dark Harvest Commandos" deposited packages of anthrax-contaminated soil outside chemical weapons facilities in Great Britain to protest the presence of the chemical facility and its alleged contamination of Gruinard Island.[l]

- In 1972, the extremist right-wing group "Order of the Rising Sun" was arrested in Chicago with 30–40 kg of typhoid bacteria. The group was planning to poison water supplies in Chicago, St. Louis, and other Midwest cities.[m] Even if the plot had not been foiled, however, water filtration systems would likely have negated any consequences.

---

[k] *Beyond Anthrax: Extremism and the Bioterrorism Threat*, p. 5; *See also*, Stern.

[l] *Beyond Anthrax: Extremism and the Bioterrorism Threat*, p. 8.

[m] Stern, p. 79.

PART II

The Global Strategy for Preventing Bioviolence

4 Strategic Foundations

There are scenarios for bioviolence that could deeply destabilize the modern era. To summarize Part I: there are capacities to do harm, and there are people who want to devote those capacities precisely to do harm.

The thesis of Part II is that there are policies that can substantially reduce risks. No proposal, of course, can provide an ironclad guarantee that a bioattack will not happen. It would seem that we will never be completely safe, but there is much that we can do to make us safer. We can pursue these policies in ways that promote the advance of bioscience and that elevate global attention to public health. Absent a prevention strategy, the threats will grow larger and more uncontrollable. Considerable improvement is better than perpetually accruing insecurity.

Prevention strategies are controversial because the limits of these strategies are uncertain. Should broad policy sectors involving health and science be bent to the objective of preventing bioviolence, an as-yet unrealized threat? The answer must be clear: preventing bioviolence is one part of a policy mélange, important but not an exclusive priority. Whatever actions are to be taken must not only improve security from biothreats, they must also promote (or at least not encumber) other values and aspirations. Putting this point more bluntly, not everything that can conceivably be done to prevent bioviolence should be undertaken. Not every preventive measure produces benefits that are worth the costs. Viewed more positively, richer and more sophisticated initiatives can ripen if we pursue bioviolence prevention in a context of broader policy paradigms.

Admittedly, this is complicated. It is also important. The answers given to – *how can international law address the intrinsic security threats posed by high science, especially the life sciences?* – say a great deal about how we can and should govern ourselves at this time.

THE INDICTMENT

Count 1. In view of the enormous opportunities for policy progress, too little is being done to make it hard to prepare and commit bioviolence. Progress is too slow on the basics: keeping dangerous pathogens and equipment out of the hands of strangers. Only a few individuals that we know a lot about should have access to items that can do vast and irreparable harm; we should be sure that no one else can get in. Laboratory security experts understand how to make rules for the conduct of bioscience that complicate access. Although scientists argue endlessly about this or that rule, no serious scientist would assert that the conduct of science is void of rules. The question is whether everyone is complying. The overwhelming majority of scientists in developed countries operate according to these rules and procedures. But there are holes especially in countries less scientifically advanced. Why?

The problem is that these rules are not really rules, they are *guidelines*: scientists should behave in this or that way, but it is difficult to find out about violations. Guidelines have served the world well; there is remarkably scant evidence about rogue scientific activity. Yet, there are benefits to making them law:

> If these rules about science are binding, then every authority (whether governmental or professional) will have to educate its members about those rules. A large problem in bioscience today is not malevolence but negligence; too few scientists are actively trained to be aware of bioviolence risks. The best defense from bioviolence is a bioscience community where everyone understands the seriousness of working with dangerous capabilities. Converting these guidelines into rules would compel that training. Law can institute requirements of courses, certification, etc. Although it may readily be conceived that law can go too far in this context, it need not.
>
> It will be easier to develop tools to detect intentionally wrongful conduct and, therefore, to leave everyone else alone. There very well might be culprits who can inflict an unprecedented harm, and both bioscientists and law enforcers have a professional responsibility to stop them; cooperation between these two communities is essential to preventing bioviolence. Without a legal framework, cooperation can take place here or there on an *ad hoc* basis, but the gaps in coverage are imperiling. Simply put, it is very difficult to envision global cooperation between bioscience communities and law enforcement communities unless there is some legal framework of rules and standards.

Today, there is too much that is unknown. We do not know where every well-equipped laboratory is; we suspect that not all dangerous pathogens can be accounted for; we have inadequate systems for tracking the movement of pathogens and equipment; and we have grossly inadequate capabilities of putting information together to give us the best chance to stop bio-offenders. Not enough is being done to track bioscience so that there is a basis for detecting wrongful conduct. Even if there are only a handful of people sufficiently hateful to commit a catastrophic bioviolence attack, we should improve the odds of finding and stopping them. Accordingly, the international community should consider how bioscience standards should be best universalized – that is, how law should help to fill gaps through which bioviolence might too easily emerge.

The obstruction here is not resistance from scientific or pharmaceutical communities; although these communities resist heavy-handed regulation, they appreciate the value of universalized scientific standards that are developed by and for scientists. It is the States that resist international standards as an intrusion on sovereignty or because their enforcement would disadvantage developing economies that have less resources to devote to security. The first objection – sovereignty – is absurd in view of the laundry list of internationally recognized standards in other areas of science and technology without which we would all be far worse off. The objection based on inadequate resources for security is short-sighted; it misses the shrewd assessment that burdens can be opportunities and that, in fact, international law upholds processes for enabling developing countries to gain capacities as they undertake obligations to achieve security.

Count 2. We are insufficiently taking advantage of the many law enforcers worldwide who should serve as the primary line of detection. Many of these law enforcers are inadequately trained and ill-equipped to pursue bioviolence. More important, law enforcers operate only where there are legal rules and processes that define illegal behavior. The absence of appropriate legal prohibitions against bioviolence makes every other initiative vastly harder to accomplish. There are too many flaws in law enforcement's readiness, whether at the conceptual level – how should international legal assistance work effectively to ensure cooperation to discover and interdict bioviolence? – or at the most operational level – how should police be trained to use protective gear? Not enough is being done by specialized organizations, Interpol excepted, to introduce bioviolence concerns to their constituents; not only do we lose the benefit of local police, we lose those organizations' capabilities for taking decisive action.

The obstructors here are leaders who argue that fundamental international security decisions should not be grounded on law enforcement. For example, although the U.S. government strongly supported United Nations Security Council Resolution 1540 – legally obligating all States to criminalize development of weapons of mass destruction and to adopt legal measures to prevent proliferation of WMD precursors to terrorists – it has been adamant that international security initiatives relevant to bioviolence must leave a very sizeable escape hatch for unilateral *realpolitik*. While the U.S. government has embraced the need to train and equip police, it has resisted bringing the full legal weight of the international community to bear on this issue. Although many laudable U.S. government personnel have been trying to make the world safer from bioviolence, they have had to carve out a niche of accomplishment virtually in hiding from political superiors. Resistance to international law from U.S. officials leaves everyone vulnerable. Enormous progress could be made if political leaders make a serious commitment to strengthening global law enforcement.

Count 3. There is no effective method to address the small number of extraordinarily serious threats of bioviolence preparation. While intelligence, diplomatic, and military communities are responsible for ensuring that these threats do not materialize, the disengagement of the United Nations Security Council – the legal apparatus for addressing threats to international peace and security – weakens us substantially. For example, U.S. officials have asserted that over a dozen nations have active bioweapons capabilities that could readily be converted to a weapons program, and this number will likely increase. Moreover, these officials have asserted that terrorist networks and perhaps even criminal syndicates have the capacity or intention to pursue bioviolence. Yet, proof of these assertions is neither forthcoming nor expected. Although the United States can try to shame these nations in the diplomatic community and loudly condemn terrorism, the accusations get thrown in the stew of "problems in international affairs" with nary any progress from year to year.

There needs to be an investigative capability at the highest level – a capability that should be exercised judiciously (as should all law enforcement) but is not a paper tiger. Criteria of *threats* should be developed, and there needs to be a process by which responsible persons can get facts and decide whether laws have been violated. This is not about establishing a bioviolence prevention bureaucracy or about moving toward a global government. What is needed is a scalpel, not a ballistic missile. Today, however, hopes for making that scalpel effective are mired in the unwillingness to infuse international security issues with the rule of law. Unfortunately, that applies to many issues besides bioviolence.

Count 4. Global distribution of capacities to prevent bioviolence are woefully unjust – a product of the much larger phenomenon of economic disparity that afflicts humanity. Not enough is being done to consider how making people safer from biothreats can be accomplished with benefits to professional communities and national economies throughout the developing world. Indeed, at this time there is insufficient (essentially nil) serious discussion about how to best enable developing countries to prevent bioviolence. There has been no systematic effort whatsoever to link compliance with bioviolence prevention policies to measures for stimulating indigenous bioscience. It is unconscionable that major policy discussions about bioscience development are wholly and entirely separate from major policy discussions about biothreats to international peace and security. The result is that the entire world is more dangerous.

It is difficult to assign guilt for this global failure other than to the shameful lack of vision on the part of many world leaders. A notable exception has been former Secretary General Kofi Annan who has repeatedly called for more attention to be given to these issues, even calling for a global forum that would start the process of improving policy.[1] Yet, Secretary General Annan's call has roused little enthusiasm. So long as the developmental aspects of bioviolence prevention continue to be ignored, policy progress will be hobbled.

There is another, no less important side to this assertion. Any policy to improve bioviolence prevention, even a policy that contributes materially to development, will survive only amid a legal structure where rights and obligations are meaningfully applicable. Right now, the allure of bioscience and technology is, among too many governments, greater than the respect for the rule of law. That there are inadequate efforts to engender and deepen that respect should evoke the highest priority for legal reform.

Count 5. There's nobody in charge. No one is responsible; no one is accountable. With regard to bioviolence, no international authority defines relevant prohibitions and responsibilities. Over the years, many good ideas have not been rejected but have died for lack of a responsible official who has authority to act. There is no authorized focal point for new initiatives and no central body with clear capacity to carry out prevention responsibilities, evaluate who might be failing to meet their responsibilities, and instigate inquiry into emerging problems. As a result, even well-regarded ideas have nowhere to grow. There is not so much resistance to initiatives as there is simply an absence of initiatives, and a manifest inertia has become a significant drag on even the best public servants' calls to action. No body exists to promote reasonable, even widely shared initiatives to advance progressive policies. International alarms of bioviolence ring nowhere!

The reason why the absence of authority endangers us is that, as the following chapters make clear, bioviolence prevention requires a sizeable orchestra, made up of various instruments, to play complicated music in harmony. Today there is not a bad conductor – there is no conductor at all. Sometimes the players rise to the occasion; too often there is little more than cacophony.

There is another factor that harkens back to the distinction between rules and guidelines. Too often there has been a tendency to pursue policies in the well-intentioned belief that incremental progress is possible but then not devoting the time or political will to ensure that legalities are upheld. Policies that might be effective in addressing some small aspect of bioviolence prevention have proceeded without attending to the question of precisely how those policies can be legally firm. The result is a mixed bag of many good people working in murky official capacities to put out a fire here or there. In nearly every other comparable dimension of human activity, there are methods for professionally and legally undertaking complex initiatives. Policies for preventing bioviolence are noticeably different. The failure to respect the need for a legal system with clear lines of authority and responsibility is the worst count of this indictment.

OBSTACLES TO POLICY PROGRESS

The remaining chapters' recommendations are not revolutionary; they do not call for a sweeping metamorphosis in how we live or how science is conducted. To implement them requires profound efforts, but it is not the difficulty of their implementation that is the primary barrier against progress. Instead, the following obstacles should be appreciated as explaining why so many of these recommendations are not in force and why potentially valuable proposals are so remarkably knotted.

First is *the bioscience paradox*. Bioscience that is beneficial is identical to bioscience that is potentially horrifying. Emerging possibilities of bioviolence are inherent in its progress – it is therefore problematic to say, "this is prohibited" or "this is not prohibited." The science that arguably should be prohibited is exactly the same science that should be encouraged. Moreover, science changes rapidly. Any set of legal prohibitions or regulations are likely to require nuanced applications and constant updating.

Attention should focus, therefore, on the process by which those precepts can perpetually emerge through evolving contexts. This is a remarkable legal challenge.

Second is *bureaucratic fragmentation*. Bioviolence evokes no single discipline or specialization. It cuts across the sciences, law, and politics; across academia, government research, and the private sector; across developed and developing States; and across planners who focus on military prowess, on public health, on law enforcement, and on emergency preparedness and management. The result is not that the issue has too many homes; it has no home at all. Traditional bureaucracies either step on each other's turf or pass responsibility through a maze of departments. In the U.S. government, there has been no authoritative office for coordinating a broad array of policies to prevent bioviolence. They vanish in the bureaucratic labyrinth. On the international level, the situation is immensely worse.

Third is *conflict over priorities*. Arms controllers and military strategists haggle about whether policies to reduce bioviolence threats should be addressed before policies to reduce other strategic threats (e.g., nuclear weapons). Developed States' advocates urge prompt action, but developing States' spokespersons argue that bioviolence threats should not divert attention from threats of natural disease, famine, and poverty. Law enforcers recognize that bioviolence is a crime but resist efforts to divert resources and attention away from core police functions. Bioscientists welcome resources to develop vaccines against biothreats but rebuff suggestions that their work should be governmentally supervised to reduce risks of misapplication. These and many similar conflicts over priorities serve to muddy the policy waters thereby impeding policy makers' ability to see where synergies can be usefully created and inappropriately engendering resistance to ideas that simultaneously advance multiple agendas. Instead, bioviolence prevention is a policy domain that is riddled with priority fortresses; entrenched defense of these fortresses impedes progress.

Fourth is the awesome *rate of change in bioscience*. Changes in the underlying science are absolutely beyond the rate of progress in diplomacy. Even if State-to-State diplomacy suddenly rang of harmony and shared commitment about what should be done, these diplomatic interactions are simply incapable of keeping pace with changing threat parameters. Bioviolence is an international security threat that is too dangerous to leave to political realists; they are simply too slow to undertake progress or respond to evolving dangers. Needed is an international legal capacity for rapidly making extremely sophisticated decisions at the very edge of human intellect – decisions that have humanity-wide implications.

Fifth is a *poverty of foresight*. Bioviolence prevention policy tends to be reactive as if the next problem will mimic recent experience. The 2001 anthrax attacks prompted a colossal shift of resources toward developing anthrax vaccines; expert attention to smallpox likewise provoked widespread concern about the paltry stockpiles of smallpox vaccine. A plague attack would likely incite stockpiling of appropriate antibiotics; if ebola is perilously manipulated into a terror device, an entirely different set of initiatives will ensue. Policies are event driven, and bio-offenders can outwit us by changing their attack mode. Nowhere is there systemic evaluation of today's bioviolence threats, much less the threats that we might face in only a few years. There is no widely accepted coherent framework of principles or obligations to guide prevention policies.

BIOVIOLENCE IS A CRIME!

A lot about preventing bioviolence is complicated, yet the keystone is clear. This book opened by defining bioviolence as a crime – quite literally, treason against humanity. For humans to pervert scientific progress into a catastrophic human loss is treachery most vile: members of our species using other species to devastate our species. It is a crime regardless of who the bio-offender is. There should be no ambiguity on this point anywhere for any reason whatsoever.

Designating behavior as a crime against humanity – as an act committed as part of a widespread or systematic attack directed against any civilian population – is the clearest and most forceful articulation of a prohibitory norm. This term includes murder, extermination, or other inhumane acts intentionally causing great suffering or when committed as part of a widespread or systematic attack or on a large scale directed against a civilian population.[2]

Criminalizing the misuse of pathogens for hostile purposes clarifies that such conduct is absolutely intolerable. Many scientific associations have condemned activity that contributes to commission of a bioviolence attack; there are a long list of *Codes of Ethics* and *Declarations* attesting to the universality and seriousness of this prohibition. It is wrong, therefore, to refer to biological weapons as "the poor nations' nuclear weapons"; no one should even suggest that their use might be rationalized in the name of self-determination. There are no legitimizing exceptions or national security justifications; no ideology or belief system can provide cause for ignoring the prohibition.

Setting clear norms and criminal prohibitions forces nations to choose: be a member of the global community or be a pariah. As global integration becomes ever more economically pivotal and as membership in regional associations increasingly depends on compliance with internationally recognized tenets of behavior, clear normative prescriptions gain weight. Criminalization means that global opprobrium must befall a State that adds bioweapons to its military arsenal. It means that the international community must take necessary and proportional action to thwart any nation from obtaining the materials and equipment and conducting the tests required for a bioweapons program.

Criminalization offers even greater benefits for confronting non-State terrorists or outlaws. It means that law enforcers must cooperate worldwide to be watchful of bioviolence preparations, and they must sustain vigilance for preventing those preparations' consequences. On this issue at least, there is no alternative to and no dispute about the need for international law enforcement cooperation. To their everlasting credit, some preeminent law enforcers and their institutions have forthrightly exercised leadership in regard to bioviolence prevention. This bodes well for future cooperation and, more generally, for the global spread of the rule of law.

Ultimately, the status of "crime against humanity" means that every State has responsibilities. Every State must criminalize bioviolence under its national laws, attach strict penalties, develop mechanisms to detect illegal behavior, authorize law enforcers to interdict that activity, and cooperate to bring bio-offenders to justice. No State can legally approve such conduct or grant impunity for any bio-offenders irrespective of where it is committed, against what category of victims, and whether it occurs during peace or war. A State that refuses to conduct an investigation or request support to interdict criminal bioviolence in its jurisdiction will be signaling through its inaction that it condones the illegal conduct. In that case, the State should be accountable for whatever harm follows from that crime.

OVERVIEW OF THE PREVENTION STRATEGY

From the straightforward premise that bioviolence is a crime grows an intricate strategy that can be expressed as follows:

$PREVENTION =$

$COMPLICATION + RESISTANCE + PREPARATION + NONPROLIFERATION$

These dimensions of the prevention strategy, discussed more fully in the next four chapters, should be thought of as successive and mutually reinforcing filters. Each captures or erases some risks of bioviolence and in coordination will likely deter malevolent actors from its pursuit. No one set of measures will be altogether effective, yet the risks of bioviolence can be substantially reduced by activating the strategy comprehensively. This is complex and must be pursued carefully. Most importantly, all of these dimensions must be subject to the rule of law.

Complication

First, *denial measures* should make it hard for a bio-offender to get what he needs to commit bioviolence, and if he tries, *interdiction measures* should make it more likely he will be discovered and stopped. The bio-offender needs pathogens and a capability to weaponize them. It will be harder for him to get these items if only legitimate scientists who need to work on highly refined and dangerous pathogens using sophisticated equipment in very secure laboratories are allowed to have access to such items. Cutting off or limiting wrongful access to sophisticated and refined agents, equipment, or laboratories would pose complicated obstacles for bioviolence that likely will discourage potential offenders from pursuing this catastrophic mode of attack.

Correctly structured denial measures should be linked to observable signals so that an offender will more likely make a mistake that alerts law enforcers. This is how interdiction measures can be beneficial. Law enforcers (police, customs and border control officials, regulatory inspectors, etc.) should be authorized, trained, and equipped to look for such indicative behavior so that they will stop a bio-offender before he has a chance to carry out his plans. The key challenge facing law enforcers is to know where and at whom to look; more precisely, it is to know how to distinguish bio-offenders from legitimate bioscientists.

If denial measures pose obstacles to getting necessary items for bioviolence, and if interdiction measures raise the risks of getting caught, then malevolent persons will likely be dissuaded from bioviolence altogether. A potential bio-offender has to think about the costs and benefits of various schemes; uniquely difficult and risky schemes will, in that equation, appear unattractive. By implementing effective denial and interdiction measures worldwide, we would go a long way to preventing bioviolence. But we must not stop there.

Resistance

Perhaps more than any other threat facing humanity, bioviolence is inherently linked to explosively changing science that perpetually transforms the types of threats as well as our capacity to withstand attacks. Advancing bioscience can discover vaccines and medications that deprive some diseases of their horrifying impact and thereby reduce options for bioviolence. Bioscience can also create novel pathogens that are unaffected by those vaccines. Thus, bioscience is simultaneously a critical component of the solution and an impetus for the problem.

The concept of resistance, therefore, is double-edged. First, there are policies that can encourage creation of drugs that will enable us to resist pathogens more effectively, but there is no cure-all that will immunize us from harm. Second, there are policies that can resist bioscience's potential for developing dangerous capabilities whether inadvertently or malevolently, but these policies must not constrict the fundamental pursuit of scientific knowledge. Resistance measures can contribute to complication. By denying potential offenders various easy-to-accomplish methods of bioviolence through widespread immunization of target populations, complication measures can focus on more challenging attack methods. Yet, resistance policies carry costs both overt and hidden that must not be ignored. Moreover, there are remarkable challenges in extending these policies worldwide.

Preparedness

As repeatedly explained in previous chapters, it is getting easier to commit ever more horrible bioviolence. Even if complication and resistance measures are implemented, risks remain that someone will successfully commit a bioviolence attack despite our best efforts. We must be ready to mitigate the damage. Worldwide, we need to enable early detection and response to an attack once it has happened. If all else fails, it is socially responsible to ensure that an attack's consequences will be containable.

Preparedness measures are closely linked to resistance measures. The vaccines and medicines that scientists discover have to be produced in sufficient quantities, distributed globally, and allocated with respect for adverse side effects. Other preparedness measures such as hardening buildings against pathogen dissemination can also heighten our resistance to attack.

Preparedness measures can also contribute to complication measures. By establishing lines of communication between public health authorities and law enforcers, we can more quickly identify a bioattack and respond more effectively. After an attack, preparedness measures will be critical for treating victims. Especially for attacks involving contagious pathogens, preparedness measures can limit an attack's spread and encourage public health–law enforcement cooperation to contain the consequences and maintain order. The challenge is how to advance systems where more secure bioscience and better law enforcement capabilities are integrated with and complementary to promoting global public health preparedness.

Nonproliferation

The three sets of measures just mentioned (complication, resistance, and preparedness) are together the most effective way to address threats of terrorists, criminals, and lunatics. There remains, however, the rarer but very serious threat of State military programs. Because States have unique capabilities for committing violence and making covert preparations, consideration must be given to measures for preventing proliferation of military bioviolence programs.

The Biological Weapons Convention (BWC) establishes the global norm against bioviolence, but its operational vagueness and political rancorousness have denuded it of real power to prevent State bioviolence. Three controversial issues should be the centerpiece of prospective BWC deliberations. First, what process should decide precisely what is a bioweapon; most especially, how should so-called nonlethal bioagents be considered? Second, how can States be confident of their mutual compliance and be assured that burgeoning national biodefense programs are not covers for bio-offensive initiatives? Third, how can the BWC process encourage and oversee the dismantlement of existing bioweapons stockpiles particularly in the former Soviet Union. Notably, two other issues that exceed the BWC's scope have received substantial yet unproductive attention; they should be removed from its ambit: what should be the trade and economic incentives for developing States in the treaty regime; and should a governance authority be associated with the BWC. The importance of these issues has weighed down BWC progress and should, therefore, be considered elsewhere more productively.

The final chapter of this book considers perhaps the most important challenge facing anyone concerned with bioviolence. Few aspects of this strategy can emerge and be sustainable if pursued without any type of international governance, yet no modicum of governance currently exists. The global strategy for bioviolence prevention comprising complication, resistance, preparedness, and nonproliferation must proceed, therefore, by establishing specialized oversight bodies within the United Nations.

Guiding Principles

As the remaining chapters explore the bioviolence prevention strategy, three core principles deserve paramount attention:

- *Comprehensive security* – Decisions and activities should reflect global rather than national interests and should consider the future linkages among scientific, developmental, and security issues. As the 1995 Commission on Global Governance stated, "Global security must be broadened from its traditional focus on the security of states to include the security of peoples and the planet." Security from bioviolence is an essential priority that intersects diverse efforts to promote international peace.

- *Distributive justice* – Decisions and activities should strive to equitably distribute obligations and benefits according to the principle of common but differentiated responsibilities. Comprehensive security from bioviolence is a common "humanity" right in the sense that it is possessed by all, for all. International policies should reflect appreciation for the uneven distribution of opportunities among States. More broadly, the pursuit of sustainable development should include respect for bioviolence prevention and vice versa.

- *Fair participation in legal process* – The formation and application of rules should propound basic principles of procedural justice – access to information, right of interested parties to participate, and accountability. As all humanity is directly concerned with bioviolence prevention, all should have a say in the policy options and the distribution of benefits and burdens. A structured governance system will need effective collective decision-making processes as well as mechanisms to monitor and enforce compliance with rules. Much attention throughout this book focuses on the need for *legitimacy* – no decision can satisfy everyone, but every decision must manifest that it is the product of an objectively reasonable process.

Viewed even more broadly, the bioviolence prevention strategy attempts to grapple with the potential dangers emerging from bioscience, fully recognizing that preventing bioviolence must be a facet of a broad international commitment to promote that science – not just its products (pharmaceuticals) but the science itself – as a global good. Yet, the bioscience undertaking poses inherent and unavoidable dangers, and the more that bioscience spreads the greater the need for global controls to prevent a humanity-wide catastrophe. Therefore, access to and participation in modern bioscience should be conditional on performance of that bioscience according to international standards. With the commitment to encourage the global spread of bioscience comes an obligation to undertake scientific activities according to standards that reflect an appreciation of the unfortunate but nontrivial potential that a fraction of those so engaged could wreak disaster out of all proportion to their numbers or resources.

Synthesizing a global strategy of bioviolence prevention requires, therefore, a broad international commitment to the spread of legitimate bioscience; recognition that countering bioviolence must be a facet of that commitment; and an obligation to establish and implement international legal standards and measures as a prerequisite of global bioscience guardianship. Inappropriately addressing bioviolence concerns could undermine development of bioscience and technology with catastrophic effects. Developing bioscience but failing to address bioviolence concerns could lead to disaster and undermine confidence in science. Addressing all these concerns in harmony is mandatory for humanity's security.[3]

5 | Complication: What Law Enforcers Should Stop

Law enforcement's potent crime-fighting capabilities should be committed worldwide to detect and interdict bioviolence preparations. In most nations, however, police and other law enforcers are inadequately authorized and woefully lack information that would enable effective action. Recently, the United Nations Security Council and Interpol have each taken impressive strides to improve law enforcement authority and capacity, but the problem is far too vast for these measures to fill the void. Much more is needed.

A recent incident highlights this need. In June 2006, *The Guardian* newspaper reported that it easily obtained some smallpox DNA through the mail. It used an invented company name, a mobile phone number, a free e-mail address, and a house in north London to receive a plastic bag containing a small vial holding a white gel – the DNA. The source, VH Bio Ltd., did not know that the supplied material is part of the smallpox genome. VH Bio's chairman said that it is impossible to screen orders for short genetic sequences; in any event, no laws require background checks on potential customers. *The Guardian* reported that five of twelve gene synthesis companies that it surveyed in North America and Europe always screen their orders for suspect sequences; three said they never do.[1] Fortunately, this DNA sample was only a tiny fraction of a smallpox genome. There is scant risk that someone could order consecutive links and patch them together to make a whole virus. Yet, the full sequence map is freely available on the internet as are the DNA sequences of other dangerous pathogens that are far easier to assemble. For example, the genome of the 1918 Spanish Flu is only about 7 percent the length of the smallpox genome.

This chapter is about how law enforcement should complicate the pursuit of bioviolence. It should be difficult for bio-offenders to gain wrongful access to refined pathogens, sophisticated bioequipment, and advanced biolaboratories that could make it easier for them to carry out serious bioviolence scenarios. If they get access, there should be clues that enable law enforcers to stop them before the attack. There are many recommendations here and many elaborate details need to be addressed, yet all these recommendations can be achieved quickly and without great expense if there is the will to do so.

IRRESPONSIBLE GAPS

There appear to be huge opportunities for bio-offenders to gain lethal capabilities. Getting sophisticated equipment is trivial, and there are an untold number of biolaboratories containing refined pathogen seed stocks. How readily might any of these labs deliver pathogen samples in response to a fraudulent request? How many labs have appropriate safeguards for complicating diversion of pathogens or wrongful use of their facilities? Maybe there are many – maybe only a handful. No one knows for sure. Yet, one thing is certain: in most places around the world, if pathogens are diverted or if labs are malevolently used, it is extremely unlikely that law enforcers would find out in time to stop a catastrophe! Like the rest of us, the police will find out after the attack is carried out and the victims pile up.

It is alarming that we do not know where are *all* pathogens and laboratories that could facilitate bioviolence. More precisely, we know an enormous amount about *some* pathogens and laboratories; most worrisome is what we do not know about. As bioscience increasingly proliferates throughout regions near and far, the gaps of critical information expand. In truth, we have no real idea of what we do not know.

Worse, many States have not legally restricted accumulation of agents or critical equipment that bio-offenders might use. In many States, cultivation or transfer of deadly pathogens is not a criminal act. It is perfectly legal to obtain the most lethal agents and the equipment with which modestly trained scientists could assemble a functional bioweapon. In many nations, even if police learn that someone has an amateur laboratory, that laboratory violates no law. Police lack authority to inspect legal behavior and therefore lack authority to investigate amateur bioscience activities. A bio-offender can prepare, transport, and even export agents that could be lethally misused without running afoul of any legal constraint. Refining pathogens for easy dissemination is also not prohibited. Only the final act – the actual commission of an attack – is a crime.

This is irresponsible. We would not accept a system where anyone could fly a commercial airplane virtually anywhere without informing authorities or in violation of safety standards. We would not accept a system where nuclear laboratories have open doors that might allow anyone to carry materials or equipment in and out. We most certainly would not accept a system where, despite knowing that there is potential for criminality, law enforcers are incapable of doing much to prevent a most horrible crime. Most of us respect the need for scientific freedom, but there has to be a difference between freedom and anarchy especially when the consequences of misuse could be cataclysmic.

Bioscientists are not to blame for this condition, although some scientists are perhaps too complacent about the potential for bioviolence. Most scientists are engaged in a headlong competition to make a new discovery and publish the next paper. It is a competition where ethical precepts hold powerful sway but where compulsory standards are deficient. At root here are legal gaps throughout major regions of the world and ignorance about what is going through those gaps. Some States enforce relevant standards; most do not. Cavernous holes in national legislation undermine any authority to enforce basic security standards. These holes in nations' laws are magnified by the legal void at the international level. There is no authoritative system for keeping records and no way to know about compliance with even properly enacted laws. There is no coherent international oversight structure that can make fine, nuanced decisions much less determine whether everyone is obeying those decisions.

Most importantly, there is essentially no mechanism whatsoever for detecting bioscience activity that is intentionally evasive of standards, that is, criminal bioscience. While bio-offenders are becoming more focused and organized, policies to deny them the capabilities for bioviolence are vague, gap-ridden, backward-looking, unsupervised, and largely inattentive to the threat posed by intentional malefactors. More dismayingly, there is no process whatsoever to anticipate the policies that might suitably cope with tomorrow's challenges – a most striking deficiency in view of bioscience's accelerating rate of change. The crisis here is not in science – the crisis here is in law. There is a systemic failure to clarify and enforce even rudimentary legal obligations that could make it harder to commit bioviolence.

THE LOGIC OF COMPLICATION

It should be hard for a bio-offender to get the pathogens and technology that he needs to commit bioviolence. If he can obtain refined pathogens and readily weaponize them using advanced equipment and facilities, he will more likely succeed than if his preparations are unremittingly obstructed. Global implementation of measures that deny the more straightforward ways to commit bioviolence will compel a bio-offender to pursue more precarious and expensive routes that raise the odds of botching his plans. Therefore, he should be barred from obtaining refined laboratory specimens of dangerous pathogens. If he wants to refine natural pathogens himself, then his acquisition of refining equipment should leave an obviously detectable trail. If he tries to enter sophisticated bio-laboratories, he should confront multiple security checks. In general, the higher the hurdles that the bio-offender has to overcome and the greater the risk of alerting law enforcers, the more likely he will take his evil intentions in other directions.

Denial + Interdiction

Raising barriers to bioviolence makes sense. Indeed, national and international laws apply similar barriers in comparable contexts to deny access to dangerous items. Neither nuclear materials nor extremely toxic chemicals can be casually obtained by people who lack permission or skills to have them. In the biological sciences, minimally obtrusive methods to keep pathogens and equipment secure could readily be implemented. Only scientists who need such key items for legitimate purposes should have access to them.

Many technologically advanced nations have effectively implemented mandatory standards for restricting access. All nations should follow suit, but most have not; the proliferation of bioscience is far outpacing the spread of appropriate security standards. In many countries, denial measures for preventing bioviolence are supposed to be observed on a "voluntary" basis. Voluntary compliance is fine for the many scientists who are attentive to bioviolence risks, but their observance is not very useful for stopping real bio-offenders who want to manipulate the system for hostile purposes.

If denial measures are not in place everywhere, then bio-offenders will exploit the gaps. Moreover, these measures must not only be legislated; officials must have authority and capability to actually enforce them. The challenge, therefore, is not to design novel controls that can be experimentally applied to bioscience to see if they might be effective. It is to ensure that well-understood security controls are implemented and enforced wherever bioscience is dynamically emerging.

Binding obligations to comply with denial measures have an additional benefit: implementing them generates a lot of information. To assess compliance with denial measures, legitimate bioscientists and their institutions will have to report data about where laboratories are and what pathogens are stored or handled in them. These reports will produce data flows that can generate a global census of biofacilities, location of pathogens, and the traffic in pathogens and equipment. Such data is essential for effective interdiction.

To stop bioviolence, law enforcers have to know where and at whom to look. One purpose of denial measures is to gather enough information about legitimate bioscience to have a clear picture about who is engaged in sensitive activities and where those activities are carried out. With better data about legitimate bioscience, law enforcers can distinguish bio-offenders from scientists, enabling them to optimally focus scarce resources. Absent that information, movements of pathogens and access to laboratories will be just a blur.

By knowing where legitimate science is practiced and what is the traffic in critical items, law enforcers can look for anomalies – unusual situations that might be a clue of covert bioviolence preparations. Correctly structured denial measures should, therefore, be linked to observable signals so that an offender trying to overcome those barriers will leave clues. It is critical that law enforcers be authorized, trained, and equipped to look for such clues so that they will stop a bio-offender before he executes an attack. Data reporting has a double benefit here: legitimate bioscience can help law enforcers focus scarce resources on interdicting outlaws, and law enforcers will leave those bioscientists alone.

Simply expressed, denial measures should make it very difficult to get necessary items to commit bioviolence so that a bio-offender should have to leap over high hurdles to prepare a bioviolence attack. Interdiction measures should enable law enforcers to observe leapers and quickly move against them. Facing difficult obstacles and high risks of getting caught, potential bio-offenders will likely view bioviolence as excessively risky. Worldwide implementation of these measures would, therefore, go a long way to dissuading pursuit of bioviolence.

Bioscience's Anxieties

Some bioscientists become anxious when discussions of bioviolence evoke proposals for regulating their activities. They are understandably concerned that legal monitoring and enforcement of bioviolence prevention policies might raise the specter of snaring legitimate, even compelling activities in a dragnet whereby law enforcers will interfere with their work or insinuate that their work is linked with bioviolence. Controls on distribution of pathogens means that they might not be able to get what they need for experiments or that a scientist will be prosecuted for having a bottle in back of the refrigerator that might be found to hold a lethal but unregistered pathogen. Graver worries are that persons of certain ethnicity or nationality will be altogether barred from potentially sensitive scientific research.

In this view, regulating laboratories and the people working in them means that police will be constantly supervising scientific activity, ready to pounce on the merest transgression, stifling the relaxed atmosphere that is conducive to good science. If working with pathogens – refining them into pure strains, manipulating them into uniform shape and density, and studying their processes of lethality – is suspicious, then thousands of bioscientists could face legal inquiry or worse. If having lethal pathogens and equipment for preparing bioviolence agents is enough to initiate an inquiry, then all sorts of bioscientists, including high school science teachers, might have to explain themselves.

Overbroad regulation would not serve any beneficial purpose and could stifle life-saving and lucrative progress. Indeed, if regulations are imposed without criteria, it is not far-fetched to envision police barging into laboratories and interrogating scientists. We must acknowledge that bioscientists have a history of substantial abuse when officials enter their realm or circumscribe their research. The miracle discovery of small-pox vaccine was widely denunciated as immoral amid calls to stop inoculations. Today, the U.S. government resists stem-cell research while various European governments resist exposure to genetically modified organisms.

It is important to stress that bioscience has made (and continues to make) outstanding contributions to humanity. Bioscientists strongly value their independence. Many believe that this progress is directly related to minimal government intrusion and constraint by law enforcers who have little understanding of what they do. Indeed, a degree of anarchy has always characterized the pursuit of bioscience that, until recently, could be conducted with minimal resources. Bioscientists trace their art to Mendel whose breakthrough discoveries took place in his garden. Worth emphasizing is that bioscience has immediate and direct entrepreneurial implications for the pharmaceutical sector – a sector that, to put it mildly, has issues with legal supervision.

Moreover, the bioscience/pharmaceutical sectors are crucial allies in preventing bioviolence. They share a common interest with law enforcers in reducing vulnerabilities. These sectors must undertake research on pathogenicity and virology, produce vaccines and antidotes and instruct first responders on their use, and join with other disciplines to create sensors and other instruments to assist law enforcement. In the event of a bioviolence attack, law enforcers and scientists will have to cooperate with public health personnel to limit the spread and severity of consequences. It would be counterproductive to view bioscience as dangerous or bioscientists as suspects for potential bioviolence. More broadly, it is ridiculous to think that there is widespread interest among bioscientists to engage in bioviolence.

Part of the difficulty here is that bioscientists and law enforcers do not communicate with each other especially well. Each community regularly sponsors workshops on bioviolence, but only recently have representatives of one community participated in the other community's discussions. Even their terminology is different. Terms like "surveillance" have very different meanings in each context. Broadly viewed, the fact that bioscientists and law enforcers are mutually leery and averse to seeing the other's perspective is a dangerous impediment to preventing bioviolence. It is pivotal to forge supportive linkages between scientists and law enforcers that enhance cooperation yet are respectful of each other's domain.

Looking forward, bioscience will proliferate throughout the world and increasingly offer opportunities for bio-offenders to hostilely misapply that science. Necessarily therefore, all the arguments in favor of free scientific inquiry are not limitless. No freedom is absolute. Society has a right – indeed an obligation – to protect its members from harm or crime. It is imperative to pursue well-defined criteria that apply objectively to real security concerns without regard to dogma or political preference and that are minimally necessary to further a legitimate social purpose. The selection of criteria should be guided by a strict calculation of what measures can actually be beneficial. There is no reason to waste resources investigating innocent persons and activities. But transfers of lethal agents and sophisticated equipment to persons lacking a legitimate need for them could have horrifying consequences. Thus, scientists should embrace reasonable security standards that can diminish the risk of bio-offenders obtaining and weaponizing pathogens as the price of living in a dangerous world.

Moreover, bioscientists must recognize that an actual bioattack will inevitably provoke calls for draconian oversight measures. That was the immediate reaction to the anthrax attacks of late 2001. If there is any evidence of bioscience involvement in a future attack, even inadvertently, the clamor for controls is likely to be deafening. President of the National Academies of Science Bruce Albert said, "We'd all be haunted if some publication in my [NAS] journal were used to make a biological weapon."[2] If bioscientists are truly concerned that law enforcers will cite bioviolence to justify interfering with their work and falsely characterize their possession of pathogens and critical equipment, it would be tactically wise to help design reasonable prevention mechanisms before an attack occurs rather than stubbornly resist any oversight whatsoever until a nightmare scenario unfolds. More broadly, it would be cavalier to ignore the unfortunate but nontrivial potential that a few bioscientists could, if wrongfully motivated, wreak disaster out of all proportion to their numbers or resources.

Registration and Census

Complication policies must be directed at misuses of biology and place only minimal burdens on legitimate science. Broadly stated, complication policies should focus on: 1) census functions – knowing where sensitive items are and how they are moving; and 2) thwarting wrongful diversion, access, or smuggling of such items. Complication policies should not focus on: 1) monitoring individual bioscientists' activities; or 2) impeding participation in the biosciences by persons based on their nationality or ethnicity.

Companies and academic institutions working with dangerous pathogens should be registered, and that registration should be declared to international and national authorities. Registration serves two purposes. First, lawful entities must comply with strict security safeguards for impeding misuse or diversion. Second, registration authoritatively distinguishes lawful possessors of select pathogens from outlaw possessors. Properly registered entities are presumably legitimate, and their possession of pathogens is therefore not inherently suspicious. By negative implication, anyone having listed pathogens without proper registration has violated the law and may be punished; no further evidence of malevolent intent is needed.

The message to scientists who seek to work with such microbes is: Identify yourself, comply with explicit standards for safety and security, and agree to transfer these microbes only to scientists who are similarly identified and complying with such standards. If so, law enforcers will not have reason to bother you. Bio-offenders are unlikely to come forward and register.

The scientists who overtly declare their intentions to conduct research should face little more than routine paperwork obligations. For all the bioscientific entities that are not working with dangerous pathogens or uniquely critical equipment, the obligations should be trivial. Only the few entities that handle items of concern should face more onerous requirements. Even for these few entities, the consequences of missing a regulatory detail should be trifling unless there is hard evidence that the oversight was deliberate. By their act of self-identification, they enable attention to be devoted to persons or institutions who deliberately do not identify themselves. By contrast, the consequences of someone's willful refusal to participate in the regulatory system should be very stiff. It is this type of secret bioscience that is troubling. Most importantly, the entire system must be consistently mandated and enforced globally.

DENIAL TACTICS

In some countries with advanced bioscience sectors, laws effectively control access to particularly lethal pathogens, unique equipment, and facilities.[3] Many of the controls proposed here are standard operating procedures for bioscience in these nations.

Denying Access to Pathogens

Access to specimens of readily weaponizeable pathogens should be controlled. If bioviolence offenders cannot get these specimens, they would have to gather natural pathogens that would need to be refined, raising both technical challenges and risks of detection.

The first question is which pathogens should be controlled? Smallpox and anthrax would likely be on everyone's list. After that, scientists disagree. No list will be perfectly satisfactory or without dispute. Even if a list could be synthesized here, it would be quickly out of date as new pathogens are discovered or someday constructed. Properly framed, the question is who should determine the list of controlled pathogens. These decisions must be perceived as "legitimate." There should be firm criteria for decisions, an explicit decision-making process that welcomes expert input, and opportunities to review decisions.

In the United States, the CDC makes authoritative judgments. Its "select agent list" now has forty-one pathogens (the 1918 Spanish Flu genome was recently added) divided into Class A (high threat) and Class B (medium threat) biological agents.[4] No doubt, some scientists disagree with some of the CDC's listing decisions, but few scientists dispute the CDC's legitimacy. The process applies elaborate criteria and engages esteemed scientific intellect. Legal grounds to challenge a decision are limited to abuse of process – exceptionally rare in these circumstances. Because the CDC's process for composing the list is legitimate, its authority to impose obligations for handling and transferring select agents is undeniable.

How can this type of oversight be internationalized? The CDC has analogues in other nations, but no comparable authority exists at the international level. The World Health Organization (WHO) could stipulate which pathogens should be controlled but has refused, to date, to do so. Instead, it alerts States about potential risks and suggests that each State identify the agents *it* believes pose a threat worthy of preventive and responsive measures. States should focus on the "biological agents known to have entered the process of weaponization during the Cold War, in other words, agents which have been used in the past" and "agents condemned under the BWC."[5] The WHO expects some disparity as to agents of concern: "[A]ppraisals and priorities will certainty differ from country to country, but ... prudent Member States will have at least some organization and some plan in place to deal with deliberate releases of biological and chemical weapons."[6]

The WHO's position is suffused with diplomatic timidity that leads to the lowest and most worthless level of permissiveness. If each State defines its own list of violence-relevant pathogens, then there is no standardized list whatsoever. Because specimens are readily transferred across national borders, different lists of agents produce incoherence that undermines rational regulatory controls. Very recently, the WHO has taken a small positive step: its newly adopted International Health Regulations specify diseases that "may constitute a public health emergency of international concern."[7] This list does not pertain directly to possession of pathogen seed stocks, yet it is an initial step toward WHO assumption of authority in this context. Notably, the Animal Health Organization (Office des Epizooties, OIE) has done better with regard to animal pathogens.[8]

An international body (presumably the WHO for human pathogens and the OIE for animal pathogens) should be authorized to compile a list of "select" pathogens, with prescribed processes for promptly expanding or revising the list. Whether that body would adopt the CDC "select agent list" or a different list of pathogens is not the point here; any chosen list will soon change. What is important is that an official body comprised of well-informed scientists must be authorized to make determinations pursuant to law.

Pathogen Census

A globally accepted list of potentially dangerous pathogens is the necessary basis for a census of those pathogens' location and movement. Every State should identify the facilities within its territory that have stocks of any listed pathogen. Maintaining international databases is absolutely essential to properly record information about these pathogens. Today, databases of culture collections are incomplete. The good news is that the World Federation for Culture Collections (WFCC) has established guidelines for operating micro-organism culture collections;[9] organisms listed in its World Data Centre for Micro-organisms (WDCM) are available only to bona fide users who maintain proper records. The bad news is that the WFCC is a voluntary organization – a club – of well-meaning bioscience institutions. It does not govern nonmember activities. The problem, of course, is that bio-offenders are unlikely to join the WFCC – its guidelines are not directed at finding or stopping them.

Lacking comprehensive records about pathogens' locations, law enforcers cannot optimally prevent or prosecute bioviolence. Without records that might suggest who possessed pathogens, when, and what has become of them, it is essentially impossible to investigate suspected criminality. Conventional law enforcement would be far less effective if there were no data collection systems (e.g., fingerprints, gun registration, felony records, etc.). Yet, in connection with bioviolence, no comparable systems exist.

Pathogen Marking

One innovative step that could help prevent bioviolence is to require selective pathogen marking. On DNA strands, there are spaces that serve no apparent biological purpose. Bioscientists could insert "markers" or "barcodes"; this technique could enhance identification and tracking of specific pathogen strains. If each registered laboratory has a distinctive marker, and if an additional marker could be added if the strain is transferred to another laboratory, then there would be a set of markers that indicate where the pathogen came from and who might have worked with it. If that pathogen is later found in an inappropriate location or if it has been used to instigate bioviolence, there would be information that could be very relevant for holding bio-offenders accountable.

Pathogen marking has provoked controversy among bioscientists. It is a bother, although it is unclear how much. Only the small minority of biological substances that are select agents would have to be so marked, and the costs of emplacing and tracking such markers are not considered to be substantial.[10] The major objection is that such markers would be imperfect. Many pathogen strains already in circulation could not reasonably be marked (much less be retroactively marked), and it would be easy to remove markers on strains that are marked. (It is curious that, according to these objectors, marking pathogens would be a burden but removing those markers would be trivial.)

These objections to marking select pathogens belie a profound misunderstanding of how to prevent crime, especially crime that involves sophisticated techniques. Although pathogen marking would be initially incomplete and subject to manipulation, a potential bio-offender who wants to avoid accountability would be deterred. Seeking to covertly weaponize a laboratory strain yet knowing that many pathogen strains are marked, bio-offenders could be certain that the strain is unmarked only if they scrutinize that strain and remove any existing markers – another hurdle that would need to be surmounted.

There is another virtue. Worldwide, some managers of legitimate laboratories might be less than perfectly attentive to their security responsibilities, not out of malevolence but just because they are lazy or wanting to avoid expense. However, if dangerous pathogens are marked, then diversion followed by misuse could be traced back to the lab from where they were diverted; the lackadaisical facility director could be held accountable for dereliction of oversight responsibilities. Under many nations' laws, a facility that is the source (even unwittingly) of diverted pathogens that are catastrophically used would be liable for the ensuing losses. Knowing that possibility, these scientists might take their responsibilities far more seriously – at least their lawyers or insurers will.

More generally, it is imperative to know where the most dangerous pathogen strains are located, and police must have records that can readily be used to conduct investigations and pursue suspicions. Even if these measures are only partially effective, bio-offenders will have to consider the heightened risk of exposure and punishment, and scientists responsible for security will have to consider their potential accountability if something that they could have prevented goes horribly wrong.

Denying Access to Laboratories

Improving security at biolaboratories is critical to preventing bioviolence. At which laboratories? It would waste resources to regulate every site that *could* cultivate pathogens including, for example, school science laboratories. Only the very few laboratories that pose the most serious concern should receive substantial attention. Importantly, safeguards to foil criminal diversion, including physical security and identification of potential risks, should be graduated based on the assets that require protection. Three factors should comprise this equation.

1. What agents could be diverted? How potentially dangerous are the agents, and how easily can they be used as a weapon? Relevant factors include the availability of weaponizeable strains, their hardiness and ease of production, how they could be disseminated, and how much specialized knowledge is needed to use the agents as weapons.
2. What could be the consequences of using those agents for bioviolence? Relevant factors here involve infectious dose, incubation period, pathogenicity, modes and ease of transmission, and availability of post-exposure treatments.
3. What are the risks associated with the facility? Relevant factors here include its location, its design, the number of people who have open access, and whether there are physical security devices (e.g.,cameras, locks, and so forth.).[11]

Security standards for laboratories are well understood. There are globally accepted measures to prevent injury to laboratory employees or to the surrounding environment. These measures, generically referred to as *biosafety*, include procedures for handling lethal pathogens to avoid accidental release. The *WHO Laboratory Biosafety Manual* provides in-depth guidelines for maintaining safe laboratory conditions. The WHO and various other international organizations encourage States to prepare codes of practice for safely handling pathogens and to assess risks.[12] Moreover, the WHO and the OIE each have reference and collaborating facilities that standardize laboratory practices within a cooperative international network.

Biosafety measures are already in practice in many nations and could be expanded to address bioviolence concerns. External threats can be averted by physical barriers such as guards, gates, closed circuit cameras, and electronic access codes or biometric security devices. Internal threats can be averted by data and IT system security, security policies for personnel, policies for accessing select agent areas, and specimen accountability. Additional measures include prohibiting scientists to work alone with especially dangerous pathogens and monitoring exits to ensure that no materials are illicitly removed.[13] Transit threats can be averted by requiring confirmation of receipt of select agents into the laboratory as well as tracking transfer or shipping of select agents from the laboratory. If threats materialize, there should be emergency response plans and reporting mechanisms for security breaches. Altogether, improved security should be aimed at the most likely threats that have the most capacity to cause harm.[14]

The problem is not a lack of guidelines – the problem is that the guidelines that exist are not binding. In some countries, especially countries with maturely developed bioscience sectors, national laws effectively require compliance with comparable standards. In most parts of the world, however, these standards are at best aspirational; there are no consequences for noncompliance. For example, in a recent study of biolaboratories holding extremely lethal pathogens in Asia, most pathogens were supposed to be kept under biosafety level (BSL) 3 conditions; however, almost two-thirds of researchers admitted that they comply with only BSL-2 practices.[15] More generally, the flaw of voluntary standards is that they are observed only by the willing. Noncompliers need not be malevolent; they need only be careless. There is no way to know about labs that fail to implement or fully observe these standards.

Making laboratory security standards binding will make it easier to prosecute operators of covert facilities if and when they are discovered. Covert facilities will most likely not implement security measures much less obtain official registration. Thus, failure to comply with these requirements should, in and of itself, lead to prosecution. Indeed, many experts agree that the easiest and most immediately beneficial step to prevent bioviolence would be to make internationally recognized laboratory security standards legally binding. Laboratory administrators would be required to account for the pathogens that they possess and the personnel who have access to them. They would also have to evaluate how an adversary would attempt to divert, steal, destroy, or release those assets. Moreover, a globally enforced compliance system for biolaboratories will generate copious amounts of data that could be useful to law enforcement interdiction efforts.

Denying Access to Equipment

Worldwide, there is a virtually unregulated flow of very advanced bioequipment. As this equipment is ubiquitous, trying to limit its distribution is probably a hopeless undertaking. Export controls on this equipment are porous, and the list of potential suppliers is rapidly growing. Conscientious efforts to limit equipment exports serve primarily to disadvantage the controlling State (and its industries) to the advantage of less circumspect States.

Efforts of States to make collective decisions to control exports raises issues about freedom of trade, and actions to enforce those controls have the appearance if not the reality of a cartel. An even more important objection to restricting distribution of bioequipment has to do with the global development of bioscience. An active market in sophisticated bioequipment promotes the spread of legitimate science. Even if restraints are not meant to produce a cartel, they will likely slow down the distribution of technology – that is, after all, the basic purpose for the restraint.

Law enforcers should be able to track the traffic in bioequipment in order to detect wrongful activity. A positive idea is to tag sensitive equipment with positioning devices that expose its location wherever it goes. For legitimate science, a GPS locational device would barely be noticeable. Law enforcers could track sophisticated machinery that is operated outside of authorized facilities and be alerted to transfers of critical items. Tagging equipment is the corollary to marking pathogens, and it has evoked similar objections that it will not effectively stop misuse. Granted, the enormous amounts of equipment already in circulation cannot be tagged. Yet over time, new tagged equipment will replace older untagged equipment. Another objection is that transponders might have to be applied to a huge volume of devices and machinery, but transponder technology that was yesterday's breakthrough innovation is now remarkably pedestrian.

Databases that record the location of bioequipment could usefully contribute to understanding where threats of bioviolence might emerge.[16] If we know where biolaboratories that handle dangerous pathogens are, then lining up equipment location with those legitimate facilities is simple. Attention should focus on the equipment in places where there is not a known facility. Perhaps these anomalies can be innocently explained, yet law enforcers would have key information that might enable early interdiction.

One advantage of tracking equipment is to diminish the need for export cartels; properly registered laboratories should be able to get what they need. Equipment exporters would have to declare their exports – this information would go into an international database. An electronic trail would record its transfer cycle from carrier to national destination through import registration. Recipients would also have to be properly registered and have to declare where the equipment will be used. If the records match, there is reason to be confident that the transfer is for legitimate purposes.

Moreover, bioequipment that has outlived its useful life should be verifiably destroyed. Equipment that has lost utility for legitimate scientific or medical purposes might still have utility for misuse. Having better information about the location of equipment will facilitate monitoring and destruction of discarded equipment.[17]

Most important, a bio-offender could not know for sure if his newly obtained equipment (whether bought or stolen) is tagged; using it might reveal his covert preparations. He might, therefore, opt for older and less proficient equipment rather than risk detection of his entire plan by seeking the best equipment. If he forfeits technical capacity for secrecy, he may be left with unresolved technological challenges. From his perspective, this is one more consideration to dissuade him from pursuing bioviolence.

This highlights the power of denial measures. If producers of critical equipment must insert an unobtrusive tracking device that sets off alarms if removed, then signals from those devices could be centrally collected, perhaps by the Interpol Preventing Bioterrorism Office, where they would be linked to data about pathogen location. Altogether, a system would emerge for tracking items that could be used for bioviolence, deterring perpetrators who would fear detection of their covert activities, and substantially contributing to investigations of wrongful behavior. Tracking equipment is not a perfect prophylactic against bioviolence, yet it is an effective way to combine denial and interdiction measures against bioviolence threats.

INTERDICTION

To prevent bioviolence, it is imperative to interdict illicit preparations. Interdiction of critical agents and equipment in transit to bio-offenders is pivotal to denial measures. Interdiction of ready-to-use weapons is the last opportunity to prevent catastrophe. Whether our concern is the circulation of pathogens and equipment or the traffic in fully operational weapons, law enforcers bear enormous responsibilities. They must stop wrongful preparations before it is too late. Can they?

This question focuses on police capabilities, the scope of their legal authority, and whether effective interdiction modalities have broad international application. Fortunately, this aspect of the prevention agenda is receiving international attention. Interpol has assumed responsibility for worldwide police training through a series of workshops, train-the-trainer programs, publications and guides, and promotion of stronger national legislation. In only a few years, the Interpol Program has demonstrated the substantial benefits of specialized cooperation and organizational commitment. It will create a central information resource and reporting hub that raises awareness of bioviolence threats as it facilitates communication between experts and police officials in nations that might not otherwise draw on such expertise. Notably, Interpol is demonstrating that engaging police on this subject need not threaten legitimate bioscience but, on the contrary, is the best way to protect against inappropriate intrusions.

To effectively interdict: 1) national laws must authorize police to act, and 2) law enforcers must have enhanced capabilities for identifying covert bioviolence preparations.

Legislating the Crime

Law enforcers do not interdict legal activity. As mentioned earlier, most States lack laws that criminalize unauthorized possession of lethal pathogens or building an amateur laboratory. This has to change. Every nation must enact laws to criminalize not only the act of bioviolence but the preparations that are necessary to its accomplishment. If law enforcers have to await the completed attack, then bioviolence preparations can proceed without serious constraint. Prohibitions must reach preliminary steps.

National laws should criminalize unauthorized possession of pathogens, access to laboratories, and possession of critical equipment. It must be a crime to: construct an unauthorized facility for working with select pathogens, divert pathogens from a facility, transfer pathogens or relevant equipment to someone who misuses them, or deliberately cause pathogens to be released. If the only legal way to possess controlled pathogens is to have a license, then possession of those pathogens without a license must be, in and of itself, a criminal offense.

In addition, there are many legal measures for ensuring that law enforcers can work with foreign counterparts by sharing information and conducting investigations. But States that do not appropriately criminalize behavior undermine international legal cooperation. This problem is especially pronounced in States where proliferation and terrorism are most worrisome. For this reason, both the United Nations Security Council and the Biological Weapons Convention (BWC) require States to enact necessary laws, but most States have not met their obligations in full. This noncompliance corrodes the foundation of bioviolence prevention policy, endangering everyone.

Right now, it is extremely difficult to assess the gaps in most States' implementation of measures to keep relevant pathogens and laboratories secure or to interdict bioviolence. Even if a State has enacted regulatory measures, it is practically impossible to assess whether those measures are rigorously enforced, and, if unenforced, whether that infirmity is due to inadequate capabilities or to more sinister reasons. Each State establishes its own criteria of compliance and thereby defines itself as compliant regardless of whether it has, in fact, implemented sufficient controls to prevent a biocatastrophe. This circular logic is perilous.

The Dilemma of Pre-Attack Interdiction

Prevention demands that law enforcers act before there is an actual attack. This is not how law enforcement usually works. Most criminal laws punish a crime only after it has been committed. Laws against murder do not prohibit people from sharpening knives; only when a knife is violently used will law enforcers find, apprehend, and prosecute the offender. We do not investigate everyone who has a knife in order to identify persons with malevolent intentions – that would be a grotesque intrusion on personal privacy. Just because somewhere, anyone in a broad community can commit a crime, law enforcers do not investigate everyone to assess if someone might have criminal intent. Society awaits the crime before authorizing an inquiry.

However, the enormity of bioviolence's consequences forces us to reexamine how law enforcement operates. All crime is tragic, yet rarely does a crime threaten consequences that could disrupt civilization. Bioviolence is not a typical crime that causes an individual or small group to suffer. A biooffender could inflict a qualitative leap in devastation causing harm that could reverberate around the world well into the future. Indeed, prevention is so imperative precisely because it is insufficient to punish bioviolence after it has been committed. Law enforcers must, therefore, identify biooffenders as early as possible – well before their plans materialize.

Here's the dilemma: except in unusual cases, law enforcers will not know where to look for covert preparations. The perpetrators will not self-identify; they will do whatever they can to evade detection. Even if law enforcers stumble onto evidence, it might appear to be an inoffensive amateur lab. After an attack, inferring where preparations had occurred might be easy, but that begs the question. The challenge is accurate pre-attack identification. But how can law enforcers know what they do not know?

It is nonsense to tell law enforcers to visually distinguish a vial of lethal pathogens from a vial of innocuous liquid. Neither is it reasonable to expect a customs or border official to spot pathogens that might be carried in a common perfume bottle. Consider the challenge of detecting micro-organisms among more than two hundred million containers yearly transported by land, sea, and air. In the United States, homeland security personnel physically inspect less than 2 percent of all sea-shipped containers, yet expanding those inspections is very expensive and a burden on trade. Ports that inspect more shipments are at a competitive disadvantage. X-ray equipment or scanners that might be effective for detecting other contraband are ineffective for detecting pathogens that emit no energy. Says one analyst, "For some threats, such as biological and chemical or radiological weapons, breakthrough technologies are not available."[18]

This dilemma has been callously manipulated to justify ill-conceived plans to escalate government eavesdropping or coercive methods to extract information. Interdicting bioviolence is a complex challenge, but it should not beget facile calls for broad intrusions on civil liberties. Today's threats certainly warrant highly selective information-gathering capacities, but it is discouraging and ultimately debilitating for these threats to be asserted as rationale for ill-tailored sweeps through innocent people's affairs. Instead, there are two refined methodologies to consider: 1) enhancing law enforcement's ability to recognize the subtle clues of bioviolence, and 2) developing pattern recognition techniques.

One point is indisputable: only adequately trained and equipped police can make effective use of even the most sterling information-gathering mechanisms. Much of the following discussion calls for elaborately honed systems to collect and analyze data, which entail advanced computers, integrated electronic networks, and people who know how to operate them. These systems must be implemented globally, which calls for a prolonged commitment to augment developing nations' law enforcement. At the root of efforts to strengthen law enforcement, therefore, must be systemic and worldwide police professionalization.

Clues of Bioviolence

A bio-offender will likely leave a subtle trail that well-trained law enforcers can track. Yet, it is unlikely that a single clue will be so revealing that law enforcers can instantly deduce an illegal scheme. Multiple bits of information – virtually trivial by themselves – must be assembled into a mosaic of suspicion (see Box 5-1). Moreover, no one official domain will

BOX 5-1. CLUES OF BIOVIOLENCE PREPARATIONS

1. Unauthorized surveillance of potential targets, such as hotels, entertainment venues, trains, airplanes, water sources, office buildings, apartment buildings, or food services;
2. Purchase or theft of pathogens or equipment such as dispersal or aerosolizing sprayers;
3. Procurement or theft of suspicious items, such as growth agent, personal protective gear (latex gloves, suits, or gas masks), antibiotics, or literature on bioweapons;
4. Recruitment of scientific personnel;
5. Establishment of a secret facility that could operate as a laboratory;
6. Acquisition of animals and cell-culturing media for testing;
7. Reports of "unusual" disease outbreaks from poison control centers or emergency rooms (might indicate unintentional self-infection);
8. Reports of "unusual" environmental emissions or noxious odors not typically associated with the area;
9. Unscheduled spraying by aircraft/helicopters or individuals, or unusual or unscheduled window washing or power washing, especially when crowds are present;
10. Unscheduled presence of individuals in dust masks or other protective gear;
11. Tampering or unusual activity associated with water supplies, building ventilation systems, food supplies, or food distribution centers.

SOURCE: Bioterrorism Incident Pre-Planning & Response Guide, ICPO-Interpol (2007). *See also*, Tracee A. Treadwell et al., *Epidemiologic Clues to Bioterrorism*, PUBLIC HEALTH REPORTS, Vol. 118 (March–April 2003).

be able to gather sufficient clues. Diverse agencies with distinct responsibilities for identifying bioviolence must share information. "The problem is not, to use the old saying, 'finding the needle in the haystack,' but rather 'passing a thread through the eyes of many needles buried in several haystacks.'"[19]

Science and public health communities must work with law enforcers. Scientists understand what pathogenic agents might be used, and public health workers can help distinguish a natural outbreak from a malevolently released disease. Expert assessments by science and health communities can help identify what to look for during investigations. Law enforcers, of course, have to be able to recognize local changes (e.g., unusually heavy traffic to a remote location, complaints of disturbances, etc.) and linkages to other criminal activity. An informative lesson is the failure to identify Aum Shinrikyo, the Japanese cult that attacked Tokyo subway commuters with sarin gas in 1995. Aum left many clues that Japanese authorities failed to recognize until afterward. Disparate police, public health, counter-terrorism, and environmental officials each noticed oddities but, unable to effectively share that information, did not frame a coherent picture that could have warned law enforcers to interdict Aum's preparations. Those authorities were not careless or lacking detection tools, but discerning camouflaged bioviolence preparations requires attentiveness to combinations of unusual clues.

We can all be safer from bioviolence if police in every nation efficiently gather and share information with public health officials who monitor disease outbreaks. When there is reason for concern, the evidence should be distributed to the appropriate authorities who, in turn, can refer to international databases that track terror and criminal networks. These communities and capabilities should work as seamlessly as possible. If so, they could serve a critical triage role for diagnosing the circumstances that deserve further attention.

Pattern Recognition

Pattern recognition is the process of deducing relationships about people, organizations, and activities from broad data sources. According to a U.S. government office, it is "the application of database technology and techniques – such as statistical analysis and modeling – to uncover hidden patterns and subtle relationships in data and to infer rules that allow for the prediction of future results."[20] Small data pieces might seem innocuous, yet patterns can be detected by identifying subtle linkages among heterogeneous pools of information from huge databases. Advanced mathematical capabilities, faster computers, and innovative software applications are increasingly valuable to modern law enforcers who, to coin a phrase, are drowning in information but starved for knowledge. Pattern recognition techniques enable law enforcers to near-instantly sort through heaps of data to uncover evidence of criminality; they are widely used in tracing money laundering and terrorist financing.

Key to bioviolence prevention is better tracking of the global traffic in pathogens and bioequipment. The registration systems and census functions discussed earlier will generate broad information about locations of pathogens and laboratories as well as data about where and when critical items are moved. Orders for transfers of materials or equipment as well as all transport records are relevant. If GPS technology is affixed to sophisticated bioequipment, if pathogens are marked, and if records are kept about where these items are supposed to be, then movements of critical items could be tracked through international commerce. Also informative would be credit card records of purchases of critical equipment or materials as well as enrollment data for classes on how to handle dangerous materials or operate equipment.

All this information should be linked with data about criminal networks and smuggling operations from police and customs files. Other useful data sources would be information from health-related and environmental data sources concerning unusual outbreaks and patterns of illness. Pattern recognition involving sophisticated analyses of information from these diverse sources should be designed to recognize anomalies or inexplicable patterns. The evidence of something incongruous or devious should alert law enforcers to clarify the situation.

Application of pattern recognition techniques to identify signals of bioviolence preparations needs to be very carefully considered. Notably, accumulating aggregate data is very different from conducting targeted investigations on individuals. Indeed, in the United States, broad data mining initiatives have provoked considerable public outcry as intrusive of privacy. (Box 5-2 lists the principal U.S. data mining initiatives.) Privacy concerns are especially intense here because bioscience will be under the microscope; moreover, information will be compiled and analyzed globally. It takes little imagination to envision an ominous system where an unaccountable "big brother" monitors bioscientists' purchases, activities, and communications on the off chance of discovering illicit activity.

Privacy protections are essential to uphold due process of law. For example, law enforcers might need health data to assess a situation, but reviewing patients' medical records is extraordinarily invasive. Pattern recognition technology should, therefore, be able to focus on broad data aggregations but on no one specifically. For example, if there are health databases that preclude identification of individuals, law enforcers could less intrusively assess whether there is a threat to public security. In rare situations involving a full-scale public health emergency that poses a grave risk to society, there should be already emplaced procedures for linking generic data to individual identities pursuant to judicial approval and oversight.

Worldwide, far too little is known about bioscience. Even rudimentary pattern recognition applications cannot be effective today. Volumes of data are produced about the products of biological research including food additives, pesticides, and pharmaceuticals. However, there are not stringent data collection and analysis systems for basic science, assertedly because strict governmental oversight would be prohibitively expensive and would chill creativity.[21] As a result, however, a key tool for interdicting covert criminality on the path to bioviolence is unavailable.

BOX 5-2. PRINCIPAL UNITED STATES DATA-MINING INITIATIVES

- Two now-disbanded data-mining initiatives for combating terrorism were: 1) the Terrorism Information Awareness (TIA) conducted by the Defense Advanced Research Projects Agency (DARPA); and 2) the Transportation Security Administration's (TSA) Computer-Assisted Passenger Prescreening System II (CAPS II). The TIA program, shut down in September 2003, envisioned a centralized national database for information from government and commercial databases including bank records, tax returns, driver's license data, credit card purchases, airline tickets, gun purchases, work permits, etc. The scope of the initiative led to a public outcry that soon brought it to a close. The CAPPS II program was halted in August 2004 after legal challenges and implementation issues, including the European Union's refusal to provide data due to concerns about privacy.[a]
- Following TIA came the Multistate Anti-Terrorism Information Exchange (MATRIX), a government-funded but privately run antiterrorist initiative combining information from government and commercial databases – credit histories, driver's license photographs, marriage and divorce records, social security numbers, dates of birth, names and addresses of family members, along with neighbors and business associates – to aid law enforcement in searching for anomalies. Like TIA, the program came under heavy fire from groups concerned with privacy and civil liberties issues and was terminated in April 2005.
- The Automated Commercial Environment (ACE) and the International Trade Data System (ITDS) are used by customs to track cargo movements.
- The Custom and Border Protection's (CBP) Container Security Initiative (CSI) is a security regime to ensure all containers that pose a potential risk for terrorism are identified and inspected at foreign ports before they are placed on vessels bound for the United Sates. It relies on the National Targeting Center (NTC) to evaluate shipments' risk, and it flags certain high-risk containers for inspection before entering the United States.
- The Department of Homeland Security has launched Operation Safe Commerce (OSC) to tighten dangerous gaps in shipping security; the OSC proposes greater third-party oversight of containers at *all* ports, through the use of video cameras and biometric information. It uses multiple technologies to verify that container seals have remained intact and to verify the identity of drivers and overseers of shipments in order to build greater confidence in their reliability.

[a] CAPS II is being replaced by a new program called Secure Flight. *See generally*, *Data Mining: An Overview*, CONGRESSIONAL RESEARCH SERVICE, THE LIBRARY OF CONGRESS, p. 4–5 (December 16, 2004). *See also*, Willard Price, *Reducing the Risk of Terror Events at Seaports*, REVIEW OF POLICY RESEARCH, Vol. 21, p. 329 (May 1, 2004); *See also*, *CSI in Brief*, U.S. Customs & Border Protection (February 15, 2006).

A pattern recognition system is needed that is global in scope and can overcome the past obstacles associated with data mining and broad counterterrorism efforts: the use of data that is too general, too obvious, or incomplete. Yet, enormous complications attend implementing pattern recognition techniques internationally if only because no one is authoritatively designated to gather and analyze information. Moreover, even if a system could be effectively designed to detect potential bioviolence preparations worldwide, who would (or even could) take appropriate action to interdict those preparations' successful execution?

The Weapons of Mass Destruction Commission[22] (see Box 5-3) has proposed a system to increase transparency in transfers of biological materials and equipment. This proposal is to accredit entities engaging in such transfers and, working with States' export control authorities, aggregate data of transfers. The Commission anticipates that, in time, patterns will emerge and anomalies can be detected. Those anomalies should provoke consultations and a request for clarification. If no satisfactory explanation is given, then an inspection might be appropriate depending on the nature and seriousness of the anomaly. It is critical, according to the Commission, to centralize information about transfers precisely to enable pattern recognition at the international level. International authorization would also be mandatory both to investigate anomalies and to assist States that want to participate in the system.

Because not every State will participate and provide information to a central database, the Commission would require suppliers (who presumably are citizens of participating States) to provide extensive information about recipients. Then, relevant officials of both the supplier and recipient States would have to approve transfers. The supplier State could try to verify the items' proposed use or impose limitations on the transfer. The difficulties increase if the transfer is between two non-accredited units; there would have to be other sources of data with regard to these transfers. Obviously, the more States and economic units that choose to participate, the easier this task would be. The Commission left unresolved the question of how to impel all States to participate in the system – a potentially fatal flaw if advanced States do not participate.

Transport Security and Counter-Smuggling

The transnational traffic in pathogens offers substantial opportunities for bio-offenders to gain lethal capabilities and to move those capabilities to their eventual targets. This traffic also offers substantial opportunities

BOX 5-3. THE WEAPONS OF MASS DESTRUCTION COMMISSION

The WMD Commission was established in 2003 to set forth realistic proposals for reducing WMD proliferation. Its mandate is to foster public debate concerning weapons of mass destruction, including reaching out to nongovernmental organizations and other elements of civil society. Chaired and organized by Dr. Hans Blix, the Commission is comprised of fourteen members and operates as an independent body. Its members serve without instruction from any government or organization, and it disavows participating in any governmental or intergovernmental negotiation.

The WMD Commission released its report, *Weapons of Terror*, on June 1, 2006. It contains sixty proposals. Its recommendations concerning biological and toxin weapons include the following:

- All States not yet party to the Biological Weapons Convention (BWC) should adhere to the Convention. The States that are parties to the Convention should launch a campaign to achieve universal adherence by the time of the Seventh Review Conference to be held in 2011.
- To achieve universal adoption of national legislation and regulations aimed at full and effective implementation of the BWC, the States parties should offer technical assistance and promote best-practice models of such legislation. As a part of the confidence-building process and in order to promote transparency and harmonization, all States parties should make annual biological-weapon-related national declarations and make them public.
- States parties to the BWC should enhance the investigatory powers of the United Nations Secretary-General, ensuring that the Secretary-General can rely upon a regularly updated roster of experts, advice from the World Health Organization, and a specialist unit, which is to be modeled on the United Nations Monitoring, Verification and Inspection Commission, to assist in investigating unusual outbreaks of disease and allegations of the use of biological weapons.
- States parties to the BWC should establish a standing secretariat to handle organizational and administrative matters related to the Treaty, such as review conferences and expert meetings.
- Governments should pursue public health surveillance to ensure effective monitoring of unusual disease outbreaks and develop practical methods of coordinating international responses to any major event that might involve bioweapons. They should strengthen cooperation between civilian health and security-oriented authorities at the national, regional, and global levels, including in the framework of the new International Health Regulations of the World Health Organization. Governments should also review their national biosafety and biosecurity measures to protect public health and the environment from the release of biological and toxin materials. They should harmonize national biosecurity standards.

SOURCE: *New Proposals to Reduce Threats by Weapons of Mass Destruction*, Weapons of Mass Destruction Commission Press Release (June 1, 2006).

BOX 5-3. CONTINUED

The Commission continues to operate through consultations with governments and international organizations to promote the report's recommendations. It plans to issue a follow-up report in 2007.

for law enforcers to interdict bioviolence. From either perspective, it is imperative to consider how modes of transport can be secure against wrongful diversion and how smuggled pathogens can be intercepted.

Of all aspects of bioviolence prevention, transport oversight is where international and regional organizations, supported by many States, have most positively developed potent control measures. It is also where pattern recognition techniques are most advanced. This might best explain why catastrophic bioviolence has not yet happened. There is an important lesson here: progress has been achieved to complicate transnational biosmuggling with measures that provoked objections (ultimately unsuccessful) based on national sovereignty. As that progress is likely contributing to bioviolence prevention, serious consideration should be given to extending international controls in other potentially beneficial ways and similarly discounting protests of trespassing against sovereign domains.

It is useful to think of transport security and counter-smuggling efforts as a series of three overlaying control mechanisms. First are packaging and labeling standards that are designed to protect critical items from theft and diversion. Second, there are container shipping and port monitoring systems that are designed to enable detection of critical items that someone might try to move covertly. Third, there are intrusive activities that are designed to ferret out smuggled items when there is a basis for suspicion.

Packaging and Labeling

WHO regulations require that pathogens be shipped in a *triple packaging system*. Pathogens must be stored in a watertight, leakproof, and appropriately labeled primary container that is sufficiently absorbent to withstand a potential spill. The secondary packaging provides the same protection for multiple primary containers. The third layer should protect the primary receptacle and secondary packaging against damage during shipment and should have documentation identifying the pathogen, its source, and its destination. The packaging must be tamperproof against removal of its contents.[23] These straightforward regulations are well-observed and effective.

Proper labeling is necessary so that package handlers know that its contents are dangerous. Here is where problems can arise. Proper labeling reveals the package's contents to any malevolent thief. Another problem is that WHO guidance has the perverse effect of showing counterfeit dispatchers how to send illicit goods to counterfeit recipients in what seems to be a properly labeled package. These two problems call for more discrete labeling processes (e.g., invisible bar codes); only authorized personnel using specialized equipment should be able to identify legitimate shippers and know the package's lethal contents. There is an unfortunate irony here. The WHO issued packaging and labeling requirements in order to promote easy and transparent compliance for preventing accidents, but malevolent actors can take advantage of that transparency. Today, international standards must be more intricate and opaque to reduce misuse.

Transporters and handlers who move a package to its destination must be qualified to observe the encoded labels' markings that distinguish lethal pathogens. No longer should just anyone toss a carton on a truck or ship. Those transporters and handlers must be certifiably trained. Checks should be run for illicit connections to malevolent groups lest their knowledge and access combine to divert sensitive packages – imagine Al Qaeda personnel working in legitimate ports.

In this context, global uniformity is a paramount priority. All transporters whether in aviation or maritime shipping should obey the same standards. Logically, therefore, a United Nations body – the United Nations Committee of Experts on the Transport of Dangerous Goods (UNCETDG), advised by WHO – issues *Model Regulations for the Transport of Dangerous Goods*[24] that define global standards. Most States have adopted these standards, and relevant international shipping organizations such as the International Civil Aviation Organization (ICAO)[25] enforce them. This is effective global governance.

Shipping Security

Despite packaging and labeling standards, risks remain due to the sheer quantity of items shipped in international commerce. Pathogens are essentially invisible. Although scanning technology is improving, it is extremely unlikely that a currently operational scanner will perceive a microscopic agent that has been slipped into one of the over 250 million containers that move through global commerce per year.[26] A grim joke is that if bin Laden wants to move lethal pathogens around the world, he could put them into a container of illegal drugs with confidence that no customs control agent would ever find them.

No prophylactic solution exists, but much can be done to complicate smuggling. The integrity of containers must be maintained so that bad actors do not have ready access. Improved tamperproof seals can prevent offenders from sneaking agents into a container as it is being loaded onto a ship or after it has left the port. Sophisticated monitoring systems can alert ship and port authorities if a container is breached. The objective is deterrence as well as detection. A biosmuggler who faces a significant risk of getting caught might not want to challenge the system.

The system of global shipping security is very sophisticated. Two international organizations – the International Maritime Organization (IMO) and the World Customs Organization (WCO) – have developed intricate operating procedures known as the International Ship and Port Facility Security (ISPS) Code.[27] Transporters and port operators must assess their security measures, establish a security plan, designate agencies to execute the plan, and establish training programs for personnel who carry out the plan. Every shipper must display on each ship an International Ship Security Certificate that manifests compliance with the plan's requirements.[28] Every port operator must develop a Port Facility Security Plan (PFSP) to restrict access to particularly sensitive areas and to docked ships. The PFSP should specify procedures for handling a breach of security or an actual attack, including evacuation guidelines and how to notify proper authorities.[29]

The IMO publishes the list of ports and ships that satisfy these security standards thereby alerting governments as to which vessels pose the greatest risks. Complying shippers can move through port inspections more expeditiously – an inducement for everyone to comply. Although these standards do not force anyone to do anything, a nation that cares about the competitiveness of its export sectors and of its shipping companies will pay a steep price for its refusal if its exports and its ships cannot easily enter foreign ports. Delays in cross-through customs checkpoints can impose enormous financial costs, but these costs decline appreciably for shippers that can move goods through the "express lane." Companies will, therefore, be eager to take steps to reduce smuggling opportunities if doing so entitles their goods to proceed through customs unimpeded.

Notably, the United States leverages access to its markets to compel compliance. Under the Maritime Transportation Security Act,[30] vessels and cargo from high-risk ports or nations can be denied entry to U.S. ports. Foreign vessels of concern must provide advance notice of their arrival so that the Coast Guard can assess security risks that guide port authorities to efficiently select targets for investigation. Instead of mere random inspection, officials can concentrate attention on high-risk vessels, boarding them more frequently to ensure compliance with security and safety standards. A recently implemented program, the Customs-Trade Partnership Against Terrorism (C-TPAT), encourages companies to provide information and to engage in risk assessment jointly with the government. Over nine thousand companies are currently involved in the program.[31]

The United States has promoted comparable measures internationally. The Container Security Initiative (CSI)[32] – a series of bilateral and multilateral agreements – allows U.S. Customs officials to have access to foreign ports to prescreen high-risk containers bound for the United States. Ports must transmit cargo manifests twenty-four hours before cargo is loaded. This information is checked against other intelligence data through the National Targeting Center in order to assess the security risk. In order to track shipments as they move around the world, the U.S. Automated Commercial Environment (ACE) uses mass data storage and analysis in order to provide expansive information sharing and intelligence in real time.[33] By collecting data from customs trade systems, inspectors determine which shipments and containers are low risk that need not be investigated; attention can be focused on fewer high-risk shipments. Similar initiatives are being undertaken by the European Union and the Asia Pacific Economic Cooperation (APEC), yet ACE is perhaps the most ambitious data mining system to track global trade, costing about $3 billion.

Intrusive Counter-Smuggling

The most aggressive part of transport security and counter-smuggling is interdiction. Defensive security measures are crucial, but there are occasions when law enforcement must go on the offense. Who should undertake intrusive measures? In the United States and various other nations, domestic authorities carry out those responsibilities, but who may interdict smuggling either in common areas (e.g., the high seas) or in nations that are unable to take necessary action on their own?

In the post 9/11 environment, one of the most controversial steps to prevent terrorism (and, by implication, bioviolence) is the Proliferation Security Initiative (PSI). The PSI is a series of bilateral arrangements between the United States and other governments to prevent WMD smuggling.[34] As such, it signifies perhaps the best and worst of current counter-smuggling efforts. The PSI fosters international cooperation. States agree to exchange information concerning suspected proliferation efforts and

BOX 5-4. STATEMENT OF INTERDICTION PRINCIPLES

In September 2003, PSI States met in Paris and agreed to commit themselves to the following interdiction principles:

1. Undertake measures to interdict the transfer or transport of WMD;
2. Adopt streamlined procedures for rapid exchange of relevant information concerning suspected proliferation activity and dedicate appropriate resources and efforts to interdiction operations and capabilities, and maximize coordination among participants in interdiction efforts.;
3. Review and strengthen their relevant national legal authorities where necessary to accomplish these objectives, and work to strengthen when necessary relevant international laws and frameworks in appropriate ways to support these commitments;
4. Take specific actions to interdict cargoes of WMD to the extent consistent with their obligations under international law and frameworks, to include:
    a. Not to transport or assist in the transport of any such cargoes to or from States or non-State actors of proliferation concern, and not to allow any persons subject to their jurisdiction to do so.
    b. To take action to board and search any vessel flying their flag in their internal waters or territorial seas, or areas beyond the territorial seas of any other State, that is reasonably suspected of transporting such cargoes to or from States or non-State actors of proliferation concerns, and to seize such cargoes that are identified.
    c. To consider providing consent to the boarding and searching of its own flag vessels by other States, and to the seizure of WMD-related cargoes in such vessels.
    d. To take appropriate actions to 1) stop and/or search in their internal waters, territorial seas, or contiguous zones (when declared) vessels that are reasonably suspected of carrying such cargoes to or from States or non-State actors of proliferation concern and to seize such cargoes that are identified; and 2) enforce conditions on vessels entering or leaving their ports, internal waters, or territorial seas that are reasonably suspected of carrying such cargoes, such as requiring that such vessels be subject to boarding, search, and seizure of such cargoes prior to entry.
    e. At their own initiative or upon the request and good cause shown by another state, to 1) require aircraft that are reasonably suspected of carrying such cargoes to or from States or non-State actors of proliferation concern and that are transiting their airspace to land for inspection and seize any such cargoes that are identified; and/or 2) deny aircraft reasonably suspected of carrying such cargoes transit rights through their airspace in advance of such flights.

SOURCE: *Statement of Interdiction Principles*, Paris (September 2–3, 2003).

f. If their ports, airfields, or other facilities are used as transshipment points for such cargoes to or from States or non-State actors of proliferation concern, to inspect vessels, aircraft, or other transport modes reasonably suspected of carrying such cargoes, and to seize such cargoes that are identified.

to reform their domestic laws in order to crack down on proliferation. A primary virtue is that the PSI is not a treaty – it does not impose a specified set of criteria on participating States. It is impossible to imagine that the arrangements contemplated by PSI would have come into effect if it had to await diplomatic consensus. Its second virtue is that, in the face of modern terror and criminal threats, it inverts whatever priority had been given to freedom of shipment over prevention of WMD proliferation. Indeed, it stipulates common action in the face of global threats and provides guidelines as to how that action should be undertaken so as to limit potential abuse.[35] PSI's objectives are promoted through multinational training exercises that enable PSI States to put their capacities to work with one another and to develop measures to intercept ships and planes.

> The [PSI] reflects the need for a more dynamic, proactive approach to the global proliferation problem. It envisions partnerships of states working in concert, employing their national capabilities to develop a broad range of legal, diplomatic, economic, military, and other tools to interdict threatening shipments of [WMDs].[36]

Yet the PSI operates without force of law. Its foundation inheres in the diplomatic power of the United States but is unconnected to the mandates of international organizations. Moreover, discovery of evidence of wrongful conduct would not necessarily lead to prosecution. Linking the operation of the PSI to the police and other law enforcers worldwide is, therefore, *ad hoc*, but systematic cooperation is limited. In this regard, the PSI exemplifies what is increasingly true of global complication policies generally: many good ideas with the best of intentions but insufficiently integrated within an effective strategy. See Box 5-4 for more information about the specific principles outlined for the PSI States.

6 Improving Resistance through Science

Bioscience is not just an activity or set of knowledge. It is a uniquely accelerating phenomenon that evokes inquiries about humanity's most existential search – what is the architecture of life? Our era is witnessing an unprecedented revolution in human comprehension of the physics of life. Yesterday's flights of imagination are today's reality. Only the best scientific minds can predict where the rush of scientific advance will take us tomorrow, and even they can only guess at what might be conventional wisdom in a few brief decades.

> Knowledge of fundamental life processes has progressed to the point that extensive human intervention in the course of natural evolution has apparently become feasible, not only to determine particular outcomes but to redirect the process itself. . . . As a result, the human species is relentlessly acquiring power far in excess of its vision and this is thereby posing monumental problems of prudential judgment – problems that society is not yet conceptually or institutionally equipped to handle.[1]

This bioscience revolution offers enormously beneficial prospects for curing disease that necessarily expose how pathogens exploit human vulnerabilities. Unfortunately, these scientific advances could supply knowledge for the commission of heinous violence. Thus, at the core of research to protect against bioviolence is a paradox: To learn how to defeat disease is to learn how it works. As the 21st Century opens, bioscience's precious potential is intertwined with cascades of new threats. Techniques that generate life-saving progress are the same techniques that could generate catastrophic bioviolence. The essence of discovering protective medicines opens ever more fascinating windows into the structure of life itself that necessarily makes bioviolence easier, more lethal, more untreatable, or more contagious. This intertwining of promise and threat cannot be disentangled at the level of fundamental science. To try to separate them is to try to separate sides of a coin.

> In principle all biological knowledge can be used both for civil and military purposes. The knowledge needed to weaponise a germ is essentially the same as is needed to understand how that germ causes disease and how to create an effective vaccine against it.[2]

This chapter's two sections explore the bioscience paradox by asking: how should bioresearch be supervised in order to forestall pursuits with uniquely dangerous implications; and how should bioresearch be promoted to encourage global development of vaccines and medicines that enhance resistance against bioviolence.

DUAL-IMPLICATION RESEARCH

The discovery of knowledge or its release could enable bio-offenders to accomplish something that otherwise might pose a real barrier. Research to produce vaccines might enable creation of a profoundly more powerful bioweapon. For example, if research could identify how to alter anthrax's genetic code to make it contagious, malevolent persons might be able to profoundly escalate the bioviolence threat. This might now be somewhat fanciful, yet the United States has genetically engineered an immune-resistant strain of anthrax.[3] Other research innocently intended for beneficent purposes could be cruelly manipulated. For example, advancing processes for assembling DNA strains into functioning viruses might guide a bio-offender to synthesize a viral strain that is unaffected by available vaccines.[4]

Should research proceed into the genetic properties of ebola, for example, to determine what properties make it so lethal and to intermix genes of ebola with related hemorrhagic diseases? Ebola is approximately 90 percent lethal, but it has disadvantages for purposes of bioviolence (already discussed in Chapter 2). Although it is contagious, new victims would have to come into contact with a sufferer's bodily fluids only once symptoms have emerged when he would be too sick to move and the need to isolate him would be obvious. Related hemorrhagic diseases are less lethal yet more contagious than ebola; a victim might be less debilitated for a longer period and spread the disease more widely. Should a scientist be allowed to pursue research into how the ebola virus could be fused with more contagious viruses that might result in a superbug with ebola's lethality but far more readily spread? If so, should he be allowed to publish the results of his work?

The breakthrough need not involve pathogens. Particle physicists cooperating with pulmonary scientists have improved the efficiency of how drugs can evade the respiratory system's usual defenses and be inhaled into the lung's deep alveoli. Other advances in modeling airflow in the human lung have transformed vaccine delivery. Newly invented organic coatings dramatically increase the uptake of particles within the lungs where microbes could settle and begin replication. These breakthroughs could make it easier for an aerosolized pathogen such as anthrax to be deposited into the lower airways. Thus, various technologies that improve small drug aerosols and that generate specialized coatings for enhancing the body's absorption of vaccines could also make an anthrax weapon more effective by reducing how many anthrax spores are sufficient to cause infection. These discoveries do not enhance pathogens, but they could offer new techniques for weaponization.

The Challenge of Overseeing Bioresearch

If the same knowledge underlies great progress and horrible violence, how might we prevent the destructive applications of bioscience while encouraging the conduct of legitimate research? How can policies to control the direction and application of bioresearch be promoted without constricting progress? Should policies to regulate the content of bioresearch even be considered? These questions are among the most controversial in the entire policy arena of bioviolence prevention.

A facile suggestion would be to prohibit research that could open or augment dangerous capabilities. Another suggestion would be to prohibit publication of research findings because worldwide circulation could enhance the lethal capabilities of otherwise unsophisticated offenders. These "suggestions" are patently wrong. Distinguishing what research should be allowed from the research that should be prohibited is exceedingly difficult, and that distinction would likely change in a short time. Moreover, how would such a prohibition be enforced? Every advanced laboratory would have to be equipped with monitoring technology, and scientists would have to extensively report their activities. Even then, noncompliance would be difficult to detect. In short order, scientists would likely devise ways to evade the prohibition.

The issue here is what should be done if the essence of scientists' work – opening ever more fascinating windows into the structure of life – necessarily opens more dire potential for bioviolence? This concern is different from what has been discussed in Chapter 5: how to enhance security of pathogens, labs, and equipment. Telling bioscientists to pursue science in compliance with security measures is reasonable; telling them that their science might produce dangerous knowledge implies that their endeavor is threatening and should be corralled.

There is a further dilemma. The exponential pace of scientific progress drastically outstrips the incremental growth of law. The quantum disparity of pace is intrinsic to the respective disciplines of science and law. Science is inherently accelerative; received truths should be aggressively challenged. Law is inherently conservative; change derives incrementally from precedent. With the passage of time, the gap between scientific risks and legal controls widens. Increasingly, there is a real danger that law just can't keep up. The ramifications here are critical. Even if we could devise optimal answers to the bioscience paradox that maximize opportunities for beneficial science while minimizing risks of its deliberate misuse, those answers would quickly be obsolete. Even if we could weave a net of controls sufficiently elastic and permeable to let science flourish while sufficiently sensitive to warn us of criminal preparations, there is the dilemma of how to catch a torpedo by casting that net from a rowboat.

Accelerating globalization adds to the quandary. If all bioscience was taking place in the United States, the pace of scientific progress would still outpace legal reform, but at least such reform could proceed in a consistent authoritative framework. However, emerging bioresearch is extensively distributed worldwide – both a product of and a stimulant to globalization that takes advantage of rapid trade in ideas and materials. The more that science spreads, the more that a discovery that enables bioviolence could come from anywhere on Earth. Over a million scientific articles are published yearly, increasingly from nations that a decade ago had little participation in cutting-edge science.[5] Of course, whatever research that is published can be instantly disseminated via the internet to other scientists, students, and anyone else.

It makes no sense to supervise bioscience in one nation or even a few. Whatever threats derive from emerging bioscience demand an international approach – legal controls must be implemented worldwide. If not, scientists who are stopped from doing research in one jurisdiction would simply take that research elsewhere.[6] Consider the following perspective offered by the United States National Research Council:

Without international consensus and consistent guidelines for overseeing research in advanced biotechnology, limitations on certain types of research in the United States would only impede the progress of biomedical research here and hinder our own national defense. It is entirely appropriate for the United States to develop a system to provide oversight of research activities domestically, but the effort will ultimately afford little protection if it is not adopted internationally. This is a challenge for governments, international organizations, and the entire international scientific community.[7]

Yet, it is a daunting challenge to try to harmonize laws among all nations so as to consistently balance scientific freedom and security. The complexities of these highly nuanced issues are exponentially multiplied in the international arena among radically incompatible notions of scientific freedom as well as of governmental authority to restrict that freedom for the sake of security. Even benign initiatives in international law must tread gingerly through the thickets of an anarchic State-centric system. Indeed, as the globalization of science stimulates ever more dynamic pressure for international regulation, the impediments of propelling law in a contentious and disorderly environment impair development of comprehensive control mechanisms.

In the end, scientific progress must win. Policies to address emerging bioscience risks must admit that science will proceed regardless of legal norms or constraints. Moreover, no nation that has capabilities and political will to develop vaccines and other measures for resisting bioattacks will abide by internationally imposed constraints on those defensive pursuits. Even if rational approaches could be identified, who should supervise their implementation? Few of us would consider legislating constraints on bioscience, but even if we wanted to pass a law to contain bioscience, the law would soon be washed away by an inexorable surge of knowledge.

With every passing day, the temptation rises to either give up efforts for strengthening law or to impose retrogressive controls on science that alienate the scientific community from the rule of law. Neither option is attractive. Answers here are intricate and provocative, yet one assertion stands beyond any modicum of doubt: positive or negative, potent or trivial, the implications of advancing bioscience currently face a legal system that is wholly archaic and incapable of organizing institutional responses to promote either security or justice, unnecessarily imperiling us all.

Constraining Science?

Do we really want to devise international legal controls that, at their core, are supposed to stop science? To even raise this question is to enter into a sensitive area. A repeated theme throughout this book is the need to impose only such minimal standards of good scientific conduct that are essential to carry out denial and interdiction policies but to avoid weighing down legitimate research. It is imperative to carefully weigh regulation's benefits for preventing bioviolence against the cost to scientific innovation.

At stake here is something far more profound than a utilitarian weighing of costs and benefits. Scientific research is human thought at its most elevated, and its free pursuit is fundamental to humanity's exploration of our world. Restraint of that pursuit is repugnant to the dignity of human freedom. Said Dr. Joshua Lederberg, "The profession of science is the search for truths about the natural world; more precisely, it seeks verifiable generalizations that simplify human comprehension and prediction of natural phenomena."[8] At the core of concepts about freedom of thought is respect for analytical investigations that comprise the pursuit of truth, including unbridled inquiry that challenges traditional wisdom; scientific experimentation is thought par excellence. To limit science, even in the name of security, is to restrict what people think about and therefore to constrict human intellect.

Discussions of whether to limit publication are no less troubling. This concern was the basis of an uproar when Australian scientists working with mousepox (a nonlethal [to humans] relative of smallpox) injected a gene – Interleukin-4 – and produced a "supercharged disease" for which vaccines were ineffective and that, as a result, had a 100 percent fatality rate among exposed mice. The methodology and its success provoked anxiety because it showed how to intensify diseases by injecting a gene into a virus and thereby spawn decimating consequences.[9]

Many scientists were troubled by the experimenters' seeming indifference to the potential malevolent applications of their discovery as well as their publishing the results in the popular science press. Similar concerns arose about the publication of the fully decoded genetic sequence of the 1918 Spanish Flu[10] (discussed in Chapter 2). Few scientists objected to the research, but a vigorous debate ensued as to whether the decoded genetic sequence should have been so widely exhibited.[11] Although samples of the virus are strictly controlled, its component DNA strands are widely available, and few viruses are so easily subject to regeneration as influenza.

Yet, constraints on publication are problematic. There are inseverable links between the act of research and freedom of expression.[12] Science is

BOX 6-1. NATIONAL ACADEMIES OF SCIENCE'S LIST OF "RESEARCH OF CONCERN"

1. Experiments that would demonstrate how to render a vaccine ineffective;
2. Experiments that would confer resistance to therapeutically useful antibiotics or antiviral agents;
3. Experiments that would enhance the virulence of a pathogen or render a non-pathogen virulent;
4. Experiments that would increase transmissibility of a pathogen;
5. Experiments that would alter the host range of a pathogen;
6. Experiments that would enable the evasion of diagnostic/detection modalities; and
7. Experiments that would enable the weaponization of a biological agent or toxin.

SOURCE: *Biotechnology Research in an Age of Terrorism*, NATIONAL RESEARCH COUNCIL OF THE NATIONAL ACADEMIES, p. 5 (2004).

not merely the work of a lone scientist as much as an interchange of theories to explore hypotheses. Scientists conduct experiments to refine their ideas and to test a theory's validity. A central tenet of the scientific method is the independent reproducibility of experimental findings; communication of the knowledge learned to other scientists is essential. Scientific publications must include enough technical detail so that other investigators can repeat the experiment to verify results. Of all types of communication, scientific expression is likely to open avenues of understanding that might otherwise not have opened and that, once opened, cannot be reclosed.[13] It undermines scientific exploration, therefore, to suggest that a scientist may undertake an experiment to demonstrate a theory but communication of its results must be restricted. (See Box 6-1.)

Not to be ignored is the right of others to receive the research results, including scientists, policy makers, and the general public. Doctors who must decide if a drug should be prescribed must have access to the research product of other physicians, scientists, and academics. More generally, intelligent public debate depends on the free flow of scientific ideas. Many scientific advances (from Galileo's observations to stem-cell research) have proceeded from initiatives that some members of society have sought to constrict. If the only messages that may be disseminated are those already in the public domain, then a government could drastically restrict the flow of information by merely restricting activities that are prerequisite for publication. The government could control access to ideas by placing restraints at the point where the information is initially developed or obtained. Research is so intimately connected with the scientist's goal of generating and exchanging information that, without protection, the right to communicate about science would be meaningless.

Moreover, it bears acknowledging that for a restriction to be implemented and enforced, there must be someone doing the restricting. Should that someone be a national government, an international authority, someone else? Even more ominous is the "slippery slope" of authoritative restrictions on science. In one context, a restriction might be purportedly justified by concerns for bioviolence. In another context, the impetus might be opposition to stem-cell research or to the teaching of evolution. If political authorities can decide the direction of science, then there is a substantial risk that they will make those decisions according to the wishes of the constituencies that put them in power, not necessarily according to what is scientifically true.

Yet another objection to secrecy stems from a very different direction. If experiments on the lethality of pox diseases or reconstructing the 1918 flu are performed within or supported by a government facility, barring publication of that research might provoke suspicions of a covert bioweapons program, especially if the research is accompanied by preparations of vaccines for distribution to troops and citizens. Tightly guarding the information suggests that it contributes to preparing hostile capabilities. Today, as governments finance most research, distinguishing between bioresearch that is pure science from research that is done for military purposes is increasingly difficult. This issue is discussed more fully in Chapter 8.

Virtues and Limitations of Codes of Ethics and Self-Regulation

Questions about how to address bioscience's risks have occupied enormous attention in the past few years. In the United States, these issues have been hotly debated with respect to the First Amendment. A National Academies of Sciences panel devoted serious intellectual energy to this question,[14] which led to the establishment of a new advisory body within the U.S. government.[15] The essence of that panel's approach is that there are innate risks in the progress of bioscience, and those risks are best addressed through intra-science awareness, not overt regulation.[16] Moreover, there should be opportunities for the scientific community to inject its concerns into relevant governmental decisions.

Altogether, the commitment to improving intra-science awareness has commendably been pursued in the United States and elsewhere. Numerous global organizations are devoutly on record for raising sensitivity to the risks of malevolent bioscience and the need for bioscientists to voluntarily self-regulate. These proposals advocate that scientists who are best informed about the implications of their work are, therefore, best able to avoid doing research that might contribute to violence. Moreover, voluntary self-regulation keeps the lawyers and police at bay, insulating the scientific endeavor from harassment or tedious inquiries. In the name of self-regulation, codes of scientific ethics (see Box 6-2) have rapidly proliferated in recent years – a phenomenon worth praise.

Indeed, if ethical codes could solve the security questions associated with advancing bioscience, these questions would have already faded into irrelevance. But these codes have inherent structural flaws. Initially, what do they cover? The criteria of dangerous research must be globally uniform – if States have different criteria of potentially dangerous bioresearch, there will be a "race to the bottom" as States compete to be the least restrictive and therefore most enticing for emerging bioscience. Crucially, scientists (as well as law makers) must precisely know what criteria apply to specific activities. The principle of legality requires that for a prohibition to be enforceable, its application must be judiciously limited and specifically defined so that potential violators should know if their conduct crosses permissible lines.

Yet, experts have differing opinions on the definition of potentially dangerous bioresearch.[17] Box 6-1 explores some issues compiled by the National Academies of Science regarding "research of concern." None of the proposed codes define what type of research is covered, that is, what type of research is potentially dangerous or could lead to production of bioweapons. The problem is not so much the difference of opinions but the absence of any authoritative process to resolve them. No code provides any mechanism of how applicable research will be overseen. What is the criterion of review, the methodology of review, the administrative process of review, the rights and responsibilities of persons being reviewed? These codes offer no answers.

Moreover, even if precise criteria could be identified, their application to specific experiments would demand constant renewal. The scientific issues change over time as does the community of scientists who might undertake relevant dangerous research. For example, nanoscientists are not commonly thought of as bioscientists, but their work is increasingly linked to bioscience's risks. Which group of tomorrow's scientists should

BOX 6-2. PRINCIPAL CODES OF CONDUCT

For a representative list of codes of ethics, *see* Biosecurity Oversight and Codes...Biosecurity Information[a]

- UNESCO Declaration on Science and the Use of Scientific Knowledge, adopted by the World Conference on Science, 1 July 1999.
- International Committee of the Red Cross (ICRC) *Preventing Hostile Use of the life Science: From Ethics and Law to Best Practice*, November 11, 2004.
- American Society for Microbiology, *Code of Ethics*, 2005.
- American Medical Association, *Guidelines to Prevent Malevolent Use of Biomedical Research*, June 2004.
- Council for Responsible Genetics (CRG), *Campaign for The Peaceful Development of the Biological Sciences.*
- InterAcademy Panel on International Issues, *Statement on Biosecurity*, December 1, 2005.
- International Union of Microbiological Scientists (IUMS). Code of Ethics against Misuse of Scientific Knowledge, Research and Resources, 28 April 2006.
- Global BioBusiness, *Code of Conduct for Life Science Professionals*, University of Southern California Global Business Initiative.

[a] Available at http://www.biosecuritycodes.org/codes_archive.htm.

be included? There is no authoritative process to anticipate forthcoming challenges.

The bigger problem has to do with the effect of codes that are exclusively commitments of the willing that ignore the real problem: the activities of the unwilling. Even among code-adopting groups, there is no way to know if members are really observing the code. We might believe that persons who declare their commitment to the code are in fact being observant, but how are we to know if there are others who should be observing but are not? Nothing in these codes would even begin to enable detection of someone who is intentionally outside whatever code or system might apply. At best, these codes relate exclusively to those persons and entities that accept them. By definition, these codes have no application to anyone who rejects them.[18]

Ethical declarations that lack capacity to internationally manage risks inevitably create something of a Swiss cheese of protections. Most bioscience is conducted according to the highest safety and security standards, but it is absurd to argue that there are no exceptions. No one – not a single serious commentator – would argue that the bioresearch phenomenon will long be a monopoly of a few States that require rigorous scientific standards. It isn't now. From the prevention perspective, as science evolves, the presence of cheese in some places becomes less important than the holes in others. The issue is not how the overwhelming majority of ethical scientists behave. The issue is how to stop intentionally malevolent perpetrators who are unlikely to be swayed from their illicit undertakings by taking an oath to abjure harmful behavior. Prevention must be made of sterner stuff.

The Need for Translucency

The challenge here, ultimately, is analogous to counter-espionage. We are really not so interested in checking the activities of the overwhelming majority of scientists; we are interested in detecting a traitor's activities.

The term *transparency* refers to policies that enable verification of compliance with legal obligations. If stipulated activities are transparent, then observers can know what others are doing and can promptly enforce rights in a controversy. The mechanisms of transparency, developed in connection with superpower nuclear weapons control, involve inspections – specially authorized inspectors are entitled to scrutinize facilities having capacity to make prohibited weapons. To achieve transparency with regard to bioscience would require gathering copious information about facilities capable of producing bioweapons. The extreme expense of monitoring bioresearch in order to distinguish peaceful purposes from hostile purposes must be weighed against the low likelihood of fully verifying compliance or detecting noncompliance.

In contrast to nuclear weapons verification, there are virtually limitless bioscience facilities, and illicit preparations can be easily hidden even at monitored facilities. Perhaps thousands of inspectors could oversee activities at key bioscience installations. Yet even highly trained and broadly authorized United Nations inspectors failed to discover Iraq's bioweapons program in the 1990s until an Iraqi weapons official tipped them off. It borders on the absurd to devote comparable resources to inspection of every sophisticated bioscience facility.

Moreover, the kinds of places and activities that would likely be inspected are not where bioviolence preparations are expected to occur. To focus on them would far more likely interfere with legitimate bioscience pursuits than on potential criminality. Thus, even if massive resources were devoted to monitoring declared bioscience activities, those resources would at best prove that legitimate bioscience is not, in fact, engaged in bioviolence preparations. It would not tell us much about where illicit preparations are taking place or give us much insight about how to stop them. Implementation of transparency policies is, therefore, inappropriate.

The term *translucency* may be offered as a middle ground between transparency and opacity. Translucency refers to a set of policies that are designed to generate an information flow for deterring and detecting wrongful activity. The prime directive of translucency policies is that bioscience that is designed for or poses a unique threat of weapons applications must not be performed in absolute secrecy. Notably, these policies are hardly novel for bioscientists operating in States with highly developed science sectors; indeed, the concept here is to globalize these policies for enabling non-intrusive oversight.

The central reason to prohibit secrecy is to compel accountability. Someone should always be able to trace research activity back to its source. Secret bioscience programs raise suspicions and could promote a race for offensive capabilities under the cover of "defense."[19] Prohibiting secrecy raises confidence that bioresearch is not undertaken to advance bioviolence. Prohibiting secrecy also has deterrent value especially for national biodefense programs by escalating the challenge of keeping wrongful intentions secret. Accordingly, no bioresearch should be black-box, *i.e.*, totally out of sight. Even where national authorities deem it appropriate to classify (hold confidential) bioresearch, classification should be limited to the details of that research; keeping secret the fact of classification should be prohibited.

Some scientific disciplines (notably nuclear physics) have long been subject to government classification that restricts the unfettered dissemination of ideas. That some research is "classified" is not an unjustifiable constraint on scientific freedom. Indeed, a government's interest in circumscribing the flow of potentially dangerous information is distinguishable from its attempt to constrain what someone might speculate about. Limiting the audience of certain scientific information is clearly different from censoring what research a scientist might undertake. The intricate classification system that safeguards information having international security implications does not prevent scientists from pursuing or sharing ideas, only from disseminating the information they generate through unapproved channels. In this context, there are very well-understood processes that could promote reasonable regulation. This issue is raised again in Chapter 8.

Prohibiting secrecy also has ramifications for important proprietary and privacy interests. Most research has value – proprietary value for developing pharmaceuticals and career value to the researchers. There must be criteria about what information should be disclosed and the process of handling and storing that information. Accordingly, it is essential to differentiate: 1) research with significant implications for bioviolence from the vastly larger amount of research that does not; and 2) the existence of that research from its specific contents or results. In truth, very little research need be disclosed; it is the *fact* of research not its *content* – its location and basic purpose not its methodology or results – that should be disclosed.[20] Disclosure would be made to national authorities except in rare cases involving extremely dangerous research or research overtly focusing on military applications that should involve international disclosure.[21] Moreover, protections should be developed to ensure that the process of disclosing information does not intrude into professional and personal privacy. Confidentiality is essential; distinguishing secrecy from confidentiality is mandatory.[22]

Bioscientists as the First Line of Defense

Although codes of ethical conduct are inadequate to fully address bioresearch's potential dangers, there are more formal mechanisms of self-supervision – short of legal regulation – that could contribute to reducing risks, especially if such mechanisms are implemented worldwide. These mechanisms include: 1) requirements for education and training with regard to research responsibility, 2) professional certification requirements, and 3) protection and encouragement of whistleblowers.

Bioresearch Education and Training

Every bioscientist should be required to successfully participate in a program of study that highlights ethical responsibilities for research that could be catastrophically misused. No scientist should be able to claim that he or she was unaware of the dangerous implications of doing particular research; "competency in research entails responsible conduct and the capacity for ethical decision making."[23] Accordingly, the National Academy of Sciences (NAS) Panel on Scientific Responsibility and the Conduct of Research has recommended that scientists and research institutes "integrate into their curricula educational programs that foster faculty and student awareness of concerns related to the integrity of the research process."[24] Mentors should monitor trainees for misconduct and instill by example the highest ethical standards.[25]

According to the United States Commission on Research Integrity, education on ethical research practices for scientists should begin in the early stages of training and continue through the most senior career stages.[26] Researchers more often engage in responsible professional conduct when they can: 1) identify ethical aspects of research situations and applicable legal standards, 2) develop defensible rationales for a choice of action, 3) integrate the value of professional discipline with personal values and appropriately prioritize those values, and 4) perform complex tasks with integrity.[27] Courses that emphasize ethical responsibilities should be a mandatory part of Ph.D. programs; other professions such as law and medicine have comparable requirements for ethics courses. For practicing bioresearchers, continuing professional education could make available such courses, and professional accreditation could compel scientists to participate.

Professional Certification

In sharp contrast to physicians who must be licensed to practice medicine and lawyers who must be licensed to practice law, there is no formal process for licensing or certification to approve career entry in the life sciences. In general, bioresearch institutions are supposed to identify persons who are capable of committing scientific misconduct – a mandate that is lacking both criteria and legal obligation.

Instead of insisting on global certification for bioresearch professionals, the U.S. government has initiated selective and arguably ill-designed efforts to limit risks. There are additional security checks on visa applications for foreign nationals with expertise in certain chemical and biological technologies; these students' programs of study are tracked through the Student and Exchange Visitor Information System (SEVIS).[28] Besides obviously ignoring risks that American students might be motivated to commit bioviolence, these efforts to limit access of foreign students often turn the best and the brightest away from the ethical training that American institutions could provide in favor of education outside the United States.

Another controversial initiative is the United States Security Risk Assessment (SRA) which requires scientists who work with potential bioviolence agents to turn over their fingerprints and personal information to the Federal Bureau of Investigation (FBI) for background checks.[29] The FBI searches relevant databases and other sources to determine if an applicant is a "restricted person" that is, a citizen of a country suspected of supporting terrorism, a person with a history of mental illness, illegal drug use or felony convictions, or has been dishonorably discharged from the military.[30] In its first two years of operation, over 13,000 background checks had been completed; 72 applicants were considered to be "restricted persons" of whom the vast majority – 53 of the 72 – were restricted due to a prior felony conviction.[31]

Many scientists object to these initiatives that are thought to have questionable value for preventing bioviolence. However, the impetus for these initiatives is that although bioresearch entails activity that could be enormously dangerous, there is little support within the profession for a global certification system with records detailing who is working in which institutions and what each scientist is qualified to undertake. Calls for self-regulation that do not include mechanisms to identify individual scientists and to keep track of their activities are calls for no real oversight at all. In that vacuum, scientists might be disappointed but should not be surprised when the government's heavy hand intrudes on their anonymity.

Whistleblowers

Scientists correctly assert that they are best positioned with the greatest opportunity to detect misconduct and report it in its early stages. It will likely be a scientist who notices when a colleague works on strange projects at odd hours or moves vials without returning them.[32] Will scientists see it as their responsibility to report their misgivings; if they do, will they be protected against potential retaliation? If whistleblowers who report a colleague are punished by their institutions or if their identity is widely aired to those colleagues who, after all, might be associated with reprehensible activity, other scientists will be discouraged from ever reporting misconduct.[33] To expect members of the scientific community who have knowledge of misconduct to come forward because it is their ethical responsibility to do so requires fair systems of review and effective protection from retaliation.

The U.S. Commission on Research Integrity (CRI) has recommended a Whistleblower's Bill of Rights to strengthen whistleblower protections by encouraging institutions to treat whistleblowers fairly, protect them from retaliation, and to articulate the responsibilities one incurs when accusing another of misconduct. The CRI also recommended notifying all research scientists of acceptable and unacceptable procedures, making available an independent ombudsman, and appointing a senior advisor to both accuser and accused.[34] At this time, these recommendations are merely advisory.

All these initiatives – improving bioresearch education, professional certification, and whistleblower protection – could be implemented in the near term and would be beneficial. Yet, if bioscientists sincerely assert that they can operate as a first line of defense that fends off the need for more intrusive supervision, then they should demonstrate a more substantial commitment. In this regard, the following words from noted experts deserve attention:

> Over time, we must construct a network of "checks and balances": regulations, incentives, cultural expectations, and practices that encourage and enable progress in scientific understanding so that knowledge can be brought to bear on human needs, while simultaneously assuring responsible stewardship of powerful knowledge so that it is not used for malevolent purposes. Such stewardship will have to evolve – rapidly, in concert with the pace of advances in the life sciences – to embrace a network of international agreements, legal regulations, professional standards, ethical mores, and catalogues of "best practices" pertinent to various fields and disciplines. Scientists and the scientific community must be integral participants in the design and implementation of such a network.[35]

DEVELOPMENT OF VACCINES AND MEDICINES

It is critical to develop more vaccines and medicines. Yet, throwing money at scientific research in the blind faith that shields and cures will immunize us from bioviolence is a strategy of dubious value. These doubts are deeply rooted in the challenge of trying to get ready for an attack that could involve any of a large array of pathogens and could arise anywhere in the world.

As discussed in Chapter 1, a widespread attack throughout developing nations would have catastrophic economic and political consequences for the developed world and, of course, even more catastrophic health consequences for those targeted. Yet, in the entire bioviolence prevention arena, the need to encourage development of new medical methods for resisting an attack is perhaps the most graphic manifestation of tensions between policies that make sense for developed nations and policies that are appropriate for developing nations.

The United States and its comparably developed allies have devoted huge resources to protect their citizens from some bioviolence acts. It is simply irresponsible to blithely suggest that most developing nations should undertake comparable steps to protect against bioviolence. Moreover, discovering medicines without building capacities for getting them to the people who need them, especially in developing regions, is truly wasteful. Today, for lack of global distribution capacities, millions die from diseases for which medical treatments already exist. In the chaos of a bioviolence catastrophe, it is not credible to believe that these deficiencies will suddenly be overcome.

According to the WHO, low- and middle-income countries bear a disproportionate share of the global disease burden, yet 90 percent of the expenditures on health across the globe are concentrated on only 10 percent of the world's population.[36] Of the 1,233 new drugs marketed between 1975 and 1999, only 13 were for diseases that commonly afflict those in developing or underdeveloped countries. Only four deal with tropical diseases. Altogether, developing countries make up roughly 20 percent of the global pharmaceutical market. This hardly makes them attractive for biotechnology firms – mostly private and western.

Some developing countries devote as little as $2 per capita per year to health care, and the overwhelming threats of natural disease present an already tremendous burden. For example, India spends nearly half of its annual health budget combating malaria. The sub-Saharan African region, with the highest rates of child mortality on the planet, accounts for only 0.1 percent of the global health expenditure. Diseases like malaria along with diarrhea and pneumonia overwhelmingly afflict developing countries and yet receive only a fraction of the global expenditure on health. Given how destitute some of these countries are, casual calls for more research, testing, and distribution of biotechnology to prevent bioviolence are unacceptable.

Economics is not the only barrier. There is also a "brain-drain" problem. Development of new vaccines requires unique combinations of scientists and bioengineers plus sophisticated equipment operating in modern laboratories. Worldwide, these combinations are positioned to rapidly produce vaccines only in a few nations.[37] This condition generates a vicious cycle: competent scientists and researchers in developing countries feel compelled to leave to seek more gainful employment elsewhere. Even if these regions could offer basic funding for research and development, it is unlikely they could match the dollars that are offered to scientists and trained professionals in developed nations.[38]

Only in the last few years have enormous amounts of money and effort been poured into producing and stockpiling medicines for combating pandemic disease, including bioviolence threats. Wealthy nations, international health and financial organizations, generous foundations and individuals, scientific associations, and prominent academic centers are rallying to provide assistance. Perhaps most prominent is the WHO Global Immunization Vision and Strategy, a joint program with UNICEF whose goal is to cut illness and death caused by vaccine-preventable diseases by two-thirds by 2015 compared to the 2000 levels. Its three main aims are to immunize more people against more diseases, introduce new technologies and vaccines, and provide critical health interventions with immunizations. By assisting governments in designing, financing, and implementing immunization programs, the program's goal is an 80 percent vaccination rate in underdeveloped areas by 2010. One-third of the estimated $35 billion cost will be allocated to vaccines; two-thirds will be spent on immunization delivery systems.[39]

Not surprisingly, the programs that focus on mass production and distribution of already-known medicines appear to have greater impact than programs that seek to create new medicines. Important from this book's perspective is that initiatives for elevating resistance against bioviolence have had sporadic success at best and have arguably deprived global efforts to combat natural disease of resources that could do more good. More certain is that key policy decisions are not made at the highest level of global governance with consideration of those decisions' global impacts or with a strategy that effectively anticipates emerging priorities.

The remainder of this chapter examines the challenge of developing medicines from the perspective of three related barriers: financial constraints, threats of liability, and patent protection. In combination, these problems and the recent efforts to overcome them demonstrate the pitfalls and confusion that derive from partial approaches to the challenge of enhancing resistance against bioviolence.

Financial Barriers

Development of new medicines entails unique investment risks. Substantial resources must be devoted, and any single effort has a low probability of success. For private investors, there must be a high payoff when a useful medication is identified. In the United States, successfully developing a new drug takes nearly 10 years and between $400–800 million; 5,000 compounds will, on average, be identified for one approved drug. Even developing the yearly flu vaccine involves a costly production method.[40] Moreover, the permitting process for new vaccines is time-consuming under the best of conditions; any misstep entails expensive corrections.[41]

Weighing this enormous cost and failure rate against a drug's likely market impact presents a harsh reality: treatments for chronic conditions with large patient populations who can afford a steep price justify greater investment than treatments for disease outbreaks caused by unanticipated pathogens, especially if the treatment does not have wide-spectrum applicability. In the context of bioviolence that has yet to occur, the economics of vaccine development lead inevitably to underinvestment. From society's perspective, having a wide array of medicines on hand makes sense, but this logic is very different for bioresearch companies that must invest enormous sums for compounds that might never be bought.

Many analysts, therefore, call for government funding and a precommitment to purchase new medicines so as to ensure a market even if the disease that it treats does not appear.[42] For example, the United States Orphan Drug Act (ODA)[43] increases incentives to develop drugs for patients with rare illnesses and guarantees longer than usual market exclusivity. Yet, while government assumption of risks can stimulate research investment by creating larger and more reliable markets, such programs are not certain to lead to optimal allocations and do little to encourage drugs that address vulnerabilities disproportionately affecting poor countries. Moreover, this approach forces governments to "pre-pick winners" in a wasteful manner that likely benefits a few wealthy recipients rather than serves the public benefit.[44] Political considerations could also be distorting. For example, it would be politically unforgivable to be unprepared for a well-understood disease (e.g., anthrax), but citizens might be more forgiving if authorities are caught off guard for something more novel (e.g., bio-engineered ebola). Even if an impartial economic analysis justifies research on antiviral medications rather than anthrax vaccine, the political analysis would favor addressing the better known threat.

Since 2001, the solution to the underinvestment problem has been massive government allocations. In the United States, spending to develop vaccines and medicines increased from $418 million in 2001 to $3.7 billion the next year in view of the anthrax attacks that followed 9/11. In 2001, the National Institutes of Health (NIH) operated with a $50 million budget; in 2005, its budget was $1.7 billion, a 3,400 percent increase.[45] In the most recent FY 2007 budget, federal funding for civilian biodefense increased to $5.24 billion.[46] Project BioShield, begun in 2004, allocates $5.6 billion for research to counter WMD attacks (chemical, radiological, and nuclear as well as biological) by contributing to the Strategic National Stockpile (SNS), which includes vaccines and other medical tools procured and stored by

---

BOX 6-3. BIOSHIELD AT A GLANCE

BioShield provides a reserve fund for the HHS Secretary to procure a countermeasure where the Secretary determines that it is: 1) a priority measure against harm from chemical, biological, radiological, or nuclear agents; and 2) a "necessary" measure that is either a) approved or licensed under applicable law; or b) a countermeasure that will be approved or licensed within eight years of the funding approval. This reserve fund may also be used if the measure is authorized for emergency use. The HHS Secretary can simplify procurement if a "pressing need" is identified, bypassing the stringent requirements of government contract law and can spur development by paying up to 10 percent of the negotiated price. This support fosters development and relieves some of the burdens associated with research by offering drug developers the incentive of longer contracts.

If an appropriate countermeasure is unavailable, then the President should "call" for these items to be produced. A call would estimate the financial cost involved and determine how much would be needed. The HHS Secretary then decides whether to allocate the special reserve fund depending on: 1) quantities of product needed to meet stockpiling needs; 2) feasibility of production and delivery within eight years; and 3) whether there is a lack of a commercial market for the product other than as a countermeasure that could be procured from the reserve fund. The President may then either deny or approve the request; HHS handles the actual ins-and-outs of procurement, such as negotiating costs, delivery, payment, etc.

SOURCE: Frank Rapoport, Christopher Bouquet, & Scott Flukinger, *Project BioShield Act of 2004: Dawn of a New Industry?* 40-SPG PROCUREMENT LAWYER 3 (2005).

---

the government to respond to major health emergencies. See Box 6-3 for more information about BioShield. The Secretary of Health and Human Services (HHS) is empowered to promote research and development of drugs and to recommend their procurement from a special reserve fund; in some critical situations, there are simplified procurement procedures that can make available new and promising treatments without awaiting normal regulatory approval.

Criticisms of BioShield focus on its meager achievements.[47] As of 2006, officials had spent less than a quarter of their budget.[48] In December 2006, HHS cancelled its sole supplier $877 million contract with VaxGen, Inc. for delivery of 75 million doses of an anthrax vaccine beginning in early 2006. The company had not started human clinical trials because of FDA concerns about the vaccine's potency.[49] Other pharmaceutical companies have smaller contracts with the U.S. government to produce vaccines and antitoxins, but it is unlikely that they can deliver the large amount required under the VaxGen contract.[50] BioShield's efforts to address other potential threats have not been much more successful. Cangene has delivered the first of 200,000 doses of an antitoxin for botulism but is not currently planning to pursue a vaccine.[51] For smallpox, there were two hundred million doses of vaccine stockpiled before BioShield began, but an initiative to develop a smallpox vaccine safe for persons with impaired immune systems has, as of this writing, yet to begin. The NIH has begun research on vaccines for tularemia, plague, and ebola, but the government has yet to contract with any pharmaceutical companies through BioShield to address these threats.[52]

Cancellation of the VaxGen contract, despite its having spent over $175 million to develop the vaccine, may make other pharmaceutical companies hesitant to get involved with BioShield.[53] According to one expert, "The inept implementation of the program has led the best brains and the best scientists to give up."[54] BioShield's problems might not be fairly attributable to "inept implementation" as much as to the inanity of hoping that billions of dollars will promptly generate medical protections from bioviolence. Enduring support for scientific research will likely be beneficial over time, but to pour in cash and expect an immediate return is to misunderstand the unique economic aspects of pushing vaccine production. The recently enacted Pandemic and All-Hazards Preparedness Act repairs certain aspects of BioShield such as by allowing contractors to receive milestone payments, but few experts believe that it will solve the problems inherent in this effort.[55] This lack of success has transpired during relatively calm conditions – the odds of the system suddenly fixing itself during a crisis are dim.

Liability Barriers

It is virtually inevitable that wide use of vaccines and other medications to build resistance to bioviolence will have harmful consequences for a small minority of the population. Should victims of adverse effects be compensated? Vaccines are among the greatest achievements of biomedical science and public health. Vaccinated individuals are protected, and even unvaccinated persons are better off because the circulation of disease is reduced.[56] In many societies, schoolchildren must be vaccinated against contagious diseases. When the government requires vaccination for the purpose of promoting public health, who should be liable if there is an adverse reaction – the government or the vaccine industry?

Whether victims should be compensated at all raises important questions of individual versus community welfare. How should unpredictable reactions to properly manufactured and administrated vaccines be handled? Several vaccines have brought this issue to the fore, including the risks of Guillain-Barré syndrome (GBS) associated with the swine flu vaccine and of Sudden Infant Death Syndrome (SIDS) associated with the diphtheria-tetanus-pertussis (DTP) vaccine.

In many nations, victims of those consequences might seek to recover damages against producers. This risk of liability is a cost that weighs heavily against expending vast sums to produce vaccines; vaccine producers could stay out of the market altogether. In the early 1980s, adverse reactions to vaccines created liability concerns for U.S. manufacturers which caused them to stop producing vaccines that, in turn, led to declining child vaccination rates. Remaining manufacturers increased their prices to cover liability costs which led to significant vaccine shortages.[57] The number of vaccine producers in the U.S. market has decreased significantly from twenty-six companies in 1967 to five companies today.

Providing liability protection could ease pharmaceutical companies' concerns, especially during an emergency. How much harm to the population is appropriate in attempting to mitigate the effects of a bioattack? While most scientists would agree that the benefits of vaccination outweigh the harms, what sort of compensation should be available to those harmed by these vaccines?

Four policy approaches have emerged to ease disincentives that manufacturers face in producing vaccines.[58] First, the government can assume liability either by administering the vaccine itself or by substituting itself as a defendant if a victim sues the vaccine producers. The United States National Swine Flu Immunization Program in 1976–1977 took this approach by providing an exclusive remedy against the government for "personal injury or death arising out of the administration of swine flu vaccine under the swine flu program and based upon the act or omission of a program participant."[59] Vaccine producers were protected, but the government eventually paid more than $73 million to claimants out of general revenues.[60]

Second, the government can establish a no-fault compensation program. The victim may be compensated from the program if the vaccine caused the harm regardless of whether the vaccine producers or administrators were at fault. According to a recent study, fourteen vaccine injury compensation programs exist worldwide, exclusively in highly developed countries.[61] The United States National Vaccine Injury Compensation Program (VICP), discussed below, takes this approach.

Third, the government can indemnify vaccine producers who might be held liable for harm. An objection to this approach is that it does not provide the vaccine industry with enough liability protection because the government may not cover the costs of litigation, and in some instances indemnification is limited to only "reasonable" liability costs.[62]

Fourth, the government can alter the normal liability rules. For example, the Support Antiterrorism by Fostering Effective Technologies Act (SAFETY) of 2002[63] prohibits punitive damages and limits liability to the amount of insurance that is "reasonably available."

The United States has combined approaches in the National Childhood Vaccine Injury Act that establishes the Vaccine Injury Compensation Program (VCIP), a no-fault compensation scheme that provides liability protections to producers of vaccines against childhood diseases.[64] The Vaccine Injury Table lists injuries presumed to be caused by vaccines and the time period in which they generally occur; listed injuries are compensable.[65] Victims who accept compensation are paid through the program trust fund raised from taxes on each vaccine delivered in the United States. Victims who suffer an injury that is unlisted or does not occur during the designated timeframe may recover but only if they provide additional proof of harm.[66] Victims who are denied compensation or are dissatisfied with their compensation may appeal the decision or may sue the manufacturers directly.[67] Although manufacturers seem content with the program, some victims' advocates claim that proving causation complicates getting compensation.[68]

Notably, only vaccines that are recommended for routine administration are included. Biodefense vaccines are left out, most likely because the harms associated with such vaccines are largely unknown. An important question, therefore, is whether these policies should similarly limit liability of companies that produce vaccines or medications as countermeasures for use in bioviolence emergencies. The United States has recently enacted the Public Readiness and Emergency Preparedness (PREP) Act that establishes the "Covered Countermeasure Process Fund" to compensate persons who suffer serious injuries or death due to a countermeasure's use. Producers and distributors are protected from liability if there is an officially declared public health emergency or a credible threat, except if the harm results from their "willful misconduct."[69]

During the 2003 smallpox vaccination campaign, three cardiac deaths occurred; all victims (two civilians and one person in the military) were in their mid-fifties.[70] Thereupon, the Smallpox Emergency Personnel Protection Act of 2003[71] was passed to encourage medical and public health workers to get vaccinated. The Act establishes the Smallpox Vaccine Injury Compensation Program which provides compensation for listed injuries to specific personnel (health care workers, law enforcement officers, firefighters, security personnel, emergency medical personnel, and other smallpox emergency response personnel) who receive the vaccine. As under the VCIP, victims of unlisted injuries may receive benefits but must provide additional proof that the vaccine caused their injuries. For Department of Defense (DoD) civilian employees and contractor personnel, however, adverse events that occur under the U.S. Department of Defense Anthrax Vaccine Immunization Program are covered under either federal or state worker's compensation programs.[72]

This brief account of recently enacted law in only one nation – the United States – is confusing. Consider the multiple levels of confusion and disconnect for a pharmaceutical producer who seeks to market drugs worldwide. These matters are indeed complex, but there is no valid reason why legal solutions are not identified globally. Harmonization of liability rules and protections worldwide should be an immediate priority.

Patent Barriers

A huge legal issue vexing global distribution of vaccines concerns the intellectual property rights associated with vaccine production. From the perspective of vaccine producers and government officials in developed nations, the high risks of making safe and effective vaccines would make no economic sense if, having configured a critical drug, someone could readily copy and sell it for a price that need not reflect the sizeable research investment plus a reasonable profit. From developing nations' perspective, paying a price that reflects research costs plus profit is virtually impossible. They could produce the drug at a fraction of the cost, and their populations desperately need these medications; they argue that the pharmaceutical sector's pursuit of exorbitant profits should not be a death sentence for millions of innocent people. Indisputably, any restriction on access to medicines necessarily advantages developed nations' producers that account for over 90 percent of new pharmaceutical patents.[73]

This conflict of perspectives is being played out in the rarified context of the World Trade Organization's (WTO) Trade-Related Aspects of Intellectual Property Rights (TRIPS).[74] States must extend patent protection to micro-organisms and microbiological processes, albeit not to diagnostic, therapeutic, or surgical methods. States that allow infringement of a patented vaccine risk losing their coveted WTO privileges.

There are exceptions. States may grant *compulsory patent licenses* that permit domestic producers to manufacture a patented item without the patent holder's consent so long as licenses are nonexclusive and granted only on an individual basis, and the producer must have sought the original patent holder's approval on reasonable terms. These restrictions need not apply in cases of national emergency. Compulsory licenses must be limited to meeting domestic needs, not for export, and the original patent holder is to be paid adequate compensation.[75] See Box 6-4 for the steps required for compulsory licensing of pharmaceuticals.

The issue here is whether a State may grant a compulsory license to a domestic producer of a vaccine against a bioviolence threat, say anthrax. The answer is very much unresolved.

Two recent events shape this issue. In 2001, the WTO Ministerial Conference adopted the *Declaration on the TRIPS Agreement and Public Health* ("Doha Declaration"), which states that TRIPS "can and should be interpreted and implemented in a manner supportive of WTO Members' right to protect public health and, in particular, to promote access to medicines for all.... WTO Members with insufficient or no manufacturing capacities in the pharmaceutical sector could face difficulties in making effective use of compulsory licensing under the TRIPS Agreement." The Council pledged to find "an expeditious solution to the problem."[76]

Two years later, the WTO Council announced that a country may produce generics of patented drugs for export if another country is in need. The exporter must include unique characteristics on the product that distinguish it from the patented version, and the products must not be diverted for an alternative use. The importing country must inform the Council about the types and quantities of the products it seeks, but there are complaints that the time-consuming procedure to inform the TRIPS Council could be a significant obstacle during an unforeseen public health emergency when patented products are immediately needed.[77] Patented vaccines for rarely occurring diseases might not be available in needed quantities when a bioviolence emergency arises.

The issue of compulsory licensing has been contentious. In the 1990s, South Africa and Brazil each allowed generic manufacturing and parallel importation of needed drugs, especially to combat AIDS. Brazil grounded its argument for a TRIPS emergency exception on its need for cheap drugs to combat HIV/AIDS; South Africa simply ignored the TRIPS provisions on compulsory licensing. The United States initially disputed both

---

BOX 6-4. TEN REQUIRED STEPS FOR COMPULSORY LICENSING OF PHARMACEUTICALS

Developing countries must go through ten steps before patented drugs would be available to them. Each step must be followed every time a drug is exported even if the same drug is being exported to another country. Some experts argue that this *procedural nightmare* is not in the spirit of the Doha Declaration because it impedes countries trying to provide relief for their citizens who are in desperate need of life-saving pharmaceuticals. The ten steps are as follows:

1. A country that is seeking to import a drug through a compulsory license must seek a voluntary license on commercially reasonable terms for a reasonable period of time.
2. If the importing country is unsuccessful in obtaining a voluntary license, it must apply to the WTO for a compulsory license.
3. If the compulsory license is for import, the importing country must assess its industry's capacity to produce the medicine locally.
4. If its capacity is insufficient, it must notify and explain to the WTO the reason for its decision.
5. The importing country must notify a potential exporter.
6. The exporter must, in turn, seek a voluntary license on commercially reasonable terms for a reasonable period of time.
7. The exporter must seek a compulsory license from its own government on a single-country basis.
8. Royalty compensation must be set based on standards of reasonableness in the importing country.
9. If a license is granted to a generic producer, the exporter must investigate pill size, shape, color, labeling, and packaging of the patent holder's product in the importing country and differentiate its new product in all respects, regardless of cost.
10. The generic producer would need to seek product registration and prove bio-equivalence based on a pill of different size and shape.

---

countries' actions but later retracted its objection in recognition of the extent of the AIDS crisis.[78] In 2005, Brazil announced that it planned to produce a generic version of the antiretroviral drug Kaletra. The patent holder, Abbott, agreed to supply the drug to Brazil at a discounted price.[79]

The threat of bioviolence has impacted the perspective of developed countries, especially the United States, toward compulsory licensing. After the anthrax attack in 2001, both Canada and the United States considered circumventing the patent protection of the drug Cipro – the "drug of the hour" for combating anthrax. Canada overrode the patent.[80] The Bush administration's threat to circumvent Cipro's patent protection evoked a promise from Bayer, the patent holder, to supply the drug at a deeply discounted price. More broadly, the U.S. pharmaceutical industry protested against such threats to circumvent patent protections yet promised to help the United States build a stockpile of drugs.[81] Developing nations criticized the United States in view of its past "hard-line" position on compulsory licenses for developing countries. This policy shift was a primary reason for the Doha Declaration and its subsequent interpretation: if the United States and other developed nations claim that a public health emergency forces them to choose between their welfare and honoring patents, similar claims of developing nations must be respected as much if not more.[82] However, the WTO has not officially ruled on the matter.

What conditions should enable claims of compulsory licensing? Under the latest TRIPS rulings, States are freer to pursue compulsory licensing to address their public health emergencies. In 2002, the United States argued that the compulsory licenses for public health emergencies should be limited to only a few infectious diseases such as tuberculosis, malaria, and AIDS.[83] The European Union offered a much more expansive list.[84] Other countries, such as India and Singapore, have argued against narrowly defining which infectious diseases amount to a public health emergency – any limitation on the list of diseases may limit a country's capacity to respond to a threat through the use of compulsory licensing.

Through 2006, there had been no legal challenge concerning use of compulsory licensing to stockpile drugs or vaccines for responding to bioviolence. Apparently, drug manufactures would prefer to supply cheaper drugs than to risk having their patent overridden by a compulsory license or resort to costly litigation against a county that violates the patent protection. The "threat" of a compulsory license has become a bargaining tool for countries to press patent holders to meet their needs. The situation is too new to accurately assess whether the specter of compulsory licensing under the TRIPS agreement to negotiate for cheaper medicines will prove to be balanced or will adversely impact the manufacturing of drugs and vaccines for responding to bioviolence. The untested issue is whether a country can claim an emergency exception to issue a compulsory license if an attack has *not yet occurred*. The threat of HIV/AIDS is a clear reality in Brazil and South Africa. Can the same be said for anthrax in the United States? Presumably, as to threats that appear more remote, countries' claims to an emergency exception are unlikely to qualify for exemption under the Doha Declaration.

In sum, too little attention has been devoted to how global efforts for promoting biotechnology can have positive implications for enhancing resistance against bioviolence and how much bioviolence should be a driver for those programs. As this book goes to press, a group of wealthy nations has announced a new initiative to prepare vaccines for developing regions. This is an important step forward in global efforts to combat disease generally, and it suggests ways that developed nations can reduce risks of vaccine production, at least for vaccines that are likely to have widespread use. It is far too early to even wonder if this proposed initiative will grapple with bioviolence threats.[85] Until the issue of how to promote bioviolence resistance measures is addressed globally and in connection with broader efforts to combat pandemic disease, real hope for progressive measures is stalled.

7 Public Health Preparedness

Public health preparedness can reduce vulnerability to some types of bioviolence. It would be the height of folly to not be as prepared as possible. Of course, better that an attack not happen at all, but it would be reckless to rely exclusively on complication and resistance measures. Mitigating harm to potential victims is mandatory. If all else fails, we should be able to contain bioviolence's consequences.

Preparedness measures include pre-attack efforts to reduce vulnerability by distributing vaccines and hardening potential attack sites. A perpetrator is unlikely to inflict a disease against an effectively immunized population or try to spread it in a guarded site. Also, preparedness measures include rapid detection and post-attack commitment of public health resources to treat victims. An intentionally perpetrated disease will less catastrophically ruffle a community whose medical professionals can promptly apply counter-measures. Finally, preparedness measures include establishing quarantines to limit the spread of contagion.

Preparedness measures have indisputable virtues, yet serious questions abound. Can they be sufficiently effective to reduce the need for the complication measures (discussed in Chapter 5)? How should vaccines be fairly stockpiled and distributed worldwide? Which targets should be hardened? Which persons should be vaccinated, perhaps without their consent? How can quarantines operate without trampling civil liberties?

This chapter propounds a note of skepticism. Reliance on preparedness measures raises unhappy choices, and to ignore their implications by offering a false palliative for security is disingenuous. Preparedness measures can be modestly effective for preventing bioviolence, but there is no magic pill that will inoculate us against threats or promptly cure us if threats materialize. Moreover, preparedness refers to a bottomless grab bag of things to do that government officials often brag about doing, but dangers lurk in unanswered quandaries and in disconnects among a hectic potpourri of activity. And to repeat a constant refrain: worldwide, preparedness measures are dismally ill-prepared to meet even limited expectations.

PREPAREDNESS VS. COMPLICATION – THE FALSE DEBATE

Preparedness measures operate differently than the complication measures earlier discussed. Complication measures focus on the perpetrator: there should be thorny obstacles to his attempts to carry out his malevolent plans, and law enforcers should have optimal tools to interdict him. Preparedness measures focus on the victims: we want to reduce their exposure and limit harm. Complication measures are primarily the concern of law enforcement; preparedness measures are primarily the concern of medical and health care communities.

Ideally, preparedness, resistance, and complication measures should be mutually reinforcing. Vaccinations and rapid response preparations can diminish some pathogens' utility for bioviolence, which would force perpetrators to choose other agents that might be harder to deploy or covertly prepare; law enforcers would be able to concentrate on fewer attack varieties. After an attack, preparedness measures can abet coordination between health care providers and law enforcers to mitigate harm and maintain order.

Yet, some public health proponents, focusing on natural diseases' real horrors, argue that scarce resources should be devoted exclusively to distributing medicines and to installing early warning surveillance. Resources should not be diverted to strengthening law enforcement efforts to stop bio-offenders. In this argument, the alternatives are zero-sum – a dollar spent for police is a dollar less for public health. This would be an unwise trade-off because the risks of bioviolence are lower than the risks of natural disease, especially in developing regions. After all, bioviolence's historical toll is negligible, but natural disease kills millions yearly, and many casualties could be avoided with even a modicum of resources. Says the Commission on Macroeconomics and Health: for additional annual health outlays of $57 billion by 2007 and $94 billion by 2015, approximately 330 million disability-adjusted life years (DALYs – one disability-adjusted year is defined as the loss of one year of healthy life to disease) could be saved for every eight million deaths prevented, generating economic benefits of $186 billion per year as of 2015.[1]

If bioviolence occurs, continues the argument, enhanced public health capacities would be useful; even if bioviolence never happens, these capacities will beneficially mitigate natural disease outbreaks. In sharp contrast, law enforcement measures to impede, disable, or interdict bioviolence preparations will have no significant impact against natural epidemics and therefore will have scant value if bioviolence threats never materialize. Unlike public health measures that are worthwhile for multiple purposes, denial and interdiction measures can never be completely effective. They would likely produce bloated legal bureaucracies that deprive on-the-ground public health providers of what they need to save lives now and tomorrow regardless whether bioviolence ever occurs.

No one should disagree that global disease fighting capabilities must be improved, whether against disease that is natural or human-inflicted. Here is a *dual-use opportunity*. Devoting resources to strengthen medical response and health interventions will save lives from the inevitable onslaught of natural disease and, if bioviolence happens, such preparedness will limit the damage. In the face of dreadful emerging disease threats, there is every reason to promote preparedness measures – if the rationale for increasing public health budgets is portrayed as preparedness against bioviolence, so be it.

There is yet another argument for preparedness measures: they do not entail profound changes in international law and governance. Complication measures require global harmonization of laws, bureaucratic structures, and police capabilities; compliance mechanisms must be emplaced. If those structures and mechanisms are inconsistent, bio-offenders can exploit the weakest link. Preparedness measures, by contrast, can be beneficial at the national or local level. A community that chooses to protect itself from disease by investing more resources in public health will realize benefits even if other communities make different choices. Globalization of preparedness measures is hardly irrelevant, but compared to complication measures there is much less need to substantially reconfigure governance systems.

It is not surprising, therefore, that the U.S. government views bioviolence as a subset of disease threats generally, eliciting consistent disease surveillance and response efforts. By so characterizing bioviolence threats, U.S. policy devotes billions to drug development and local preparedness while sidestepping international legal commitments to harmonize standards for denying access to lethal pathogens or to enhance global law enforcement. From the Bush administration's perspective, there is a convenient convergence of policy agendas that call for strengthening the domestic population's preparedness yet eschew diplomacy to strengthen international law and institutions.

Yet, can preparedness measures, even if substantially upgraded, keep us safe from human malevolence? The argument against looking at bioviolence as predominantly a problem of disease containment is that intentionally inflicted disease differs from natural disease precisely because the bio-offender has strategic agility. The attacker can choose where to pierce society's preparedness, even pierce it repeatedly. Government officials persistently assert that they can predict risks and adequately protect us, but it is preposterously naïve to suppose that a bio-offender will cooperate by choosing a disease that is readily responsive to medical counter-measures and attack where public health is prepared to respond. In connection with bioviolence, the attacker holds the advantage because it is easier and cheaper to create new ways to commit an attack than to develop and field defenses.[2]

Certainly, preparedness measures have value. There are effective vaccines for some diseases that are easily spread and devastating; of course we should stockpile such vaccines for rapid distribution. For example, there should be smallpox vaccine aplenty. Smallpox would be an imperiling bioviolence threat against unvaccinated populations but will cause only limited harm to a vaccinated population. Precluding a smallpox pandemic by preparing to mitigate vulnerability makes obvious sense.

If there were only a few bioviolence agents and effective immunities or antidotes against each of them, then preparedness measures might suffice. But there are innumerable bioviolence threats; full-spectrum immunization against many of them would likely kill the people we are trying to protect. Moreover, emerging bioscience increasingly enables scientists to bioengineer around even the best defenses, opening vast risks of misuse with ever easier ways to target victims. Given the range of available agents, the agent-specific nature of most defenses, the long time needed to develop new vaccines, and how easily an attacker can achieve surprise, protecting large populations against numerous threat agents is a dauntingly expensive undertaking that might readily be eluded. Simply stated, preparedness measures have substantial benefits, but without comprehensive denial and interdiction policies they are a Maginot Line: unreliable for containing the suffering, loss, and ensuing panic ignited by a well-designed bioattack.

It is imperative to view complication measures and preparedness measures as complementary – each makes the other stronger. Asserting that resource allocation choices are zero-sum perpetuates a false debate that distracts pursuits of beneficial synergies and makes adversaries out of potential partners. It is possible and productive to sustain two parallel agendas simultaneously. The vital question, therefore, is how to impel systems for integrating promotion of public health with making bioscience more secure and strengthening law enforcement.

The remaining sections of this chapter discuss how to harden targets so that conducting attacks is more difficult, how to encourage prompt and effective medical response measures, and how to maintain social order in the face of a bioattack.

HARDENING TARGETS

Bioviolence attacks (other than agroviolence) will likely take place in confined spaces: buildings, airplanes, subways, or sports arenas. Making it harder to penetrate these targets is therefore a preparedness priority. Of course, enhancing building security generally – positioning trained guards and security cameras at entry points and in front of sensitive areas – is useful whether the threat is explosives, chemicals, or something else. This section, however, focuses on two types of measures that are uniquely appropriate for preventing bioviolence. First, there are ways to make it harder to circulate pathogens through air (and less so, water). Entry points for circulation systems can be locked and guarded; filters can collect pathogens. Second, sensors for identifying undue concentrations of pathogens can enable rapid and accurate response. Sensors cannot stop an attack from happening, but they might help mitigate its consequences.

Unfortunately, all these guards, filters, and sensors are porous. There are essentially an infinite number of targets, but which targets should be protected? Major transportation hubs including airports and central train stations likely top the list, followed by parliaments, major entertainment venues, and large (and symbolically significant) office towers. Yet, as most targets will not be adequately protected, it must be asked whether protecting any target makes sense. If an offender can pass one building and immediately go to another, protecting the first but not the second is a strategy of questionable value. Hardening targets is an excellent proposition in theory, but doing it worldwide is daunting. Even a very selective list of high-priority sites would number in the thousands.

Moreover, while some pedestrian devices make obvious sense (e.g., putting locks on access points to air filtration systems), more cutting-edge technologies should be met with a healthy dose of skepticism. Much money is being spent on sensors, but like vaccines they tend to be pathogen-specific and evadable. As to all these technologies, difficult questions arise: are the benefits worth the costs? If so, how can those benefits be fairly distributed worldwide?

Protecting Air Circulation Systems

Air filters can be installed in heating, ventilation, and air-conditioning (HVAC) mechanisms to capture and remove aerosolized agents, but it is not easy or cheap to retrofit facilities. Moreover, various filters work differently against many potential agents. Depending on the agent and how it is weaponized, it might be too small to be caught within a filter. Most effective are HEPA (high-efficiency particulate air) filters that provide efficiencies greater than 99.99 percent for their particulate size range.[3] Yet, because of the wide range of buildings and HVAC systems, no single off-the-shelf filter can be installed in all buildings to protect against all agents. Some system components have multiple and flexible applications, but they work best if custom designed for a specific building.[4] Filters used in confined spaces could have great utility especially in high-profile targets such as parliament buildings. However, filtering air in open areas such as airports would be extremely costly, and it is uncertain if they would protect against various attack agents. Moreover, determining which filters to use and how to use them might differ due to regional variations in building construction or climate conditions.

There are recent reports that air filtration technology is improving.[5] Globally viewed, however, it would be overwhelming to retrofit airports, train stations, government buildings and entertainment venues with effective air filters and maintain them to work at high efficiency. All these considerations do not negate the value of using air filtration systems in prime sites or suggest that the technology is defective (see Box 7-1 for guidelines on installing air circulation filters). Over time, new construction codes can be envisioned that would incorporate these systems. For the foreseeable future, however, it is questionable whether the high cost of filter research and development has benefits that are comparable to traditional law enforcement interdiction techniques and medical response measures.

Protecting Water Supplies

Widespread bioattacks against water supplies are more difficult to do successfully than aerosol attacks. An attack would have to be well-planned to put enough agent into water supplies and circumvent filtration systems in order to sicken large populations. Some experts assert, however, that even in the United States there are serious weaknesses in protecting water distribution systems from a bioattack; better security measures such as installing cameras, sensors, or guards are necessary.[6] Moreover, water-quality testing methods for detecting intentional contamination,

---

BOX 7-1. CONSIDERATIONS FOR INSTALLATION OF AIR CIRCULATION FILTERS

The National Institute for Occupational Safety and Health (NIOSH) has identified the following "important questions" concerning installation of filtration systems:

- How are the filters held in place and sealed? Do the filter frames provide for an airtight, leakproof seal?
- What types of air contaminants are of concern? Are the air contaminants particulate, gaseous, or both? How toxic are they?
- How might the agents enter the building? Are they likely to be released internally or externally, and how can various release scenarios best be addressed?
- What is needed? Are filters or sorbents needed to provide protection in an accidental or intentional release or from a potential terrorist attack using CBR agents?
- How clean does the air need to be for the occupants, and how much can be spent to achieve that desired level of air cleanliness? What are the total costs and benefits associated with the various levels of filtration?
- What are the current system capacities (fans, space for filters, etc.) and what is desired? What are the minimum airflow needs for the building?
- Who will maintain these systems and what are their capabilities?

SOURCE: *Guidance for Protecting Building Environments from Airborne Chemical, Biological, and Radiological Attacks*, NATIONAL INSTITUTE FOR OCCUPATIONAL SAFETY AND HEALTH (April 2003).

---

although improving throughout developed nations, would probably fail to detect a bioattack until changes in disease trends and illness patterns are noticed. Far more severe consequences can be expected if pathogens are disseminated through water systems in developing areas where overcrowded populations rely on water that is inadequately cleansed of microbes. Even without the threat of bioviolence, there is a compelling case for improving drinking water supplies worldwide. The vulnerability of sizeable populations to bioviolence via water contamination only heightens the urgency of this priority.

Sensors

Accurate sensors, especially in enclosed spaces, could be helpful if inserted into air circulation systems. Sensors could detect the presence of intentionally disseminated agents before they are widely inhaled. Such devices are being developed for airplanes to enable early detection of pathogens; in that case, the plane could land and passengers given immediate medical treatment. In office buildings or subways, evacuation alarms could be sounded. High-intensity, pulsated Advanced UV Source (AUVS) sensors are being developed that rapidly sense and then destroy biological agents. They can be placed in air ducts to eliminate biological agents or be used to purify water, but they are expensive.[7]

Environmental sensors can help detect agents in large open areas. Installed at especially sensitive targets or deployed around a suspicious facility, such sensors could pick up evidence of illicit bioviolence preparations. However, weather conditions can disturb their measurements. Other problems include "false positives" – the sensor indicates the presence of lethal agents when, in fact, there is nothing untoward. As pathogens are everywhere, a sensor that can detect low concentrations of lethal agents would likely pick up ambient germs. Yet, reducing its sensitivity risks detecting an attack only after amounts of agent are so high that people are already sickened.

The experience of the BioWatch system in the United States illustrates some pitfalls of relying on sensors. At a cost of $129 million, sensors were designed to detect agents at high-profile events such as the Olympics. These sensors are now used in over thirty cities with an annual cost of about $2 million per city. However, the devices trap airborne particles in filters that are then collected and analyzed 24–36 hours later. This is not useful as an immediate alarm system. Moreover, these systems require highly proficient maintenance by trained personnel to sustain continuous monitoring, and mishandling the devices could readily contaminate samples.[8]

Sensors are most effective for focusing on a few types of agents – typically threats that experts believe pose the gravest danger, but they are less effective for detecting rare or "engineered" agents. According to a recent report, "Sensors would ideally be multifunctional, robust, low cost, accurate, reliable, used with little training, able to remotely discern signals in a high background environment, and would provide definitive information to decision makers and require little special care such as refrigeration or power."[9] Sensors that are available now, however, are more likely to overlook exotic agents. New technologies are being developed to address this problem (see Box 7-2). Yet, striking an optimal balance between over- and under-sensitivity is an enormous challenge.

Sensors' greatest utility is in small devices that can be carried by emergency responders and law enforcers. Every police first responder unit worldwide could be equipped with such sensors for costs that are well within acceptable levels. Although not designed for hardening targets, a handheld sensor can help a responder rapidly determine if a suspected site is contaminated. It might signal the need to deploy personal protective

BOX 7-2. SOME MODERN SENSORS

- The Autonomous Pathogen Detection System (APDS, "BioWatch in a Box") is designed for use in critical or high-traffic areas such as airports, subways, and government installations. Collected samples can be immediately analyzed and results sent to monitoring authorities.
- Differential Mobility Spectrometry (DMS) technology is "a sensitive, handheld device that can detect multiple biological and chemical agents, even in the presence of interferents."[a]
- Surface Plasmon Resonance (SPR) technology enables development of inexpensive, portable biosensor systems for detecting microbes while minimizing risks of false positives.[b]
- The Triangulation Identification for the Generic Evaluation of Risks (TIGER) biosensor system, funded by the NIH and the CDC, detects emerging infectious diseases, helps identify unexpected agents, and may be beneficial for large-scale testing of food products.[c]

[a] Melisa D. Krebs et al., *Detection of Biological and Chemical Agents Using Differential Mobility Spectrometry (DMS) Technology,* IEEE SENSORS JOURNAL, Vol. 5, No. 4, pp. 696–703 (2005).

[b] Scott D. Soelberg et al., *A Portable Surface Plasmon Resonance Sensor System for Real-time Monitoring of Small to Large Analytes,* JOURNAL OF INDUSTRIAL MICROBIAL BIOTECHNOLOGY,Vol. 32, No. 11, p. 669 (December 2005).

[c] Lawrence B. Blyn, *Biosensors and Food Protection,* FOOD TECHNOLOGY, p. 36 (February 2006).

equipment, to seal the site, or otherwise appropriately respond; hand-held sensors could certainly boost responders' confidence about how to cope with suspect situations.

Innovative filters and sensors can contribute to preventing bioviolence if they are integrated with other facets of preparedness. This contribution is likely to be more significant the more specifically it is applied. Hoping for broad protective umbrellas of sensors and filters, however, is not realistic for the foreseeable future.

RESPONSE INTERVENTIONS

Effective response is as valuable against bioviolence as it is for any emergency (fire, flood, etc.) or any other type of terror attack. Many of the same elements of response – trained and equipped personnel with a clear command authority all following an elaborate plan – apply to bioviolence. Critically, the essence of effective response is that it is not reactive; effective response is a function of preparation. Response cannot be optimal if it is formulated only when the situation presents itself. Response needs to be planned. If not, precious time and lives might be lost while isolated bureaucracies try to make *ad hoc* and uncoordinated determinations.

Effective bioviolence response requires that multiple agencies coordinate and promptly share information so that they know in advance who should carry out particular tasks. Many experts routinely recommend that nations should develop response plans with input from all relevant bodies: health, medicine, law enforcement, transportation (land, air, and sea), environmental protection, and the military. Indeed, the elements of an effective response plan are well understood. It should designate which agencies will be needed in an emergency, where these agencies will be deployed, and what their responsibilities will be; private entities should be engaged with incentives and reasonable liability protections. These aspects of planning are commendable. Yet, suggesting that planning should be comprehensive and inclusive is easy; assessing the implications of that suggestion for different political, legal, and economic systems is far more problematic; constructing a plan that is adjustable as conditions warrant is, for most of the world today, a remote aspiration.

A bioviolence response plan must confront three unique demands. First, bioviolence presents difficult challenges of detection and analysis that might not be satisfactorily overcome if personnel are inadequately trained or equipped. Second, if an attack entails a contagious agent, first responders must contain the attack's consequences; carriers – whether culprits or victims – must be isolated to stop the spread of disease. Third, the extraordinary level of panic that disease typically engenders must be considered. All emergencies incite fear, and violence accelerates that fear precisely because it is caused by human malevolence. Yet, bioviolence will likely raise panic levels to the point that fear becomes a chaotic force itself unless authorities are prepared for it.

These three demands can be addressed, and progress can be made, as the following discussion explains. But abstract exposition of rational approaches should not disguise the fact that now and for the foreseeable future, response planning is in many respects a self-congratulatory myth perpetuated by developed nations' officials.

Detecting and Analyzing a Bioviolence Attack

Most emergencies are immediately detectable and understandable. Whether a hurricane or planes flying into skyscrapers, the event may be a surprise but it rarely remains a secret. A bioattack, however, is an insidious

BOX 7-3. CLUES OF A BIOVIOLENCE ATTACK

- A disease caused by an uncommon agent (e.g., glanders, smallpox, viral hemorrhagic fever, inhalational or cutaneous anthrax), or an atypical (or genetically engineered) strain of a disease without adequate epidemiologic explanation.
- Unusual presentation of the disease (e.g., inhalational anthrax or pneumonic plague), unusual geographic or seasonal distribution of disease (e.g., tularemia in a non-endemic area, influenza in the summer), or an unexplained increase in incidence of a disease.
- Atypical disease transmission through aerosols, food, or water, in a mode suggesting deliberate sabotage (i.e., no other possible physical explanation).
- Unusual preponderance of a disease among a large, disparate population, unusual clusters of disease, or appearance of illness in unusual patterns (e.g., measles among adults).
- Higher morbidity and mortality in association with a common disease or failure of patients to respond to usual therapy.
- Several unusual diseases coexisting in the same patient without any other explanation.
- Outbreak of disease among persons exposed to a common environment (e.g., workers in the same building or spectators of the same event).

SOURCE: *See* DOMESTIC WMD INCIDENT MANAGEMENT. *Legal Deskbook* (December 2003).

enigma. Initially, emergency rooms report they are teeming with many patients showing atypical symptoms that natural disease processes cannot explain. Police will not start to investigate until public health authorities notify them that the disease pattern suggests a criminal cause. The inherent similarity between bioviolence and natural disease makes this especially difficult and tends to slow emergency response. (See Box 7-3 for clues of a bioviolence attack.)

Technological innovation can contribute to making detection of a disease outbreak (whether natural or man-made) faster and more accurate. Indeed, substantial resources and attention have been devoted to detection technology in the last few years,[10] arguably more than to developing uniform standards for effectively using innovative technology and certainly faster than the legal codification of those standards. For example, linking communication nodes has proven easier than ensuring that diverse users of those links enter complex data in a consistently usable format. In the United States and comparably developed nations, the lack of such standards has caused glitches and delays. Effective globalization of early detection techniques has proven to be a more severe challenge that to date has received little more than polite acknowledgment.

Law Enforcement – Public Health Cooperation

Police and public health share a major concern that a bioattack will not be appreciated for what it is and that lives will be lost unnecessarily. It is critical that these two communities establish cooperative bonds in advance to mutually reinforce their detection capabilities so as to minimize delays from inefficient information exchange. Following an attack, these communities will seek to identify the source of infection – both the perpetrator and the means of attack. Identifying the perpetrator is essential for criminal justice and to prevent further attacks. Moreover, assessing the means of attack – the type of agent, its form, its dissemination method, and its likely dispersion path – enables public health officials to design a medical response strategy, select appropriate protective and decontamination equipment, decide whether to evacuate or quarantine, and oversee effective recovery.

These responsibilities are overlapping. Law enforcers should understand medical and epidemiological investigation procedures; public health responders should preserve the crime scene. Cross-discipline training would introduce police responders to their public health counterparts. Sharing critical information on self-protection would reduce errors and enable weaknesses to be addressed before they have tragic consequences. In many nations lacking resources, however, this is more aspirational than realistic. The international community should emphasize the importance of police–public health coordination by establishing teams of public health and law enforcement professionals and by equiping them with rapid deployment capabilities including portable laboratories for performing basic forensic analyses at the scene.

Coordination between law enforcement and health is improving in highly developed nations. Some bioviolence response planners, concerned about the lack of comparable preparation in developing nations, are conducting training programs. Most notably, Interpol is encouraging police throughout the world to reach out to public health and to establish bioresponse protocols. Interpol's police training programs are the first truly global effort to connect these communities. There remains, however, a widespread lack of mutual appreciation between public health and law enforcement that could impede bioviolence response and investigation.

Biosurveillance

Health information networks that connect doctors, public health providers, and emergency response personnel with near-instantaneous data about disease outbreaks could help combat both natural pandemics and bioviolence. Databases that receive data from emergency responders should be connected to an incident command center so that law enforcers, medical professionals, hospitals, and medical suppliers can receive near real-time information.[11]

In April 2004, President Bush ordered the development of a strategic plan to guide nationwide implementation of inter-operable health information technology.[12] In response, the U.S. Department of Health and Human Services has been developing a national health security information infrastructure,[13] but the goal of having a pilot program operational by 2006 has not been met. Establishing massive linkages has proven to be a substantial undertaking; there are multiple information systems lacking a uniform standard and format for entering medical data. Local networks have demonstrated success with experts believing that a medical symptoms surveillance network could be achieved soon for $100–200 million.

Biosurveillance networking might improve rapid detection of bioviolence, yet there are concerns that increasing electronic exchanges of health information may lead to inappropriate disclosure of individuals' personal health records. The challenge, therefore, is to create and manage access controls for large health databases, some of which must be classified, that minimize risks associated with a breach in security. Protections for health information should ensure that only the minimum data necessary is disclosed and only to those entities authorized to receive it, and individuals should be entitled to have access and make changes to their own health data.[14]

Microbial Forensics

A bioattack investigation team will have to identify what organism was used and locate its source. Once samples are obtained from both victims and the environment microbial forensics techniques can identify the intentionally released pathogen's "fingerprint." Forensic investigators will have to distinguish it from many pathogens that are naturally in the environment, including innocuous strains of the same disease agent. It would be helpful, therefore, to have reasonably good data about what is "normal" in particular environments so that if a crisis occurs, measurements can be made against that baseline.

Problems can arise concerning the rights of victims (or their families) to resist having samples taken. In most jurisdictions, taking blood or tissue samples from corpses does not present serious legal challenges, especially when there is manifest evidence that the cause of death was unnatural.[15] Taking samples from live victims, however, involves a careful balancing of public safety interests with individual privacy rights. These issues are addressed more fully in the following discussion of compulsory medical interventions.

Samples must be properly collected, packaged, and stored lest pathogens perish as ambient conditions change on the way to laboratory testing. However, because a bioattack might not be instantly recognizable, key evidence might initially appear to be routine medical data. The need for specialized collection and handling of samples might be appreciated only after it becomes clear that an attack has occurred. Microbial forensic investigators must also protect the chain of custody of evidence to ensure that samples can be used effectively to prosecute offenders. A missing link or an undocumented examination by someone handling the sample could break the chain, perhaps rendering the evidence inadmissible at trial.[16] To ensure that this does not occur, tamperproof containers should be used with a bar-coded label, and information about collected samples should immediately be entered into a secure database.[17] Standard operating procedures need to be established with responders trained to meet these challenges. Fortunately, these procedures are well understood and, with the tools of modern genomics, are ever improving in many countries. (See Box 7-4.) These tools and procedures need to be globalized.

Notably, in March 2007, a significant new G-8 initiative has drawn attention to the challenges of disease forensics in the global environment. These eight richest and most powerful nations sponsored a workshop to identify methods of sampling and to consider issues related to multinational sharing of forensic information. This exercise is noteworthy not only for whatever substantive contributions it might offer to improve detection and response capabilities but because these leading States are taking an initial step to augment preparedness in connection with bioviolence and other disease threats.

Containing Contagion

First responders are trained to be heroes, to run into dangerous situations and help victims. This instinctive response, however, might be exactly wrong amid a bioattack because unprotected responders could be

BOX 7-4. U. S. GOVERNMENT PATHOGEN SAMPLING PROTOCOLS, STANDARDS, AND RECOMMENDATIONS

- HUMAN PATHOGENS – *Molecular Diagnostic Methods for Infectious Diseases; Approved Guideline – Second Edition*, The National Committee on Clinical Laboratory Standards (NCCLS).
- ANIMAL PATHOGENS – *The Significance of Surveillance to Safeguarding American Animal Health*, APHIS Fact Sheet, Veterinary Services (July 2003); and *National Animal Health Monitoring System*, Animal and Plant Health Inspection Service, U.S. Department of Agriculture.
- FOOD PATHOGENS – *United States Food Safety System*, U.S. Food and Drug Administration, U.S. Department of Agriculture (March 3, 2000).
- PLANT PATHOGENS – *Plant Health: Crop Biosecurity and Emergency Management*, Animal and Plant Health Inspection Service, U.S. Department of Agriculture; and *Plant Protection and Quarantine: Importation of Plants for Planting, Protocols and Critical Issues*, USDA Animal and Plant Health Inspection Service, U.S. Department of Agriculture.
- PATHOGEN CHAIN OF CUSTODY – *Guidance on Initial Responses to a Suspicious Letter / Container with a Potential Biological Threat*, Federal Bureau of Investigation, Department of Homeland Security, Centers for Disease Control and Prevention (November 2, 2004).
- PUBLIC SAFETY WMD RESPONSE – SAMPLING TECHNIQUES AND GUIDELINES, *Public Safety WMD Response – Sampling Techniques and Guidelines (Participant Manual)*, National Center of Biomedical Research and Training, Academy of Counter-Terrorist Education.

exposed to the disease. Moreover, the objective in most crises is evacuation (e.g., NYPD entering the World Trade Towers on 9/11), but in a bioattack it might be more appropriate to keep people inside. The already exposed victims might have to be kept away from the larger population that might yet be unaffected.

Interpol's Bioterrorism Prevention Program is training police to respond in these circumstances. It recommends that every nation develop a specially trained cadre of police first responders to implement defense, evacuation, decontamination, and first aid. These responders must be trained to use protective equipment; clearly, there is little point to invest in such equipment unless responders know how to use it properly. Albeit rightly focused, the scale of the challenge facing policing responders far exceeds the Interpol Program's limited resources.

First responders also include public health personnel who must treat victims and limit the spread of disease. There must be enough trained personnel available in the event of an attack, enough supplies to distribute to victims, and a plan for mobilizing and allocating resources during emergency conditions. Depending on the agent, medical personnel might have to administer antibiotics or vaccines to responders, but these medical personnel might be overwhelmed with civilian victims (to say nothing of protecting themselves). An effective plan should provide personal protective equipment including respiratory protection to these responders; equipped personnel are less likely to shirk responsibility during a bioattack out of fear of exposure. The protective equipment must eventually be brought to a decontamination facility that, again, must have multiple capabilities for dealing with various agents.

Wealthy nations are aggressively developing and distributing protective equipment, but not all equipment is appropriate for all biothreats. For most developing nations, the public health infrastructure is insufficient to address crushing natural disease threats much less to prepare for bioviolence. Having a variety of equipment on hand to meet an unpredictable and low-probability event is unrealistic. Even in the United States, public health advocates complain that 90 percent of the first $3.8 billion that Congress appropriated for biothreats was devoted to vaccine stockpiling, leaving only $350 million for improving public health infrastructure.[18]

Compulsory Vaccination for First Responders

Should first responders be vaccinated now, before there is an attack? There is obvious logic to pre-attack vaccination. First responders must react immediately and would not have time to get vaccinated much less to wait for the vaccine to take effect. They must, for everyone's welfare, be able to work at the scene. Vaccination not only limits the spread of a bioattack but can assure first responders that, by offering assistance, they would not risk harm to them or their families.

There are two critical objections against pre-attack vaccination: 1) with so many potential disease agents, which diseases should responders be vaccinated against? and 2) many vaccines have serious side effects, and these side effects might be unevenly distributed among subpopulations. The most clichéd suggestions for how best to cope with these objections are better communication and risk assessment. Of course, it is imperative to communicate risks associated with vaccines and to inform health care workers why they are being vaccinated. Moreover, risk assessment is mandatory because policy makers deciding who should be vaccinated with what vaccines are aware that informed health care professionals will carefully scrutinize their decisions. But bioviolence risk assessment is not easy. Among the relevant factors are:

1. How likely is a bioviolence attack?
2. If a bioviolence attack occurs, how likely is it that any particular disease agent will be inflicted?
3. For any particular disease agent, how effective might an available vaccine be?
4. How quickly can a vaccine be applied and take effect?
5. What are the costs and side effects of an available vaccine?
6. Can costs and side effects be reduced by selective allocation to particular responders?
7. Will a particular vaccine have wide-spectrum benefits against various diseases or will its benefits be limited to a single disease?

Occasionally these questions might lead to a consensus answer; most often, they do not. Moreover, there may be more logic in their conception than in their execution. For example, in the anthrax attack of 2001 in which five people died, thousands of people who were not likely at risk of exposure were encouraged to take prophylactic antibiotics (mainly Cipro). Problems arose from the government's poor communication as to why prophylactic medicines were necessary, who should have received them first, and how they corresponded to the actual threat level.[19] A recent study concerning costs and benefits of anthrax vaccine questioned the value of pre-attack distribution:

> [The] net health benefit and cost-effectiveness depended critically on the probability of an attack and on the proportion of the population exposed during the attack. For a large metropolitan U.S. city, vaccination provides reasonable value for the health care dollar only when the probability of clinically significant exposure reaches about 1 in 200 (for example, when the probability of attack is 0.01 and the probability of exposure during an attack is 0.5, the joint probability of clinically significant exposures would be 0.005 or 1 in 200). Our findings highlight the inherent difficulties in decision making about anthrax vaccination. Several factors influence the probability that an individual will receive a clinically significant exposure during an attack, including the quantity of spores released, method of dissemination, and environmental factors (such as geography, wind conditions, and time of day of the dispersal).[20]

A more systemic dilemma of pre-attack vaccination pertained to the Bush administration's plan to support smallpox vaccinations even though the WHO, the CDC, and other public health authorities have long opposed mass inoculation with vaccines that can endanger some recipients. Phase 1 of the plan was to vaccinate half a million armed forces personnel and half a million health care workers. Phase 2 was to vaccinate ten million emergency responders. However, the program was pulled due to political and safety pressures. Most health care professionals chose not to participate in the program – less than 8 percent of the original half a million workers in Phase 1 participated. Indeed, despite efforts to not vaccinate persons who might have a heightened risk of suffering adverse effects, 145 persons experienced serious effects resulting in hospitalization, permanent disability, life-threatening illness, and at least three deaths.[21]

Many medical experts believe that because smallpox spreads slowly, it would be better to vaccinate only after a first case is detected and then only medical workers in close contact with infected patients. In view of the rare but potentially fatal effects of the vaccine, "[a]ny policy that increases vaccinations will lead to an increase in morbidity and mortality associated with vaccinia."[22] An Institute of Medicine committee later reasserted the traditional opposition to pre-attack smallpox vaccination, citing not only the health risks but the drains on other financial, medical, and personnel resources.[23] Further:

> The smallpox vaccinations harmed others beyond those who suffered side effects. Considerable public health resources were used in the campaign.... During the height of the smallpox vaccination effort, a number of state health officials complained that important work, including tuberculosis screening and standard children's inoculations, had to be scaled back. The siren song of dual use – that bioterrorism funding would strengthen public health infrastructure – has shown itself to be an empty promise, as preparedness priorities have weakened rather than strengthened public health.[24]

All of these considerations might lead to precisely the opposite result from what is intended. They may counteract or even negate the advantage of encouraging first responders to participate. Mandatory pre-attack vaccination could induce workers to quit at the training stage. Health care workers such as nurses and physician assistants might resist pre-attack vaccination, especially if the vaccination carries substantial risks and the likelihood of the type of attack that the vaccination is aimed to protect does not appear imminent. Widespread discussion of the risks associated with medicines may also arouse suspicion toward mass vaccination programs among support workers receiving little recompense (e.g., ambulance drivers, clerical workers, and other entry-level health care assistants). More broadly, terms like "compulsory or mandatory vaccination" sound inherently pejorative especially in societies where informed consent, freedom from undue government coercion, and bodily integrity are upheld as fundamental rights.

The anthrax and smallpox experiences highlight these challenges. With anthrax, poor communication and information sharing led people at low risk to seek medical interventions and people at higher risk to be wary of them. With smallpox, the vaccine's risk persuaded many targeted health care workers to opt out of the program. At minimum, therefore, any program of pre-attack vaccination for health care workers must be accompanied with clear guidelines of the risks involved, data on which populations may have a heightened risk, and measures that would not reveal the medical conditions of those unwilling to participate in the program. Also, measures should be in place to compensate for any unforeseen consequences of pre-attack vaccinations.

Placement of Victims

Having sufficient hospital space and other medical facilities is obviously critical, yet it is a luxury that is rarely available even in developed nations, much less in developing nations. During more conventional emergencies, the lack of such facilities might call for temporary conversion of schools and community centers. In a contagious bioattack, however, there are concerns about exposing public spaces to a victim's affliction; the goal is to limit human-to-human transmission of the disease.[25] Health care providers must shift from doing what is best for individual patients to what is best for other patients inside the hospital as well as for the surrounding population and beyond.[26] Infected victims might have to be isolated from everyone else, including family and friends. There is a real potential for disruption as parents demand access to sick children, as the ill who are treatable seek to escape confinement next to terminal patients, as shortages of supplies or space seem (with or without justification) to be unfairly allocated among particular groups.

On the basis of information available during the crisis, a specially adapted triage process would need to divide the public into five categories, those who are: 1) susceptible but not exposed; 2) exposed but not yet infectious; 3) infectious; 4) removed by death or recovery; and 5) protected by vaccination or prophylactic medication.[27] Susceptible persons, likely the largest category, should be evaluated and sheltered-in-place. Exposed persons should receive time-sensitive vaccinations and antibiotics. Infectious persons should receive supervised care in inpatient, negative-pressure isolation. Persons who are removed (or next of kin) should receive assistance to deal with stigma, survivor guilt, and other issues. Vaccinated persons should receive confirmation of their protection and may serve as critical personnel for surge capacity.

Hospitals should deal predominantly with exposed and infectious individuals.[28] Isolating these groups in the hospital could reduce transmission to the rest of the community. However, modern hospitals are not designed to accommodate a large number of highly contagious patients. Experts have identified the need to cohort patients, adjust HVAC systems, and use personal protective gear to protect health care providers and patients from infection. Alternative care sites such as schools and community centers could be used to decrease the demand on hospitals, but these sites do not have the capabilities to manage respiratory support, intravenous medication, and supplemental oxygen.[29] These alternative care sites might more usefully function as primary triage sites, sites for limited supportive care, locations for isolation, and recovery clinics.[30] All this should, of course, be pre-planned. Amid widespread panic, there will be little opportunity to consider how to allocate scarce space among untold numbers of victims.

Stockpiling and Distribution of Medical Resources

Creation of vaccines and medicines is meaningless unless the products of that research can be pushed quickly and widely as needed. The biggest challenge is knowing what to stockpile. For most natural emergencies where victims likely suffer bruises, breaks, or burns, the priorities for stockpiling medicines are well understood, but a bioattack can entail any of a long list of pathogens dispersed by a wide variety of methods. An anthrax vaccine will not be very useful to have on hand if the attack involves a virus. If the attack involves a genetically modified organism or an exotic disease strain, all known vaccines may be frustratingly for naught. Manifesting true bureaucratic perspective, most officials have sought to stockpile medicines that are relevant to diseases known to have been prepared by past bioweapons programs. In an effort to widen the scope of public health preparedness, the United States Department of Health and Human Services (HHS) recently released the Public Health Emergency Countermeasure Enterprise Implementation Plan. According to the plan, acquisitions of emergency medications through and beyond FY 2013 will include: broad spectrum antibiotics; broad spectrum antivirals for ebola, junin, marburg, and variola viruses; anthrax vaccine and antitoxin; smallpox vaccine and antivirals; point-of-care diagnostics for all biological threat agents; and filovirus medical countermeasures.[31] Despite the progressive agenda of the plan, however, to assume that perpetrators will repeat what has been done before is likely a fallacious wager with thousands of lives hanging in the balance.

Even if a country knows what to stockpile, there are no guarantees that it will be able to meet the demand. In 2004 and 2005, the United States experienced a flu vaccine shortage when a principal supplier, Chiron, had contaminated facilities. Procuring more vaccines was difficult; only ten vaccine companies produce over 80 percent of the world's influenza vaccine. Multiple entrants into the sector face regulatory standards that vary from country to country.[32] The United States Food and Drug Administration (FDA) has resisted recognizing foreign clinical trials toward vaccine approval (although European nations have been more flexible in this regard, and international organizations that certify test results are moving toward more uniformity.[33]) Moreover, nations have different market structures for manufacturing vaccines. Japan's system, for example, is almost entirely government sponsored whereas the U.S. and western European nations rely on varying forms of private-public partnerships to generate needed vaccines.

Most critical is that few nations have vaccine manufacturers within their borders; most rely on external suppliers, though at levels that might be inadequate in a pandemic. The onus of responsibility for supplying vaccines rests with the few countries capable of surge production (the United States, Japan, and European nations), and there is no legal obligation that these countries extend humanitarian assistance. There are serious questions as to how willing any State might be to provide "excess" medical resources to other nations if domestic populations are suddenly threatened by unforeseeable circumstances. It is reasonable to expect that in a truly cataclysmic bioviolence pandemic, whatever atmosphere there is for global cooperation will be tensely strained as political pressures rise in favor of isolation and as curing us becomes a higher priority than curing them.[34]

If there is a shortage, who should receive vaccine? Should health care workers and responders have priority? If so, how can such people be readily identified? It is troubling to prioritize persons to receive vaccines or medications, and the specter of bigotry (real or imagined) is hard to avoid. Having clear criteria and rules for applying that criteria in advance can help preclude the view that decisions are unjust. Even so, questions remain. How will vaccine be distributed to priority groups? How will vaccination of priority groups be enforced; must people "prove" their rightful membership in a priority group? What can be done to reduce risks of fraudulent assertions? Is there widespread confidence in these judgments? How will security of the vaccine supply be maintained? Will force be used to deny vaccines to nonpriority groups? These questions have no good answers, but they are unavoidable especially if States rely exclusively on preparedness measures to combat bioviolence. Planning to respond with vaccines is essential, yet a severe bioattack might cataclysmically reveal the holes in these preparations. [35]

Compulsory Medical Interventions

In the wake of a contagious outbreak, it might be necessary to conduct medical tests and administer medications to mass populations. Unlike any other type of attack, there are two categories of victims: there are the people who have been injured or exposed, and there are people who might yet be exposed by inadvertent contact with victim carriers. In any other attack, a victim's refusal to accept medical assistance has implications for himself, perhaps for his family, but not really for society at large. Yet following a contagious attack where significant numbers of persons are exposed to harmful agents, a victim's refusal to accept medical intervention intolerably endangers everyone else. This raises a tension between public safety and individual liberties. Moreover, during an outbreak, authorities will have little time to discuss the issue much less to engage in a protracted legal process to get authority for forceful administration of medical interventions.

Nations and communities have the right, if not the moral mandate, to protect citizens against disease even if such protection requires intrusive tactics.[36] Lives can be saved if authorities have a limited sphere of power over individuals thought to be exposed to a pathogenic agent. The public health concept of *herd immunity* asserts that a contagious disease will less easily take hold in a population if the majority is immune – even an unprotected individual will therefore fare better amid a protected population. Accordingly, for a population to be protected from disease, members of that group must be immunized, and infected victims within a group must be isolated from the whole. To allow individuals to exercise autonomy conflicts with the concept of herd immunity and is particularly perilous in the context of intentionally inflicted contagion.[37]

Do some reasons for refusal deserve respect even if other reasons should be ignored? If an individual's refusal does not deserve respect, what should be done to overcome his or her resistance? There may be any number of reasons why a person refuses examination and treatment or both – religious, political, or borne out of a sincere concern for one's own safety. Forced testing and medical intervention violates deeply held principles of rights to privacy and bodily integrity. If public officials exercise compulsion in an emergency, their use of force may well be perceived as truly coercive. This may erode trust in the public health system and law enforcement during an emergency at the very moment when trust is most urgently needed.[38]

There is a related issue. In a bioviolence crisis, especially one that involves a novel pathogen, the only potential treatment might be drugs that have not yet been thoroughly tested. If so, public health officials will have incomplete information about the medications' efficacy or risks. In effect, their use will be akin to experimental interventions. To compel people to receive unapproved medicines would seem to violate long-held ethical objections to coerced medical experimentation.[39] The rationale that forceful intervention appropriately serves the public interest is weaker if, absent thorough testing, it is uncertain whether the medication will actually be beneficial. Conceivably, the medication might cause more harm than the disease. To abandon the principle of informed consent in such circumstances might not be the best way to protect the public, much less the individual.[40]

That various nations respect these principles to different degrees is an impediment to a multinational response. If a national plan's objective is to perform medical interventions on as few persons as possible, then responders must be allowed to diagnose potential victims to determine if there is an actual need for treatment and to determine if the individual can tolerate the treatment. Mass inoculation avoids the thorny task of testing but is intrusive and perhaps dangerous for some people who have not been exposed to the disease. During normal times, it is easy to say that no person should be forced to receive drugs or a vaccine if it could cause harm or even death. Amidst a global health crisis, however, there will likely be pressures to view unprotected individuals as a significant danger to the community and to believe that treating everyone identically is the best way to avoid charges of discrimination.

One option here is to offer persons a choice: accept medical intervention or be quarantined. In other words, forfeit your personal control over your body or your liberty. This choice will likely be called a protective measure as distinct from punishment, but that distinction might be lost on the person to whom the choice is posed. Due process concerns may arise if officials are authorized to determine that someone who refuses inspection or treatment ought to be quarantined. According to one expert:

> How will the government and health professionals determine if a person is at risk for adverse effects? Prior to being vaccinated, will all individuals receive a battery of diagnostic tests and fill out a detailed medical history to determine if they are HIV positive, had eczema as a child, are pregnant, or have a yet-undiagnosed immune deficiency? Who will perform the testing, and under what conditions will the information be collected, stored, and disclosed? Will the patient have access to the medical records, and who else will have access? What penalties will be in place if the information is misused?
>
> If a person is deemed to be at risk, and a decision is made not to vaccinate, will that person be isolated or quarantined to shield her from the live virus carried by her vaccinated family members, co-workers, and neighbors? Or will those at risk be forced to be vaccinated if the government determines that the risk of adverse effects is outweighed by the greater risk of death if infected?[41]

The legal standard here is not difficult to articulate: a designated, competent body should quarantine on the basis of a reasonable suspicion that an individual has been exposed to and may have contracted a communicable disease if that individual is unwilling to submit to examination and possible treatment, at least until the symptoms of the disease reveal that the person quarantined does not continue to pose a potential risk. Yet application of this legal standard in conditions of extraordinary pressure where there is no opportunity for judicial oversight presents a far more complicated reality. One legal expert offers four principles

> as a basis for the appropriate exercise of public health powers consistent with human rights norms: necessity, effective means, proportionality, and fairness. Compliance with these principles will not necessarily prevent all instances of government overreaching or abuse, but, at least, they require adherence to the rule of law, while enabling government to protect the public's health and security."[42]

These principles have extensive and well-appreciated meaning in international law, but there is little reason to believe that most nations are prepared to maintain them.

Maintaining Public Confidence

Preparedness must also take into account public confidence and willingness to cooperate with authorities in the event of a bioattack. The traumatic atmosphere induced by an attack might rapidly break down civil order as persons attempt to flee exposed areas. If fleeing persons have already been infected, the disease might spread uncontrollably. Moreover, studies indicate that health disasters spawn mass psychogenic illness (MPI – due to panic, many people complain of an illness even though they were never at risk of infection).[43] Preparedness must include disseminating as much information as possible before a bioattack so that the public understands what the response will be, why it will be that way, and how they can contribute to its effectiveness.

Moreover, communication is essential for the plan to operate as intended. Recipients of needed medicines must know where and how to get them, and persons who are not entitled to them must understand why and what they should do. Policy makers should decide in advance how transparent to be about the development and availability of medications. Agencies with specialized competence should handle particular needs and set up a plan for what ought to be done once an attack has been declared. The more that people willingly go to designated medical sites or simply stay within the confines of their own homes until the threat passes, the less resources must be allocated to deal with these matters. The more controversial the response actions – mandated quarantines, medical isolation, and medical interventions such as vaccines – the greater the need for accurate information to abate resistance.

In most societies, communication will be through the media, but this raises more issues. The media is not merely a channel for passing emergency messages to an awaiting public. It is a host of commentators and *de novo* experts whose speech, in some States, is legally protected even if what they say is palpable nonsense. Yet, reporting incorrect facts or pointing blame can incite panic; the media can deflate or escalate that panic whether intentionally or inadvertently.[44] Worth remembering here is that few attacks cause panic comparable to a contagious disease. Said one leading expert, "[P]ublic health is a trust. That's all it is: a trust between government and the public it serves. The media can be that bridge, keeping that trust intact, or it may not be."[45]

Official government news outlets or reports created and hosted by government organizations are tried tactics. They inform the public in a clear and coherent manner. The obvious problem with government news outlets is that they can be manipulated to serve the government's political ends. During the SARS outbreak, the Chinese government was slow to react and was even slower to allow its media to broadcast bad news as it occurred. The same outbreak, however, showed to the world that information promulgated transparently and accurately can be an effective measure for slowing the spread of disease.[46] The WHO issued guidelines about the outbreak and gave recommendations and alerts pertaining to SARS.[47] Notably, the Hong Kong Department of Health website attracted 7.2 million viewers in April 2003, fifteen times the number of viewers two months before.[48]

One legal expert suggests that the best way to balance civil liberties with the public's need for order during times of crisis is an emergency constitution that would allow governments to use extraordinary measures in terrorist attacks for only short periods of time.[49] Authorities would be required to report to the public all information that could be disseminated safely (safeguards are necessary to protect investigations).[50] By forcing the government to produce information, an emergency constitution would allow the public to hear the information it needs to stay calm. However, it is a snarled and probably impossible exercise to envision what that emergency constitution might provide for a truly global catastrophe involving bioviolence.

QUARANTINES

Quarantines are a heavy-handed response to bioviolence. They necessarily rope in the affected and unaffected, the innocent, and hopefully the culprits into a confined space where their affliction cannot harm others outside the boundary. In contrast to isolating those persons who are clearly exposed, a quarantine draws a larger circle to include persons who might have had contact with the exposed, that is, potential carriers. Quarantines add the burdens of confinement to the medical burdens of the outbreak. Says one expert, "[No matter how intelligently and humanely a quarantine is administered] it is surely worse to live, and indeed to contract an infectious disease, within a quarantine than without it."[51] The difficulties of imposing and sustaining quarantine rise exponentially as the number of confined persons and locales rises. Yet, many public health officials believe that quarantines could be valuable tools in some situations. Significantly, smallpox

> ... could theoretically be contained by quarantine, although the time it would take (from 8 weeks to 6 months) and the high numbers quarantined (25% to 50% of the daily numbers that show symptoms) makes it unlikely it could ever be fully enforced.... [Q]uarantine, when combined with other response modalities, could be an effective adjunct to contain a smallpox epidemic. If public health officials determine the risk for mass vaccination is justified, the model shows using a limited, 10-day quarantine of at least half the population that show symptoms while a mass vaccination program is prepared could contain the epidemic within 60 days and completely terminate it after 120 days.[52]

Considerations of a Quarantine's Efficacy

There are various key conditions for quarantine's success. First is early detection. If the disease has already dispersed widely, then quarantine would not be effective. There are concerns, therefore, that a slow-acting pathogen whose symptoms appear well after the initial contamination will not be readily amenable to quarantine – by the time that public health authorities know what is going on, the victims will have circulated worldwide. In the case of SARS where quarantines were successful in containing the disease's spread, it is estimated that if another week had passed, travel embargoes would not have limited the disease's spread. Speed is also relevant to the duration of the quarantine. Quarantine cannot effectively last a long time – the longer it lasts, the less successful it will be. Because quarantine without a means to treat those confined can be tantamount to a death sentence, speedy and secure means to deal with infected people are critical. These challenges can be mitigated by having mechanisms to update protocols as conditions change and as further infections are observed.

Second, there must be a clear command authority with trained personnel who know how to deal with emergency conditions. Quarantine is siege operation in reverse – the objective is not to keep the invaders out but to keep the victims in. Quarantine, by definition, restricts personal freedom in favor of the larger community's interest; some persons will be inclined to disobey. The basic rules of military engagement are useful here. A trained command serves various purposes: 1) it operates according to predefined and therefore likely temperate rules of engagement concerning the use of force; 2) it should have considered and prepared for people's needs so that there is less incentive to disobey; and 3) strict adherence to quarantine protocols will help to isolate symptomatic individuals quickly so as to minimize the number of infections.[53]

Exercise of this authority during the SARS outbreak of 2003 was effective but raised questions for the future. In Singapore, three thousand people were ordered to stay in their homes. The "government called at random times during the day and those quarantined had to present themselves before a camera (installed by the government) and check their temperature. Those who violated the quarantine were tagged with an electronic device that notified authorities if they left their house."[54] Taiwan quarantined 150,000 people for ten days; 30,000 persons in Ontario were quarantined. There was widespread cooperation.[55] It is uncertain whether the tactics that were effective in Singapore would be effective in, for example, the United States where government monitoring and constraint are less tolerated. Further, it is reasonable to ask if a global quarantine system might work if each nation implements particular restrictions that reflect its unique cultural distinctions and concepts of individual liberties.

Third, the modes of mass transportation must be effectively constrained especially where access to transportation is easiest. In the 19th Century model of quarantines, people could exit a city on foot or horseback, or via ship or train. Today, airplanes radically change the calculus of quarantines, taking many people everywhere. No less important, they bring people into hubs even if that hub is neither the origin nor destination of the travel. A quarantine that restricts the movement of airplanes will have monumental financial and other secondary consequences. For instance, an outbreak of a contagious disease that provokes a prolonged quarantine at Heathrow Airport (London) will not only constrain travel in and out of the United Kingdom; it will substantially impede virtually all air transport as systems of interconnected routing break down. A successful quarantine, therefore, involves planning not only by public health and law enforcement personnel but by transportation officials as well.

Fourth, the public must support quarantine as necessary to contain the epidemic. Information regarding the status of the epidemic should be accurate and made available to the public as soon as possible.[56] Moreover, quarantine planners should consider how they will meet the health care needs of those in quarantine and how the economic hardship of being confined in quarantine might be alleviated. Public health officials should be prepared to deal with the general public's concerns about safety and appropriateness of care for those quarantined.

Fifth, there should be mechanisms for redress that can be invoked after the quarantine is passed. A lengthy and widespread quarantine is inevitably going to provoke claims of wrongful treatment, discrimination, or denial of basic human needs. Note should be taken of the fact that minorities tend to be more concerned about quarantines than do politically dominant majorities. They might be less willing than others to trust government authorities and comply with recommendations because of concern about prior discrimination, experimentation, and inadequate public health services. Critically, whether those claims have merit under the circumstances should be decided after the quarantine, not during it. Judicial intrusion (perhaps by issuing an injunction against the quarantine) could provoke excessive chaos and disrespect for necessary emergency measures. However, if there is no remedy whatsoever for mistreated persons, there is likely to be pervasive resistance to authority. The promise of deferred accountability enables responders to fight the disease with minimum interference and also soothes self-perceived sufferers who can take solace that their day in court will come. According to one expert:

> When public health emergencies break out, we need action, not talk.... Because action is essential, courts reviewing emergency measures are even more than usually deferential to public health agencies. Courts do not demand perfect information and will usually support public officials who err within reason on the side of caution. In regard to due process, the courts generally read it into the statute when it is not there, interpreting the law consistently with other laws to make it work.[57]

Quarantines and the World Health Organization's Authority

In the event of a truly cataclysmic pandemic, the WHO has "the authority to adopt regulations concerning... quarantine requirements and other procedures designed to prevent the international spread of disease."[58] *Quarantine* is defined as the restriction of activities and/or separation from others of suspect persons who are ill or of suspect baggage, containers, conveyances, or goods in such a manner as to prevent the possible spread of infection or contamination. In the SARS context, the WHO's support for implementation of fair and effective quarantine laws has received high marks. The WHO recommended specific measures to control infection, including isolation procedures. The information posted on the WHO website received up to ten million hits per day at the height of the outbreak, highlighting the importance of its communications capability for the future.[59]

The WHO issues International Health Regulations (IHR) – binding legal obligations that are a rare example of international law promulgated by a United Nations body. The newly adopted IHR (2005) defines "a public health emergency of international concern" as "an extraordinary event which is determined: (i) to constitute a public health risk to other States through the international spread of disease and (ii) to potentially require a coordinated international response."[60] Under Article 6.2 of the new IHR, States must notify the WHO of all events that may constitute a public health emergency of international concern within its territory:

> Following a notification, a State Party shall continue to communicate to WHO timely, accurate, and sufficiently detailed public health information available to it on the notified event, where possible including case definitions, laboratory results, source and type of the risk, number of cases and deaths, conditions affecting the spread of the disease and the health measures employed; and report, when necessary, the difficulties faced and support needed in responding to the potential public health emergency of international concern.[61]

The IHR authorizes the WHO to "implement quarantine or other health measures of suspect persons" with "respect to persons, baggage, cargo, containers, conveyances, goods, and postal parcels." Also specified are the "core capacities" required to designate airports, ports, and ground crossings including being able "to provide for the assessment and, if required, quarantine of suspect travelers, preferably in facilities away from the point of entry."[62] Guidelines are provided for how countries should deal with travelers entering their countries, including requiring the traveler "to undergo: (a) the least invasive and intrusive medical examinations that would achieve the public health objective; (b) vaccination or other prophylaxis; or (c) *additional established health measures that prevent or control the spread of disease, including isolation, quarantine, or placing the travelers under public health observation*"[63] (emphasis added). States must, however, "treat travelers with respect for their dignity, human rights, and fundamental freedoms and minimize any discomfort or distress associated with such measures," including "providing or arranging for adequate food and water, appropriate accommodation and clothing, protection for baggage and other possessions, appropriate medical treatment, means of necessary communication if possible in a language that they can understand, and other appropriate assistance for travelers who are quarantined, isolated, or subject to medical examinations or other procedures for public health purposes."[64]

Some experts argue, however, that the new IHR insufficiently protects human rights. The new IHR only requires States to apply the least intrusive and invasive measure in connection with medical examinations but not to vaccination, prophylaxis, isolation, or quarantine. If compulsory measures are imposed, States need not accord due process protections to affected persons.[65] More broadly, says one expert:

> [I]nfectious disease powers curtail individual freedoms, including privacy (e.g., surveillance), bodily integrity (e.g., compulsory treatment), and liberty (e.g., travel restrictions and quarantine). At the same time, public health activities can stigmatize, stereotype, or discriminate against individuals or groups. The draft revised IHR improve human rights protection but do so in a generalized, oversimplified fashion, stating that health measures should be applied "without discrimination" and persons have "rights in international law."
>
> The draft revised IHR should elaborate the specific rights that people possess, set science-based standards and fair procedures for public health measures, and require states to actively prevent stigma and discrimination. Notably, the draft revised IHR lack guidance as to the appropriate use of compulsory powers. The draft states that no invasive medical examination, vaccination, or prophylaxis can be imposed without prior express informed consent. This is an oversimplified statement of international law and ethics. . . . At the same time, the draft revised IHR are silent regarding the legal standards and fair processes necessary for isolation, quarantine, and other compulsory measures.[66]

Human rights in this context are not merely something to be protected after there is a biocatastrophe when restricting movement is mandatory; human rights considerations should be built into quarantine preparedness measures. This is borne out by a recent study of public attitudes in four countries to the widespread use of quarantine.[67] The study found that public health authorities need to prepare trusted spokespeople to explain to the public the steps that need to be taken to halt the spread of the disease and to stress the need for compliance. Moreover, as being unable to communicate with family members is a major concern, establishing communication systems to allow those in quarantine to keep in touch with relatives will help to ease the public's anxieties.

In the end, more effective means should be put in place to not only monitor outbreaks before they have a chance to spread, but also to protect society as a whole from any biological weapons attack period. Otherwise, it may only be a matter of time before even the best set plans are laid to waste in the wake of unforeseen health devastation. Quarantines, like so many public health response measures, raise more questions than they answer.

8 International Nonproliferation

State bioweapons programs are no longer the exclusive center of bioviolence concerns, having been eclipsed by threats from terrorists and criminals. Yet we dare not ignore State bioweapons threats both because States have unparalleled capacities for making bioweapons and because State programs can be the source (wittingly or not) for non-State bioviolence.

State threats pose unique challenges for devising a prevention strategy. There is not much to be gained by trying to deny States access to critical pathogens and equipment; these items are widely available. Most States could, on their own, make bioweapons today. Law enforcement interdiction of covert preparations is irrelevant; police will not pursue their own government's activities. Also, State use of bioweapons is apt to be of a size and scale to overwhelm even the best preparations. International nonproliferation measures must fill the space left thin by complication and preparedness measures.

From the perspective of preventing bioviolence, international nonproliferation means steadfastly reinforcing the global prohibition against bioweapons as a threat to international peace and security. It means that any State that develops or assists others in developing bioweapons must be unequivocally denounced as an international criminal, and any State that puts them to hostile use must know that it will suffer the harshest consequences permissible under international law. For international nonproliferation to be effective, States must be able to know whether other States are foregoing bioweapons, and there must be an objective process to investigate suspicious activity and to hold violators accountable.

Fortunately, the normative prohibition against bioweapons is propounded by the Biological Weapons Convention (BWC).[1] The BWC's great accomplishment has been to ensconce into international law the centuries-held opprobrium against deliberate infliction of disease. Its entry into force thirty-five years ago was a nonproliferation landmark. For the first time, a treaty outlawed an entire class of weapons and compelled destruction of weapons stockpiles. It broadened the Geneva Protocol's prohibition against use of bioweapons by outlawing their development, production, acquisition, or retention.

This normative prohibition against bioweapons has since become more profoundly entrenched. Proclamations by a few developing States during the 1980s of a "right" to bioweapons – *the poor nation's nuclear weapons*[2] – have long ceased in the face of United Nations resolutions that condemn biological and other weapons of mass destruction. Most legal experts agree that the BWC's normative prohibition against bioweapons extends to all States, a position long avowed by the United States.[3]

Unfortunately, the BWC has been politically scorned and abused to a degree that is striking even in an environment that is pervasively disparaging of multilateral commitments. (Box 8-1 explores the BWC Protocol and the Fifth Review Conference debacle.) Today, in the broad scope of bioviolence prevention, the BWC has been relegated to the status of an infirm elderly relative worthy of affection and respect yet not really expected to provide meaningful answers to current challenges. As a broad signal of its strategic insignificance, the BWC Sixth Review Conference in December 2006 (the once-every-five-year event that is the centerpiece of efforts to sustain the treaty) generated negligible attention.[4] Its principal outcomes were to establish a three-person Implementation Support Unit and to outline a work program for one-week meetings for 2007 through 2010.[5]

International diplomacy's persistent efforts to erode the BWC imperil the foundation of nonproliferation. Reforms that could strengthen the treaty regime are being forsaken. The larger issue, however, is how to integrate that regime into a broad network of global norms and rules. Indeed, nonproliferation is not an isolated pursuit but is instead a reinforcing fiber in an intricate policy tapestry for preventing bioviolence. To that end, four sets of policies are recommended.

First, there is a deep structural conflict in the BWC's prohibition of bioweapons: the definition of "bioweapon" is increasingly unclear due to the onslaught of scientific advance. A process should be established for continuously delineating the category of prohibited bioweapons.

Second, national biodefense programs, purportedly to promote bioviolence resistance measures (discussed in Chapter 6), are undermining States' mutual confidence that is essential to international nonproliferation. A process should be established that can continuously distinguish legal biodefense programs from illegal bio-offensive programs.

BOX 8-1. THE BWC PROTOCOL AND THE FIFTH REVIEW CONFERENCE DEBACLE

In the early 1990s, the BWC's weaknesses were exposed by the Soviet and Iraqi bioweapons programs. An *Ad Hoc Group*, led by Hungarian Ambassador Tibor Toth, was tasked to draft a new Protocol with effective verification measures for reinforcing the BWC. It faced complicated hurdles:

- Could a verification system produce useful information about the countless and exponentially increasing civilian biofacilities where weapons preparations could easily be disguised or erased?
- Would an intrusive inspections system endanger scientific and pharmaceutical intellectual property?
- Should a verification system address the proliferation of scientific knowledge and genetic engineering techniques that are rapidly changing the landscape of what must be verified? and
- Most contentious, how could a system to verify States' compliance help detect emerging bioweapons threats from non-State violators who do not join treaties?

The *Ad Hoc Group* worked for ten years to produce the *BWC Protocol*, which called for: States to declare their biodefense programs and other bioresearch and commercial pharmaceutical facilities; site-check visits to encourage honest declarations; and challenge inspections to investigate alleged noncompliance. Its completion in early 2001 anticipated the BWC Fifth Review Conference later that year and coincided with President Bush's inauguration that brought to U.S. policy a far more distrustful view of international commitments.

Experts of widely disparate political perspectives argued that the Protocol would not likely detect the few States or terrorists that might want to make or use biological weapons. It was no surprise when U.S. negotiator Donald Mahley announced the U.S. rejection of the Protocol saying that it would "misdirect world attention into non-productive channels" and "will not enhance our confidence in compliance and will do little to deter those countries seeking to develop biological weapons, [and] would put national security and confidential business information at risk."[a] The international community fumed and sputtered; years of negotiations had passed without strengthening the BWC. Moreover, the United States did not present a rich array of substitute ideas, and offered embarrassingly shallow alternatives.

Yet, no one was prepared for the eruption that ended the Fifth Review Conference, perhaps the most dramatic debacle in arms control history. The central issue, as it evolved over the three-week conference, was how to continue efforts to strengthen the treaty. Some diplomats wanted yearly meetings to address particular issues, but the United States disagreed. At the second week's end, agreement was in doubt. The third and final week was devoted to assessing proposals and preparing a final consensus statement. By diplomatic custom, no new proposals were welcome during the final week.

On the final Friday at 4:30 p.m. moments before the conference was to conclude, Under Secretary of State John Bolton, who had arrived only the night before, unexpectedly proposed to terminate the *Ad Hoc Group*. Thus, in a tense conference that had focused for weeks on how to advance the BWC process despite the Protocol's initial rejection, the United States at the very last minute proposed disbanding the only extant forum for considering progressive measures.

A standard of civility in diplomatic meetings often covers even the most heated disagreements. However, when Under Secretary of State Bolton proposed disbanding the *Ad Hoc Group* – effectively abandoning efforts to strengthen the BWC – the room erupted. Profanity was hurled at U.S. diplomats. In the ensuing chaos, diplomats retreated to meet in their regional groupings (the standard organizing scheme for UN conferences). The entire Western Group, including all its European allies, boycotted the U.S. delegation. After ninety discordant minutes, the States Parties agreed to the unprecedented tactic of suspending the Review Conference for a year.

The Conference's resumption in 2002 adopted a plan for yearly experts' meetings to consider: national legislation to implement treaty obligations; biosecurity measures for protecting pathogens; response measures for disease outbreaks, natural or manmade; and a bioscience code of conduct. These meetings did not produce profound reform proposals for the 2006 Sixth Review Conference.

---

[a] Donald Mahley, Special Negotiator for Chemical and Biological Arms Control, Head of the U.S. AHG Delegation, Statement at the Hearing on *The Biological Weapons Convention Protocol: Status and Implications*, The House Government Reform Committee, Subcommittee on National Security, Veterans Affairs, and International Relations (June 5, 2001), *quoted in* Nicole Deller & John Burroughs, *Arms Control Abandoned: The Case of Biological Weapons*, WORLD POLICY INSTITUTE WORLD POLICY JOURNAL (June 22, 2003).

Third, the stockpiled remnants of State bioweapons programs, notably those of the former Soviet Union, pose a unique bioviolence threat. Although a few nations are trying to dismantle that threat, the international community has not been explicitly engaged. This is a role that the BWC should undertake.

Fourth, various issues that have perpetually encumbered the BWC should be sheared away; they divert attention and provoke diplomatic wranglings that ensnare opportunities for real progress. The BWC is an inappropriate context for resolving these issues; they should be addressed outside the treaty in connection with larger undertakings.

DEFINING BIOLOGICAL WEAPONS

Deep within the BWC is uncertainty about what the treaty prohibits: what exactly is or is not a bioweapon. This uncertainty was intended to provide flexibility so that, as bioweapons evolve, the prohibition would continue to be vital regardless of any specific pathogen or method of dissemination. However, in the prevention context, flexibility equates to ambiguity which equates to dysfunctionality.

The General Purpose Criterion

BWC Article I prohibits States "in any circumstances to develop, produce, stockpile, or otherwise acquire or retain: Microbial or other biological agents, or toxins whatever their origin or method of production, of types and in quantities that have no justification for prophylactic, protective, or other peaceful purposes."[6] In other words, all bioscience and related activities are disallowed *unless justified*. The meaning of "prophylactic, protective, or other peaceful purposes" turns on a State's intentions. Possession of bioagents is prohibited if the possessor intends to use them as weapons. After an attack, the user's intent would be clear from the fact that bioweapons were used. But retrospective characterization is meaningless from a prevention standpoint. Malevolent preparations must be identifiable prior to hostile use.

Sometimes, determining "intent" is easy. For example, assembly or loading of a warhead or other mass dissemination device with lethal bioagents is prohibited. However, these clear situations do not define criteria that satisfactorily characterize the myriad commercial, law enforcement, or military applications of bioagents. The gray areas are rapidly expanding as progressing bioscience blurs any functional distinction between manipulating pathogens for legitimate research or for creating a lethal weapon. Moreover, a potential weaponeer no longer needs to produce a lot of agent for loading into warheads. A weapon could now be milligrams of a highly contagious agent in a test tube. Of course, that bioagent could be the basis of an experiment that will lead to life-saving discoveries.

It is unsatisfactory to say that whether the test tube is a prohibited weapon depends on a scientist's intentions. If law enforcers discover a scientist with a test tube, should he be arrested or commended for his research? In Chapter 5, a regulatory scheme was described that distinguished legal from illegal possession of bioagents on the basis of whether the scientist has a proper license. If not, his activities are illegal; if so, his activities are presumably legal. Extending this answer to States, however, ignores that a State could license the scientists who are helping it to pursue prohibited bioweapons.

Moreover, new bioagents are constantly being discovered and engineered. There is no "list" or "schedule" that could permanently distinguish among the ever lengthening number of pathogens. It is important, therefore, to design a process that sustains a capability over time for distinguishing justifiable from unjustifiable items. Critically, for purposes of preventing bioviolence, the distinction between an illegal bioweapon and a legal bioagent must be objective, that is, based on the item's characteristics rather than who possesses it and what their intentions are. An immediate priority for that process would be to address the escalating category of so-called nonlethal bioagents.

"Nonlethal" Bioagents

One of the greatest challenges facing the BWC has to do with so-called *nonlethal* bioagents (NLBAs). The moniker is misleading. Some bioagents (e.g., anticrop pathogens) can unquestionably be weapons even if they do not cause human fatalities. Other agents that typically do not cause fatalities might do so under particular conditions. An agent that would merely disable or temporarily incapacitate one person might kill someone else. Many observers regard the term *nonlethal* as an oxymoron, referring instead to sublethal, less lethal, less than lethal, or disabling. The International Committee of the Red Cross (ICRC) disfavors the term 'nonlethal.' With regard to 'incapacitants,' a category of nonlethal chemicals, the ICRC states (unhelpfully) "While the ICRC does not claim that all incapacitants are problematic, we firmly believe that the absolute prohibition in warfare of all forms of chemical and biological agents is of crucial importance and must be maintained."[7]

The U.S. Department of Defense Joint Nonlethal Directorate (JNLWD) defines nonlethal weapons as "explicitly designed and primarily employed so as to incapacitate personnel or material, while minimizing fatalities, permanent injury to personnel, and undesired damage to property and the environment."[8] Nonlethal weapons are intended to have reversible effects on personnel or material.[9] Unlike conventional lethal weapons that destroy their targets principally through blast, penetration, and fragmentation, nonlethal weapons employ means other than gross physical destruction to prevent a target from functioning. The term typically excludes ways of disrupting an enemy's capabilities without impeding troops or impairing material, for example information warfare.[10]

Arguments For and Against Nonlethal Bioagents

Regardless of terminology, the problem is how to define the scope of the prohibition against bioweapons. Antagonists to NLBAs argue that the BWC admits of no exception that would permit NLBAs nor are there exclusions in the BWC for riot control or for other law enforcement purposes.

> Nor does it appear that any "nonlethal" intent behind the use of biological agents that degrade matériel changes the analysis. The United States' implementing legislation for the BWC clearly places use of biological agents for deterioration of food, water, equipment, supplies, or any kind of material within the prohibition contained in the BWC.[11]

To allow NLBAs, the argument continues, would poke a hole through the normative ban against bioweapons, a hole so gaping that it would swallow the prohibition. Preservation and strengthening of norms against these types of weapons is the only way to stop militarists from self-justifying whatever weaponry they find potentially useful. The fact that technology is opening new possibilities reinforces the need to prohibit any military application of a bioagent. Antagonists argue the problem of the slippery slope: if any step is taken down the path of permitting hostile applications of bioagents, there will be no logical basis for stopping the cascade to full and unfettered development of bioweapons. To ensure observance of the norm against bioweapons, the entire category must be banned.

The counter-argument is couched in humanitarian terms. Modern technology enables development of weapons that can cause far less harm than guns and explosives. If a treaty prohibits the use of newer, less lethal weapons, then older and more lethal weapons will be used. Military leaders are, of course, tasked to use force. International law requires they accomplish their missions without causing unnecessary suffering or noncombatant casualties.[12] NLBAs are far less damaging than the weapons for which they would substitute and therefore are more consistent with international humanitarian law.[13] It is more humane to incapacitate the enemy than to kill him.

> Another advantage of NLWs [nonlethal weapons] is that they provide a military commander a way to take action when the use of lethal weapons would violate rules of engagement. NLWs create less material damage and are thus less provocative than conventional munitions. . . . Additionally, NLWs allow commanders to take the political and moral high ground in circumventing the strategy of terrorists. An added advantage is that they may replace lethal weapons, such as land mines, that are condemned by the international community because of their potential to cause, long after a conflict, damage to the environment and death or injury to people.

Nonlethal weapons may well serve the intended function of such munitions without their long-term negative impacts.[14]

Notably, noncombatant casualties have risen as a percentage of total casualties in armed conflict as increasing numbers of refugees, immigrants, and civilians are caught in the crossfire of civil and ethnic strife.[15] Military forces are often given missions other than large-scale, force-on-force combat. If troops are performing humanitarian tasks (e.g., distributing meals and medical services), what should be done if local unrest prevents them from accomplishing their assigned mission? It makes little sense to use deadly force against the very people that military forces are trying to aid. What should be done if a shot is fired? Use of indiscriminate force is forbidden, but should soldiers be asked to stand by "while allowing the perpetrators a safe haven to keep fighting"?[16] Nonlethal capabilities may offer a way to limit friendly troops' vulnerability more effectively than is possible with lethal weapons.[17] It is reasonable to ask: is the use of bioagents in hostile contexts invariably more objectionable than bullets even if using bioagents might in some contexts save lives? Box 8-2 discusses this issue as it relates to Operation United Shield.

Antagonists of NLBAs respond that their availability might worsen warfare, not ameliorate it. The term deludes the public and politicians about the horrible nature of all armed conflict and reinforces a government's claims for secret weapons development. Civilian leaders might order military operations more blithely if they believe that nonlethal weapons enable pursuit of a kinder, gentler warfare without unsettling displays of injured victims that tend to undermine political resolve at home for military action abroad.[18] Thus, the concept of nonlethal weapons obscures the potential lethality of the weapons themselves and misleads people about how the military is actually thinking about the weapons. According to a United States weapons expert:

> Adoption of nonlethal technologies may create the risk that these nonlethal weapons will proliferate to hostile States and terrorist organizations. Reliance on nonlethal technologies for strategic attack will generate continuing research and refinement of existing concepts. As second- and third-generation weapons are fielded, current generation nonlethal capabilities will diffuse throughout the world and be targeted against U.S. personnel and interests. Nonproliferation measures will be difficult to implement because the technologies and equipment are not unique to nonlethal technologies. The real danger may be American vulnerabilities.

BOX 8-2. OPERATION UNITED SHIELD

The first significant use of nonlethal weapons in modern military history arose in a situation where U.S. forces could not adequately differentiate between threatening and nonthreatening groups. In 1995, during Operation United Shield, the 13th Marine Expeditionary Unit had to provide protection for the withdrawal of 2,500 UN peace-keepers from Somalia. Lieutenant General Anthony C. Zinni included various nonlethal weapons in the marines' training and equipment arsenal including: sticky foam (used to create temporary barriers); caltrops (sharp-edged pyramids for puncturing the tires of vehicles following too closely); flash-bang and stinger grenades; low-kinetic energy bullets (firing beanbags and wooden plugs); laser dazzlers and target designators; and chemical riot control agents. The mission had some success, due in part of the effect of the unfamiliar weapons. Said Zinni, "I think the whole nature of warfare is changing."[a]

Quoted in David Koplow, *Tangled up in Khaki and Blue: Lethal and Nonlethal Weapons in Recent Confrontations*, 36 GEO. J. INT'L L. 703, p. 727 (Spring 2005).

The U.S. reliance on advanced technology and sophisticated electronics makes us more susceptible to a nonlethal attack by a variety of hostile actors.[19]

Types of NLBAs

Nonlethal bioweapons can be either anti-organism (personnel, animals, or plants) or anti-material. Nonlethal anti-organism weapons are designed to have temporary effects that dissipate over time or with relatively minor treatment. Today, the nonlethal anti-organism weapons that raise the most concern are chemical agents that affect cellular processes or neurotrans-missions – often termed *biochemical weapons*.[20] Incapacitating chemicals such as the fentanyl derivative used during the siege of a theatre in Moscow in late 2002 fall into the category of toxic chemicals. However, due to advances in biotechnology and new drug discoveries, the boundary distinguishing chemicals, 'bioregulators,' and 'toxins' is increasingly blurry. In time, the debate over nonlethal chemical agents will likely spill over into the bioweapons context.

More difficult to characterize are anti-material weapons. Many micro-organisms can degrade materials causing deterioration of food, wood, stone, or conversion of organic waste into soil. *Bioremediation* refers to the use of microbes to metabolize waste or environmental contaminants that are otherwise difficult to remove, for example, by releasing them to clean up an oil spill. Indeed, thirty years ago, at the dawn of genetic engineering, the first patent ever granted on a living organism was for a genetically engineered microbe that degrades oil.[21] Now, hundreds of kinds of hydrocarbon-eating bacteria are particularly interesting to industry.

Genetic engineering to manipulate processes of microbial degradation could open new possibilities for bioagents that destroy materials. Genetically engineered microbes can be envisioned to degrade petroleum supplies, to corrode rubber tires and gaskets on vehicles, or to abrade moving parts. Critics question the feasibility of these microbes as weapons (could they work quickly enough to affect combat?), their controllability (might they spread beyond the target area?), and their military value (if personnel can get close enough to enemy forces to deploy these microbes, why not just use explosives?). Yet, these questions do not answer whether research should be permitted to develop specifically targeted, faster-acting, more predictable microbes.

It is not at all clear how to distinguish research for industrial purposes from research for military purposes. The problem is that the same research initiatives that could make many genetically altered microbial agents (GAMAs) useful in bioremediation and other applications might also enhance their weapons potential. In most research on organisms that can be used as weapons, scientific discoveries and facilities can be dual purpose; any difference between a peaceful and hostile use is exclusively a matter of intent.

A specific problem concerns taggants: micro-organisms modified to exhibit an unusual behavior (for example, "glowing" genes). A microbe can be secretly placed on a building, vehicle, or other object of concern; its unique signature can be remotely detected thereby enabling surveillance, target identification, or precision destruction of the object.[22] In more advanced conceptions, taggant weapons could be engineered to destroy upon command, for example, by triggering an inducible promoter system (known as "terminator technology") that stimulates production of a corrosive agent.

Again, characterizing a microbe as a weapon or as an industrial tool is simpler after it is put to use than while it is in a research laboratory. Thus, if motivations are well understood, it is possible to distinguish organic farmers' dispersion of microbes on food crops from a State's dispersion of microbes to wipe out illegal drug crops; both actions might further be distinguished from a military dispersion of microbes on an enemy's crops in order to undermine its war-fighting capability. However, because the actual substance that is dispersed might be identical, it is impossible to distinguish these actions simply on that basis. From a prevention perspective, if intentions are unknown, may the substance be stockpiled? By similar logic, if a military is permitted to use microbes to clean up oil spills and other hazardous waste releases but may not use the same substances against an adversary's oil supplies, is it permitted to stockpile those microbes?

Most problematic here is the prospect, not far on the horizon, that bio-microprocesses will drive information technologies (computer chips) and manufacturing (nanotechnology).[23] Is it realistic to tell the world's militaries that they may not take advantage of technologies that are widely used in commercial sectors? Should preliminary research or assessments of efficacy be categorically banned? The "slippery slope" implications here are enormous. If military use of any bioagent is permitted for war-fighting purposes, how can the prohibition against weaponization – the primary bulwark against biowarfare – be sustained? These questions cannot be satisfactorily answered by reference to the BWC's general purpose criterion.

U.S. Military Nonlethal Programs

It is impossible to know what nonlethal biocapabilities the U.S. military is pursuing because, of course, such pursuits are highly classified.[24] This is part of the problem in and of itself. To understand why some bioagents should be characterized as bioweapons, it is necessary to understand what they are. So long as these agents are cloaked in secrecy, there is little way to assess them. Moreover, secrecy spurs suspicion that the label "nonlethal" is a deceptive cover for offensive bioweapons. It is unlikely that the U.S. military would accept a North Korean claim that it is developing nonlethal bioagents for use only in humanitarian applications without divulging further information or allowing any international authority to investigate.

A substantial amount of the following information about U.S. military NLBA programs comes from a single nongovernmental organization (NGO), the Sunshine Project, based on released government documents. Not surprisingly, neither it nor the U.S. military accord each other much credibility.

The U.S. government has been curious about GAMAs since the early 1990s when a military-funded program at Los Alamos Laboratory recognized the vast number of targets – highways, metal equipment, vehicles, fuel supplies, plastics, and body armor – that are vulnerable to biodegradation.[25] By 2001, the U.S. Army's patent 6,287,844 claimed "new killing genes and improved strategies to control their expression" for the purpose of "controlling genetically engineered organisms in the open environment, and in particular, the containment of microorganisms that degrade. . . ."[26] Various facilities have been developed for GAMA research and production including a significant testing and bioreactor (fermenter) capacity.

In 2002, one response to the 9/11 attacks was to form Scientists Helping America, a cooperative effort among the Special Forces, the Defense Advanced Research Projects Agency (DARPA), and the U.S. Naval Research Laboratory (NRL) that asked American scientists to produce new materials and technologies including genetically engineered and material-eating organisms for use in covert military operations.[27] Notably, the Joint Nonlethal Weapons Program (JNLWP) requested the Navy Judge Advocate General's approval of research on offensive uses of anti-material bioagents; it was denied because it would violate the BWC.[28]

The NRL has a program "focused on identifying and characterizing the degradative potential of products from naturally occurring microorganisms."[29] Without articulating any specific threat, the Navy says it must provide "novel defense measures" for U.S. troops. NRL has genetically engineered natural organisms with "focused degradative capabilities" for destroying plastics, notably polyurethane that is used as protective coatings on aircraft. One type of NRL microbe can "cause hundreds of blisters on mil[itary] spec[ification] polyurethane paints in 72 hours."[30] The NRL principal investigator described military applications for such weapons: "It is quite possible that microbial derived or based esterases might be used to strip signature control coatings from aircraft, thus facilitating detection and destruction of the aircraft."[31] Another NRL group on bioremediation is developing delivery techniques that could be used with such agents, including micro-encapsulation of bacteria. These systems have a unique advantage: because their effects closely mimic natural microbial processes, it would be easier to deny their use if that later becomes an issue.[32]

The Army has worked on suicide gene systems specifically tailored for use in biodegradative microbes.[33] The microbes die when the target substance is no longer nearby.[34] The purported justification is to "prevent their persistence in the environment beyond predetermined limits of space and time," although biosafety experts debate such reasoning.[35] A more sinister justification is that this technology could help target offensive weapons because it would prevent organism spread to unintended targets including one's own forces; organisms that survive longer could impede cleanup or, worse, be put to use by the enemy.[36]

Perhaps most disquieting is the Department of Energy's Microbial Genome Program that focuses on genomics of classical bioweapons and material-degrading organisms. The program's goal is to create "super bugs" to "uncover applications relevant to DOE missions"[37] including bioremediation and industrial processing as well as weapons design. The program has sequenced more than twenty microbes that degrade metals, hydrocarbons, cellulose, and industrial chemicals. At the Lawrence Livermore National Laboratory in California, the Environmental Microbial Biotechnology Facility features a high-tech, industrial-sized production system for biodegradative microbes.[38] In addition, Oak Ridge National Laboratory in Tennessee, working with the Center for Environmental Biotechnology of the University of Tennessee, has conducted field tests of genetically engineered bioremediation bacteria.[39]

Implications for the Biological Weapons Convention

The root difference between protagonists and antagonists of NLBAs is over perceptions of the inevitability of strife. Underlying proponents' arguments is a belief that warfare is an inherent human condition; we should strive to reduce its casualties. Antagonists argue that an interwoven net of prohibitions against weapons development is necessary to corral militarists' capabilities and options. These positions are irreconcilable.

Unfortunately, this long-running and intractable stalemate does not help identify criteria of permissibility that could keep pace with advancing bioscience. Indeed, it has led to the worst possible situation where national militaries decide on their own, usually behind a veil of secrecy, which agents are permissible and which are not. In this context, antagonists' absolutist opposition to military use of any bioagent is a principled but ultimately vain stance that bioscience will inevitably leave behind. The cumulative effect of both sides' arguments is to weigh down the already weak BWC regime – an outcome that is wholly unproductive.

It would be more helpful to consider what the process of making and enforcing decisions about constantly changing technology should be. To try to decide for all time which bioagents and which uses of those bioagents might be prohibited is a counterproductive exercise that defies the pace of change in bioscience. A process that establishes the same rules for everyone and that compels translucency is preferable. So that legal rules and norms can fulfill their purpose effectively, an authorized and capable body should make decisions about their applications. Most important is to shift the locus of decision making from national to international authorities and to promote outcomes that are common for all. That is, if using bioagents to eradicate coca fields is permissible for one State's military, it should be permissible for any State's military. If one State may use taggants, every State should be allowed. For activities that directly engage the BWC prohibition against weaponization, the standards should be global and the authority who decides where to draw the line should be international. To promote consistency, conduct of bioresearch programs without disclosure should be illegal – as discussed in Chapter 6.

COMPLIANCE, VERIFICATION, AND CONFIDENCE BUILDING

Nations will agree to forego military capabilities only if they can reasonably trust that other nations are making a similar sacrifice. They will more likely accept nonproliferation obligations if there are agreed methods to build confidence that other States are in compliance. President Reagan famously said of agreements to control weapons of mass destruction, "Trust, but verify." The BWC, however, in sharp contrast to comparable agreements to control nuclear or chemical weapons, has no mechanism to verify State compliance. Cheaters retain maximum technological flexibility and political deniability. States that want to covertly produce bioweapons face little risk of discovery.

Thus, among BWC proponents, demands that a bioweapons' verification system be created have become something of a mantra. The logic is elementary: there are three types of weapons of mass destruction. Two of them (nuclear and chemical weapons) have intensive verification systems to prohibit proliferation; there should be a similar system for bioweapons. In these contexts, *verification* includes: 1) State declaration of facilities that could constitute a prohibited weapons capability; 2) regular reports about each facility's activities to enable monitoring that critical items are not wrongfully produced or diverted; and 3) on-site inspections of those facilities to verify the reports' accuracy. As the BWC contains no comparable system, the regime for preventing bioweapons proliferation is asserted to be uniquely deficient.

However, bioweapons do not neatly fit the nuclear or chemical nonproliferation paradigm where only a select number of uniquely specialized facilities have materials or equipment that, if diverted, could readily foster development of illegal weapons. A near-infinite number of biological facilities lacking distinctive features could readily produce offensive weapons. Few experts take seriously, therefore, the idea that States or non-State actors will produce bioweapons at select declared sites. More likely, if bioweapons emerge, their source will be any of the indistinguishable locales that are never declared or inspected. Therefore, verification modalities – declaration of critical facilities that must report on their activities and be inspected – would provide information about sites where bioweapons risks are negligible but would provide scant information about where bioweapons are being prepared.

Although expending vast resources on superfluous verification systems is unwise, States need to have information that sustains confidence about each other's compliance. Better information can: 1) lend credibility to States' claims that they are obeying their obligations, and 2) enhance legal cooperation to interdict criminal activity. Indeed, many of this book's recommendations are designed to augment data collection and investigatory authority. Chapter 5 discussed why it is important to gather information that might help detect covert bioviolence preparations.

In the context of nonproliferation, sophisticated international capabilities to track pathogens and equipment and to create a translucent picture of laboratories and their activities would make it harder for a State to disguise a weapons program. A State pursuing bioweapons would be compelled to have a wholly indigenous program lest its importation of pathogens or equipment be recorded. Although not foolproof, it is certainly better than the current situation. Robust information-gathering systems that target wrongful activity make far more sense than verification of legal activity.

Throughout the 1990s, BWC States Parties propounded *confidence-building measures* (CBMs). They agreed to provide information about: 1) bioscience activities including data on research scientists, biodefense programs, past offensive programs, and vaccine production facilities; 2) infectious disease outbreaks; and 3) their national legal infrastructure relevant to preventing wrongful bioscience activity. States also agreed to encourage bioresearch publication as well as scientific contacts and joint research. However, most States do not provide this information or encourage contacts; participation in the CBMs, never high, has been declining. Only a handful of countries including Australia, the United Kingdom, and the United States have made their reports public. Indeed, these reports are not publicly reviewed.

Little political attention is paid to these measures so States have little incentive to report. The reasons reflect much about what the BWC fails to require. To collect relevant data, States must have legal authority to collect information consonant with privacy and proprietary rights – this information could contain confidential business information that might be lost when transmitted to other States or to an international secretariat. The information must be reasonably complete and accurate, and failure to report should be punishable. Altogether, States can comply with confidence building measures only if they have elaborate laws in place; most do not, and the BWC lacks any mechanism to require that they do.

Complementary to these information-gathering systems should be a process for States to substantiate or disprove their doubts about another State's possible violation. Questions could be submitted to the suspected State – a process more useful in detecting inadvertent misdeeds than outright criminality. Yet, this process would be a deterrent, even more so if there were a process to investigate those suspicions. A State that tried to proliferate prohibited weapons would know that another State could compel an intrusive inquiry (a topic discussed more fully in Chapter 9). Granted, no international mechanism can guarantee that a totalitarian regime which intensely pursues bioweapons will be discovered. Saddam Hussein's bioweapons program was not obvious to dozens of inspectors having essentially unfettered powers (as discussed in Chapter 3). National technical means of gathering intelligence must not, therefore, be discounted. Yet a system of inquiry backed by international investigation can effectively reinforce the normative prohibitions against bioweapons. This process should be supervised by an objective international authority. For example, protections are needed if a State harasses another State by raising unsubstantiated suspicions or calls for investigations of wholly legitimate activities.

The Biodefense Dilemma

National biodefense programs present the greatest challenge to building mutual confidence that States are foregoing bioweapons. In the bioviolence policy arena, no term is used more often with less meaning than *biodefense*. Its proponents say biodefense is research on new vaccines and other protective measures that will limit harm from bioviolence attacks. Critics use the term to describe government-funded research into potentially new military applications of bioscience. Both agree that developing vaccines to inoculate troops from anthrax, for example, is legitimate. Harder to characterize is research seeking to understand anthrax's mechanism of lethality. More troubling is research that entails designing a "mock" bomblet to test anthrax and the efficacy of vaccines against it.

May a government engage in bioresearch in order to devise protective measures against biothreats if that research has direct and obvious potential for a bioweapons program? Many biodefense projects could generate an offensive capability, and a State that might truly want bioweapons may try to cover its experimentation as biodefense. By the same logic however, a State might, in the name of biodefense, perform research on how offensive bioweapons operate to determine what defenses or responses are appropriate. Should nations be permitted to undertake research that entails weaponizing a pathogen in order to prepare protective antidotes? From a scientific perspective, that research is essentially indistinguishable from research on how to make a better bioweapon.

There is very little in a pathogen itself or the research that clearly reveals whether the State is pursuing a bioweapons capability or a defense from that capability. A vaccine against anthrax or plague is not only a defensive tool, it can also support development of an offensive bioweapons capability by enabling an aggressor to vaccinate its own troops. The dual-purpose problem makes it very difficult to draw a clear line between legitimate and illicit research; the distinction is often only a matter of intent. Yet, if a State can evade normative prohibitions against bioweapons by labeling its weapons program as "biodefense," then the prohibition against bioweapons will quickly become a chimera.

The problem here harkens back to how the BWC has sidestepped a precise definition of what a bioweapon is. As scientific advances are eroding what little standardized meaning had attached to the term "bioweapon," it is increasingly difficult to distinguish defensive from offensive research. Historically, "bioweapon" denoted a warhead with massive quantities of refined agents that were specifically designed for instant and catastrophic release; it was fairly straightforward to distinguish pure science from weaponization. However, now a biological weapon might be merely a test tube of pathogens that are capable of wild replication or a tiny device that can carry a pathogen through the body. It is decreasingly realistic, therefore, to physically distinguish a legitimate product of bioscience from a weapon and, accordingly, to distinguish research for purposes of biodefense from research to produce a weapon. As this situation evolves, the prohibition against bioweapons will get more difficult to apply, providing more room for States to develop hostile capabilities under the cover of biodefense.

Moreover, it used to be that weapons research would likely be done in a government laboratory, but in today's scientific environment, there is little reason why only such facilities should be provocative. Research, whether for weapons purposes or for benign health purposes, is routinely conducted in the private sphere. In the modern world of bioresearch – where governments finance most private/academic researchers who often perform research on behalf of the government – trying to distinguish the motivations of research based on its location is illusory.

No government should be castigated for trying to protect its people from biothreats. The political implications of foregoing available research opportunities and then suffering an attack's unprotected consequences are beyond calculation. Any international law that would command a State to refrain from such research is destined to be violated. Yet, some States' biodefense activities, although truly intended to be defensive, might appear to be offensive such that another State feels threatened. U.S. security officials are extremely skeptical that purported biodefense programs of some States, notably Iran and North Korea, are truly defensive. Presumably, security officials in those countries share a parallel skepticism of U.S. biodefense initiatives.

The Problem of Secrecy Reprised

Should it be permissible to classify biodefense research and thereby strictly limit its circulation? In Chapter 6, it was suggested that bio-offenders might take advantage of research findings to make better bioweapons. Although considerations pertaining to freedom of thought and speech counsel against restrictions, there is precedent for classifying information so that it is available only via secure channels. Here, the question of whether to restrict dissemination of biodefense research cuts precisely in the opposite direction. Classifying defensive research in order to prevent its wrongful acquisition and manipulation by bioweaponeers could be perceived as something quite different: an effort to hide offensive research.

The more tightly that research on lethal pathogens is kept secret, the more it suggests that it is contributing to hostile capabilities. A State that wants to pursue bioresearch secretly so that malevolent bio-offenders do not gain useful scientific knowledge might pose no threat to another State. Yet, other States might view secrecy not so much as a security technique to deprive bio-offenders of breakthrough knowledge but as a ruse to cover an offensive bioweapons program. Secret biodefense might amplify anxiety of hostile bioweapons capabilities shrouded from sight. The problem is that suspicions grow in darkness.

Heightened translucency is a virtue. The more that we know about a program, the easier it will be to distinguish offense from defense and to understand the intentions of the researcher (and his State). Open exchange of ideas encourages scientific progress and builds confidence that purported peaceful intentions are not a ruse. Yet, serious questions attend any system that might enable the international community to peer directly into sophisticated biodefense operations. The purported justification of an inquiry might be to satisfy potential suspicions that no offensive program is underway, but the reality might be to accomplish the precise opposite by furnishing key information to malevolent actors.

Out of all this has emerged a rhetorical and unhelpful three-way controversy among arms controllers, bioscientists, and counterterrorism experts. Arms controllers stress threats of State bioweapons programs and call for access to information in the name of making biodefense programs transparent. They believe nations should divulge substantial amounts of data to international authorities to build confidence that they are not pursuing illicit weapons programs.[40] Bioscientists tend to support the idea of openness lest restrictions on the free flow of scientific information lead to censorship of publications and constraints on the direction of their work. Yet, they are concerned that broad disclosure and transparency might jeopardize the confidentiality and hence proprietary value of their work; they are therefore troubled by arms controllers' de-emphasis of protection of such information. Counterterrorism experts stress threats of malevolent groups and call for more aggressive application of classification procedures to limit the flow of potentially dangerous information. They side with bioscientists' concerns for loss of proprietary information but disapprove of scientists who propound their free speech rights and who routinely share new research with foreign colleagues. Viewed separately, each side propounds a logical position; there are reasons to object both to full secrecy and to full revelation. Yet, a policy resolution that accommodates all sets of objections is difficult to decipher.

For its part, the United States has rhetorically pursued a policy of maximum transparency. On September 21, 1985, the Reagan administration issued National Security Decision Directive 189 which set forth a national policy on the transfer of scientific, technical, and engineering information. It states, "It is the policy of this Administration that, to the maximum extent possible, the products of fundamental research remain unrestricted." More recently, U.S. policy was described by the Library of Congress:

> Fundamental research is defined as basic and applied, nonproprietary or national security research, the results of which are generally published and shared broadly within the scientific community. The directive also states as policy that "where the national security requires control, the mechanism for control of information generated during federally funded fundamental

research in science, technology, and engineering at colleges, universities, and laboratories is classification." In a November 1, 2001 letter to the Center for Strategic & International Studies, National Security Advisor Rice stated that . . . "the policy on the transfer of scientific, technical, and engineering information set forth in NSDD-189 shall remain in effect, and we will ensure that this policy is followed." . . . In a May 12, 2003, memorandum to all department heads, Energy Secretary Spencer Abraham recommended the re-issuance of NSDD-189, citing Dr. Rice's letter as confirmation that "unless a legal basis exists to control basic research (either by classification or some other means), it shall not be controlled."[41]

Biodefense Projects of Concern

Not surprisingly, it is U.S. policy that provides the grist of controversy. Critics of some U.S. biodefense activity suggest that U.S. military initiatives might, if pursued to their logical end, undermine the scope of and commitment to the BWC. In response, U.S. biodefense proponents suggest that the BWC is sufficiently flexible to tolerate some defense applications of bioscience. If it's not, the BWC should be adjusted, not biodefense efforts. Questionable U.S. government initiatives include:

- building and testing a cluster munition for spreading bioagents (See Box 8–3);[42]
- constructing a facility to produce microbial anthrax simulants;
- developing plans for genetic engineering of a vaccine-resistant strain of anthrax arguably in amounts unjustifiable for peaceful purposes;
- pursuing a long-term effort to produce weaponized anthrax spores for defensive testing;[43]
- secretly operating leading-edge bioresearch programs at former nuclear weapons facilities; and
- pursuing a program to sequence over twenty classical bioweapons microbes.[44]

Concerns go beyond classified military research. Substantial funding has been allocated to defenses against weaponizeable agents and is radically escalating. From 2002 to 2004, research funding for military and civilian programs on predatory bacteria and extremely lethal viruses increased by over 2,000 percent.[45] Altogether, 300 institutes and 13,000 individual scientists have direct access to bioweapons pathogens including anthrax, brucellosis, glanders, plague, melioidosis, and tularemia. On bioterrorism-related research alone, the United States has increased spending more than

BOX 8-3. PROJECT CLEAR VISION

In a program named *Clear Vision*, the Central Intelligence Agency built and tested a model of a Soviet-designed germ bomb that officials feared was being sold on the international market. Hundreds of bomblets were made, although they lacked a fuse that would enable them to work. A related project focused on "data that appear to have considerably greater offensive than defensive potential," such as "models to predict agent distribution and potency as a function of the dispersal method, variations in the source over time, the agent type, the amount of agent and its state (dry or wet), size distribution, environmental conditions, etc." – Infectious agents and simulants were to be used. "[T]he bomblets were filled with simulant and tested both for the way they would fall after release from a warhead and for their dissemination characteristics. To test dissemination of the BW agent simulant, the bomblet must have been detonated, if not via its own fuse, then by some external means."

SOURCE: Barbara Hatch Rosenberg, *Defending Against Biodefense: The Need for Limits*, DIS-ARMAMENT DIPLOMACY, No. 69 (February/March 2003); *See also*, Judith Miller, et al., GERMS: BIOLOGICAL WEAPONS AND AMERICA'S SECRET WAR, pp. 290–296 (2001).

thirty-fold from $53 million in 2001 to $1.6 billion in 2004. The current program includes research to develop medical biological agent counter-measures, including efforts to:

- Characterize molecular biology and physiology of biological threat agents;
- Investigate the pathogenesis and immunology of diseases;
- Determine, through modeling, how the threat agent operates;
- Identify new medical biological defense products by understanding their interaction with and mechanisms of action against BW agents;
- Establish safety and efficacy data for new medical biodefense products; and
- Establish the validity of new medical biodefense products against battlefield use.[46]

Some of these funds are going to construct new biocontainment lab-oratories equipped with filters, barriers, and air-handling systems so that researchers can handle lethal pathogens while minimizing the risks of acci-dentally infecting lab workers or of releases that could endanger public health or the environment.[47] This research might facilitate pursuit of var-ious developments – for example, rapid diagnostic methods for the most likely biological weapons, new or improved antibiotics, antiviral therapies for smallpox and ebola virus, and new vaccines for anthrax. According to a senior official, these "research and development efforts constitute an indispensable investment toward proper domestic preparedness against potential uses of biological or chemical weapons."[48]

Yet, recent initiatives raise novel concerns. For example, the National Biodefense Analysis and Countermeasure Center (NBACC) at Fort Detrick in Maryland has the mission to anticipate, prevent, respond to, and recover from current and next-generation biological threats by advancing the scientific community's knowledge of potential bioterrorism. The NBACC aims to achieve efficient interagency and private sector cooperation with five research and operation centers that integrate technical expertise in biodefense characterization, bioforensics, and agricultural security.[49] The Chemical and Biological Defense program is studying how advances in technology, specifically genetic engineering and recombinant DNA, can be used to develop countermeasures to bioagents.[50] This entails investigating the pathogenesis of biothreat agents, modeling their mechanism of causing illness, simulating pathogen releases, analyzing an agent's transmissibility including tissue culture models, and identifying new medical defense products by understanding their interaction with bioagents. It is troubling that the very same techniques and pathogens that have been seen as bioweapons are currently used in defense research.

The U.S. government has without exception avowed its support for the BWC. Critics allege, however, that the U.S. government's hostility to measures for strengthening the BWC is in fact a cover to hide classified research that is exploring applications of biotechnology for designing bioweapons. As one expert has pointed out, when you "start modeling or mimicking actual weapons, you come into very sensitive areas" that can imply offensive preparations, especially if the details are kept secret.[51]

Strengthening Confidence

Successful international nonproliferation requires that nations are confident that foreign biodefense programs are not offensive bioweapons preparations. The accelerating capabilities of emerging bioscience make that imperative more compelling. With time, the ability to hide offensive weapons behind purported biodefense programs will increase as will the risks of blind reliance on State avowals of benign intentions. Failure to provide confidence must inevitably doom any realistic prospects of strengthening international nonproliferation of bioweapons.

An appropriate policy resolution derives from the concept of *translucency* introduced in Chapter 6. Fundamental to that concept is that no activity that could contribute to bioviolence should be done in absolute secrecy. Shrouded programs inflame suspicions even if the true intent is peaceful. Moreover, without any way to assess these activities, there is no way to hold anyone, including government officials, accountable. Yet, it is nearly impossible to verify the negative proposition – in other words, no reasonable policy could prove that bioweapons are *not* being produced somewhere. Also as discussed, widespread revelation of advancing bioscience's capabilities, while perhaps enhancing confidence about nations' intentions, could readily contribute to bioviolence. In other words, *transparency* could lead to precisely the opposite of the central policy objective.

Translucency policies should be designed to elicit some informative yet nonspecific knowledge about what bioresearch activities are undertaken, where, and for what purpose. Put simply, all bioresearch can be neatly divided into two categories: unclassified and classified. BWC experts have long argued about what specific types of research should be classified and what should be open to public access, but this issue is irrelevant for translucency policies. A better answer is offered by the Chemical Weapons Convention: any information that a government classifies is treated accordingly;[52] whether someone else or some other nation might disagree with that classification is beside the point. By definition, any unclassified research is visible – even if its content is kept confidential for proprietary interests, its existence is not opaque. It is no oversimplification to say that doubts about biodefense activities are predominantly about classified activities.

The proposition here is to take advantage of the global governance architecture that is described in Chapter 9. Any bioresearch activities that a government deems worthy of classification should be confidentially declared to the United Nations Bioviolence Prevention Office. A government that chooses to classify a large quantity of information about relevant research will declare more than if it chooses to classify only a few data pieces; that is a choice reasonably left to each State. The important point is that whether classified or unclassified, the information will not be absolutely hidden. Information withheld from public access in order to keep it away from malevolent actors will be known to United Nations authorities. If, on the other hand, information about classified activities is withheld from international authorities, then there is every reason to ascribe to the State in question an illegal weapons-related motive.

The unresolved question inherent in this proposal is: Can potentially dangerous information, once declared to the United Nations, be kept away from other persons and States? Can it be protected from misuse? Again, the Chemical Weapons Convention provides a strong basis for confidence. For a decade, most nations including all of the world's major powers have declared classified information to the Organization for the Prohibition for Chemical Weapons (OPCW) pursuant to an elaborate Convention Annex[53] that accords classified information confidential protection for an unlimited duration.[54] The OPCW is charged with establishing a strict regime governing the handling of such information "to handle and store confidential information in a form that precludes direct identification with the facility it refers to."[55] Moreover, detailed regulations on security breaches give States confidence that the information they submit will remain confidential.[56] Notably, no serious claims have been made that disclosure of classified information to the OPCW has led to a proliferation risk.

DISARMING SOVIET BIOWEAPONS STOCKPILES

The Soviet Union's bioweapons program, described in Chapter 3, was humanity's largest and most extensive foray into the misuse of biology. At least 50 facilities employing more than 60,000 workers constituted the Soviet bioweapons complex. When the Soviet Union collapsed, that program left stockpiles of remarkably dangerous agents as well as thousands of highly trained scientists and technicians. It is reportedly the world's largest virus storehouse; in addition to smallpox, there are alleged to be stockpiles of marburg, ebola, and various encephalitis strains. From the perspective of a rogue State or terrorist organization, gaining access to those stockpiles or personnel could be an express route to lethal capabilities.

Major facilities include Vektor in western Siberia which produced smallpox (discussed in Chapter 3) and Obolensk in Russia. Facilities at Stepnogorsk in Kazakhstan, and Vozrozhdeniya Island in the Aral Sea, Uzbekistan, both generated antibiotic-resistant anthrax. An American team that visited Stepnogorsk in 1995 estimated that three hundred tons of anthrax spores could have been produced in less than a year.[57] The security of these bioweapons facilities varies greatly by location. Many laboratories are reported to be in poor physical condition and cannot maintain advanced biological containment measures. Many are in substantial financial distress yet have not received the attention and resources that have been devoted to securing former Soviet Union nuclear facilities. Most Russian institutes now have less than 65 percent of laboratory instruments, 75 percent of the needed computers, and only 10 percent of the heavy equipment needed to fulfill various research programs.[58] According to a recent assessment, "Some facilities, such as Vektor, have erected fences and installed security cameras with U.S. assistance, but others are awaiting security overhauls leading to concerns that pathogens might be accidentally released or stolen. It is estimated that fewer than 40 percent of bioweapons facilities have received any security upgrades."[59]

Total stockpiles of biological pathogens are unknown. Similarly unclear are how many scientists have unique weapons-relevant skills; perhaps they number in the thousands. For years, these professionals were poorly paid, generating fears that they might be motivated to steal or sell pathogens and weapons technology. In recent years, the acute level of financial distress has abated; whether improving economic conditions reduces concerns about theft or diversion is unclear.

Certainly not known (outside highly classified bureaus) is whether these materials or persons have already been acquired by States or organizations that want to commit bioviolence. Worries about a smallpox epidemic inevitably focus on Soviet facilities, but the veracity of rumored movements of lethal agents cannot be confirmed. There are extremely disquieting incidents. For example, Iran is known to have tried on several occasions to acquire information or materials from Russian biological institutes. One deal with Vektor was stopped when American officials discovered it and threatened to cease all financial assistance to Russia if the deal was not cancelled.[60] Of course, the deals we know about are the ones that are interdicted; the ones that are carried out covertly are the real concern.

The United States and other western governments have developed cooperative programs to enhance security at Russian biofacilities and to engage former weapons scientists in peaceful scientific pursuits. The Department of Defense (DoD) has bioweapons nonproliferation projects, known collectively as the Biological Weapons Proliferation Prevention Program, that address the destruction of bioweapons facilities and development of bioweapons defense mechanisms. During the 1990s, the United States and other countries established the International Science and Technology Center in Moscow and the Science and Technology Center in Ukraine to develop and fund science and technology projects that could absorb the talents of former weapons scientists. (See Box 8-4 for more information regarding strengthening biotechnology in Russia.)

U.S. efforts have focused on providing and installing equipment at critical sites. Installation of fences, sensors, and video surveillance cameras can enhance security against external threats but are less effective at reducing threats that insiders will walk off with a very dangerous vial. Moreover, the sheer scale of the effort in comparison to the magnitude of the threat is striking. As of September 2002, DoD estimated that it had obligated $14 million to help improve security at four of the forty-nine biological sites in Russia that may require such assistance.[61]

U.S. efforts to help secure former bioweapons facilities in Russia face many challenges. Merely negotiating agreements to facilitate assistance has proven difficult. Nine Russian bureaucratic organizations have jurisdiction over sites possessing extremely dangerous pathogens; American officials cannot work with a single focal point. A more intractable problem has been the reluctance of Russian authorities to allow U.S. inspectors to evaluate security at various bioweapons sites. Access has been granted to some nonmilitary institutes, but the Russian Ministry of Health has denied access to other sites, and the Defense Ministry has refused access to key bioweapons facilities.[62]

Likely, Russian officials are uncooperative because participation in U.S.-directed security programs would risk publicity about a very dark chapter in their history.[63] The asserted reason is that U.S. inspections of those sites could leak information that ultimately might help terrorists target those locations. Russian authorities, reflecting the difficulties associated with biodefense programs discussed earlier, attribute their resistance to allow access to these facilities to the United States' unwillingness to allow reciprocal visits to U.S. laboratories; this unwillingness has fed Russian concerns about the true intent and scope of the U.S. biodefense program. Because of Russian resistance as well as a more pervasive belief that U.S. resources were being squandered, the Bush administration suspended assistance for eight months in 2002. Although U.S. assistance has resumed, spending on these programs is widely considered to be insufficient. Senator Richard Lugar (R-Ind., a principal initiator of the Nunn-Lugar program) has estimated that at current funding levels, some facilities might not be fully secure for twenty-seven years.[64]

More dismaying than complaints about inadequate American funding or that Russian officials resist cooperation is the nonexistent role of international authorities, most notably any authority associated with the Biological Weapons Convention. Worth noting here is that when Argentina, Brazil, and South Africa voluntarily dismantled their nuclear weapons programs, the International Atomic Energy Agency was there to verify and to assist. For the past decade, efforts to destroy chemical weapons stockpiles in the United States, Russia, and elsewhere have been monitored by the Organization for the Prohibition of Chemical Weapons, the international body established by the Chemical Weapons Convention. Most definitely, these bodies have not acted alone, and there are reasons to complain that

BOX 8-4. STRENGTHENING BIOTECHNOLOGY IN RUSSIA

In 2003, the National Research Council initiated a study to set forth a realistic vision of bioscience and biotechnology in Russia over the next ten years. The Committee on Future Contributions of the Biosciences to Public Health, Agriculture, Basic Research, Counterterrorism, and Non-Proliferation Activities issued a report entitled "Biological Science and Biotechnology in Russia – Controlling Diseases and Enhancing Security." This report recommended the following principles to strengthen Russia's public health and security programs:

- Focus on surveillance, laboratory diagnostics, and development of countermeasures (e.g., drugs and vaccines) capable of addressing diseases;
- Improve capabilities to detect and diagnose new, re-emerging, and antibiotic-resistant pathogens;
- Upgrade communication systems to provide timely and accurate information;
- Integrate human and animal disease surveillance;
- Monitor food and water supplies for safety and potability;
- Support well-focused research projects that strengthen fundamental scientific knowledge;
- Strengthen programs to commercialize scientific findings within a regulatory framework that supports public health and protects agriculture;
- Develop improved understanding of the relationships between infectious agents and important noncommunicable chronic diseases;
- Support the emergence of a strong domestic biotechnology sector that enhances efforts to combat infectious diseases;
- Develop and implement effective security procedures at hundreds of facilities that can propagate, store, or distribute pathogens that could be used for bioterrorism;
- Conduct nationwide inventory and consolidate many collections where appropriate;
- Promote broad transparency of Russian research and other public health prevention and control activities involving dangerous pathogens;
- Recruit, train, and retain an expanded cadre of biomedical scientists, medical doctors, veterinarians, plant pathologists, epidemiologists, and other relevant specialists equipped with modern technology and positioned to deal with infectious disease threats.

SOURCE: *Biological Science and Biotechnology in Russia: Controlling Diseases and Enhancing Security*, Committee on Future Contributions of the Biosciences to Public Health, Agriculture, Basic Research, Counterterrorism, and Non-Proliferation Activities in Russia, NATIONAL RESEARCH COUNCIL OF THE NATIONAL ACADEMIES, p. 36 (2005).

weapons destruction has not proceeded sufficiently fast enough. Yet, there should be no doubt about these bodies' contributions in bringing expertise, transparency, and confidence to weapons dismantlement efforts.

With regard to former Soviet bioweapons stockpiles, it is imperative to ask why Russian officials should have the authority to deny access to these horrifying sites, at least without raising the greatest outcry from international supervisors up to and including the Security Council. In the same vein, why should the predominant financial burden for securing these sites fall to the United States (the European Union has developed its own assistance programs, but these predominantly focus on nuclear materials) and therefore be subject to the political vicissitudes of the American budgetary process? This is not intended to be a critique of the important work being done by many U.S. and Russian personnel trying to cope with a potential source of bioviolence threats. Instead, the criticism is directed toward the international community, notably the BWC, which is wholly disengaged from what should be its most important priority.

A high objective for international nonproliferation policy is to prevent the proliferation of already fashioned weapons. There is no more important role for the BWC, which embodies the norm against biological weapons, than to aggressively assert humanity's common imperative that previous generations' worst crimes must not inflict a monstrous toll against children and generations yet to come. All the current debates about strengthening the BWC are trifling and ultimately will be pointless if this central obligation is not at the very pinnacle of its agenda. The fact that former Soviet bioweapons stockpiles were not the pivotal issue at the 2006 BWC Review Conference is unimpeachable testimony to the attending diplomats' irrelevance.

TWO ISSUES FOR REMOVAL

Two issues that have traditionally been considered as within the purview of the BWC have never been satisfactorily addressed: How should policies to advance the free exchange of bioscience be balanced with the BWC's nonproliferation imperative? and; Should there be established a global authority structure directly in connection with the BWC? Failure to make progress on these issues over the passage of years has propounded a sense of diplomatic failure, all the more so because these issues carry important implications. Indeed, those implications are so important that they should be lifted out of the BWC to be pillars of the global governance architecture that is discussed in Chapter 9.

Protecting the Free Trade in Bioscience

The issue of incentives for developing States has inflamed BWC debates. BWC Article X allows parties to participate freely in the exchange of bioscience equipment, materials, and information for peaceful purposes. Many developing States argue that developed States' export restrictions on biotechnology are therefore prohibited. The real controversy surrounds the "Australia Group," an alliance of thirty-nine developed nations plus the European Commission to enforce common export controls for dangerous items. Developing States claim it is a cartel for limiting access to lucrative technology in violation of BWC Article X.[65] Developed States, including the United States, assert that the BWC's prohibition against bioweapons proliferation supersedes Article X's weakly stated preference for bioscience's unrestricted spread. This debate has evolved into an arcane tussle over treaty terminology and interpretation of little interest to anyone other than the diplomats whose living depends on arguing about it.

The truly important controversy, discussed throughout much of this book, is how to promote the global spread of bioscience and the free trade in advancing biotechnology consistently with preventing the proliferation of bioweapons capabilities. This is complicated. Much of Chapter 9's proposal for establishing oversight and assistance bodies in the United Nations is devoted to addressing this issue. It suffices to say the BWC – a treaty that is predominantly a set of normative commitments lacking enforcement mechanisms – is altogether unsuited to make progress on such multifaceted and nuanced matters. What should be clear is that Article X is too simplistic to integrate the aspirations for free trade in bioscience with the treaty's basic purpose of prohibiting proliferation of bioweapons. In fact, Article X actually requires no one to do anything; it is an empty provision. Unquestionably, the global expansion of peaceful bioscience for development is a fundamental pillar of the bioviolence prevention strategy, but the BWC is ill-suited to sustain a development agenda that far exceeds its scope or mandate.

A Global BWC Organization

An even more longstanding debate has centered on whether a BWC organization should be created. Certainly, a global authority structure for preventing bioviolence is needed. The argument for building that structure around the BWC is that both the treaty prohibiting proliferation of nuclear weapons (the Nuclear Nonproliferation Treaty) and the treaty prohibiting proliferation of chemical weapons (the Chemical Weapons Convention) have authority structures (respectively, the International Atomic Energy Agency and the Organization for the Prohibition of Chemical Weapons). But this argument ignores the countless reasons why threats of bioviolence are different than threats of nuclear or chemical weapons proliferation. The need for an authority structure for preventing bioviolence has metastasized far beyond the BWC's scope. More systemic United Nations governance is needed as will be discussed in Chapter 9.

International investigative capabilities are necessary, but this is more sensitive than the BWC can manage. The BWC requires consultations when there are doubts about a State's compliance and submission of a complaint against a violator to the UN Security Council, but this nebulous process has never been used. The only formal accusation of a BWC violation involved a Cuban accusation that the United States attacked it with insects dropped from an aircraft – a charge that is discounted by experts.[66] Recently, senior diplomats have hurled accusations of covert bioweapons programs, yet no one has seen fit to use the BWC process to judge alleged perpetrators. These allegations – mostly from American intelligence sources and diplomats – should be investigated through a far more elaborate legal process that will also be discussed in Chapter 9. Until that process is established, diplomatic allegations about bioweapons proliferation are unresolvable.

In brief, effective nonproliferation is essential to bioviolence prevention; strengthening the BWC is imperative. The thesis here is that the BWC should focus on the three issues that nonproliferation mechanisms can contribute to resolving: How should bioweapons be defined? How should States build mutual confidence that they are not making bioweapons? and How should dismantlement and destruction of weapons stockpiles be verified? Issues concerning the free trade in bioscience and concerning the establishment of a bioviolence prevention organization deserve enormous attention as discussed shortly. Right now, the BWC is in jeopardy that, in turn, jeopardizes nonproliferation efforts generally. Selective progress can and should be pursued immediately.

9 The Challenge of Global Governance

Throughout this book is a persistent plea to establish a global governance architecture for preventing bioviolence – its absence induces policy inertia. It is difficult to envision how prevention policies can advance without some entity to make decisions, supervise their implementation, and monitor compliance. Identifying who or what should undertake those responsibilities is a crucial challenge for international law.

To make this challenge manageable, a useful admonition is that form follows mission.

GOVERNANCE MISSION: THE GLOBAL COVENANT

Nearly one million children under the age of five died last month, mostly in developing countries. Most of these deaths were due to malnutrition or diseases that are readily preventable.[1] Next month, another million children will die. The month after ... In some developing countries, average life expectancy is sinking below forty years; in developed countries it is rising above eighty.[2]

In contrast to these appalling statistics is the undeniable fact that preventing bioviolence is expensive. States must enact new regulatory laws, equip and train police, implement and enforce controls on pathogens and laboratories, facilitate development of and access to vaccines, and empower the domestic penal system to detect and prosecute behavior designed to cause catastrophic harm. Large quantities of information must be gathered and analyzed by trained officials. First responders and public health networks need to be prepared. All these systems must be linked to counterparts in other States and to relevant international organizations. Arrays of secondary systems should be established, from whistle-blowing and anticorruption mechanisms, to making biodefense capabilities translucent, to assigning diplomats to represent the State's interests in multilateral arenas.

From the perspective of many economically developing States, meeting all these obligations presents herculean challenges that will strain bureaucratic attention even if everything proceeds smoothly. If things get muddled, the costs of enforcing compliance and ironing out disputes will be substantial. Moreover, extensive regulations designed to deny access to pathogens or critical equipment might forestall the anticipated benefits of pharmaceutical development or basic bioresearch. For developing nations' policy makers trying to cope with malaria, AIDS, tuberculosis, and other maladies, a legitimate question of priorities arises when developed nations propound dreadful bioviolence scenarios. Where mass public health challenges are daily phenomena, the risks of terrorists using pathogens have to be weighed against more tangible threats from nature.

Simply stated, it is illegitimate to discuss policies for preventing human-inflicted disease without acknowledging the *silent genocide*[3] that is responsible for so many deaths from natural disease. But neither is it legitimate to view bioviolence threats as distractions from efforts to combat natural disease and therefore to put off beneficial measures until those afflictions are defeated. To do so would leave developing nations wholly vulnerable to a deliberate attack. More generally, this view frustrates forward movement even on limited and cost-effective initiatives that could help build an international security framework for advancing science and health.

The essence of the governance mission for bioviolence prevention, therefore, is that preventing bioviolence must be a facet of a broad international commitment to: 1) prevent the spread of disease (e.g., public health); 2) enhance protection against and cures for disease (e.g., vaccination and drug therapies); 3) supervise the conduct of biological science and; 4) criminalize unauthorized or improper use of pathogens. Once bioviolence prevention is seen in this larger context, and once the inherent and unavoidable global character of disease challenges are appreciated, decisions about how to allocate responsibilities and opportunities can be rationally considered. In this context, bioviolence prevention measures need not siphon resources from other priorities but are instead critical cords in the fabric of humanity's pursuit of security and scientific development.

From this foundation should flow a policy commitment to the growth of bioscience as a global public good, and policies to encourage its worldwide spread deserve support. Bioscience's advance is extremely important to meeting many of humanity's most essential needs, and it can be an accelerator for economic development.[4] It has become an increasingly important component in the United Nations' development activities and, by implication, intricately intertwined with international security.[5] The UN Millennium Project's Task Force on Science, Technology, and Innovation has identified emerging bioscience as a powerful tool in meeting global challenges posed by food insecurity, industrial underdevelopment, environmental degradation, and disease. Bioscience provides opportunities for training scientists, stimulates foreign investment, and can be commercially profitable.[6] Future synergies among nanotechnology, biotechnology, information technology, and cognitive science offer multiplying opportunities. Accordingly, the United Nations General Assembly has urged international bodies engaged in bioscience to work cooperatively and has called for an integrated framework to promote bioscience development within the United Nations system.[7] According to the Organization for Economic Cooperation and Development:

> [B]ioscience has the potential to enable better outcomes for health, the environment, and for industrial, agricultural, and energy production.
>
> Innovative products and services with improved economic and environmental performance will draw on renewable resources and biological processes to meet the needs of society. If delivered successfully, they have the potential to help decouple industrial growth from environmental degradation and deliver a more resilient, more biobased economy, less susceptible to uncontrollable global events and less dependent on large-scale distribution systems.
>
> Life science research and biotechnology also promise more effective and efficient products to help deliver better health, whether in developed or developing countries, that are based on a fuller understanding of the human body and its ailments and diseases and of the interventions required to deal with them. These products can deliver on two vital and inextricably linked goals – improved health and more sustainable growth and development.[8]

Yet, bioscience carries an inexorable potential for catastrophe. Respect for policies to prevent that harm is a humanity-wide obligation. The commitment to encourage the global spread of bioscience should be fused, therefore, with an obligation to undertake bioscientific activities according to standards that appreciate those activities' unfortunate potential for wreaking disaster. With opportunities and encouragement necessarily comes responsibility – no matter how great the need, no one should be able to obtain benefits by ignoring risks. As will be discussed, gaping disparities of resources and capacities are relevant to decisions as to how to allocate burdens. Those disparities should not, however, be cited to excuse disregard or even delay in implementing reasonable measures to prevent malevolent use of pathogens.

The governance mission should thus be conceived as a global covenant. All communities must strive to prevent bioviolence, and all communities must strive to promote bioscience as a fundamental pillar of humanity's progress. Responsibilities should be common to all, even as the burdens associated with those responsibilities are differentiated according to wealth and capability – a well-recognized precept of international law in general. From everyone according to their abilities; to all for the benefit of all.

Accordingly, communities that embrace responsible bioviolence prevention measures should receive support for developing bioscience. Resources should flow to communities that manifest their compliance with bioviolence prevention measures, thereby accelerating the globalization of responsible science that, among other virtues, is key to early detection of bioviolence preparations. Willingness to abide by international standards for securing pathogens and labs, strengthening police, preparing for outbreak response, and nonproliferation should bring tangible benefits. These benefits could include: assistance for universities and centers of bioscience excellence; investment in indigenous biotechnology; access to bioscience information networks; and expansion of capabilities to produce vaccines and therapeutics for infectious diseases. These partnerships should be recognized by international development and funding institutions including the World Bank and its regional counterparts.

If that undertaking cannot be sustained for lack of capacity, then assistance should be forthcoming. If, however, a community disregards its obligations or bypasses opportunities for assistance as needed, then that community necessarily signals its unjustifiable rejection of the global covenant and should be denied access to those benefits.

The interwoven and sometimes competing considerations that have been discussed throughout this book – the ubiquity and undetectability of pathogens, the shared vulnerability of humanity to disease, and the global interactivity of bioscience – all suggest that preventing bioviolence is a shared human endeavor, demanding a shared human response through shared institutions. Thus, the global covenant that is the governance mission decrees the commonality of the human species' most basic and most long-lasting struggle against lethal microbes and offers a new vision of how to harmonize the advance of bioscience, development, and security.

GOVERNANCE AGENCIES

The governance architecture must be global with legitimate authority that is commensurate with the gravity of bioviolence threats. It should serve, fundamentally, to coordinate disparate organizations and professional disciplines. Bioviolence prevention is not the responsibility of only scientists or only police. It is implausible, however, that scientists, law enforcers, and other professional disciplines will reach across their different perspectives by merely a spirit of solidarity.

In parallel, the governance architecture must enable worldwide coordination of the State authorities and international organizations. It would be simplistic to propose that all nations should come together in a spirit of diplomatic harmony for advancing so many complex policies. Nations have critical roles, but it is far-fetched to believe that much progress can be made without a global body that designs goals and obligations, gathers information, builds capacity, and enforces compliance. By the same logic, to expect the more than thirty international organizations that have relevant responsibilities, led by Interpol and the World Health Organization, to seamlessly harmonize their standards and missions without explicit direction is naive. Each of these organizations has a demarcated mandate, and interweaving disparate bureaucracies with separate agendas and sustaining coordination over time is not realistic. Looming over all States and organizations is the larger question of who should address the hardest cases – who should wield enforcement power if there are actual suspicions of bioviolence preparations or, worse, a bioviolence attack.

These two coordination roles – among professional communities and among States and international organizations – are something of a double helix. They wind around each other with virtually infinite linkages that mutate over time. Ultimately, this is why policies for preventing bioviolence are so complicated and have proceeded so unproductively.

It is proposed, therefore, that critical coordination responsibilities for bioviolence prevention be executed by three new bodies within the United Nations: 1) a Commission on Bioscience and Security (*Commission*); 2) a Bioviolence Prevention Office (*Office*) within the United Nations Secretariat; and 3) a Bioviolence Committee of the Security Council (*Security Council Committee*).

The *Commission* should promote secure bioscience worldwide and assist countries to use bioscience consistent with policies for preventing bioviolence. It should be designed to stimulate bioscience development by incorporating security concerns into the fabric of scientific undertakings, embodying the principle that science, development, and security can and must be mutually reinforcing. Its primary responsibilities would be to promote and distribute knowledge and, along with the *Office*, build capacity to fulfill obligations, especially in developing nations.

The *Office* within the UN Secretariat should be the fulcrum of coordination among the relevant parts of the United Nations system as well as other international/regional organizations, professional networks, and expert bodies. It should supervise long-term bioviolence prevention strategies, yet it should have no power in and of itself. It will be the steering mechanism to coordinate many organizations that have specialized expertise but that infrequently work together on their own initiative. Its primary functions would be to harmonize rules from these organizations and to gather and analyze data about compliance.

These cooperative functions must be separated from investigatory and response activities concerning bioviolence preparation or attack. Situations that call for investigation or response arise rarely but carry disproportionate significance for international peace and security. The *Security Council Committee*, therefore, should pursue and investigate biothreats and coordinate assistance following a bioviolence attack. It should not advance programmatic agendas, but it should wield expertise and political muscle in volatile situations. Its primary mission would be to enable the Security Council to sustain global order in the face of a bioviolence challenge.

Placing governance responsibilities in the United Nations is consistent with its recent pronouncements. The United Nations High-level Panel on Threats, Challenges and Change[9] recommended a global strategy for international peace and security based on: dissuading people from resorting to terrorism and violence, denying capabilities to carry out attacks, deterrence, developing capacity to defeat terrorism, and defending human rights. The Panel recognized that disease, hunger, and environmental degradation are inextricably linked to security. This recognition built upon the eight United Nations Millennium Development Goals for eradicating poverty and hunger, combating disease, and ensuring environmental sustainability.[10] The eighth goal is to establish a global partnership for achieving these objectives. Said then-Secretary General Annan, "What is common to all of these elements is the indispensability of the rule of law, nationally and internationally."[11]

A cautionary comment must be offered. Creating new offices and committees within the United Nations will accomplish nothing absent political commitment and resources to carry out that commitment. Clearly, adding to the United Nations bureaucracy will not, in and of itself, lessen global biothreats.

This chapter makes the inverse argument: essential political commitments and resources are far harder to mobilize if policy makers lack a vision of how to usefully allocate them. Indeed, one part of the problem in addressing bioviolence is that, while some policy makers appreciate the threat and are willing to take action, they lack architecture for how policy pieces might be synchronized. This chapter, therefore, does not prescribe three United Nations bodies as the "solution" for preventing bioviolence, but if there are committed leaders who agree that bioviolence prevention is a challenge that must be met, it is useful to specify realistic plans for how to put ideas and initiatives into operation.

The United Nations Commission on Bioscience and Security (*Commission*)

The *Commission* should undertake the largest and most visibly active part of bioviolence prevention. Standing at the junction of the global bioscience community and States, it would assist developing countries to take advantage of bioscience. It also would follow legal, scientific, and technical developments relating to bioscience and technology in order to advise States, international organizations, and other United Nations offices. Its three programmatic components would be to promote bioscience, to define standards for the conduct of bioscience, and to increase national capacity for developing bioscience.

Promote Bioscience Research

The *Commission's* highest priorities would be to define strategies for coping with critical bioscience policy issues and to frame perspectives of key constituencies. Accordingly, the *Commission* would be the world's primary body responsible for upholding a right to bioscience development and promoting its sustainable and peaceful uses. It would do so by stimulating research and identifying promotional strategies and by arranging for technical advisory services especially in States with emerging bioscience sectors.

The *Commission* need not undertake primary research, but it could usefully coordinate various UN institutes that do research on relevant concerns such as economic planning and information management. It could work, for example, with various United Nations research institutes that are deeply engaged in analyses of social development issues (the Research Institute for Social Development), that contribute to international security and disarmament initiatives (the Institute for Disarmament Research), and that undertake genetic engineering training and research (the Institute for Genetic Engineering and Biotechnology). The *Commission* would thereby highlight the significance of some types of inquiries and help shape social perception of new discoveries and applications. By distributing the products of research, it would help equalize global information asymmetries. This process has a multiplier effect: disseminating knowledge stimulates extensive interaction which catalyzes experimentation that evokes new knowledge.

The *Commission* should configure channels for exchanging bioscience knowledge. It should prepare and distribute reports on international bioscience activities and on international law pertaining to bioscience. An important implication here is that State and international officials who need to understand critical matters of bioviolence prevention policy typically have other responsibilities in other issue arenas; they will inevitably turn to internationally respected and neutral bioviolence experts when an issue in this domain arises. The *Commission* plays a particularly strong role here by credentialing "experts" to provide critical knowledge. Thus, by structuring research priorities, the *Commission*, albeit drawing formal authority from States and other organizations, could become the locus of power within its issue purview.

A key quandary will be determining how nongovernmental sources can contribute perspectives. There are strong virtues to encouraging such contributions, but the *Commission* must be selective as well as inclusive; input from irresponsible sources could impede the *Commission's* mission. Rules of procedure, therefore, should govern how expertise is admitted. Equitable geographical representation, different trends of thought, and varying degrees of development should all be taken in account. This should be compatible with formal processes to encourage expert and public participation that are a growing feature of international law. The Convention on Access to Information, Public Participation in Decision Making and Access to Justice in Environmental Affairs demonstrates how to usefully enable public participation in the decision making processes of States and of international organizations.[12] An analogy here is to the World Health Organization's (WHO) "Regulations for Expert Advisory Panels and Committees" that limits how many experts may participate in discussions on a given subject while obtaining relevant input from diverse branches of knowledge and local experience.[13]

To enable global communication of scientific and technical issues, the *Commission* should supervise a Scientific and Technical Advisors' Network that has the following responsibilities:

- To review reports or agreements by other organizations on bioscience and collate that information into an accessible database; and,
- To act as a forum to bring together scientists and technical experts in order to facilitate delivery of advice and assistance on how to address scientific developments that may pose a risk.

Another important function of the *Commission* will be to establish a Global Resource Center for Bioviolence Prevention that would be a library of manuals, training materials, scholarly papers, and reports for States and expert researchers. The Center could help distribute information and materials worldwide and provide analyses of these documents for useful application to new issues and controversies.

Define Standards for Bioscience

To the minimal extent that bioscience needs to be "governed" – for example, developing standards for research having uniquely dangerous implications – the *Commission* should undertake relevant responsibilities. The *Commission* should be the nucleus of bioscience policy formulation, prescribing ways to promote sustainable bioscience development that incorporate policies to prevent bioviolence. In that context, it would work closely with development institutions (e.g., the World Bank, UNESCO, UNDP, etc.) to ensure that those institutions appropriately understand how their activities affect bioviolence prevention.

Thus, the *Commission* should define and prioritize tasks to be performed by governments and other organizations. As the world's principal disseminator of bioscience knowledge, the *Commission* would also be responsible for restricting access to that knowledge. As discussed in Chapter 6, there may be experiments that reveal capabilities so potentially lethal that their circulation would need to be corralled, thereby superseding the normal preference to consider information a public good. Because the integration of information dissemination systems is global, the challenge of controlling that dissemination befalls the global authority.[14]

For a body to limit access to knowledge, it will not only have to hold that knowledge securely – it must also monitor communications and other information distribution networks. Bioscientists and others might be troubled by the possibility that the *Commission* could restrict the dissemination of information. As the pace of science accelerates, and as avenues for disseminating knowledge multiply, there will be a growing need to highly particularize the *Commission's* authority so as to enable it to operate effectively without overstepping its mission's boundaries.

Promote Capacity Building and Resource Mobilization

Bioviolence prevention requires States to devote scarce resources. Therefore, international assistance should be provided to developing States that lack capabilities. Gaping disparities of resources and lack of capacity to undertake requisite measures should inform decisions as to how to allocate burdens. But lack of capacity should not be cited to excuse disregard or even delay compliance with reasonable international standards. Under no conditions should emerging bioscience be promoted where bioviolence prevention is inadequate yet where assistance is neither sought nor accepted.

"Capacity building" refers to gaining skills to foster modernization.[15] The term sometimes is incorrectly used as a synonym for "technology transfer" – that is, developing States could build capacity if they were allowed access to modern technology. Increasingly, this view distorts the role of technology in promoting development, especially at the frontiers of science. Transferring biotechnology from developed nations to developing nations would not, in and of itself, build much capacity. Instead, it is necessary to reach far into the scientific community, including enhancing a research capacity for devising solutions for local diseases and conditions. Notably, these efforts should coordinate with the international organizations that are already engaged in capacity building, including the Global Environment Facility (GEF), the United Nations Environment Programme (UNEP), the United Nations Development Programme (UNDP), the WTO, and the World Bank.

The *Commission* need not be the actual provider of assistance. Instead, it can coordinate training courses, workshops, and conferences on bioscience applications; organize fellowships for bioscience specialists; and raise awareness of bioscience's potential contributions to sustainable development. The *Commission* can work with the *Office* to address health and natural resources management issues by encouraging institutional coordination among government bodies, universities, research centers, NGOs, and private companies. These efforts should weave networks among national and regional expert institutions in order to define an adaptable action plan for research support and to facilitate information exchange. Recipients of capacity building assistance should maintain control over strategies to create a productive institutional framework where work programs can be clearly defined, information readily exchanged, decisions efficiently taken, and officials held accountable. No less important, these strategies must help police to interdict wrongful preparations.

A recent UN report emphasizes the linkage between receipt of bioscience capacity-building assistance and a State's implementation of basic bioviolence prevention measures into their national law.

> Bioterrorism, if not properly handled, could emerge as [a] barrier to technology transfer. Countries with advanced technology may be less willing to provide the knowledge to countries whose capacity to manage and monitor its use is weak. Therefore, countries must take deliberate steps to build in-house capacity to manage and develop biotechnology. There will be nothing more dangerous to world peace than having countries whose backyards could be used, without their knowledge due to a lack of monitoring capacity, to manufacture deadly agents.[16]

Three components of capacity building deserve attention in connection with bioviolence prevention policies. First, there must be a knowledge base of scientists who can lead research initiatives, a technically trained support network, and well-equipped facilities to sufficiently sustain research. To support national capacities for research and biotechnology applications, assistance could focus on establishing regional centers for bioscience education. Such centers of excellence could undertake research thereby engaging scientific personnel, resources, and skilled managers. Most bioscience clusters grow near university communities where fundamental research occurs. Accordingly, nations that currently have limited bioscience capabilities could use universities to pursue partnerships with external research centers in order to jointly produce innovations and contribute to biotechnology development.[17]

The second component of capacity building is access to capital. Ripening a deeply entrenched science community requires sustainable investment. However, developing countries lack mature venture capital markets, and new bioscience is risky. The lack of funding for institutional, infrastructure, and personnel development is the main barrier. Indicating the need to overcome this barrier, the Commission on Macroeconomics and Health has suggested that $1.5 billion should be allocated to existing institutions for research and development on drugs, vaccines, and medical intervention. It further recommended the establishment of a Global

Health Research Fund to operate also with a $1.5 billion budget to support scientific research and development.[18]

Last, it is critical to have strong legal and regulatory institutions to enhance markets by protecting property rights, impartially enforcing contracts, and fostering competition through antitrust enforcement. Political institutions – especially in developing countries – are fragile, and if these countries lack a strong rule-of-law foundation, then there is an increased risk of corruption.[19] Designing accountability and transparency mechanisms and building effective checks and balances to guard against corruption is crucial for markets to smoothly function.

The Bioviolence Prevention Office (*Office*)

Bioviolence prevention's many domains – health, law enforcement, science, development, trade, etc., each with its own bureaucratic supervisor – testify to the need for coordination of many activities and actors. The *Office* could help States develop their own legal and scientific infrastructures to implement regulatory standards. It could also serve as an essential administrative tool by providing necessary secretariat services to States and to other UN bodies dealing with bioviolence prevention issues. The *Office* would organize global efforts to prevent bioviolence under a unified work plan and reorient the work of various programs by establishing broad priorities, assessing progress of prevention policies, and making recommendations to relevant organizations.

These primary missions of the *Office* suggest powers that could readily be overstepped, even abused. This is why the *Office* should have no *de jure* authority. Its design must carefully traverse a tightrope, being neither an unaccountable decision maker citing biothreats to justify exercise of governmental power, nor an irrelevant closet full of datasheets and ignored manifestos on the other side. This is also why the *Office* should be separate from the *Commission* and why potentially sensitive responsibilities should be in its domain. Whereas the composition of committees in the United Nations is controlled by the States, the Secretary General appoints the staff of an office. Being removed from the political influences of States means that the *Office* would be a legally independent component of the United Nations as a whole that does not serve any particular State interest.

The *Office* should not displace or supersede what a few dozen international organizations and countless professional associations are already accomplishing to reduce biothreats. Its role should be to harmonize bioviolence prevention policies by organizing and filling in the blanks of this jumbled mélange. Indeed, by harmonizing the activities of other programs, the *Office* would observe a trend within the United Nations system to enhance existing programs' efficacy rather than to replace those programs with new bureaucratic structures. Programs such as the Joint United Nations Program on AIDS/HIV (UNAIDS – recommends priorities to organizations with AIDS-prevention responsibilities)[20] and the United Nations Development Group (UNDG – helps countries reach the Millennium Development Goals)[21] have productively coordinated organizations in their respective fields to tackle major global issues.

The *Office* would have two critical missions that require precise delineation lest the parameters of bioviolence prevention policy be exceeded: 1) information gathering and analysis, and 2) harmonization of and compliance with international standards.

Information Gathering and Analysis

A bedrock of the entire bioviolence prevention strategy is the need to gather enough information to know the location of pathogens and laboratories, the international traffic in relevant items, and States' internal oversight and monitoring mechanisms. All this information must be effectively correlated with information about criminal and terrorist networks. Accordingly, the *Office* could augment law enforcement interdiction and international compliance assessments by establishing criteria for uniform data sets, core informational requirements, and timely monitoring and reporting mechanisms.

The *Office* must do more than passively receive data; it should develop mechanisms to integrate and analyze data from diverse sources. This function could suggest establishing independent collection capabilities. However, a quandary here is how much the *Office* should make use of modern surveillance technology to gather its own sources of data – a capability that might raise concerns about the *Office* having unsupervised surveillance powers. The *Office's* information gathering and analysis responsibilities should, therefore, be limited and certainly not be confused with treaty verification. It should gather and analyze three distinct types of information:

1. Information about standards that are set by specialized organizations and associations. The *Office* should determine if policies coming from all these diverse sources are consistent and should address discrepancies or gaps.

2. Information that might suggest potential threats. Chapter 5 discussed the importance of detecting anomalous situations that call for further inquiry. In brief, the *Office* should be where information to enable such detection is amassed and analyzed.

3. Information about emerging issue arenas that will call for new policies. Chapter 6 discussed why bioscience's radical acceleration poses altogether unique difficulties for designing legal measures to reduce risks. The *Office's* responsibility in this context would be to track and even predict tomorrow's trends.

A useful analogy here is the information gathering capabilities of the Office for Outer Space Affairs (OOSA). Its International Space Information Service (ISIS) houses various directories, documents, and the *Register of Objects Launched into Outer Space* that tracks which States launch satellites, each satellite's general function, and its orbital parameters. The ISIS can track both objects registered with the UN and others by obtaining additional information from external sources.[22] Analogously, the *Office* should maintain a register that can be updated to keep track of dangerous pathogens and their intended purpose. This register can be supplemented with information from the World Federation for Culture Collections and other national culture collection agencies, various transportation monitoring agencies, and law enforcement bodies.

As the repository of information, it is important that the *Office* respect privacy and proprietary interests. The risk of revealing valuable or sensitive information could engender resistance from persons who must provide it. For example, access to health records and monitoring of the internet might help the *Office* fulfill its responsibilities but at a price that scientists and perhaps the general public find unacceptable. These quandaries call for formulation of nuanced policies that are carefully honed to be consistent with the *Office's* pivotal yet limited role. It could learn lessons from multilateral initiatives to control nuclear and chemical weapons proliferation that have developed intricate confidentiality mechanisms. Most experts agree that these mechanisms satisfy both the need for information and the imperative to keep that information out of public view.[23]

Impelling Implementation

As the harmonizer of various organizations' standards concerning bioviolence prevention, the *Office's* most sensitive role would be to impel States to properly implement and comply with these standards. The *Office* will not have any power over States, but there are subtle methods to impel States to adhere to progressive international standards. The *Office's* responsibility, in this context, would be to help States observe common standards and to design realistic analyses for assessing compliance.

The *Office's* staff should comprise legal and scientific experts tasked with guiding sound policy decisions and working within the frameworks of existing organizations to harmonize common standards. Although the *Office* will not be authorized to adopt rules, it could leverage its expertise and networks to persuade key players who do have authority to implement particular standards that the *Office* has helped to shape. Through this process, the *Office* could accelerate coordination of international bioviolence rules.

The *Office's* extensive network of contacts could open opportunities for experts to provide input when proposals are drafted. Today, there are disconnects among many expert bodies who mutually disregard each other's objectives; these disconnects handicap effective bioviolence prevention policies. The *Office* should, therefore, establish processes that facilitate transinstitutional communication and that solicit insight about emerging concerns. According to one expert, "[G]iving all who have relevant information and positions a chance to advance their ideas in the policy-making process helps to bring expertise to bear, test the prevailing wisdom, and ensure neutrality within the decision-making framework."[24]

Moreover, the *Office* should assist a web of local, national, and international actors to develop appropriate bioviolence laws and practices. Through quiet diplomacy exercised by an experienced core of experts, the *Office* could explain to States why accession to widely accepted rules is in their best interest; this is akin to how the International Union for the Conservation of Nature and Natural Resources (IUCN) operates in the field of international environmental protection.[25] The *Office* should keep abreast of recent developments and upcoming activities so that it can help apprise organizations of the implications of bioviolence considerations for their decisions. By working with nations, the *Office* could also provide fact finding and investigatory support such as special rapporteurs for documenting violations of international obligations.

Global financial institutions could play an important role in impelling bioviolence prevention, and the *Office* should be capable of working with these institutions. The World Bank and regional development banks give substantial funding support to health-related projects including programs to build public health infrastructure. These funders can supervise how the

BOX 9-1. CAPACITY BUILDING UNDER THE CARTAGENA PROTOCOL ON BIOSAFETY

A useful analogy is capacity building to implement the Cartagena Protocol on Biosafety. Biosafety capabilities should be enhanced by establishing a roster of experts, reviewing appropriate capacity-building activities, identifying mechanisms of multilateral cooperation, engaging the private sector, defining the Secretariat's role, and assessing financial resources. All this should be devoted to:

- Risk assessment and management with regard to living modified organisms
- Institution building including funding laboratories/equipment and developing regulatory frameworks
- Scientific, technical, and institutional collaboration including mechanisms to share experiences and provide access to information on opportunities for collaboration
- Human resources development including training in scientific skills and regulatory processes
- Identification of living modified organisms
- Raising awareness and participation by enabling seminars and access to communication networks
- Data management through participation in the Biosafety Clearinghouse.

borrower implements relevant standards. For example, the World Bank promotes international regulations on biosafety in developing countries. It has helped Columbia and India implement biosafety frameworks in connection with their agricultural sectors and natural resources management. This project, known as the Capacity Building for Implementation of the Cartagena Protocol (see Box 9–1), has inspired a multi-country approach for biosafety implementation by the World Bank in West Africa and Latin America. The World Bank, already engaged in policies concerned with biosafety, has recognized its role in implementing relevant treaty obligations:

> The World Bank's role is to assist countries build their capacity to meet treaty obligations by implementing necessary measures for minimizing possible environmental and health risks from the transfer, handling, use, or release of GMOs. . . . It is therefore crucial that assistance continues to concentrate on building the capacity and knowledge base of all relevant stakeholders in order to permit countries to make informed choices on how to assess and manage both the potential risks and the benefits associated with the use of modern biotechnology.[26]

United Nations Bioviolence Committee (*Security Council Committee*)

The *Security Council Committee* would be a subsidiary body of the Security Council, serving to: 1) pursue and investigate suspicious activity related to bioviolence; 2) respond to Security Council resolutions and other instructions concerning biothreats; and 3) assist in mitigating the effects of a bioattack. Attaching the *Committee* to the Security Council is explicitly both an empowerment and a constriction. It would draw its power from the Security Council's legitimacy, yet it would not deal with concerns that the *Commission* or *Office* could address. The *Committee* would operate only in extreme circumstances when States are suspected of being in material breach of their bioviolence prevention obligations or in the grave instance of a State-sponsored, terrorist, or criminal bioattack.

The alternative of investing the *Commission* or the *Office* with these responsibilities would entail combining functions that should not mix and would weaken each body's respective cooperative functions. When enforcement action is required, however, cooperation will be a secondary priority. The principal objective will be to determine if a threat exists and, if so, to erase it.

Institutionalizing investigative functions in connection with the Security Council has important virtues. First would be to internationalize some intelligence gathering functions. An information gathering capacity linked to the Security Council could use information gathered from national intelligence agencies along with other data to compile a systematic threat assessment. Second, the *Committee's* determinations would carry the Security Council's legitimacy. According to the U.S. Institute of Peace, "In certain instances a decision by the United Nations, including the legally binding decisions of the Security Council under Chapter VII, may be more acceptable to other governments than pressure from any single nation or group of nations."[27]

There has long been discussion about vesting the UN Secretary-General with monitoring and investigative capabilities. Notably, this discussion has focused on the need for action against "alleged violations of the 1925 Geneva Protocol (banning the use of biological and chemical weapons) or of the Biological Weapons Convention (BWC)."[28] The Secretary-General's power, however, is limited by the United Nations Charter. The Secretariat may act in an investigatory capacity only when "entrusted" by the Security Council (Article 98), although the Secretary-General may "bring to the attention of the Security Council any matter which in his opinion may threaten the maintenance of international peace and security" (Article 99).

The Charter confers on the Security Council the "primary responsibility for the maintenance of international peace and security" (Article 24). Only the Security Council has legitimate authority to ensure that prompt and effective action is taken when needed and to "investigate any dispute, or any situation which might lead to international friction or give rise to a dispute ... likely to endanger the maintenance of international peace and security" (Article 34).[29] Moreover, only the Security Council is authorized to "call upon the parties concerned to comply with such provisional measures as it deems necessary or desirable" (Article 40) and to decide what measures are to be employed to give effect to its decisions. To that end, the Charter explicitly confers to it the authority to "establish such subsidiary organs as it deems necessary for the performance of its functions" (Article 29).

Predecessors

United Nations inspectors' experience investigating alleged WMD programs offers important lessons. After the first Gulf War in 1991, the Security Council established the United Nations Special Commission (UNSCOM) to verify Iraq's compliance with its disarmament obligations by inspecting Iraq's biological, chemical, and missile capabilities. UNSCOM pursued this mandate using information gathered from documents, interviews with officials, on-site inspections, and sampling and forensic investigations.[30] These investigations are credited for impeding Iraq's reconstruction of its biological weapons program.[31]

In late 1999, Security Council Resolution 1284 established the United Nations Monitoring, Verification and Inspection Commission (UNMOVIC) to replace UNSCOM. Unlike UNSCOM inspectors who were selected by States, UNMOVIC inspectors were international civil servants recruited from a broad geographical base and from international arms control organizations. They worked directly in accordance with the United Nations rules on impartiality and professionalism. Moreover, UNMOVIC was equipped with more powerful tools and broader authority. It could designate sites for on-site inspections, conduct interviews with Iraqi officials, analyze documents, and conduct sampling and aerial surveillance of designated areas.[32] Notably, UNMOVIC continued to exist until 2007, nearly four years after the withdrawal of inspectors from Iraq. In those years, UNMOVIC assumed an active epistemic role, hosting seminars and training sessions, attending workshops and participating in conference discussions.

In addition to these inspection bodies, Security Council Resolution 1540 (discussed in Chapter 5) established a Committee to report on how States are adopting and enforcing laws to prohibit WMD proliferation to non-State actors. Although the Committee was initially mandated to endure for "a period of no longer than two years," Security Council Resolution 1673, adopted in April 2006, extended its mandate for an additional two years, commanding it to "intensify its efforts" for implementation and to explore "the availability of programmes which might facilitate the implementation of Resolution 1540." Yet, the 1540 Committee is not an investigatory body, and its focus on all WMD means that it would be ill-suited to undertake the responsibilities of the proposed *Security Council Committee*.

A New Inspectorate

This book has attempted to highlight why preventing bioviolence is more complex than other challenges facing the international community, even more than preventing other types of WMD violence. Thus, while both UNMOVIC and the 1540 Committee provide important lessons, in their respective incarnations neither is a substitute for the proposed *Committee*.

There have been suggestions that UNMOVIC become a permanent investigatory arm of the Security Council so that its knowledge and experience could continue to address concerns about noncompliance with international nonproliferation obligations.[33] A report entitled *American Interests and UN Reform* recommends that the Security Council "consider the creation of a permanent nonproliferation inspectorate using UNMOVIC's standing expertise in chemical and biological weapons and missile systems." UNMOVIC "could be converted into a body able to launch verification and inspection operations on short notice when directed by the council or UN Secretariat."[34] Another suggestion from Hans Blix is that a "small standing group under the Security Council would be very useful":

> It would not be an intelligence body. There is plenty of stuff in open sources. However, it would be as objective as you can be. It would thus be of interest for Great Powers to check how their intelligence compares and it could help the [nonpermanent ten], who mostly do not have a great deal of information of their own. In addition, it would have a roster of inspectors and could 'surge' quickly, if needed.[35]

Whether as a new body or as a transformation of an existing body, the *Committee's* role would be to monitor, verify, investigate, and ensure compliance with international measures for preventing bioviolence. It would report directly to the Security Council and issue recommendations as necessary. Because the Security Council Committee is to act only in extreme circumstances, it would not have *carte blanche* authority to investigate any State it chooses but would act only upon the Security Council's specific instructions to investigate activity deemed to threaten international security. The *Committee* must have capacity, expert personnel, and authority to make country visits if there are suspicions that bioviolence prevention obligations are being violated. Whether State consent is a prerequisite for any particular visit is for the Security Council to decide.

Notably, the *Committee* would both provide information to the Security Council about possible bioviolence concerns and receive instructions from the Security Council that derive from intelligence gathered from States. The *Committee* should develop tools to keep information that is provided to it confidential even as it holds consultations and briefings for interested States and other relevant international actors. Once a bioviolence attack happens, the *Committee* should devote its expertise to helping States and international organizations mitigate harm, limit the spread of disease, and apprehend perpetrators. With regard to a severe attack having global ramifications, the *Committee* can, at the Security Council's discretion, coordinate response activities of relevant international organizations such as the WHO and Interpol as well as the law enforcement and health care communities of national governments to ensure prompt and effective response.

A Final Note on Governance

During preparation of this chapter, various experts offered alternative formulations for the governance structure, for example that there should be only two bodies with a combined *Commission-Office* and a separate *Committee*; or there should be a single body with three subsidiary offices. It may be readily acknowledged that, within the UN's intricate structure, there might well be different ways to arrange relevant responsibilities. What is important is that the priority of global governance is recognized, that the primacy of the UN as the venue of that governance is accepted, and that the multiple security-science-development challenges in preventing bioviolence are pursued in harmony.

Conclusion

Advancing bioscience offers a future of endless possibilities – a consummation devoutly to be wished. But it also affords emerging methods of devastation that are ever harder to control. Today, a few undeterrable people could use pathogens to inflict massive damage, and there are many reasons to believe that someone will try. These people could be anywhere on Earth.

Here may be seen the future of challenges to international peace and security at the beginning of the third millennium: scientific progress intertwined with malevolent threats that have consequences for all humanity. Across scientific disciplines, progressing capabilities – initially for managing and communicating information, now for medicine, and soon for industrial applications (nanotechnology) – improve our lives and yet carry, inextricably, escalating risks to humanity. These growing threats do not argue for braking scientific progress, but they undercut notions that new threats can be effectively addressed with yesterday's policies.

Our era is witnessing a scientific revolution which calls for a revolution in how we conceive of security. Historically, scientific revolutions that have prompted critical changes in the means and methods of executing violence have stimulated new security paradigms, but too often these paradigms were appreciated only when their obsolete predecessors had painfully failed. With regard to bioviolence, the consequences of learning through horrible experience are unacceptable.

This book has discussed approximately three dozen bioviolence prevention measures that could reduce risks of that unacceptable experience. There are common cords running through these recommendations that might be conveniently designated as three "I's": information, integration, and international.

Every prevention measure requires better information. It is too easy for bio-offenders to hide and too hard to identify or interdict their activities. Comparable gaps of information would be intolerable in the nuclear sciences or in other domains that pose high risks, and they should not be tolerated in bioscience. These information gaps are especially striking in view of the extraordinary progress of information technology that could enable effective detection capabilities.

The challenges of gathering information deserve substantial thought and attention. Collecting information can transgress personal and institutional privacy. Analyzing information can generate conclusions that are perhaps corrupted by political perspective or that are just wrong. Sharing information can leak critical capabilities to the people who should be stopped. For these and other reasons, implementing mechanisms for gathering information without carefully designed safeguards could be counterproductive. Indeed, every measure discussed in this book carries potential for intrusion into scientific freedom or personal privacy; any measure could consume vast and unwarranted resources.

An intemperate approach to bioviolence prevention that disregards the negative ramifications of information gathering and analysis would be ill-advised; discretion is certainly a virtue deserving respect. Yet, it would be extremely imprudent to wait until bioviolence occurs and then respond as if the dangers could not have been anticipated. Indeed, a very real concern throughout this book is that, if there ever is a bioviolence catastrophe, discretion will be an early victim. Too late to devise reasonable prevention policies, there will likely be a clamor for ill-considered reactions that drown out wiser counsel for nuanced approaches. This is why it is vital to establish the foundations for progressive policies now, before an attack.

The second "I" is integration. Each of this book's recommendations offers potential benefits, but none will accomplish much by itself. Each measure, if viewed in isolation, has substantial limitations and can be sidestepped by someone who is sufficiently motivated to commit bioviolence. Policies must, therefore, be integrative; each measure gains strength from pursuit of all the others. It is a challenge, however, to knit a comprehensive and interwoven policy fabric with threads from three dozen skeins.

Fortunately, across a broad range of technical issues, we know how to augment safety from bioviolence. Virtually every proposed measure is well understood and doable; there is some organization, expert, or government agency that is vigorously trying to do something positive. These activities are certainly making a beneficial contribution – albeit less advantageously than if part of a larger tapestry. We know less, however, about how to integrate technical knowledge and experience into a global system that can keep pace with the advance of science and its accompanying perils. The conundrum is how to arrange disaggregated expertise and energy and how to align a critical mass of constituencies so that bioviolence prevention initiatives are mutually reinforcing. Thus, the issue is not *why doesn't somebody do something* as much as *how can we effectively create synergies among what a lot of people are already doing.* How can *activity* be organized into *strategy*?

Most needed today are not so much definitive answers to discrete problems but rather parameters that help decision makers create and implement multiple policies over time. Today's leaders, lacking clear experience and hearing fractured proposals to take action, have been dissuaded from moving forward by a pervasive ambiguity about how policy pieces fit together. Rather than stumble counterproductively among hidden pitfalls of ill-considered policies, it may have seemed safer to wait and react instead of focusing on prevention. This book has sought, therefore, to clarify how potentially beneficial initiatives might be more comprehensively embraced.

There is another context for highlighting *integration* – bioviolence prevention policies must be integrated with other important policy agendas. Indeed, the important implications of bioviolence – for international security, for the future of science, and for combating pandemic disease – call for appreciating bioviolence prevention as one agenda priority among others. Just as the many measures discussed in this book gain strength from mutual integration, the pursuit of bioviolence prevention gains strength from integration with other global priorities including the advance of bioscience and health.

The fact that various bioviolence prevention measures should be integrated with each other as well as with separate policy agendas is not a justification for moving slowly. At some point, the lack of policy initiative must be viewed more harshly. As dangers mount, the inescapable conclusion must be that a lack of political commitment to advance prevention policies is testimony to our leaders' feeble unwillingness to face the major threats that confront our era. Bluntly offered, this situation must not long continue.

The third and most important "I" is international. For centuries, destructive power was primarily an attribute of States. Although State conflict certainly posed security nightmares, at least there was a clear idea of the enemy's identity. Borders separated friend from foe and defined imminent threats. Advancing science, however, has eviscerated the nation-State's monopoly of destructive force, and national borders are decreasingly relevant to the pursuit of security. Globalization is disseminating productive and destructive capabilities around the world.

Bioscience is promoting and benefiting from globalization. In an even more profound sense, bioscience is the palpable manifestation of our common genome and our shared existence. Our era's increasing agility in manipulating the genetic tools of life opens potential for improving the human condition as well as for inflicting horror. Bioviolence is, accordingly, tightening the fabric of humanity with irreversible implications about what can threaten all of us; the very life force that connects us all simultaneously imperils us all.

Human existence, of course, has always been a struggle against disease, but the introduction of human knowledge and intention on the side of disease is threatening to reconfigure this struggle. It's us against them in the eternal war between humans and microbes; the prospect of traitors tipping the balance demonstrates that the rest of us are in this together. We will be more secure if we can get better organized to pursue our common objectives. Ultimately, therefore, the pathways for bioviolence prevention demand governance structures and processes for all humanity.

This need for a new humanity-governance evokes this book's intended thesis: the imperative of security from bioviolence is fundamentally transformative of international law. The predominant view of international law has long been that sovereign States define the law's content through their treaties or customary practices; international law is the law of nations. A weaker, alternative view is that international law is a set of organizing principles embodying a categorical imperative to advance humanity's survival and progress. The difference between these two perspectives has to do with States: for proponents of the law of nations, States are the fundamental units of human organization; for proponents of the law of humanity, States can be useful mechanisms for establishing order amid evolving yet still anarchic conditions, but their parochial interests are not the law's primary concern. Unquestionably, the first view has dominated political affairs and scholarly thought for centuries.

Looking to the future of bioviolence and the mechanisms of its prevention is to open visions of an evolving paradigm of international law where the imperative of advancing the human community must be ascendant. In the same sense that fortressed cities became obsolete when the security they offered became a mirage, today's security challenges erode the illusion that separate sovereign States can keep us safe from impending catastrophe. Bioviolence is not the only challenge that calls for worldwide collaborative action, but perhaps it most graphically crystallizes the shortcomings of our inherited allegiance to divisive concepts of State sovereignty. Humanity is now compelled to turn to a broader conception of international law so that arrays of policies and initiatives can be effectively focused. This is not a preference or a choice; it is the inherent implication of scientific progress.

The need to prevent bioviolence has emerged from the confluence of radically accelerating progress in bioscience along with the post-2001 pre-eminence of non-State violence atop the world's strategic agenda. Preventing bioviolence is increasingly too complicated for two hundred squabbling sovereigns to accomplish, and the consequences of getting it wrong are too dire for us to long tolerate their imprudence. Thus, bioviolence prevention portends a new chapter in the human species' most basic and most long-lasting struggle against lethal microbes and offers a new vision of how to globally organize strategic security under law. As this is a struggle we must win, international legal pursuit of prevention policies is a paramount priority.

Notes

Introduction

1. A recent and noteworthy exercise was "Black Ice" (Bioterrorism International Coordination Exercise), which the United States and Switzerland co-hosted in Montreux, Switzerland, in September 2006, with high-level officials from twelve international organizations. The exercise involved a smallpox scenario, focusing on the international community's capabilities and challenges to bioterrorism response coordination, including public communication, information sharing, operational readiness, and the impact of national interests on organizational missions.
2. *See* G. John Ikenberry & Anne-Marie Slaughter, FORGING A WORLD OF LIBERTY UNDER LAW: U.S. NATIONAL SECURITY IN THE 21ST CENTURY, The Princeton Project Papers, The Woodrow Wilson School of Public and International Affairs (September 27, 2006).
3. Michael Foucault set forth the term *biopolitics* to refer to "that mode of organizing, managing, and above all regulation 'the population' considered as a biological species entity." Biopolitics refers to the object of governing as "addressed to a multiplicity of men, not to the extent that they are nothing more than their individual bodies, but to the extent that they form, on the contrary, a global mass..." *See generally*, Eugene Thacker, THE GLOBAL GENOME, MIT Press, pp. 21–36 (2005).
4. Gro Harlem Brundtland, *Global Health and International Security; Global Insights*, GLOBAL GOVERNANCE (October 1, 2003).

Chapter 1. Why Worry?

1. *Proliferation of Weapons of Mass Destruction*, Office of Technology Assessment, US Congress, OTA-ISC-559, pp. 53–55 (1993), *cited in, Anthrax as a Biological Weapon: Medical and Public Health Management*, JOURNAL OF THE AMERICAN MEDICAL ASSOCIATION, Vol. 281, No. 18, p. 1735 (May 12, 1999).
2. According to the Stockholm International Peace Research Institute, the cost to inflict civilian casualties is $2,000 per square kilometer with conventional weapons, $800 with nuclear weapons, and $1 with biological weapons. In 1999, the U.S. Defense Threat Reduction Agency built a small facility that could be used to produce biological warfare agents for only $1.6 million. *See* Judith Miller *et al.*, GERMS: BIOLOGICAL WEAPONS AND AMERICA'S SECRET WAR, Simon & Schuster, pp. 297–298 (2001).

Chapter 2. Methods of Bioviolence

1. *Smallpox as a Biological Weapon: Medical and Public Health Management*, JOURNAL OF THE AMERICAN MEDICAL ASSOCIATION, Vol. 281, No. 22 (June 9, 1999).

2. CDC, *Smallpox Fact Sheet: Side Effects of Smallpox Vaccination, available at* http://www.bt.cdc.gov/agent/smallpox/vaccination/reactions-vacc-public.asp.

3. *Smallpox as a Biological Weapon: Medical and Public Health Management*, JOURNAL OF THE AMERICAN MEDICAL ASSOCIATION, Vol. 281, No. 22 (June 9, 1999).

4. *See* K. T. Chelvi, *The Pox Maybe on You*, NEW STRAITS TIMES (April 4, 2005); *See also*, Ewen MacAskill et al., *Threat of War: Powell's Evidence Against Saddam: Does It Add Up?* THE GUARDIAN (LONDON) (February 6, 2003).

5. *Quoted in* Meridith Wadman *US Scientists Split on Smallpox Decision*, NATURE, Vol. 398, p. 741 (April 29, 1999), *available at* http://www.nature.com/wcs/b32.html.

6. Ken Alibek, *Behind the Mask: Biological Warfare*, PERSPECTIVE, Vol. IX, No. 1 (September–October, 1998).

7. *See generally*, Myrna Watanabe, *The Bioterror Error*, HARTFORD COURANT (September 5, 2004).

8. See *WMD 411 Chronology – 2002*, NUCLEAR THREAT INITIATIVE, *available at* http://www.nti.org/f_wmd411/2002.html, stating "The *Washington Post* reports that U.S. intelligence believes that France, Russia, Iraq, and North Korea maintain stockpiles of weaponized smallpox. Days later, France officially denies the charges, maintaining that France has always strictly adhered to the 1972 BWC."; *See also*, Barton Gellman, *4 Nations Thought to Possess Smallpox; Iraq, N. Korea named, Two Officials Say*, WASHINGTON POST (November 5, 2002), stating "The CIA now assesses that four nations – Iraq, North Korea, Russia and, to the surprise of some specialists, France – have undeclared samples of the smallpox virus."

9. U.S. Department of Defense, Smallpox Vaccination Program Information Statement and Acknowledgement, available at http://www.smallpox.mil/documents/118Smallpoxack.pdf.

10. *The Ecology of Flu*, ZKEA EMERGING DISEASES: BIOLOGICAL TERRORISM: BIOLOGICAL WARFARE, *available at* http://www.zkea.com/articles/flu2.html.

11. Michael T. Osterholm, *Preparing for the Next Pandemic*, FOREIGN AFFAIRS, p. 24 (July–August, 2005).

12. *See* Laurie Garrett, *The Next Pandemic?* FOREIGN AFFAIRS, p. 3 (July/August 2005); *See also*, Klaus Stohr & Marja Esveld, *Will Vaccines be Available for the Next Influenza Pandemic?* SCIENCE, Vol. 306, No. 5705 (December 24, 2004).

13. K. Y. Yuen & S. S. Y. Wong, *Human Infection by Avian Influenza A H5N1*, HONG KONG MEDICAL JOURNAL, Vol. 11, No. 3 (June, 2005).

14. *The Ecology of Flu*, ZKEA EMERGING DISEASES: BIOLOGICAL TERRORISM: BIOLOGICAL WARFARE, *available at* http://www.zkea.com/articles/flu2.html; *See also*, David A. Relman, *Bioterrorism – Preparing to Fight the Next War*, NEW ENGLAND JOURNAL OF MEDICINE, p. 113 (January 12, 2006).

15. Graeme Laver & Elspeth Garman, *The Origin and Control of Pandemic Influenza*, SCIENCE, Vol. 293, No. 5536, p. 1,776 (September 7, 2001).

16. *Researchers Reconstruct 1918 Pandemic Influenza Virus; Effort Designed to Advance Preparedness*, CENTERS FOR DISEASE CONTROL AND PREVENTION, Press Release (October 5, 2005) *available at* http://www.cdc.gov/od/oc/media/pressrel/r051005.htm.

17. *Influenza (Flu) Questions and Answers: Reconstruction of the 1918 Influenza Pandemic Virus*, CENTERS FOR DISEASE CONTROL AND PREVENTION, *available at* www.bt.cdc.gov/scripts/emailprint/print.asp.

18. *The Ecology of Flu*, ZKEA EMERGING DISEASES: BIOLOGICAL TERRORISM: BIOLOGICAL WARFARE, *available at* http://www.zkea.com/articles/flu2.html; *See also*, Terrence M. Tumpey et al., *Characterization of the Reconstructed 1918 Spanish Influenza Virus*, SCIENCE, Vol. 310, pp. 77–80 (October 7, 2005).

19. R. J. Webby & R. G. Webster, *Are We Ready for Pandemic Influenza?* SCIENCE, Vol. 302, No. 5650, pp. 1519–1522 (November 28, 2003).

20. Mohamad Madjid et al., *Influenza as a Bioweapon*, JOURNAL OF THE ROYAL SOCIETY OF MEDICINE, Vol. 96, p. 345 (July 2003); *See also*, *Flu Bioweapon Fears*, BBC NEWS (July 1, 2003), *available at* http://news.bbc.co.uk/1/hi/health/3031488.stm.

21. Michael T. Osterholm, *Preparing for the Next Pandemic*, FOREIGN AFFAIRS, p. 24 (July/August, 2005).

22. Robert M. Krug, *The Potential Use of Influenza Virus as an Agent for Bioterrorism*, ANTIVIRAL RESEARCH, Vol. 57, No. 1–2, pp. 147–150 (January 2003).

23. Laurie Garrett, *The Next Pandemic?* FOREIGN AFFAIRS, p. 3 (July/August, 2005).

24. *Flu Bioweapon Fears*, BBC NEWS (July 1, 2003), *available at* http://news.bbc.co.uk/1/hi/health/3031488.stm.

25. Graeme Laver & Elspeth Garman, *The Origin and Control of Pandemic Influenza*, SCIENCE, Vol. 293, No. 5536, p. 1776 (September 7, 2001).

26. *See* Klaus Stohr & Marja Esveld, *Will Vaccines be Available for the Next Influenza Pandemic?* SCIENCE, Vol. 306, No. 5705 (December 24, 2004); *See also*, I. M. Longini et al., *Containing Pandemic Influenza with Antiviral Agents*, AMERICAN JOURNAL OF EPIDEMIOLOGY, Vol. 159, No. 7, p. 623–633 (April 1, 2004); *See also*, Monica Schoch-Spana, *Implications of Pandemic Influenza for Bioterrorism Response*, CLINICAL INFECTIOUS DISEASES, Vol. 31, p. 1413 (December 2000).

27. *See* Gigi Kwik Gronvall & Luciana L. Borio, *Removing Barriers to Global Pandemic Influenza Vaccination*, BIOSECURITY AND BIOTERRORISM: BIODEFENSE STRATEGY, PRACTICE, AND SCIENCE, Vol. 4, No. 2 (2006); *See also*, Laurie Garrett, *The Next Pandemic?* FOREIGN AFFAIRS, p. 3 (July/August, 2005).

28. Klaus Stohr & Marja Esveld, *Will Vaccines be Available for the Next Influenza Pandemic?* SCIENCE, Vol. 306, No. 5705 (December 24, 2004).

29. Michael T. Osterholm, *Preparing for the Next Pandemic*, FOREIGN AFFAIRS, p. 24 (July 2005–August 2005).

30. Graeme Laver & Elspeth Garman, *The Origin and Control of Pandemic Influenza*, SCIENCE, Vol. 293, No. 5536, p. 1776 (September 7, 2001).

31. World Health Organization, *Global Stockpile of H5N1 Vaccine 'Feasible,' 26 April, 2007*, *available at* http://www.who.int/mediacentre/news/releases/2007/pr21/en/index.html.

32. Luzi Ann Javier, *Bird Flu May Result in $200 Billion in Losses Worldwide*, available at http://www.bloomberg.com/apps/news?pid=20601086&sid=aCl7Rm0bVxlY&refer=latin_america.

33. The CDC groups the hemorrhagic fever viruses into a "High-Priority," "Category A Disease/Agent" because: (a) it can be easily disseminated or transmitted from person to person; (b) it can result in high mortality rates and has the potential for major public health impact; (c) it might cause public panic and social disruption and; (d) it requires special action for public health preparedness. See *Bioterrorism Agents/Diseases*, THE CENTERS FOR DISEASE CONTROL AND PREVENTION, *available at*: http://www.bt.cdc.gov/agent/agentlist-category.asp#adef; *See also*, *Hemorrhagic Fever Viruses as Biological Weapons: Medical and Public Health Management*, JOURNAL OF THE AMERICAN MEDICAL ASSOCIATION, Vol. 287, No. 18 (May 8, 2002).

34. Staff statement, U.S. Senate Permanent Subcommittee on Investigations (Minority Staff), *Global Proliferation of Weapons of Mass Destruction, A Case Study on the Aum Shinrikyo*, Hearing before the Permanent Subcommittee on Investigations, 104th Congress, 1st Session (October 31, 1995).

35. *Marburg Hemorrhagic Fever Fact Sheet*, THE CENTERS FOR DISEASE CONTROL AND PREVENTION, *available at* http://www.cdc.gov/ncidod/dvrd/spb/mnpages/dispages/Fact_Sheets/Marburg%20Hemmorhagic%20Fever%20Fact%20Sheet.pdf.

36. Roman Biek et al., *Recent Common Ancestry of Ebola Zaire Virus Found in a Bat Reservoir*, PLoS PATHOGENS, Vol. 2, No. 10, p. 885 (October, 2006).

37. *Hemorrhagic Fever Viruses as Biological Weapons: Medical and Public Health Management*, JOURNAL OF THE AMERICAN MEDICAL ASSOCIATION, Vol. 287, No. 18 (May 8, 2002).

38. *Marburg Haemorrhagic Fever: Fact Sheet*, WORLD HEALTH ORGANIZATION (March, 2005), *available at* www.who.int/mediacentre/factsheets/fs_marburg/en/print.html.

39. In a reported case of Bolivian hemorrhagic fever, where students observing a nurse instructor changing bed sheets of an infected individual contracted the disease even though the students did not physically touch the person or any contaminated object and stood at a distance of 6 feet or greater from the patient at all times. See *Hemorrhagic Fever Viruses as Biological Weapons: Medical and Public Health Management*, JOURNAL OF THE AMERICAN MEDICAL ASSOCIATION, Vol. 287, No. 18 (May 8, 2002).

40. COUNTERING AGRICULTURAL BIOTERRORISM, National Academies Press, p. 67 (2002).

41. *See* Henry S. Heine et al., *Determination of Antibiotic Efficacy Against Bacillus Anthracis in a Mouse Aerosol Challenge Model*, Report prepared for the United States Army Medical Research Institute of Infectious Diseases, Division of Bacteriology, ANTIMICROBIAL AGENTS AND CHEMOTHERAPY, doi:10.1128/AAC.01050-06 (2007).

42. *Anthrax as a Biological Weapon: Medical and Public Health Management*, JOURNAL OF THE AMERICAN MEDICAL ASSOCIATION, Vol. 281, No. 18 (May 12, 1999).

43. *Anthrax as a Biological Weapon, 2002: Updated Recommendations for Management*, THE JOURNAL OF THE AMERICAN MEDICAL ASSOCIATION, Vol. 287, No.17, p. 2237 (May 2002); *See also*, Rick Weiss, *A Terrorist's Fragile Footprint; Letter's Anthrax Spores Pose Many Obstacles to Analysis*, WASHINGTON POST (November 29, 2001); *See also*, Gary Matsumoto, *Anthrax Powder – State of the Art?* SCIENCE, Vol. 302, No. 5650 (November 28, 2003) *available at* http://www.sciencemag.org/cgi/content/summary/302/5650/1492.

44. Statement of Dr. Kenneth Alibek, *Russia, Iraq, and Other Potential Sources of Anthrax, Smallpox, and other Bioterrorist Weapons*, Hearing before the Committee on International Relations, House of Representatives, 107th Congress, 1st Session, p. 34 (December 5, 2001), *available at* http://commdocs.house.gov/committees/intlrel/hfa76481.000/hfa76481_0.HTM.

45. Statement of Dr. Kenneth Alibek, *Russia, Iraq, and Other Potential Sources of Anthrax, Smallpox, and Other Bioterrorist Weapons*, Hearing before the Committee on International Relations, House of Representatives, 107th Congress, 1st Session, p. 34 (December 5, 2001), *available at* http://commdocs.house.gov/committees/intlrel/hfa76481.000/hfa76481_0.HTM.

46. Steven Malloy, "The Threat of Anthrax Has Been Exaggerated," *cited in*, William Dudley (ed.), BIOLOGICAL WARFARE: OPPOSING VIEWPOINTS, Greenhaven Press (2004).

47. *See generally*, Malcolm Dando, *The Impact of the Development of Modern Biology and Medicine on the Evolution of Offensive Biological Warfare Programs in the Twentieth Century*, DEFENSE ANALYSIS, Vol. 15, No. 1, pp. 43–62 (1999).

48. *See* Douglas Beecher, *Forensic Application of Microbiological Culture Analysis to Identify Mail Intentionally Contaminated with Bacillus Anthracis Spores*, APPLIED AND ENVIRONMENTAL MICROBIOLOGY, Vol. 72, No. 8 (August 2006).

49. *See* Statement of Dr. George Painter, Chief Executive Officer Chimerix, Inc., *Biodefense: Next Steps*, before the Senate Committee on Health Education, Labor and Pensions (February 8, 2005); *See also*, Lawrence O. Gostin, *When Terrorism Threatens Health: How Far Are Limitations on Personal and Economic Liberties Justified?* Vol. 55, FLA. L. REV. 1105 (December, 2003).

50. *See* Sharon Begley, *Unmasking Bioterror*, NEWSWEEK (October 8, 2001), describing efforts by the DoE to install biodetectors in stadiums and other large areas in order to reduce the threat posed by possible bioterror attacks at these venues.

51. *See* IAS Dust Collectors website describing negative air pressure technology: "With negative pressure systems, airborne bacteria, viruses, and mould spores are confined by airflow patterns that circulate *into* and not out of these restricted areas." *See* the IAS Dust Collectors website *available at* http://www.mist-dust-collection.com/Cleanroom-Filtration/negative-pressure-systems.html.

52. *See* Penny Hitchcock, *Improving Performance of HVAC Systems to Reduce Exposure to Aerosolized Infectious Agents in Buildings; Recommendations to Reduce Risks Posed by Biological Agents*, BIOSECURITY AND BIOTERRORISM: BIODEFENSE STRATEGY, PRACTICE, AND SCIENCE, Vol. 4, No. 1, (2006).

53. Scott Shane, *Clean up of Anthrax Will Cost Hundreds of Millions of Dollars*, Baltimore Sun, December 18, 2002. The Postal Service says decontaminating Brentwood and another sorting center in Hamilton Township, N. J., will cost "in excess of $100 million." The bill for decontaminating the Hart Senate Office Building and other Capitol Hill offices cost the EPA and its contractors about $42 million, according to figures provided by the EPA to Iowa Republican Sen. Charles E. Grassley. Many millions more have been spent testing and cleaning other government and postal buildings.

54. *Botulinum Toxin as a Biological Weapon, Medical and Public Health Management*, JOURNAL OF THE AMERICAN MEDICAL ASSOCIATION, Vol. 285, No. 8 (February 28, 2001).

55. *Interim Report of the Select Committee to Study Governmental Operations with Respect to Intelligence Activities on the Alleged Assassination Plots Involving Foreign Leaders*, Senate Report No. 94–465, 94th Congress, 1st Session, p. 80 (November 20, 1975).

56. *Botulinum Toxin as a Biological Weapon, Medical and Public Health Management*, JOURNAL OF THE AMERICAN MEDICAL ASSOCIATION, Vol. 285, No. 8 (February 28, 2001).

57. *Botulinum Toxin as a Biological Weapon, Medical and Public Health Management*, JOURNAL OF THE AMERICAN MEDICAL ASSOCIATION, Vol. 285, No. 8 (February 28, 2001).

58. Lawrence M. Wein & Yifan Liu, *Analyzing a Bioterror Attack on the Food Supply: The Case of Botulinum Toxin in Milk*, PROCEEDINGS OF THE NATIONAL ACADEMY OF SCIENCES OF THE UNITED STATES OF AMERICA, Vol. 102, p. 9984 (July 12, 2005).

59. J. Kaiser, *ScienceScope*, SCIENCE, Vol. 309, p. 31 (July 1, 2005); *See also*, Alison McCook, *PNAS Publishes Bioterror Paper, After All*, THE SCIENTIST (June 29, 2005).

60. *Mad Cow Watch Goes Blind*, USA TODAY (August 4, 2006), *available at* http://www.commondreams.org/views06/0804-24.htm.

61. Mark Wheelis, Rocco Casagrande, & Laurence V. Madden, *Biological Attack on Agriculture: Low-Tech, High-Impact Bioterrorism*, BIOSCIENCE, Vol. 52, No. 7, pp. 569–576 (July 2002).

62. Mark Wheelis, Rocco Casagrande, & Laurence V. Madden, *Biological Attack on Agriculture: Low-Tech, High-Impact Bioterrorism*, BIOSCIENCE, Vol. 52, No. 7, pp. 569–576 (July 2002).

63. For a comprehensive list of animal diseases, *see* the World Organization for Animal Health (OIE) website, *available at* http://www.oie.int/eng/maladies/en_classification.htm?e1d7.

64. Mark Wheelis, Rocco Casagrande, & Laurence V. Madden, *Biological Attack on Agriculture: Low-Tech, High-Impact Bioterrorism*, BIOSCIENCE, Vol. 52, No. 7, pp. 569–576 (July 2002).

65. Michael Gips, *The First Link in the Food Chain*, SECURITY MANAGEMENT ONLINE (February 2003), *available at* http://www.securitymanagement.com/library/001379.html.

66. David A. Ashford et al., *Biological Terrorism and Veterinary Medicine in the U.S*, JOURNAL FOR THE AMERICAN VETERINARY ASSOCIATION, Vol. 217, No. 5, pp. 664–667 (September 1, 2000).

67. *See* Testimony before the United States Senate Committee on Agriculture, Nutrition, and Forester (Wednesday, July 20, 2005).

68. Michael Balter, *Prions: A Lone Killer or a Vital Accomplice? Creutzfeldt-Jakob Disease; Bovine Spongiform Encephalopathy*, SCIENCE, Vol. 286, p. 660 (October 22, 1999).

69. *International Plant Protection Convention*, TIAS 7465, (December 6, 1951), (entered into force April 3, 1952).

70. *Animal Health at the Crossroads: Preventing, Detecting, and Diagnosing Animal Diseases*, Board on Agriculture and Natural Resources, THE NATIONAL ACADEMIES PRESS, p. 256 (2005), *citing Countering Agricultural Bioterrorism*, NRC Report (2003).

71. *Plague as a Biological Weapon: Medical and Public Health Management: Consensus Statement*, JOURNAL OF THE AMERICAN MEDICAL ASSOCIATION, Vol. 283, No. 17, p. 2282 (May 3, 2002).

72. *Plague as a Biological Weapon: Medical and Public Health Management: Consensus Statement*, JOURNAL OF THE AMERICAN MEDICAL ASSOCIATION, Vol. 283, No. 17, p. 2282 (May 3, 2002).

73. *Plague as a Biological Weapon: Medical and Public Health Management: Consensus Statement*, JOURNAL OF THE AMERICAN MEDICAL ASSOCIATION, Vol. 283, No. 17, p. 2281 (May 3, 2002).

74. *Tularemia as a Biological Weapon, Medical and Public Health Management, Consensus Statement*, JOURNAL OF THE AMERICAN MEDICAL ASSOCIATION, Vol. 285, No. 1, p. 2766 (June 6, 2001).

75. *Tularemia as a Biological Weapon, Medical and Public Health Management, Consensus Statement*, JOURNAL OF THE AMERICAN MEDICAL ASSOCIATION, Vol. 285, No. 1, p. 2764 (June 6, 2001).

76. *Coxiella Burnetii*, EVANSTON NORTHWESTERN HEALTHCARE, *available at* http://www.enh.org/healthandwellness/bioterrorism/bi001000.aspx?lid=1093.

77. *Q Fever Caused by Coxiella Burnetii*, THE CENTERS FOR DISEASE CONTROL AND PREVENTION, *available at* www.cdc.gov/ncidod/dvrd/qfever/index.htm.

78. *Ricin and the Umbrella Murder*, CNN.COM (October 23, 2003), *available at* www.cnn.com/2003/WORLD/europe/01/07/terror.poison.bulgarian; *See also*, Nick P.

Walsh, *Markov's Umbrella Assassination Revealed*, GUARDIAN (June 6, 2005), *available at* www.guardian.co.uk/print/0,,5208940-103681,00.html.

79. Jeronimo Cello, Aniko V. Paul, & Eckhard Wimmer, *Chemical Synthesis of Poliovirus cDNA: Generation of Infectious Virus in the Absence of Natural Template*, SCIENCE, pp. 1016–1018 (August 9, 2002); *See also*, Rick Weiss, *Polio-Causing Virus Created in N.Y. Lab: Made-from-Scratch Pathogen Prompts Concerns about Bioethics, Terrorism*, WASHINGTON POST (July 12, 2002).

80. The National Academies of Science have just recently addressed this very topic. *See* GLOBALIZATION, BIOSECURITY, AND THE FUTURE OF THE LIFE SCIENCES, Committee on Advances in Technology and the Prevention of Their Application to Next Generation Biowarfare Threats, NATIONAL RESEARCH COUNCIL OF THE NATIONAL ACADEMIES (2006), Executive Summary *available at* http://books.nap.edu/execsumm_pdf/11567.pdf.

81. Malcolm Dando, *The Impact of Modern Biology and Medicine on the Evolution of Offensive Biological Warfare Programs in the Twentieth Century*, DEFENSE ANALYSIS, Vol. 15, No. 1, pp. 43–62 (1999); Brian Rappert, *Biological Weapons, Genetics, and Social Analysis: Emerging Responses, Emerging Issues*, NEW GENETICS AND SOCIETY, Vol. 22, No. 2 (August 2003).

82. Malcolm Dando, *The Impact of the Development of Modern Biology and Medicine on the Evolution of Offensive Biological Warfare Programs in the Twentieth Century*, DEFENSE ANALYSIS,Vol. 13, No. 3 (1999).

83. *Emerging Technologies: Genetic Engineering and Biological Weapons*, THE SUNSHINE PROJECT, Background Paper, No. 12 (November, 2003).

84. Mark Wheelis, *Will the New Biology Lead to New Weapons?* ARMS CONTROL TODAY (July 2004).

85. GLOBALIZATION, BIOSECURITY, AND THE FUTURE OF THE LIFE SCIENCES, Committee on Advances in Technology and the Prevention of Their Application to Next Generation Biowarfare Threats, NATIONAL RESEARCH COUNCIL OF THE NATIONAL ACADEMIES, p. 48 (2006).

86. *Emerging Technologies: Genetic Engineering and Biological Weapons*, THE SUNSHINE PROJECT, Background Paper, No. 12 (November, 2003).

87. *Emerging Technologies: Genetic Engineering and Biological Weapons*, THE SUNSHINE PROJECT, Background Paper, No. 12 (November, 2003).

88. *See generally*, Jonathan B. Tucker & Raymond A. Zilinskas, *The Promise and Perils of Synthetic Biology*, THE NEW ATLANTIS: A JOURNAL OF TECHNOLOGY & SOCIETY, No. 12 (Spring 2006).

89. Claire M. Fraser & Malcolm R. Dando, *Genomics and Future Biological Weapons: The Need for Preventive Action by the Biomedical Community*, NATURE GENETICS, Vol. 29, p. 253 (2001).

90. Testimony of Dr. Craig Venter, before the Senate Health Education, Labor and Pension Committee, Bioterrorism and Public Health Preparedness Subcommittee (May 11 2005).

91. Gigi Kwik Gronvall et al., *Biosecurity: Responsible Stewardship of Bioscience*, BIOSECURITY AND BIOTERRORISM: BIODEFENSE STRATEGY, PRACTICE, AND SCIENCE, Vol. 1, No. 1 (2003).

92. *See generally*, Joseph G. Perpich, *The Recombinant-DNA Debate and Bioterrorism*, CHRONICLE OF HIGHER EDUCATION (March 15, 2002).

93. GLOBALIZATION, BIOSECURITY, AND THE FUTURE OF THE LIFE SCIENCES, Committee on Advances in Technology and the Prevention of Their Application to Next Generation

Biowarfare Threats, NATIONAL RESEARCH COUNCIL OF THE NATIONAL ACADEMIES, p. 49 (2006).

94. Bill Joy, *Why the Future Doesn't Need Us*, WIRED, Issue 8.04. (April 2000), *available at* http://www.wired.com/wired/archive/8.04/joy_pr.html.

Chapter 3. Who Did Bioviolence? Who Wants To Do It?

1. The dying Tartars, stunned and stupefied by the immensity of the disaster brought about by the disease, and realizing that they had no hope of escape, lost interest in the siege. However, they ordered corpses to be placed in catapults and lobbed into the city in the hope that the intolerable stench would kill everyone inside. What seemed like mountains of dead were thrown into the city, and the Christians could not hide, flee, or escape from them, although they dumped as many of the bodies as they could in the sea. Soon the rotting corpses tainted the air and poisoned the water supply, and the stench was so overwhelming that hardly one in several thousand was in a position to flee the remains of the Tartar army. Moreover, one infected man could carry the poison to others, and infect people and places with the disease by look alone. Mark Wheelis, *Biological Warfare at the 1346 Siege of Caffa*, CENTERS FOR DISEASE CONTROL AND PREVENTION (September, 2002), *quoting* Gabriele De Mussi, a fourteenth-century notary public in Piacenza, Italy, *available at* http://www.cdc.gov/ncidod/EID/vol8no9/01-0536.htm.

2. Referring to a written correspondence: *Amherst to Sir William Johnson, Superintendent of the Northern Indian Department*, (July 9, 1793), British manuscripts project, a checklist of the microfilms prepared in England and Wales for the American Council of Learned Societies, 1941–1945. Library of Congress Call No.: Z6620.G7 U5 1968, microfilm reel 34/38, item 244, compiled by Lester K. Born, Greenwood Press (1968).

3. *The Rapport presente a la Conference des Preliminaires de Paix par la Commission des Responsabilites des Auteurs de la Guerre et Sanctions*, cited in, *The Problem of Chemical and Biological Warfare, Volume I: The Rise of CB Weapons*, STOCKHOLM INTERNATIONAL PEACE RESEARCH INSTITUTE (1971).

4. *See* Eric Croddy, CHEMICAL AND BIOLOGICAL WARFARE: A COMPREHENSIVE SURVEY FOR THE CONCERNED CITIZEN, Springer-Verlag New York, Inc., p. 222–223 (2002).

5. Jeanne Guillemin, BIOLOGICAL WEAPONS: FROM THE INVENTION OF STATE-SPONSORED PROGRAMS TO CONTEMPORARY BIOTERRORISM, Columbia University Press, pp. 6, 24 (2005).

6. Robert Gomer et al., JAPAN'S BIOLOGICAL WEAPONS: 1930–1945–A HIDDEN CHAPTER IN HISTORY, *The Bulletin of the Atomic Scientists* (October, 1981).

7. Jeanne Guillemin, BIOLOGICAL WEAPONS: FROM THE INVENTION OF STATE-SPONSORED PROGRAMS TO CONTEMPORARY BIOTERRORISM, Columbia University Press, p. 88 (2005).

8. *See* Ira Baldwin, *Special BW Operations*, Memorandum for Executive Secretary, Research and Development Board, Unclassified, THE NATIONAL MILITARY ESTABLISHMENT RESEARCH AND DEVELOPMENT BOARD (October 5, 1948).

9. *Nevin v. United States*, 696 F.2d 1229 (1983).

10. *Biological Weapons*, FEDERATION OF AMERICAN SCIENTISTS, *available at* http://fas.org/nuke/guide/usa/cbw/bw.htm; *See also*, David R. Franz, et al., *The U.S. Biological Warfare and Biological Defense Programs*, in MEDICAL ASPECTS OF CHEMICAL AND BIOLOGICAL WARFARE, *Textbook of Military Medicine*, pg. 431 (1997).

11. Statement by the President, Office of the White House Press Secretary, p. 2 (November 25, 1969); *See also*, Jonathan B. Tucker, *A Farewell to Germs: The U.S.*

Renunciation of Biological and Toxin Warfare, 1969–1970, INTERNATIONAL SECURITY (Summer 2002).

12. *See* Tom Mangold & Jeff Goldberg, *"Incident at Sverdlovsk,"* in PLAGUE WARS: A TRUE STORY OF BIOLOGICAL WARFARE, Macmillan Publishers Ltd., Chapter 9 (1999).

13. According to Dr. Ken Alibek:

> The Russians have steadfastly refused to open their military biological weapons facilities to international inspection. Pursuant to agreements between Russia, the U.S. and Britain, a series of trilateral inspections was begun in 1991. However, the facilities visited in Russia were those managed by the civilian arm of the Soviet/Russian biological weapons program, Biopreparat. The facilities of the Ministry of Defense, most notably those at Sergiyev Posad (formerly Zagorsk), Kirov, Yekaterinburg, and Strizhi, have never been inspected. Furthermore, according to the On-Site Inspection Agency, the last visits to Russian civilian facilities took place in early 1994.

Statement by Dr. Ken Alibek, *Terrorist and Intelligence Operations: Potential Impact on the U.S. Economy,* before the Joint Economic Committee, United States Congress (May 20, 1998); *See also,* Richard G. Lugar, *Symposium on Security & Liberty: Essay: Nunn-Lugar in the Second Term,* 19 NOTRE DAME J.L. ETHICS & PUB. POL'Y., 233 (2005).

14. George Post, *Biotechnology and Terrorism,* PROSPECT MAGAZINE (April 25, 2002).

15. Prepared Statement of Richard O. Spertzel, *Russia, Iraq, and Other Potential Sources of Anthrax, Smallpox, and Other Bioterrorist Weapons,* Hearing before the Committee on International Relations, House of Representatives, 107th Congress, 1st Session (December 2001).

16. *Gunning for Saddam: Saddam Hussein's Weapons of Mass Destruction,* PBS Frontline Special (Nov 8, 2001), *available at* http://www.pbs.org/wgbh/pages/frontline/shows/gunning /etc/arsenal.html.

17. *Report on Status of Disarmament and Monitoring,* Letter dated January 27, 1999, from the Permanent Representatives of the Netherlands and Slovenia to the United Nations Addressed to the President of the Security Council, UNITED NATIONS SPECIAL COMMISSION, UN Doc. S/1999/94 (January 29, 1999), *available at* http://www.un.org/Depts/unscom/s99-94.htm.

18. *Russia, Iraq, and Other Potential Sources of Anthrax, Smallpox, and Other Bioterrorist Weapons,* Hearing before the Committee on International Relations, House of Representatives, 107th Congress, 1st Session, p. 7 (December 2001); *See also,* Graham Pearson, *On-Site Investigations, available at* http://www.bradford.ac.uk/acad/sbtwc/briefing/bp1.pdf.

19. *"Dr. Death" to Be Retried,* NEW YORK TIMES (September 10, 2005); *See also,* William J Broad & Judith Miller, *Live Ammo; The Threat of Germ Weapons is Rising. Fear, Too,* NEW YORK TIMES (December 27, 1998).

20. Joby Warrick & John Mintz, *Lethal Legacy: Bioweapons for Sale: U.S. Declined South African Scientist's Offer on Man-Made Pathogens,* WASHINGTON POST, p A1 (April 20, 2003).

21. *Biological Weapons Program – Egypt,* FEDERATION OF AMERICAN SCIENTISTS, *available at* http://www.fas.org/nuke/guide/egypt/bw/index.html.

22. *Country Reports: Egypt,* MIDDLE EAST DEFENSE NEWS, Vol. 6, No. 13 (April 5, 1993) *cited in, Country Overviews: Egypt: Biological Overview,* NUCLEAR THREAT INITIATIVE, *available at* http://www.nti.org/e_research/profiles/Egypt/3438.html.

23. *Adherence to and Compliance with Arms Control Agreements,* Defense Treaty Inspection Readiness Program, ARMS CONTROL AND DISARMAMENT AGENCY

(1993), *available at* http://dtirp.dtra.mil/tic/START/st_comp.htm; *See also*, *Country Overviews: Egypt: Biological Chronology*, Nuclear Threat Initiative, *available at* http://www.nti.org/e_research/profiles/Egypt/3456.html.

24. Danny Shoham, *Chemical and Biological Weapons in Egypt*, The Nonproliferation Review, p. 50 (Spring/Summer, 1998).

25. *Country Overviews: Israel: Biological Overview*, Nuclear Threat Initiative, *available at* http://www.nti.org/e_research/profiles/Israel/Biological/index.html; *See also*, Ben-Gurion's Letter to Avriel, (dated March 4, 1948), *cited in*, Michael Keren, *Ben-Gurion and the Intellectuals*, p. 32 (Sdeh Boker: The Ben-Gurion Research Center Press, 1988 [in Hebrew]).

26. Avner Cohen, *Israel and Chemical/Biological Weapons: History, Deterrence, and Arms Control*, The Nonproliferation Review, p. 31 (Fall/Winter 2001).

27. Avner Cohen, *Israel and Chemical/Biological Weapons: History, Deterrence, and Arms Control*, The Nonproliferation Review, p. 35 (Fall/Winter 2001).

28. Testimony of Dr. Amy Sands, before the Senate Foreign Relations Committee (March 19, 2002), *available at* http://cns.miis.edu/pubs/reports/asands.htm.

29. Unclassified Report to Congress on *The Acquisition of Technology Relating to Weapons of Mass Destruction and Advanced Conventional Munitions* (January 1, 2003 through June 30, 2003), *available at* http://www.fas.org/irp/threat/cia_jan_jun2003.pdf.

30. Office of the White House Press Secretary, *Statement by the President*, p. 2 (November 25, 1969), *cited in*, Jonathan B. Tucker, *A Farewell to Germs: The U.S. Renunciation of Biological and Toxin Warfare, 1969–1970*, International Security (Summer, 2002).

31. *Country Overviews: North Korea: Biological Overview*, Nuclear Threat Initiative, *available at* http://www.nti.org/e_research/profiles/NK/Biological/index.html.

32. John Bolton, *Beyond the Axis of Evil: Additional Threats from Weapons of Mass Destruction*, Remarks to the Heritage Foundation, Heritage Lectures, No. 743, p. 3. (May 6, 2002). *available at* http://www.heritage.org/Research/NationalSecurity/HL743.cfm.

33. Testimony of Director of Central Intelligence Porter J. Goss, *Global Intelligence Challenges 2005: Meeting Long-Term Challenges with a Long-Term Strategy*, before the Senate Select Committee on Intelligence (February 16, 2005), *available at* https://www.cia.gov/cia/public_affairs/speeches/2005/Goss_testimony_02162005.html.

34. *Country Overviews: North Korea: Biological Overview*, Nuclear Threat Initiative, *available at* http://www.nti.org/e_research/profiles/NK/index_207.html#fn2, *citing* Pak Tong-sam, *How Far Has the DPRK's Development of Strategic Weapons Come?*, Pukhan, translated in FBIS Document ID: FTS19990121001655, pp. 62–71 (January 1999).

35. Jeff Goldberg & Tom Mangold, Plague Wars: The Terrifying Reality of Biological Warfare, Macmillan Publishers, Ltd., p. 330 (1999).

36. Testimony of Dr. Amy Sands, before the Senate Foreign Relations Committee (March 19, 2002), *available at* http://cns.miis.edu/pubs/reports/asands.htm.

37. *Weapons of Mass Destruction (WMD) – Biological Weapons – Iran*, GlobalSecurity.Org, *available at* http://www.globalsecurity.org/wmd/world/iran/bw.htm; *See also*, Anthony Cordesman & Khalid R. Al-Rodhan, Iran's Weapons of Mass Destruction, Center for Strategic and International Studies (2006); *See also*, *Recognizing Iran as a Strategic Threat: An Intelligence Challenge for the United States*, U.S. House of Representatives, Permanent Select Committee on Intelligence (August 23, 2006), *available at* http://intelligence.house.gov/Media/PDFS/IranReport082206v2.pdf.

38. Jonathan Spyer, *The Al-Qa'ida Network and Weapons of Mass Destruction*, MIDDLE EAST REVIEW OF INTERNATIONAL AFFAIRS, Vol. 8, No. 3, pp. 39–40 (September 2004); *See also*, Ely Karmon, *Hisballah Hand the War on Terror* (August 1, 2002).

39. Jonathan Spyer, *The Al-Qa'ida Network and Weapons of Mass Destruction*, MIDDLE EAST REVIEW OF INTERNATIONAL AFFAIRS, Vol. 8, No 3, p. 40 (September 2004), *available at* http://meria.idc.ac.il/journal/2004/issue3/spyer.pdf, *citing* Testimony of Paula A. DeSutter, Assistant Secretary for Verification and Compliance, *Iranian WMD and Support of Terrorism*, before the U.S.-Israeli Joint Parliamentary Committee (September 13, 2003).

40. *Current and Projected National Security Threats to the United States and its Interests Abroad*, Central Intelligence Agency, written responses to questions before the Select Committee on Intelligence of the United States Senate, Hearing 104–510 (February 22, 1996), *available at* http://www.fas.org/irp/congress/1996_hr/s960222c.htm.

41. *Country Overviews: Iran: Biological Overview*, NUCLEAR THREAT INITIATIVE, *available at* http://www.nti.org/e_research/profiles/Iran/Biological/2299.html, *citing* Gregory F. Giles, *The Islamic Republic of Iran and Nuclear, Biological, and Chemical Weapons, cited in*, Peter R. Lavoy, et al., (eds.), PLANNING THE UNTHINKABLE: HOW NEW POWERS WILL USE NUCLEAR, BIOLOGICAL, AND CHEMICAL WEAPONS, Ithaca: Cornell University Press, p. 84 (2000).

42. Statement of Michael D. Maples, Director of the Defense Intelligence Agency, *Current and Projected National Security Threats to the United States*, before the Senate Armed Services Committee (February 28, 2006), *available at* http://www.dia.mil/publicaffairs/Testimonies/statement24.html.

43. *Recognizing Iran as a Strategic Threat: An Intelligence Challenge for the United States*, Staff Report of the House Permanent Select Subcommittee on Intelligence Policy, U.S. House of Representatives, p. 14 (August 23, 2006), *available at* http://intelligence.house.gov/Media/PDFS/IranReport082206v2.pdf, *citing, Adherence and Compliance with Arms Control, Nonproliferation, and Disarmament Agreements*, U.S. Department of State, pp. 20–21 (August 2005).

44. *Country Overviews: Iran: Biological Overview*, NUCLEAR THREAT INITIATIVE, *available at* http://www.nti.org/e_research/profiles/Iran/Biological/2299.html.

45. *Perspectives, A Canadian Security Intelligence Service Publication, Report # 2000/05 Biological Weapons Proliferation* (June 9, 2000), *available at* http://www.csis-scrs.gc.ca/en/publications/perspectives 200005.asp.

46. *Country Overviews: Syria: Biological Overview*, NUCLEAR THREAT INITIATIVE, *available at* http://www.nti.org/e_research/profiles/Syria/Biological/3338.html.

47. *Perspectives, A Canadian Security Intelligence Service Publication, Report # 2000/05 Biological Weapons Proliferation*, (June 9, 2000), *available at* http://www.csis-scrs.gc.ca/en/publications/perspectives 200005.asp.

48. Statement of Michael D. Maples, Director of the Defense Intelligence Agency, *Current and Projected National Security Threats to the United States*, before the Senate Armed Services Committee (February 28, 2006), *available at* http://www.dia.mil/publicaffairs/Testimonies/statement24.html.

49. *Unclassified Report to Congress on the Acquisition of Technology Relating to Weapons of Mass Destruction and Advanced Conventional Munitions* (1 January Through 30 June 2003), *available at* http://www.fas.org/irp/threat/cia_jan_jun2003.pdf.

50. Statement of Gordon C. Oehler, *cited in, Beyond Anthrax: Extremism and the Bioterrorism Threat*, ANTI-DEFAMATION LEAGUE, p. 11 (2001), *available at* http://www.adl.org/learn/Anthrax/hoaxes.asp?xpicked=3&item=hoax; *See also*, Testimony of

Gordon C. Oehler, *The Continuing Threat from Weapons of Mass Destruction* (March 27, 1996), *available at* http://www.fas.org/irp/cia/product/go_testimony_032796.html.

51. Jessica Stern, *Domestic Terrorists Constitute a Potentially Serious Biological Warfare Threat, in* William Dudley (ed.), Biological Warfare: Opposing Viewpoints, pg. 80 (2004).

52. *See generally,* Milton Leitenberg, *Assessing the Biological Weapons and Bioterrorism Threat,* U.S. Army War College Strategic Studies Institute (December, 2005); *See also,* Milton Leitenberg, The Problem of Biological Weapons, Swedish National Defense College (2004).

53. Numerous books detail how anarchists and other extremists can go about acquiring biological agents. Kurt Saxon's *The Poor Man's James Bond* and Maynard Campbell's *Catalogue of Silent Tools of Justice* explain how to manufacture biological agents and poisons such as ricin. Steve Preisler's *Silent Death* and Maxwell Hutchkinson's *The Poisoner's Handbook* instruct guerrilla-warfare-type methods of producing and deploying poisonous agents. *See also, Beyond Anthrax: Extremism and the Bioterrorism Threat,* Anti-Defamation League, pp. 3–4 (2001), *available at* http://www.adl.org/learn/Anthrax/hoaxes.asp?xpicked=3&item=hoax.

54. *Terrorism: Terror Organizations,* Basics Project Website, *available at* http://www.basicsproject.org/terrorism/terror_organizations.htm. More conservative estimates conclude that Al Qaeda is active in at least twenty different countries; *See also,* Jonathan Spyer, *The Al-Qa'ida Network and Weapons of Mass Destruction,* Middle East Review of International Affairs, Vol. 8, No. 3 (September 2004), *available at* http://meria.idc.ac.il/journal/2004/issue3/spyer.pdf.

55. Speech by Interpol Secretary General Ronald K. Noble, *Interpol Asian Bioterrorism Workshop,* Singapore (March 27, 2006), *available at* http://www.interpol.int/Public/ICPO/speeches/SGBioterrorism20050327.asp.

56. *Al-Qa'ida's WMD Activities,* Chart prepared by the Weapons of Mass Destruction Terrorism Research Program, Center for Nonproliferation Studies, *available at* http://cns.miis.edu/pubs/other/sjm_cht.htm, *citing* The 9/11 Commission Report, Final Report of the National Commission on Terrorist Attacks Upon the United States; (2004) *See also, Al-Qaeda Operatives Discussed WMD Attacks While Training Prior to 9/11, Report Says,* Global Security Newswire (June 16, 2004).

57. Sammy Salama & Lydia Hansell, *Does Intent Equal Capability?: Al-Qaeda and Weapons of Mass Destruction,* Nonproliferation Review, Vol. 12, No. 3, p. 631 (November 2005), *citing* an article on *Biological Weapons* appearing in an al Tawhid Wal Jihad Website.

58. *Conversation with Terror,* Time Magazine (January 11, 1999), *available at* http://www.time.com/time/magazine/article/0,9171,17676,00.html.

59. Sammy Salama & Lydia Hansell, *Does Intent Equal Capability?: Al-Qaeda and Weapons of Mass Destruction,* Nonproliferation Review, Vol. 12, No. 3 (November, 2005).

60. Alan Cullison & Andrew Higgins, *Computer in Kabul Holds Chilling Memos,* Wall Street Journal, (December 31, 2001).

61. Sammy Salama & Lydia Hansell, *Does Intent Equal Capability?: Al-Qaeda and Weapons of Mass Destruction,* Nonproliferation Review, Vol. 12, No. 3, p. 637 (November 2005), *citing, Learn my Mujahid Brother How to Manufacture Poisons,* al-Ma'asada al Jihadiya – the Jihadi Lion's Den Website (November 13, 2004).

62. Paul Cruickshank & Mohanad Hage Ali, *Jihadist of Mass Destruction*, WASHINGTON POST (June 11, 2006); *See also*, Sammy Salama & Lydia Hansell, *Does Intent Equal Capability?: Al-Qaeda and Weapons of Mass Destruction*, NONPROLIFERATION REVIEW, Vol. 12, No. 3, p. 625 (November, 2005).

63. *Al-Qa'ida's WMD Activities*, Chart prepared by the Weapons of Mass Destruction Terrorism Research Program, CENTER FOR NONPROLIFERATION STUDIES, *available at* http://cns.miis.edu/pubs/other/sjm_cht.htm, *citing, U.S. Biological Attack Imminent – Taliban*, IAFRICA.COM (December 12, 2001); *See also, Walker Lindh: Al Qaeda Planned More Attacks*, CNN (October 3, 2002).

64. Sammy Salama & Lydia Hansell, *Does Intent Equal Capability?: Al-Qaeda and Weapons of Mass Destruction*, NONPROLIFERATION REVIEW, Vol. 12, No. 3, p. 627 (November, 2005), *citing* Michael Scheuer, *Imperial Hubris: Why the West is Losing the War on Terror*, p. 153 (2004).

65. *Al-Qa'ida's WMD Activities*, Chart prepared by the Weapons of Mass Destruction Terrorism Research Program, CENTER FOR NONPROLIFERATION STUDIES, *available at* http://cns.miis.edu/pubs/other/sjm_cht.htm, *citing The Base of the Vanguard*, an Al Qaeda manifesto posted on the Internet; *also citing, Counter-Insurgency in the Middle East*, MIDDLE EAST NEWSLINE MORNING REPORT, Vol. 6, No. 23 (January 19, 2004).

66. Ross E. Getman, *Modus Operandi: Pouring Musk on Barren Land, in* VANGUARDS OF CONQUEST: AL QAEDA, ANTHRAX AND AYMAN ZAWAHIRI, Chapter IV, *available at* http://members.bellatlantic.net/~vze43v8m/alqaedaanthraxay.html# RequirementofWarning.

67. Paul Cruickshank & Mohanad Hage Ali, *Jihadist of Mass Destruction*, WASHINGTON POST (June 11, 2006).

68. Paul Cruickshank & Mohanad Hage Ali, *Jihadist of Mass Destruction*, WASHINGTON POST (June 11, 2006).

69. *See generally*, Paul Cruickshank & Mohannad Hage Ali, *Abu Musab Al-Suri: Architect of the New Al Qaeda*, STUDIES IN CONFLICT & TERRORISM, Vol. 30, pp. 1–14 (2007), *available at* http://www.lawandsecurity.org/documents/ AbuMusabalSuriArchitectoftheNewAlQaeda.pdf.

70. Tony Allen-Mills & Uzi Mahnaimi Tel Aviv, *Al-Qaeda Seeks Toxins for Biowarfare Attack*, SUNDAY TIMES (London) (January 2, 2005).

71. Nasir Bin Hamd Al-Fahd, *A Treatise on the Legal Status of Using Weapons of Mass Destruction Against Infidels*, (May 2003).

72. *Al-Qa'ida's WMD Activities*, Chart prepared by the Weapons of Mass Destruction Terrorism Research Program, CENTER FOR NONPROLIFERATION STUDIES, *available at* http://cns.miis.edu/pubs/other/sjm_cht.htm, *citing* Statements given by various defendants in the Egyptian *Trial of the Returnees from Albania; also citing* Al J. Venter, *Elements Loyal to Bin Laden Acquire Biological Agents 'Through the Mail,'* JANE'S INTELLIGENCE REVIEW (August 1999); *also citing* Khalid Sharaf al-Din, *Bin Ladin Men Reportedly Possess Biological Weapons*, AL-SHARQ AL-AWSAT (March 6, 1999).

73. *Al-Qa'ida's WMD Activities*, Chart prepared by the Weapons of Mass Destruction Terrorism Research Program, CENTER FOR NONPROLIFERATION STUDIES, *available at* http://cns.miis.edu/pubs/other/sjm_cht.htm, *citing* John McWethy, *Bin Laden Set to Strike Again?*, ABC NEWS (June 16, 1999); *also citing* Muhammad Salah, *Bin Ladin Front Reportedly Bought CBW From E. Europe*, AL-HAYAH (April 20, 1999); *also citing, U.S. Said Interrogating Jihadist Over CBW*, AL-HAYAH (April 21, 1999).

74. *Al-Qa'ida's WMD Activities*, Chart prepared by the Weapons of Mass Destruction Terrorism Research Program, Center for Nonproliferation Studies, *available at* http://cns.miis.edu/pubs/other/sjm_cht.htm, *citing Islamist Lawyer on Bin Ladin, Groups*, Al-Sharq al-Awsat (July 12, 1999).

75. *Al-Qa'ida's WMD Activities*, Chart prepared by the Weapons of Mass Destruction Terrorism Research Program, Center for Nonproliferation Studies, *available at* http://cns.miis.edu/pubs/other/sjm_cht.htm, *citing* Toby Harnden, *Rogue Scientists Gave bin Laden Nuclear Secrets*, Daily Telegraph (London) (December 13, 2001); *also citing* Peter Baker, *Pakistani Scientist Who Met Bin Laden Failed Polygraphs, Renewing Suspicions*, Washington Post (March 3, 2002); *also citing* Susan B. Glasser & Kamran Khan, *Pakistan Continues Probe of Nuclear Scientists*, Washington Post (November 14, 2001).

76. *Al-Qa'ida's WMD Activities*, Chart prepared by the Weapons of Mass Destruction Terrorism Research Program, Center for Nonproliferation Studies, *available at* http://cns.miis.edu/pubs/other/sjm_cht.htm, *citing* Paul Daley, *Report Says UBL-linked Terrorist Groups Possess 'Deadly' Anthrax, Plague Viruses*, Melbourne Age (June 4, 2000).

77. *Al-Qa'ida's WMD Activities*, Chart prepared by the Weapons of Mass Destruction Terrorism Research Program, Center for Nonproliferation Studies, *available at* http://cns.miis.edu/pubs/other/sjm_cht.htm, *citing* Maria Ressa, *Reports: Al Qaeda [sic] Operative Sought Anthrax*, CNN (October 10, 2003); *also citing* Judith Miller, *U.S. Has New Concerns About Anthrax Readiness*, New York Times (December 28, 2003); *also citing* Yazid Sufaat, The Open Source Threat Network Database (January 26, 2004).

78. *Al-Qa'ida's WMD Activities*, Chart prepared by the Weapons of Mass Destruction Terrorism Research Program, Center for Nonproliferation Studies, *available at* http://cns.miis.edu/pubs/other/sjm_cht.htm, *citing* Jeffrey Bartholet, *Terrorist Sleeper Cells*, Newsweek (December 9, 2001).

79. Suzanne Goldenberg & Nick Hopkins, *MI 5 Says Dirty Bomb Attack is Inevitable*, Guardian (June 18, 2003).

80. Tony Allen-Mills & Uzi Mahnaimi Tel Aviv, *Al-Qaeda Seeks Toxins for Biowarfare Attack*, Sunday Times (London) (January 2, 2005), *available at* http://www.timesonline.co.uk/tol/news/world/article407762.ece.

81. Allan Cullison & Andrew Higgins, *Files Found: A Computer in Kabul Yields a Chilling Array of Al-Qaeda Memos*, Wall Street Journal (December 31, 2001).

82. *Al-Qaeda Leader Calls for Scientists to Join Cause*, WCBS (September 28, 2006), *available at* http://www.wcbs880.com/pages/93915.php?contentType=4&contentId=214158.

83. James Dao, *Muslim Cleric Found Guilty in the 'Virginia Jihad' Case*, New York Times (April 27, 2005).

84. Jerry Markon, *Va. Terror Case Sent Back to Lower Court; Appeals Panel Cites Eavesdropping Program*, Washington Post (April 26, 2006); *See also*, Caryle Murphy, *Muslim Lecturer Fits Easily in Two Worlds*, Washington Post (August 8, 2003).

85. Ross E. Getman, Vanguards of Conquest: The Sheik and the BioWeaponeers, *available at* http://members.bellatlantic.net/~vze43v8m/alqaeda,anthraxa.html#SheikandtheBioweaponeers.

86. Timothy Dwyer, *Prosecution Called 'Overzealous' Guilty Verdict in Terror Case Angers Muslims Who Know Lecturer*, Washington Post (April 27, 2005).

87. Alan Cullison & Andrew Higgins, *Files Found: A Computer in Kabul Yields a Chilling Array of al Qaeda Memos*, WALL STREET JOURNAL (December 31, 2001).

88. Barton Gellman, *al-Qaida Near Biological, Chemical Arms Production*, WASHINGTON POST (March 23, 2003).

89. Allan Cullison & Andrew Higgins, *Files Found: A Computer in Kabul Yields a Chilling Array of Al-Qaeda Memos*, WALL STREET JOURNAL (December 31, 2001).

90. Harold Kennedy, *Military Officials Warn Al Qaeda to Attack with WMD*, NATIONAL DEFENSE (February 2005), *available at* http://www.nationaldefensemagazine.org/issues/2005/Feb/Military_officials.htm.

91. Translated from Arabic.

92. *Al-Qa'ida's WMD Activities*, Chart prepared by the Weapons of Mass Destruction Terrorism Research Program, CENTER FOR NONPROLIFERATION STUDIES, *available at* http://cns.miis.edu/pubs/other/sjm_cht.htm, *citing Al Qaeda Tested Germ Weapons*, REUTERS (January 1, 2002).

93. *Al-Qa'ida's WMD Activities*, Chart prepared by the Weapons of Mass Destruction Terrorism Research Program, CENTER FOR NONPROLIFERATION STUDIES, *available at* http://cns.miis.edu/pubs/other/sjm_cht.htm, *citing* Guido Olimpio, *Islamic Group Said Preparing Chemical Warfare on the West*, CORRIERE DELLA SERA (July 8, 1998); *also citing* Yossef Bodansky, BIN LADEN: THE MAN WHO DECLARED WAR ON AMERICA, p. 326 (2001).

94. *Al-Qa'ida's WMD Activities*, Chart prepared by the Weapons of Mass Destruction Terrorism Research Program, CENTER FOR NONPROLIFERATION STUDIES, *available at* http://cns.miis.edu/pubs/other/sjm_cht.htm, *citing* Dominic Evans, *U.S. Troops Found Afghan Biological Lab*, REUTERS (March 22, 2002); *also citing* Michael R. Gordon, *U.S. Says It Found Qaeda Lab Being Built to Produce Anthrax*, NEW YORK TIMES (March 23, 2002).

95. Judith Miller, *Lab Suggests Qaeda Planned to Build Arms, Officials Say*, NEW YORK TIMES (September 14, 2002).

96. Allan Cullison & Andrew Higgins, *Files Found: A Computer in Kabul Yields a Chilling Array of Al-Qaeda Memos*, WALL STREET JOURNAL (December 31, 2001).

97. *Al-Qa'ida's WMD Activities*, Chart prepared by the Weapons of Mass Destruction Terrorism Research Program, CENTER FOR NONPROLIFERATION STUDIES, *available at* http://cns.miis.edu/pubs/other/sjm_cht.htm, *citing Al-Qaeda: Anthrax Found in al-Qaeda home*, GLOBAL SECURITY NEWSWIRE (December 10, 2001); Judith Miller, *Labs Suggest Qaeda Planned to Build Arms, Officials Say*, NEW YORK TIMES (September 14, 2002).

98. *Al-Qa'ida's WMD Activities*, Chart prepared by the Weapons of Mass Destruction Terrorism Research Program, CENTER FOR NONPROLIFERATION STUDIES, *available at* http://cns.miis.edu/pubs/other/sjm_cht.htm, *citing Terrorist Attacks in Iraq*, program transcript, NBC Nightly News (March 2, 2004).

99. *Al-Qa'ida's WMD Activities*, Chart prepared by the Weapons of Mass Destruction Terrorism Research Program, CENTER FOR NONPROLIFERATION STUDIES, *available at* http://cns.miis.edu/pubs/other/sjm_cht.htm, *citing U.S. Knew of Bioterror Tests in Iraq*, BBC NEWS (August 20, 2002); *also citing U.S. Monitors Kurdish Extremists*, FOX NEWS (August 21, 2002); *also citing* Isma'il Zayir, *Ansar al-Islam Group Accuses [Jalal] Talabani of Spreading Rumors About Its Cooperation with al-Qa'ida*, AL-HAYAH (August 22, 2002); Sammy Salama & Lydia Hansell, *Does Intent Equal Capability?: Al-Qaeda and Weapons of Mass Destruction*, NONPROLIFERATION REVIEW, Vol. 12, No. 3, p. 623 (November 2005).

100. Harold Kennedy, *Military Officials Warn Al Qaeda to Attack with WMD*, National Defense, (February 2005), *available at* http://www.nationaldefensemagazine.org/issues/2005/Feb/Military_officials.htm.

101. *Al-Qa'ida's WMD Activities*, Chart prepared by the Weapons of Mass Destruction Terrorism Research Program, Center for Nonproliferation Studies, *available at* http://cns.miis.edu/pubs/other/sjm_cht.htm, *citing* Statement given by Al Qaeda operative Ahmad Rassam, in U.S. custody; also citing *Bin Laden's Biological Threat*, BBC (October 28, 2001).

102. *Al-Qa'ida's WMD Activities*, Chart prepared by the Weapons of Mass Destruction Terrorism Research Program, Center for Nonproliferation Studies, *available at* http://cns.miis.edu/pubs/other/sjm_cht.htm, *citing Sketches of Anthrax Bomb Found in Pakistani Scientist's Office*, Rediff.com (November 28, 2001).

Chapter 4. Strategic Foundations

1. *UN Secretary-General's Message to Parties to Biological Weapons Convention*, United Nations Office at Geneva (November 20, 2006), *available at* http://www.unog.ch/80256EDD006B9C2E/(httpNewsByYear_en)/246D92BF4061C961C125722C0037EA12?OpenDocument.

2. *Rome Statute of the International Criminal Court*, Article 7(2)(b), U.N. Doc. A/CONF.183/9 (July 17, 1998), *available at* http://www.un.org/law/icc/statute/99_corr/2.htm; *See also*, M. Cherif Bassiouni, Crimes Against Humanity (1999).

3. *The Kampala Compact: The Global Bargain for Biosecurity and Bioscience*, International Council for Science (October 1, 2005), *available at* http://www.icsu-africa.org/Resource_centre/KampalaCompactoct05.pdf.

Chapter 5. Complication: What Law Enforcers Should Stop

1. James Randerson, *Synthetic Biology: Lax Laws, Virus DNA and Potential for Terror: Loopholes Mean Anyone Can Order Gene Sequences: Scientists Back Voluntary Regulation as First Step*, Guardian (June 14, 2006).

2. Statement of Bruce Alberts, *quoted in* Neil Monro, *Securing Science*, National Journal (September 6, 2003).

3. For laws of the United States, see *Audit Report – Adequacy of Controls to Prevent the Improper Transfer of Sensitive Technology*, Office of Inspector General, USDA, Report No. 02601-1-Ch (September 2005); *See also*, *Inspection Report – Coordination of Biological Select Agent Activities at Department of Energy Facilities*, Office of Inspector General, Department of Energy, DOE/IG-0695 (July 2005).

4. Jennifer L. Bower, *The Terrorist Threat and its Implications for Sensor Technologies*, *available at* http://www.nato-asi.org/sensors2005/papers/brower.pdf.

5. According to the WHO Guidance:

   > [T]he agent will need to be stable enough to resist degradation during handling and storage, and during the energy-transfer processes, that will, in most scenarios, be involved in disseminating it on its targets. Once disseminated, the agent must be capable of establishing field dosages that are infective or toxic over a particular area. It must also be relatively easy to produce from readily available precursor compounds or from naturally occurring or genetically modified organisms.

   Public Health Response to Biological and Chemical Weapons: WHO Guidance, Second Edition of Health Aspects of Chemical and Biological Weapons: Report of a WHO Group of Consultants, World Health Organization, p. 25–26 (2004); *available at* http://www.who.int/csr/delibepidemics/chapter3.pdf.

6. *Public Health Response to Biological and Chemical Weapons: WHO Guidance*, Second Edition of Health Aspects of Chemical and Biological Weapons: Report of a WHO Group of Consultants, WORLD HEALTH ORGANIZATION, pp. 18–19 (2004), *available at* http://whqlibdoc.who.int/publications/2004/9241546158_chap2.pdf.

7. *International Health Regulations*, 48th World Health Assembly, Article 1 (May 23, 2005), *available at* http://www.who.int/csr/ihr/IHRWHA58_3-en.pdf.

8. The OIE has recently revamped its *world animal health information system* to include a single list of all animal diseases, both terrestrial and aquatic, of which occurrence Member States must report immediately to the OIE. The list is *available at* http://www.oie.int/eng/maladies/en_classification.htm.

9. The World Data Centre for Microorganisms (WDCM) Committee on Postal, Quarantine, and Safety Regulations recommends increased vigilance with respect to dangerous pathogens. *See Guidelines for the Establishment and Operation of Collections of Cultures of Microorganisms*, WORLD DATA CENTRE FOR MICROORGANISMS (WDCM), 2nd edition (1999), *available at* http://wdcm.nig.ac.jp/. According to the *Safety and Quality Standards*, paragraph 16.2: "Particular attention needs to be given to the containment and security aspects of strains which are potentially harmful to man, animals, or crops." See *Culture Collection Organization Statements on Biological Warfare*, WORLD FEDERATION FOR CULTURE COLLECTIONS (April 24, 2002), *available at* http://wdcm.nig.ac.jp/biowarfare.html.

10. Scientists at Cornell recently developed a new technique that could make both detection and tracking of pathogens possible where small segments of inactive DNA bind to the DNA of particular pathogens. As Cornell University News Service reports, "Researchers make synthetic DNA 'barcodes' to tag pathogens, providing an inexpensive, off-the-shelf monitoring system." *See* Bill Steele, *Researchers Make Synthetic DNA 'Barcodes' to Tag Pathogens, Providing an Inexpensive, Off-the-Shelf Monitoring System*, (June 13, 2005), *available at* http://www.news.cornell.edu/stories/June05/Luo.barcodes.ws.html; *See also*, Yougen Li, Yen Thi Hong Cu, & Dan Luo, *Multiplexed Detection of Pathogen DNA with DNA-based Fluorescence Nanobarcodes*, NATURE BIOTECHNOLOGY, Vol. 23, No. 7 (July 2005).

11. J. Gaudioso & R. M. Salerno, *A Conceptual Framework for Biosecurity Levels*, Paper presented at *BTR 2004: Unified Science and Technology for Reducing Biological Threats and Countering Terrorism*, Proceedings, (March 18–19, 2004).

12. Various smaller organizations have contributed expertise. The International Organization on Standards (ISO) has issued standards for laboratory operations pertaining to testing apparatus and information technology. The International Federation for Biological Laboratory Safety (IFBLS) provides a forum for bioscientists to train and exchange information. The IFBLS does not accredit facilities, but it is linked with regional organizations that have that authority. The Global Health Security Action Group (GHSAG) – formed after the 2001 anthrax attacks by the health ministers of the G-7 nations plus Mexico – has the objective "to improve linkages among laboratories, including Level Four laboratories, in those countries which have them." *See Health Ministers Take Action to Improve Health Security Globally*, Ministerial Statements, Ottawa, (November 1, 2001), *available at* http://www.ghsi.ca/english/statementottawanov2001.asp; *See also*, WHO *Laboratory Biosafety Manual*, Interim Guidelines 2nd ed. (2003), *available at* WHO21: http://www.who.int/csr/resources/publications/biosafety/en/Labbiosafety.pdf.

13. *Laboratory Security and Emergency Response Guidance for Laboratories Working with Select Agents*, CENTERS FOR DISEASE CONTROL AND PREVENTION, MORBIDITY AND

MORTALITY WEEKLY REPORT, Vol. 51, pp. 1–8 (2002); *See also*, Jonathan B. Tucker, *Biosecurity: Limiting Terrorist Access to Deadly Pathogens*, UNITED STATES INSTITUTE OF PEACE (2003).

14. Reynolds M. Salerno & Daniel P. Estes, *Biosecurity: Protecting High Consequence Pathogens and Toxins Against Theft and Diversion*, SANDIA NATIONAL LABORATO-RIES, Report SAND No. 2003-4274P, p. 6–7 (2003); *See also, Laboratory Security and Emergency Response Guidance for Laboratories Working with Select Agents*, CEN-TERS FOR DISEASE CONTROL AND PREVENTION, MORBIDITY AND MORTALITY WEEKLY REPORT, Vol. 51, pp. 1–8 (2002), stating that threat assessment "identifies and eval-uates each threat on the basis of different factors (e.g., the capability and intent to attack an asset, the likelihood of a successful attack, and the attack's probable lethality)."

15. Jennifer Gaudioso, *A Survey of Asian Life Scientists: The State of Biosciences, Labo-ratory Biosecurity, and Biosafety in Asia*, BIOLOGICAL WEAPONS NONPROLIFERATION DEPARTMENT, SANDIA NATIONAL LABORATORIES, Report SAND 2006–0842 (February 2006).

16. *See*, Helen E. Purkitt, *Biowarfare Lessons, Emerging Biosecurity Issues, and Ways to Monitor Dual-Use Biotechnology Trends in the Future*, INSTITUTE FOR NATIONAL SECURITY STUDIES, Occasional Paper 61 (September 2005).

17. Testimony of Shelton Young, Director Readiness and Logistics Support Directorate, Office of The Inspector General Department of Defense, before the National Security, Emerging Threats, and International Relations Subcommittee of the House Govern-ment Reform Committee (October 7, 2003).

18. Joseph S. Szyliowicz, *International Transportation Security*, THE REVIEW OF POLICY RESEARCH, Vol. 21, No. 3, p. 351 (May 1, 2004), (emphasis added); *See also*, Statement of Michael Moodie, *cited in, Smuggling of Weapons of Mass Destruction*, Senate Committee on Governmental Affairs (June 23, 2004).

19. Samuel Watson, Joe Suyama, Stefanie Fiddner Junker & Michael Allswede, *Connect-ing the Dots: Characterizing Preparations for a Bio Attack*, Unpublished Paper – Final Document (February 21, 2006).

20. *Data Mining: Federal Efforts Cover a Wide Range of Uses*, United States General Accounting Office (May 2004). For a more expansive definition, *see* Colleen McCue, Emily S. Stone, & Teresa P. Gooch, *Data Mining and Value-added Analysis*, FBI LAW ENFORCEMENT BULLETIN (Nov. 1, 2003).

21. *See*, Michael J. Malinowski, BIOTECHNOLOGY: LAW, BUSINESS, AND REGULATION, at § 1.05[D] (1999).

22. *See Mandate of the Commission*, WEAPONS OF MASS DESTRUCTION COMMISSION (Jan-uary 28, 2004), *available at* http://www.wmdcommission.org/.

23. "*Introduction to the Transport of Infectious Substances*," in LABORATORY BIO-SAFETY MANUAL, World Health Organization, 3rd ed., Ch. 15 (2004), *available at* http://www.who.int/csr/resources/publications/biosafety/Biosafety7.pdf.

24. *UN Model Regulations on the Transport of Dangerous Goods*, Committee of Experts on the Transport of Dangerous Goods, UNITED NATIONS ECONOMIC AND SOCIAL COUNCIL, 14th rev. ed., (2005), *available at* http://www.unece.org/trans/danger/publi/unrec/rev14/14files_e.html.

25. *Convention on Civil Aviation*, INTERNATIONAL CIVIL AVIATION ORGANIZATION, Annex 18 (9th ed. 2006). To similar effect, see *European Agreement concerning the Interna-tional Carriage of Dangerous Goods by Road*, UNITED NATIONS ECONOMIC COMMISSION FOR EUROPE (4th ed. 2007).

26. Martin Van de Voort et al., *Improving the Security of the Global Sea-Container Shipping System*, RAND Corporation (2004), *available at* http://www.rand.org/pubs/monograph_reports/MR1695/MR1695.pdf.

27. *International Ship and Port Facility Security Code*, SOLAS/CONF.5/34, Annex 1 (Dec. 12, 2002).

28. *International Ship and Port Facility Security Code*, SOLAS/CONF.5/34, Annex 1, Part A, Sections 2.1.4, 9.1–9.8.1; Part B, Sections 9.1–9.53 (Dec. 12, 2002).

29. *International Ship and Port Facility Security Code*, SOLAS/CONF.5/34, Annex 1, Part A, Sections 14.1–14.6; Part B, Sections 15, 16, 18 (Dec. 12, 2002).

30. *Maritime Transportation Security Act of 2002*, 46 U.S.C.S. §§ 70101–117.

31. *C-TPAT: Customs-Trade Partnership Against Terrorism*, U.S. Customs and Border Protection, *available at* http://www.cbp.gov/xp/cgov/import/commercial_enforcement/ctpat/, containing the C-TPAT Security Guidelines along with continually updated information on growth and improvements to the agreement.

32. *CSI: Container Security Initiative*, U.S. Customs and Border Protection, *available at* http://www.cbp.gov/xp/cgov/border_security/international_activities/csi/, containing an overview of the program along with information about its continual expansion to new seaports.

33. *ACE: Modernization Information Systems*, U.S. Customs and Border Protection, *available at* http://www.cbp.gov/xp/cgov/toolbox/about/modernization/.

34. *Proliferation Security Initiative*, U.S. Department of State, *available at* http://www.state.gov/t/np/c10390.htm.

35. Mark R. Shulman, *The Proliferation Security Initiative and the Evolution of the Law on the Use of Force*, 28 Houston J. Int'l L. 771 (2006).

36. Statement of John R. Bolton, Under Secretary of State for Arms Control and International Security, *U.S. Efforts to Stop the Spread of Weapons of Mass Destruction*, Testimony before the House Committee on International Relations, 108th Congress (2003).

Chapter 6. Improving Resistance through Science

1. John Steinbruner, Elisa D. Harris, Nancy Gallagher, & Stacy Okutani, *Controlling Dangerous Pathogens: A Prototype Protective Oversight System*, Center for International and Security Studies, p. 6–7 (December, 2005), *available at* http://www.cissm.umd.edu/papers/files/pathogens_project_monograph.pdf.

2. Emilio Mordini, *Conclusions of the International Conference on Ethical Implications of Research into the Prevention of Bioterrorism*, Bioethical Implications of Globalization Processes, Policy Paper 1 (April, 2004).

3. Francis A. Boyle, Biowarfare and Terrorism, Clarity Press, Inc., (2005); *See also*, William J Broad & Judith Miller, *A Nation Challenged: The Investigation; U.S. Recently Produced Anthrax in a Highly Lethal Powder Form*, New York Times. (December 13, 2001).

4. See Peter Aldhous & Michael Reilly, *Friend or Foe?; Efforts to Combat Killer Pathogens with New Vaccines and Drugs Could Be Inadvertently Writing a Handbook for Biowarfare*, New Scientist, pp. 20–23 (October 14, 2006).

5. See generally, Halla Thorsteinsdotir et al., *Health Biotechnology Publishing Takes Off in Developing Countries*, 8 Int. J. Biotechnology 23 (2006).

6. See Andrew J. Hawkins, *National Biosecurity Advisory Board Members Stress Balance, International Implications*, Research Policy ALERT (July 1, 2005).

7. *Biotechnology Research in an Age of Terrorism*, NATIONAL RESEARCH COUNCIL OF THE NATIONAL ACADEMIES (2004).

8. Joshua Lederberg, *The Freedoms and the Control of Science: Notes from the Ivory Tower*, 45 S. CAL. L. REV. 596, at p. 599 (1972).

9. See Ronald J. Jackson et al., *Expression of Mouse Interleukin-4 by a Recombinant Ectromelia Virus Suppresses Cytolytic Lymphocyte Responses and Overcomes Genetic Resistance to Mousepox*, JOURNAL OF VIROLOGY, pp. 1205–1210 (February, 2001); See also, Jeronimo Cello et al., *Chemical Synthesis of Poliovirus cDNA: Generation of Infectious Virus in the Absence of Natural Template*, SCIENCEXPRESS (July 11, 2002), available at www.sciencemag.org/cgi/content/abstract/1072266v1.

10. Terrence M. Tumpey, Christopher F. Basler, Patricia V. Aguilar et al., *Characterization of the Reconstructed 1918 Spanish Influenza Virus*, SCIENCE, Vol. 310, pp. 77–80 (October 7, 2005).

11. See Sabin Russell, *Deadliest Flu Bug Given New Life in U.S. Laboratory; Some Applaud Scientific Feat, but Others Decry Move as Reckless*, SAN FRANCISCO CHRONICLE, p. A1 (October 6, 2005); See also, Philip A. Sharp, 1918 Flu and Responsible Science, SCIENCE, Vol. 310, p. 17 (October 7, 2005).

12. See generally, Barry P. McDonald, *Government Regulation or Other "Abridgements" of Scientific Research: The Proper Scope of Judicial Review Under the First Amendment*, 54 EMORY L. J. 979 (2005).

13. *Seeking Security: Pathogens, Open Access, and Genome Databases*, NATIONAL RESEARCH COUNCIL OF THE NATIONAL ACADEMIES (2004).

14. *Biotechnology Research in an Age of Terrorism*, NATIONAL RESEARCH COUNCIL OF THE NATIONAL ACADEMIES, (2004).

15. *National Science Advisory Board for Biosecurity Charter*, DEPARTMENT OF HEALTH AND HUMAN SERVICES (March 4, 2004). General information regarding the NSABB can be found online at http://www.biosecurityboard.gov/. For further information, *see* Dana A. Shea, *Oversight of Dual-Use Biological Research*, The National Science Advisory Board for Biosecurity, CONGRESSIONAL RESEARCH SERVICE REPORT (July 10, 2006).

16. Margaret A. Somerville & Ronald M. Atlas, *Ethics: A Weapon to Counter Bioterrorism*, SCIENCE, Vol. 307, pp. 1881–1882 (March 25, 2005).

17. See Ronald M. Atlas, *National Security and the Biological Research Community; Policy Forum: Public Health*, SCIENCE (October 25, 2002).

18. *See* Brian Rappert, *Responsibility in the Life Sciences: Assessing the Role of Professional Codes*, BIOSECURITY AND BIOTERRORISM: BIODEFENSE STRATEGY, PRACTICE, AND SCIENCE, Vol. 2, pp. 164–174 (July 2004).

19. See *An Introduction to Biological Weapons, their Prohibition, and the Relationship to Biosafety*, THE SUNSHINE PROJECT, Backgrounder Series, No. 10 (April 2002).

20. See Draft Recommendations for a Code of Conduct for Biodefense Programs, FEDERATION OF AMERICAN SCIENTISTS (November 2002).

21. John Steinbruner, Elisa D. Harris, Nancy Gallagher, & Stacy Okutani, *Controlling Dangerous Pathogens: A Prototype Protective Oversight System*, CENTER FOR INTERNATIONAL AND SECURITY STUDIES (December 2005).

22. A relevant process was used by the U.S. NAS to handle the dissemination of sensitive portions of its 2002 study on agricultural bioterrorism. In response to security concerns from the U.S. Department of Agriculture, which funded the study, NAS officials developed guidelines for the types of individuals who could be given access to the controlled information. Anyone interested had to submit a written request and be interviewed by NAS staff before being provided a copy of the controlled information.

See Martin Ensirenk, *Entering the Twilight Zone of What Material to Censor*, SCIENCE (November 22, 2002).

23. *Integrity in Scientific Research: Creating an Environment that Promotes Responsible Conduct*, INSTITUTE OF MEDICINE (2002).

24. *Integrity in Scientific Research: Creating an Environment that Promotes Responsible Conduct*, INSTITUTE OF MEDICINE (2002).

25. D. L. Weed, *Preventing Scientific Misconduct*, AMERICAN JOURNAL OF PUBLIC HEALTH, Vol. 88, pp. 125–129 (1998).

26. *Integrity and Misconduct in Research*, Report of the Commission on Research Integrity, U.S. Department of Health and Human Services, USGPO 19960746-425 (1995).

27. *Integrity and Misconduct in Research*, Report of the Commission on Research Integrity, U.S. Department of Health and Human Services, USGPO 19960746-425 (1995).

28. *Biotechnology Research in an Age of Terrorism: Confronting the Dual-Use Dilemma*, INSTITUTE OF MEDICINE (2003).

29. Public Health Security and Bioterrorism Response Act of 2002, P.L. 107-188.

30. Bernadette Tansey, *U.S. Requires Scientists to Give FBI Fingerprints: Thousands who use Bioterror Compounds Must Disclose Data for Background Checks*, SAN FRANCISCO GATE (March 12, 2003).

31. Inspection of the FBI's Security Risk Assessment Program for Individuals Requesting Access to Biological Agents and Toxins, U.S. Department of Justice (March, 2005), available at http://www.fas.org/irp/agency/doj/oig/sra-bio.pdf.

32. D. L. Weed, *Preventing Scientific Misconduct*, AMERICAN JOURNAL OF PUBLIC HEALTH, Vol. 88, pp. 125–129 (1998).

33. *Responsible Science, Volume 1: Ensuring the Integrity of the Research Process*, INSTITUTE OF MEDICINE (1992).

34. *Integrity and Misconduct in Research*, Report of the Commission on Research Integrity, U.S. Department of Health and Human Services, USGPO 19960746-425 (1995).

35. Gigi Kwik Gronvall, Joe Fitzegerald, Thomas V. Inglesby, & Tara O'Toole, *Biosecurity: Responsible Stewardship of Bioscience in an Age of Catastrophic Terrorism*, BIOSECURITY AND BIOTERRORISM, Vol. 1, No. 1 (2003).

36. *Genomics and the Global Health Divide*, WORLD HEALTH ORGANIZATION, *available at* http://who.int/genomics/healthdivide/en/print.html.

37. Barry C. Buckland, *The Process Development Challenge for a New Vaccine*, NATURE MEDICINE, Vol. 11, pp. S16–S19 (April 2005).

38. See generally, Beatrice Seguin et al., *Scientific Diasporas as an Option for Brain Drain: Re-circulating Knowledge for Development*, 8 INT. J. BIOTECHNOLOGY 78 (2006).

39. *With an Additional $1 Billion per Year, Immunization Could Save Ten Million More Lives in a Decade*, UNICEF, Joint Press Release (December 9, 2005), available at http://www.unicef.org/media/media_30393.html.

40. Michelle M. Mello & Troyen A. Brennan, *Legal Concerns and the Influenza Vaccine Shortage*, JOURNAL OF THE AMERICAN MEDICAL ASSOCIATION, Vol. 294, No. 14, pp. 1817–1820 (2005).

41. Barry C. Buckland, *The Process Development Challenge for a New Vaccine*, NATURE MEDICINE, Vol. 11, pp. S16–S19 (April 2005).

42. Henry Grobowski, *Encouraging the Development of New Vaccines*, 24 HEALTH AFFAIRS 697 (2005).

43. Public Law No. 97-414, 96 Stat. 2049 (1983) (codified as amended 1988).

44. Statement by Gerald L. Epstein, Senior Fellow for Science and Security, Homeland Security Program, *Biodefense: Building a Medical Countermeasure Capability*, Testimony before the Bioterrorism and Public Health Preparedness Subcommittee, Committee on Health, Education, Labor, and Pensions, United States Senate, CENTER FOR STRATEGIC AND INTERNATIONAL STUDIES (February 8, 2005) *available at* http://www.stanford.edu/class/msande193/Handouts/Autumn_2006_07/11_13_2006_Epstein.pdf.

45. David M. Shea, *The Project BioShield Prisoner's Dilemma: An Impetus for the Modernization of Programmatic Environmental Impact Statements*, 33 B.C.ENVTL. AFF. L. REV. 695 (2006).

46. Clarence Lam, Crystal Franco, & Ari Schuler, *Billions for Biodefense: Federal Agency Biodefense Funding, FY 2006–FY 2007*, 4 BIOSECURITY & BIOTERRORISM 113 (2006).

47. *Is Bioshield Doing the Job?* 24 BIOTECHNOLOGY L. REP. 56 (February 2005).

48. Renae Merle, *Bioterror Antidote: Unfulfilled Prescription*, WASHINGTON POST, p. D01 (January 16, 2007).

49. Ken Silverstein, *Flaws in the BioShield: VaxGen Looks for Another Federal Bailout*, HARPER'S MAGAZINE (December 12, 2006).

50. Renae Merle, *Bioterror Antidote: Unfulfilled Prescription*, WASHINGTON POST, p. D01 (January 16, 2007); See also, *Anthrax: Replacement for VaxGen Vaccine Likely Years Away*, AMERICAN HEALTH LINE (December 22, 2006).

51. Renae Merle, *Bioterror Antidote: Unfulfilled Prescription*, WASHINGTON POST, p. D01 (January 16, 2007).

52. Michael Greenberger, *Choking BioShield: The Department of Homeland Security's Stranglehold on Biodefense Vaccine Development*, MICROBE MAGAZINE (June 2006), available at http://www.asm.org/microbe/index.asp?bid=43195.

53. Steve Johnson, *U.S. Dumps VaxGen: Brisbane Company Had Won $877.5 Million Contract to Develop Anthrax Vaccine*, MERCURY NEWS (December 19, 2006).

54. Eric Lipton, *Bid to Stockpile Bioterror Drugs Stymied by Setbacks*, NEW YORK TIMES, p. A1 (September 18, 2006).

55. *Pandemic and All-Hazards Preparedness Act*, S 3678, Public Law 109–417 (December 19, 2006). As this book goes to press, new legislation has been introduced to accelerate BioShield funding by making Department of Homeland Security risk assessment processes more efficient. *See* John Fox, *Legislators Propose Measure To Speed Up Biodefense Program*, GLOBAL SECURITY NEWSWIRE (February 22, 2007), *available at* http://www.govexec.com/dailyfed/0207/022207gsn1.htm.

56. *See Achievements in Public Health, 1900–1999 Impact of Vaccines Universally Recommended for Children – United States, 1990–1998*, CENTERS FOR DISEASE CONTROL AND PREVENTION, MORBIDITY AND MORTALITY WEEKLY REPORT, Vol. 48, No. 12, pp. 243–248 (April 2, 1999); *See also, Healthy People 2010, Immunizations and Infectious Disease*, U.S. DEPARTMENT OF HEALTH AND HUMAN SERVICES, *available at* http://www.healthypeople.gov/Document/HTML/Volume1/14Immunization.htm.

57. *Liability Protections for Adult Vaccines*, Reports of Board of Trustees, Report 10, AMERICAN MEDICAL ASSOCIATION, Resolution 710-I04 (June 2005), *available at* http://www.ama-assn.org/ama1/pub/upload/mm/38/a-05bot.pdf.

58. J. S. Mair & M. Mair, *Vaccine Liability in the Era of Bioterrorism*, BIOSECURITY AND BIOTERRORISM: BIODEFENSE STRATEGY, PRACTICE, AND SCIENCE, Vol. 1, pp. 169–182 (2003).

59. *Swine Flu Act*, Public Law 94-380 § 2(k)(2)(A) (1976).

60. *Vaccine Supply and Innovation*, INSTITUTE OF MEDICINE, National Academies Press (1985).

61. G. Evans, *Vaccine Injury Compensation Programs Worldwide*, HRSA Advisory Commission on Childhood Vaccines Meeting and Conference Call Minutes (March 9, 2006), *available at* http://www.hrsa.gov/vaccinecompensation/accvmin03-09-06.htm.

62. Statement of John E. Calfee, Ph.D., Resident Scholar, American Enterprise Institute, *The National Immunization Program: Is It Prepared for the Public Health Challenges of the 21st Century?* Hearings before the Senate Committee on Health, Education, Labor and Pensions, 107th Congress, 1st Session (November 27, 2001).

63. *Homeland Security Act of 2002*, Public Law 107–296, Title VIII, Subtitle G, §§ 862-865, 116 Stat. 2238-2241 (November 25, 2002).

64. National Childhood Vaccine Injury Act of 1986, 42 USC §30aa.

65. M. M. Mello & T. A. Brennan, *Legal Concerns and the Influenza Vaccine Shortage*, JOURNAL OF THE AMERICAN MEDICAL ASSOCIATION, Vol. 294, pp. 1817–1820 (2005).

66. Health Resources and Services Administration, National Vaccine Injury Compensation Program, *available at* http://www.hrsa.gov/vaccinecompensation/table.htm.

67. J. S. Mair & M. Mair, *Vaccine Liability in the Era of Bioterrorism*, BIOSECURITY AND BIOTERRORISM: BIODEFENSE STRATEGY, PRACTICE, AND SCIENCE, Vol.1, pp. 169–182 (2003).

68. C. J. Shoemaker, *Description of Vaccine Litigation: A Call to Arms*, *available at* http://www.attorneyaccess.net/CallToArms.cfm.

69. Pandemic Flu and Medical Biodefense Countermeasure Liability Legislation, Public Law 109-148, Division C (2005).

70. *Cardiac Deaths After a Mass Smallpox Vaccination Campaign – New York City, 1947*, CENTERS FOR DISEASE CONTROL AND PREVENTION, MORBIDITY AND MORTALITY WEEKLY REPORT, Vol. 52, pp. 933–936 (October 3, 2003).

71. Smallpox Emergency Personnel Protection Act of 2003, Public Law 180-20, 117 Stat. 638 (2003).

72. *Anthrax Vaccine Immunization Program (AVIP)*, Information Statement and Acknowledgment, U.S. Department of Defense, *available at* http://www.seafarers.org/members/Anthraxack.pdf.

73. Human Development Report 2001: Making New Technologies Work for Human Development, UNITED NATIONS DEVELOPMENT PROGRAMME (2001).

74. *Agreement on Trade-Related Aspects of Intellectual Property Rights*, Marrakesh Agreement Establishing the World Trade Organization, Annex 1C, (April 15, 1994), *in* WORLD TRADE ORGANIZATION, THE LEGAL TEXTS: THE RESULTS OF THE URUGUAY ROUND OF MULTILATERAL TRADE NEGOTIATIONS (1999).

75. Frederick M. Abott, *The WTO Medicines Decision: World Pharmaceutical Trade and the Protection of Public Health*, 99 A.J.I.L. 317 (2005).

76. *Declaration on the TRIPS Agreement and Public Health*, WORLD TRADE ORGANIZATION, Ministerial Conference, 4th Session, WT/MIN (01)/DEC/W/2 (November 14, 2001), *available at* http://www.who.int/medicines/areas/policy/tripshealth.pdf.

77. Anthony P. Valach Jr., *TRIPS: Protecting the Rights of Patent Holders and Addressing Public Health Issues in Developing Countries*, 4 CHI.-KENT J. INT ELL. PROP. 156 (2005).

78. See *AIDS Drugs; U.S. Offers to Help South Africa Obtain Affordable Medicines*, CHICAGO TRIBUNE (August 2, 1999); See also, Geoff Dyer, et al., *U.S. Climbs Down Over Brazil's Patent Law*, FINANCIAL TIMES (London) (June 26, 2001).

79. Andrew Jack, *Cut-price HIV Drugs Drive may Spur Patents Clash*, FINANCIAL TIMES (London) (August 11, 2006).

80. The WTO Dispute Settlement Understanding (DSU) panel ruled that Canada's Patent Act did not meet the conditions of Article 30 of the TRIPS agreement, the "stockpiling exception" that allows manufacture and stockpiling of generic drugs during the last six months of the patent term. This decision striking down the stockpiling exception *did not* touch the issue of emergencies and *did not* deal with Canada stockpiling specific generic drugs for public health purposes.

81. Arnoldo Lacayo, *Seeking a Balance: International Pharmaceutical Patent Protection, Public Health Crises, and the Emerging Threat of Bioterrorism*, 33 U. MIAMI INTERN-AM. L. REV. 295 (2002); *See also*, Barbara Dreyfuss, *Patents Pending*, NATIONAL LEG-ISLATIVE ASSOCIATION ON PRESCRIPTION DRUG PRICES (February 23, 2005), *available at* http://www.nlarx.org/policy/pages/dreyfusspatents.html.

82. Jonathan Todres et al., *International Health Law*, 40 INT'L L. 453 (2006).

83. It ultimately expanded the list to twenty-two diseases: "yellow fever, plague, cholera, meningococcal disease, African trypanosomiasis, dengue, influenza, HIV/AIDS, leishmaniasis, TB, malaria, hepatitis, leptospirosis, pertussis, poliomyelitis, schistosomiasis, typhoid fever, typhus, measles, shigellosis, haemorrhagic fevers, and arboviruses and other epidemics of comparable gravity and scale including those that might arise in the future whether due to natural occurrence, accidental release, or deliberate use." *Notes on the Scope of Diseases to be Covered in the Paragraph Six 'Solution'* (December 20, 2002), available at http://www.cptech.org/ip/wto/p6/scope.html.

84. "This covers at least HIV/AIDS, malaria, tuberculosis, yellow fever, plague, cholera, meningococcal disease, African trypanosomiasis, dengue, influenza, leishmaniasis, hepatitis, leptospirosis, pertussis, poliomyelitis, schistosomiasis, typhoid fever, typhus, measles, shigellosis, hemorrhagic fevers, and arboviruses. When requested by a Member, the World Health Organization shall give its advice as to the occurrence in an importing Member, or the likelihood thereof, of any other public health problem." *EU Draft Proposal for a Compromise Solution*, Consumer Project on Technology (2003).

85. Elisabeth Rosenthal, *Wealthy Nations Announce Plan to Develop and Pay for Vaccines*, NEW YORK TIMES, (February 10, 2007).

Chapter 7. Public Health Preparedness

1. *Macroeconomics and Health: Investing in Health for Economic Development*, Report of the Commission on Macroeconomics and Health, WORLD HEALTH ORGANIZA-TION (December 20, 2001), *available at* http://whqlibdoc.who.int/publications/2001/924154550X.pdf.

2. Gregory Koblentz, *Pathogens as Weapons; The International Security Implications of Biological Warfare*, INTERNATIONAL SECURITY, p. 84 (Winter 2004).

3. *Guidance for Protecting Building Environments from Airborne Chemical, Biological, and Radiological Attacks*, NATIONAL INSTITUTE FOR OCCUPATION SAFETY AND HEALTH (April 2003), *available at* http://www.cdc.gov/niosh/docs/2003-136/default.html#toc.

4. *See* "Recommendations Regarding Filter and Sorbent Selection, Operations, Upgrade, and Maintenance," *in Guidance for Protecting Building Environments from Airborne Chemical, Biological, or Radiological Attacks*, NATIONAL INSTITUTE FOR OCCUPATIONAL SAFETY AND HEALTH, Section 3 (April, 2003), *available at* http://www.cdc.gov/niosh/docs/2003-136/2003-136d.html.

5. Paul Dvorak, *Biodefense: The Best Defense After a Biological Attack May be a Good Filter*, MEDICAL DESIGN, Vol. 6, No. 10, p. 42 (December 1, 2006).

6. Patricia L. Meinhardt, *Water and Bioterrorism*, 26 ANNUAL REVIEW OF PUB. HEALTH 213 (April 2005); *See also, Jennifer* B. Nuzzo, *The Biological Threat to U.S. Water Supplies*, BIOSECURITY AND BIOTERRORISM: BIODEFENSE STRATEGY, PRACTICE, AND SCIENCE, Vol. 4, p. 147 (2006).

7. Wayne Clark et al., *Advanced UV Source for Biological Agent Destruction* (2006), *available at* http://www.natick.army.mil/soldier/JOCOTAS/ColPro_Papers/Stumpf.pdf.

8. *Bush Issues Medical Emergency Directive*, NEW YORK TIMES (February 8, 2007).

9. Jennifer L. Brower, *The Terrorist Threat and its Implications for Sensor Technologies*, presented at Advances in Sensing with Security Applications (July, 2005), *available at* http://www.nato-asi.org/sensors2005/papers/brower.pdf.

10. *See* David L. Buckeridge et al., *Evaluating Detection of an Inhalational Anthrax Outbreak*, EMERGING INFECTIOUS DISEASES (December 1, 2006).

11. *See* Joseph Doedert, *The Biosurveillance Evolution*, HEALTH DATA MANAGEMENT, Vol. 15, No. 2, p. 50 (February 2007).

12. *Incentives for the Use of Health Information Technology and Establishing the Position of the National Health Information Technology Coordinator*, Executive Order 13335 (April 27, 2004).

13. *See generally, Creating a Nation-wide Integrated Biosurveillance System*, Hearing of the Prevention of Nuclear and Biological Attack Subcommittee of the House Homeland Security Committee (May 11, 2006).

14. *Early Efforts Initiated but Comprehensive Privacy Approach Needed for National Strategy*, GAO REPORT, GAO-07-238 (January 10, 2007).

15. David Koplow, *Arms Control Inspection: Constitutional Restrictions on Treaty Verification in the United States*, 63 N. Y. U. L. REV. 229, 324 (May 1988).

16. Ryan McDonald, *Juries and Crime Labs: Correcting the Weak Links in the DNA Chain*, 24 AM. J.L. & MED. 345 (1998); *See also, Smith v. State*, 677 So. 2d 1240, 1245 (Ala. Crim. App. 1995).

17. Paul Keim, *Microbial Forensics: A Scientific Approach*, AMERICAN ACADEMY OF MICROBIOLOGY, p. 12 (2003), *available at* http://www.asm.org/ASM/files/CCPAGECONTENT/docfilename/0000018026/FOREN%20REPORT_BW.pdf.

18. Andrew J. Grotto & Jonathan B. Tucker, *Biosecurity: A Comprehensive Action Plan*, CENTER FOR AMERICAN PROGRESS (June 2006), *available at* http://www.mericanprogress.org/kf/biosecurity_a_comprehensive_action_plan.pdf.

19. *See* Jane Gross, *A Nation Challenged: The Doctors*, NEW YORK TIMES, p. B1 (October 17, 2001); *See also,* John Schwartz, *The Truth Hurts*, NEW YORK TIMES, Section 4, p. 1 (October 28, 2001); *See also,* Sheryl Gay Stolberg, *A Nation Challenged: Steps Against Anthrax*, NEW YORK TIMES, p. A13 (January 8, 2002).

20. Robert A. Fowler et al., *Cost-Effectiveness of Defending against Bioterrorism*, ANNALS OF INTERNAL MEDICINE, Vol. 142, No. 8, p. 601 (2005).

21. *Update: Adverse Events Following Civilian Smallpox Vaccination*, CENTERS FOR DISEASE CONTROL AND PREVENTION, MORBIDITY AND MORTALITY WEEKLY REPORT, Vol. 53, p. 106 (2003).

22. J. Michael Lane & Joel Goldstein, *Evaluations of 21st-century Risks of Smallpox Vaccination and Policy Options*, ANNALS OF INTERNAL MEDICINE, Vol. 138, p. 488 (March 18, 2003).

23. See *Review of the Centers for Disease Control and Prevention's Smallpox Vaccination Program Implementation.* Committee on Smallpox Vaccination Program Implementation, Board on Health Promotion and Disease Prevention, INSTITUTE OF MEDICINE, National Academy Press (2003).

24. Hillel W. Cohen et al., *The Pitfalls of Bioterrorism Preparedness*, AMERICAN JOURNAL OF PUBLIC HEALTH, Vol. 94, No. 10, pp. 1667 (2004). The article also draws attention to "new secret research facilities that will store and handle dangerous materials" and thus "increase [] the risk of accidental release or purposeful diversion." It also expresses concerns that such sites and programs concerned with "biodefense" might spur a "biodefense race," which would spread proliferation. Accidents can occur that may release harmful biological agents into the environment. The article also asserts, though without pinpointing exact cases, that "In short, bioterrorism preparedness programs have been a disaster for public health. Instead of leading to more resources for dealing with natural disease as had been promised, there are now fewer such resources. Worse, in response to bioterrorism preparedness, public health institutions and procedures are being reorganized along a military or police model that subverts the relationships between public health providers and the communities they serve."

25. Frederick M. Burlke, *Mass Casualty Management of a Large-scale Bioterrorist Event: An Epidemiological Approach that Shapes Triage Decisions.* EMERGENCY MEDICINE CLINICS OF NORTH AMERICA, Vol. 20, p. 409–436 (2002).

26. N. Pesik, M. E. Keim, & K. V. Iserson, *Terrorism and the Ethics of Emergency Medical Care*, ANNALS OF EMERGENCY MEDICINE, Vol. 37, pp. 642–646 (2001).

27. Frederick M. Burkle, MD, *Population-based Triage Management in Response to Surge-capacity Requirements during a Large-scale Bio-event Disaster*, ACADEMIC EMERGENCY MEDICINE, Vol. 13, No. 11, pp. 1118–1129 (2006).

28. Frederick M. Burkle, MD, *Population-based Triage Management in Response to Surge-capacity Requirements during a Large-scale Bio-event Disaster*, ACADEMIC EMERGENCY MEDICINE, Vol. 13, No. 11, pp. 1118–1129 (2006).

29. T. V. Inglesby, J. B. Nuzzo, T. O'Toole, & D. A. Henderson, *Disease Mitigation Measures in the Control of Pandemic Influenza*, BIOSECURITY AND BIOTERRORISM: BIODEFENSE STRATEGY, PRACTICE, AND SCIENCE, Vol. 4, pp. 366–375 (2006).

30. C. Lam, R. Waldhorn, E. Toner, T. V. Inglesby, & T. O'Toole, *The Prospect of Using Alternative Medical Care Facilities in an Influenza Pandemic*, BIOSECURITY AND BIOTERRORISM: BIODEFENSE STRATEGY, PRACTICE, AND SCIENCE, Vol. 4, pp. 384–390 (2006).

31. DHHS, Office of the Assistant Secretary for Preparedness and Response, Office of Public Health Emergency Medical Countermeasures, *HHS Public Health Emergency Medical Countermeasure Enterprise Implementation Plan for Chemical, Biological, Radiological and Nuclear Threats*, April 2007.

32. See David S. Fedson, *Preparing for Pandemic Vaccination: An International Policy Agenda for Vaccine Development*, JOURNAL OF PUBLIC HEALTH POLICY, Vol. 26, No. 1, pp. 4–29 (2005); *See also*, Julie B. Milstien et al., *The Impact of Globalization on Vaccine Development and Availability*, HEALTH AFFAIRS, Vol. 25, No. 4, pp. 1061–1069 (2006); *See also*, Jerome O. Klein & Martin G. Myers, *Vaccine Shortages: Why They Occur and What Needs to be Done to Strengthen Vaccine Supply*, PEDIATRICS, Vol. 117, No. 6, pp. 2269–2275 (June 2006).

33. The *International Conference on Harmonization of Technical Requirements for Registration of Pharmaceuticals for Human Use* harmonizes testing and registration

procedures for new pharmaceuticals and disseminates information as to how nations implement its guidelines.

34. *See* Gigi Kwik Gronvall & Luciana Borio, *Removing Barriers to Global Pandemic Influenza Vaccination*, 4 BIOSECURITY AND BIOTERRORISM: BIODEFENSE STRATEGY, PRACTICE, AND SCIENCE, p. 168 (2006), *available at* http://www.liebertonline.com/doi/pdf/10.1089/bsp.2006.4.168?cookieSet=1; *See also*, David S. Fedson, *Preparing for Pandemic Vaccination: An International Policy for Vaccine Development*, JOURNAL OF PUBLIC HEALTH POLICY,Vol. 26, No. 1, p. 4–29 (2005).

35. Alan Melnick et al., *Public Health Ethics in Action: Flu Vaccine and Drug Allocation Strategies*, 33 J.L. MED. & ETHICS 102 (2005).

36. Robyn Martin, *The Exercise of Public Health Powers in Cases of Infectious Disease: Human Rights Implications*, 14 MED. L. REV. 141, 142 (2006).

37. John D. Blum, *Balancing Individual Rights* versus *Collective Good in Public Health Enforcement*, 25 MED. & L. 273, 278–79 (2006).

38. Wendy E. Parmet, *Informed Consent and Public Health: Are They Compatible When It Comes to Vaccines?* 8 J. OF HEALTH CARE L. & POL'Y 104 (2005).

39. This issue was litigated in *Doe v. Rumsfeld*, 297 F. Supp. 2d 119 (2003). Active duty service members objected to inoculation with the anthrax vaccine, which, at the time the case was brought, was still in an experimental stage and not approved. The plaintiffs contended that because of its unlicensed status, they should not have to submit to it. The court granted a preliminary injunction against the nonconsensual administration of the drug on the grounds that it was both an investigational drug and was being used for an unapproved purpose. A year later, in *Doe v. Rumsfeld*, 297 F. Supp. 2d 200 (2004), the court granted a stay on the injunction after the Food and Drug Administration published a rule categorizing the anthrax vaccine as safe and effective against inhalation anthrax.

40. Wendy E. Parmet, *Informed Consent and Public Health: Are They Compatible When It Comes to Vaccines?* 8 J. HEALTH CARE L. & POL'Y 104 (2005).

41. Janlori Goldman, *Balancing in Crisis? Bioterrorism, Public Health, and Privacy*, 38 J. HEALTH L. 481 (2005).

42. Lawrence O. Gostin, *When Terrorism Threatens Health: How Far are Limitations on Human Rights Justified*, 31 J.L. MED. & ETHICS 524, 526–527 (2003).

43. Peter Vasterman et al., *The Role of the Media and Media Hypes in the Aftermath of Disasters*, EPIDEMIOLOGICAL REVIEWS,Vol. 27, pp. 107–114, at 109 (2005).

44. Thomas Glass & Monica Schoch-Spana, *Bioterrorism and the People: How to Vaccinate a City against Panic*, CLINICAL INFECTIOUS DISEASES, Vol. 34, pp. 217, 221 (January 15, 2002).

45. Laurie Garrett, *Understanding Media's Response to Epidemics*, PUBLIC HEALTH REPORTS,Vol. 116, pp. 87 (2001).

46. K. U. Menon & K. T. Goh, *Transparency and Trust: Risk Communication and the Singapore Experience in Managing SARS*, JOURNAL OF COMMUNICATION MANAGEMENT,Vol. 9, p. 375 (2005).

47. Daniel Esty, *Good Governance at the Supranational Scale: Globalizing Administrative Law*, 115 YALE L.J. 1490, 1551 (2006).

48. Cecila Cheng, *To Be Paranoid is the Standard? Panic Responses to SARS Outbreak in the Hong Kong Special Administrative Region*, ASIAN PERSPECTIVE, Vol. 28, p. 67 (2004).

49. Bruce Ackerman, *The Emergency Constitution*, 113 YALE L.J. 1029, 1047 (March 2004).

50. Bruce Ackerman, *The Emergency Constitution*, 113 YALE L.J. 1029, 1052 (March 2004).

51. Daniel Markovits, *Quarantine and Distributive Justice*, 33 J.L. MED. & ETHICS 323, 324 (2005).

52. Lieutenant Colonel Mark F. Gentilman, *An Analysis to Determine Whether Quarantine is an Effective Response to a Bioterrorist Attack in the United States*, (June 3, 2005), *available at* http://www.aameda.org/MemberServices/Exec/Articles/sum05/An-Analysis_to_Determine.pdf.

53. Troy Day et al., *When Is Quarantine a Useful Control Strategy for Emerging Infectious Diseases?* AMERICAN JOURNAL OF EPIDEMIOLOGY, Vol. 163, p. 479 (2006).

54. David Bishop, *Lessons from SARS: Why the WHO Must Provide Greater Economic Incentives for Countries to Comply with International Health Regulations*, 26 GEO. J. INT'L L. 1173, 1221 (2005).

55. Lawrence O. Gostin et al., *Quarantine: Voluntary or Not?*, 32 J.L. MED. & ETHICS 83 (2004).

56. Lieutenant Colonel Mark F. Gentilman, *An Analysis to Determine Whether Quarantine is an Effective Response to a Bioterrorist Attack in the United States* (June 3, 2005), *available at* http://www.aameda.org/MemberServices/Exec/Articles/sum05/An-Analysis_to_Determine.pdf.

57. Edward P. Richards et al., *Quarantine Laws and Public Health Realities*, 33 J.L. MED. & ETHICS 69, 70 (2005).

58. *Constitution of the World Health Organization*, Article 21, paragraph A (July 22, 1946), *available at* http://www.who.int/governance/eb/who_constitution_en.pdf.

59. Jane Speakman et al., *Quarantine in Severe Acute Respiratory Syndrome (SARS) and Other Emerging Infectious Diseases*, 31 J.L. MED. & ETHICS 83 (2003).

60. *International Health Regulations*, 48th World Health Assembly, Article 1 (May 23, 2005), *available at* http://www.who.int/csr/ihr/IHRWHA58_3-en.pdf.

61. *International Health Regulations*, 48th World Health Assembly, Article 6.2 (May 23, 2005), *available at* http://www.who.int/csr/ihr/IHRWHA58_3-en.pdf.

62. *International Health Regulations, Core Capacity Requirements for Designated Airports, Ports, and Ground Crossings*. 48th World Health Assembly, Annex 1.B, paragraph 2 (May 23, 2005), *available at* http://www.who.int/csr/ihr/IHRWHA58_3-en.pdf.

63. *International Health Regulations, Core Capacity Requirements for Designated Airports, Ports, and Ground Crossings*. 48th World Health Assembly, Annex 1.B, paragraph 2 (May 23, 2005), *available at* http://www.who.int/csr/ihr/IHRWHA58_3-en.pdf.

64. *International Health Regulations*, 48th World Health Assembly, Article 3 (May 23, 2005), *available at* http://www.who.int/csr/ihr/IHRWHA58_3-en.pdf.

65. David P. Fidler, *From International Sanitary Conventions to Global Health Security: The New International Health Regulations*, 4 CHINESE J. INT'L L. 325 (2005).

66. Lawrence O. Gostin, *Revision of the World Health Organization's International Health Regulations*, JOURNAL OF THE AMERICAN MEDICAL ASSOCIATION, Vol. 291, No. 21, pp. 2623, 2626 (June, 2004).

67. Robert J. Blendon et al., *Attitudes Toward the Use of Quarantine in a Public Health Emergency in Four Countries*, HEALTH AFFAIRS, Vol. 25, No. 2, pp. 15–25 (2006).

Chapter 8. International Nonproliferation

1. *The Convention on the Prohibition of the Development, Production, and Stockpiling of Bacteriological (Biological) and Toxin Weapons and on their Destruction*, 26 U.S.T.

583; T.I.A.S. 8062; 1015 U.N.T.S. 163, (Signed April 10, 1972; entered into force March 26, 1976), (hereinafter, BWC).

2. Al J. Venter, *Biological Warfare: The Poor Man's Atomic Bomb*, JANE'S INTELLIGENCE REVIEW (March 1999).

3. See *Case Study: Yellow Rain. Fact Sheet*. BUREAU OF VERIFICATION, COMPLIANCE, AND IMPLEMENTATION. (October 1, 2005), *available at* http://www.state.gov/documents/organization/57428.pdf.

4. For more information about the Review Conference, *see* Graham Pearson, *The Biological Weapons Convention Sixth Review Conference*, CBS CONVENTIONS BULLETIN, Issue No. 74 (December 2006).

5. These meetings will focus on: 1) domestic legislation to implement and enforce the BWC (2007); 2) biosecurity and biosafety measures including scientific codes of conduct (2008); 3) enhancement of infectious disease surveillance and response (2009); and 4) assistance in the event of a suspected attack (2010).

6. BWC Article 1.

7. Statement by the International Committee of the Red Cross, Geneva. First Special Session of the Conference of the States Parties to Review the Operation of the Chemical Weapons Convention. First Review Conference, The Hague (April 28–May 9, 2003) *available at* http://www.icrc.org/web/eng/siteeng0.nsf/html/5M4BGC.

8. DoD Directive 3000.3, *Policy for Nonlethal Weapons*, Article 3.1 (July 9, 1996), *available at* http://www.dtic.mil/whs/directives/corres/pdf/d30003_070996/d30003p.pdf.

9. Joseph Siniscalchi, *Nonlethal Technologies: Implications for Military Strategy*, CENTER FOR STRATEGY AND TECHNOLOGY (March 1998), *available at* http://www.globalsecurity.org/military/library/news/1998/03/occppr03.htm. According to the Human Effects Advisory Panel (HEAP) established by the U.S. JNLWD, a weapon can be classified as "nonlethal" if no more than 5 percent of victims suffer permanent physical damage or are killed. *See* Mark Wheelis, *"Nonlethal" Chemical Weapons: A Faustian Bargain*, ISSUES IN SCIENCE AND TECHNOLOGY (Spring 2003).

10. The relationship of information warfare to nonlethal technology is at once complex and confusing. Part of this confusion stems from the fact that the scope of nonlethal technology is so broad that some experts categorize information warfare as a subset of nonlethal technology.... Although one might argue information warfare is a subset of nonlethal technology, in reality this is not entirely accurate because both lethal and nonlethal weapons systems are used for information warfare. James C. Duncan, *A Primer on the Employment of Nonlethal Weapons*, NAVAL LAW REVIEW, XLV, p. 8 (1998).

11. David P. Fidler, *The International Legal Implications of "Nonlethal Weapons,"* 21 MICH. J. INT'L L. 51 (Fall 1999), *citing* Biological Weapons Anti-Terrorism Act of 1989, 18 U.S.C.S. § 175 (prohibitions with respect to biological agents) and 18 U.S.C.S. § 178 (definition of biological agent) (1994).

12. As Margaret-Anne Coppernoll describes, "NLWs are not 'required to have a zero probability of producing fatalities or permanent injuries,' but they are intended to reduce these probabilities significantly." The use of NLWs therefore does not limit a commander's authority to use all necessary means in self-defense, but rather serves to "reinforce deterrence and expand the range of options available to commanders." Lieutenant Colonel Margaret-Anne Coppernoll, *The Nonlethal Weapons Debate*, NAVAL WAR COLLEGE REVIEW, Vol. 52, No. 2 (Spring 1999), *available*

at http://www.nwc.navy.mil/press/Review/1999/spring/art5-SP9.htm, *citing* DoD Directive 3000.3 *Policy for Nonlethal Weapons.* Article 3.1 (July 9, 1996).

13. Margaret-Anne Coppernoll, *The Nonlethal Weapons Debate*, NAVAL WAR COLLEGE REVIEW, Vol. 52, No. 2 (Spring 1999), *available at* http://www.nwc.navy.mil/press/Review/1999/spring/art5-SP9.htm.

14. Margaret-Anne Coppernoll, *The Nonlethal Weapons Debate*, NAVAL WAR COLLEGE REVIEW, Vol. 52, No. 2 (Spring 1999), *available at* http://www.nwc.navy.mil/press/Review/1999/spring/art5-SP9.htm.

15. Joseph Siniscalchi, *Nonlethal Technologies: Implications for Military Strategy.* Occasional Paper No. 3, CENTER FOR STRATEGY AND TECHNOLOGY (March 1998), *available at* http://www.globalsecurity.org/military/library/news/1998/03/occppr03.htm. *citing* Timothy Hannigan, Lori Raff, & Rod Paschall, *Mission Applications of Nonlethal Weapons*, Jaycor Technical Study for the Office of the Assistant Secretary of Defense for Special Operations and Low Intensity Conflict (August 1996), Comparing the 1980s' 80 percent figure to that of the noncombatant fatalities in 1950, which is estimated at one-half of worldwide casualties during war.

16. David Koplow, NON-LETHAL WEAPONS: THE LAW AND POLICY OF REVOLUTIONARY TECHNOLOGIES FOR THE MILITARY AND LAW ENFORCEMENT. Cambridge University Press. p. 28 (2006).

17. Margaret-Anne Coppernoll, *The Nonlethal Weapons Debate*, NAVAL WAR COLLEGE REVIEW, Vol. LII, No. 2 (Spring 1999), *available at* http://www.nwc.navy.mil/press/Review/1999/spring/art5-SP9.htm.

18. James C. Duncan, *A Primer on the Employment of Nonlethal Weapons*, NAVAL LAW REVIEW, XLV (1998).

19. Joseph Siniscalchi, *Nonlethal Technologies: Implications for Military Strategy*, Occasional Paper No. 3, CENTER FOR STRATEGY AND TECHNOLOGY, p. 12 (March 1998), *citing* Richard L. Garvin, an eminent United States weapons expert, *quoted in* Malcolm Dando, A NEW FORM OF WARFARE, p. 9 (1996).

20. *See generally*, Mark Wheelis, *Biotechnology and Biochemical Weapons*, THE NONPROLIFERATION REVIEW. Vol. 9, No. 1 (Spring 2002), *available at* http://cns.miis.edu/pubs/npr/vol09/91/91whee.htm. *See also*, U.S. Special Forces Seek Genetically Engineered Bioweapons, THE SUNSHINE PROJECT, News Release (August 12, 2002), *available at* http://www.sunshine-project.org/publications/pr/pr120802.html.

21. *See Nonlethal Weapons Research in the U.S.: Genetically Engineered Anti-Material Weapons*, THE SUNSHINE PROJECT, Backgrounder Series, Number 9, p. 3 (March 2002), *available at* http://www.sunshine-project.org/publications/ bk/pdf/bk9en.pdf.

22. *U.S. Special Forces Seek Genetically Engineered Bioweapons*, THE SUNSHINE PROJECT, News Release (August 12, 2002), *available at* http://www.sunshine-project.org/publications/pr/pr120802.html, *citing* a May 1999 document by the Future Technology Working Group.

23. *See* Michael Kohler & Wolfgang Fritzsche, NANOTECHNOLOGY: AN INTRODUCTION TO NANOSTRUCTURING TECHNIQUES (2004); *See also*, Michael Fumento, BIOEVOLUTION – HOW BIOTECHNOLOGY IS CHANGING OUR WORLD, Encounter Books (2003).

24. *See* LAURA H. KAHN, *Biodefense Research: Can Secrecy and Safety Coexist?* BIOSECURITY AND BIOTERRORISM: BIODEFENSE STRATEGY, PRACTICE, AND SCIENCE, Vol. 2, No. 2 (2004).

25. See *Nonlethal Weapons Research in the U.S.: Genetically Engineered Anti-Material Weapons*, THE SUNSHINE PROJECT, Backgrounder Series, Number 9, p. 3 (March 2002), *available at* http://www.sunshine-project.org/publications/ bk/pdf/bk9en.pdf.

26. United States Patent No. 6,287,844, Szafranski, et al., (September 11, 2001), *available at* the United States Patent and Trademark Office at http://www.uspto.gov/patft/index.html.

27. *U.S. Special Forces Seek Genetically Engineered Bioweapons*, THE SUNSHINE PROJECT, News Release (August 12, 2002), *available at* http://www.sunshine-project.org/publications/pr/pr120802.html.

28. *Nonlethal Weapons Research in the U.S.: Genetically Engineered Anti-Material Weapons*, THE SUNSHINE PROJECT, Backgrounder Series, Number 9, p. 5 (March 2002), *available at* http://www.sunshine-project.org/publications/ bk/pdf/bk9en.pdf.

29. *Nonlethal Weapons Research in the U.S.: Genetically Engineered Anti-Material Weapons*, THE SUNSHINE PROJECT, Backgrounder Series, Number 9, p. 4 (March 2002), *available at* http://www.sunshine-project.org/publications/bk/pdf/bk9en.pdf.

30. *See* Statement of NRL microbiologist Dr. Joanne Jones-Meehan *quoted in Nonlethal Weapons Research in the U.S.: Genetically Engineered Anti-Material Weapons*, THE SUNSHINE PROJECT, Backgrounder Series, Number 9, p. 4 (March 2002), *available at* http://www.sunshine-project.org/publications/bk/pdf/bk9en.pdf.

31. J. Campbell, *Defense Against Biodegradation of Military Material*, Nonlethal Defense III Conference, p. 2 (February 1998), *quoted in Nonlethal Weapons Research in the U.S.: Genetically Engineered Anti-Material Weapons*, THE SUNSHINE PROJECT, Backgrounder Series, Number 9, p. 5 (March 2002), *available at* http://www.sunshine-project.org/publications/bk/pdf/bk9en.pdf.

32. J. Campbell, *Defense Against Biodegradation of Military Material*, Nonlethal Defense III Conference, p. 3 (February 1998), *quoted in Nonlethal Weapons Research in the U.S.: Genetically Engineered Anti-Material Weapons*, THE SUNSHINE PROJECT, Backgrounder Series, Number 9, p. 5 (March 2002), *available at* http://www.sunshine-project.org/publications/bk/pdf/bk9en.pdf.

33. According to a Sunshine Project paper,

> The Army's suicide systems have been developed by Boston University scientists working with a biotechnology research unit at Natick Laboratories (near Boston, Massachusetts), a division of the U.S. Army Soldier and Biological Chemical Command (SBCCOM). Natick's terminator system uses a lethal gene from the bacteria *Streptomyces avidinii* transferred into other organisms.

> *Nonlethal Weapons Research in the U.S.: Genetically Engineered Anti-Material Weapons*, THE SUNSHINE PROJECT, Backgrounder Series, Number 9, p. 5 (March 2002), *available at* http://www.sunshine-project.org/publications/bk/pdf/bk9en.pdf.

34. *Nonlethal Weapons Research in the U.S.: Genetically Engineered Anti-Material Weapons*, THE SUNSHINE PROJECT, Backgrounder Series, Number 9, p. 5 (March 2002), *available at* http://www.sunshine-project.org/publications/bk/pdf/bk9en.pdf.

35. J. Campbell, *Defense Against Biodegradation of Military Material*, Nonlethal Defense III Conference, p. 1 (February 1998), *quoted in Nonlethal Weapons Research in the U.S.: Genetically Engineered Anti-Material Weapons*, THE SUNSHINE PROJECT, Backgrounder Series, Number 9, p. 5 (March 2002), *available at* http://www.sunshine-project.org/publications/bk/pdf/bk9en.pdf.

36. *Nonlethal Weapons Research in the U.S.: Genetically Engineered Anti-Material Weapons*, THE SUNSHINE PROJECT, Backgrounder Series, Number 9, p. 5 (March 2002), *available at* http://www.sunshine-project.org/publications/bk/pdf/bk9en.pdf.

37. *Nonlethal Weapons Research in the U.S.: Genetically Engineered Anti-Material Weapons*, THE SUNSHINE PROJECT, Backgrounder Series, Number 9, p. 4 (March 2002), *available at* http://www.sunshine-project.org/publications/bk/pdf/bk9en.pdf. The

paper refers to an outdated website of the Department of Energy website, which has since been updated and moved to another website (*available at* http://microbial-genomics.energy.gov/brochure.pdf), which no longer describes "super bugs."

38. Livermore Lab proposed to build a biodefense lab last June. The BSL-3 permit issued by the Centers for Disease Control and Prevention would allow work on a broad spectrum of biotoxins and agents including anthrax, botulism, and plague. The safety Level-3 allows work on agents with the potential for respiratory transmission – diseases that can cause serious and lethal infection. The Energy Department's cursory Environmental Assessment says the biofacility would – among other things – and I quote, "produce small amounts of biological material such as enzymes, DNA, ribonucleic acid using infectious agents, and genetically modified agents."

"The Livermore Lab proposal includes plans to aerosolize bioagents, which makes those agents more dangerous. The lab will conduct small animal challenge tests – which mean they can kill up to 100 small animals at a time with these bioagents. The facility is allowed to work with up to one liter of a single agent and up to ten liters total at the facility. To make these numbers more meaningful, let us take an example of a likely experimental agent – *Coxiella burnetii*. This agent causes Q fever, an infectious disease in animals and humans. If you could evenly distribute one liter to every person on earth – if this were possible – it would be roughly enough microorganisms to potentially infect every living person."

Inga Olson, *Nuclear Labs Move into the "Biodefense" Business; Biodevastation 7*, Synthesis Regeneration, No. 34, p. 3 (March 22, 2004).

39. *Nonlethal Weapons Research in the U.S.: Genetically Engineered Anti-Material Weapons*, The Sunshine Project, Backgrounder Series, Number 9, p. 4 (March 2002), *available at* http://www.sunshine-project.org/publications/bk/pdf/bk9en.pdf.

40. *See generally, Seven Good Reasons to Stand Up for Information Freedom on Bioweapons Research: And What Agendas may be at Work to Squelch the Public's Right to Know*, The Sunshine Project, News Release (October 30, 2001), *available at* http://www.sunshine-project.org/publications/pr/pdf/pr301001.pdf.

41. *Laws and Regulations Governing the Protection of Sensitive but Unclassified Information*, A Report Prepared by the Federal Research Division, Library of Congress under an Interagency Agreement with the NASA Office of Inspector General, p. 3 (September 2004), *available at* http://www.loc.gov/rr/frd/pdf-files/sbu.pdf.

42. Judith Miller et al., Germs: Biological Weapons and America's Secret War, p. 292 (2001).

43. Judith Miller et al., Germs: Biological Weapons and America's Secret War, pp. 308–310 (2001).

44. Ron Russell asserts, "The Bush administration is pursuing plans to build advanced labs of its own to experiment with some of the deadliest pathogens known to humankind, including anthrax, bubonic plague, botulism, and Q fever." Russell further explains:

DOE officials say it makes sense to engage in germ research at high-security nuclear labs, especially Lawrence Livermore, which already is involved in studies aimed at detecting and identifying biological weapons. They say the existing Biotechnology Research Program at Livermore is helping to develop defenses against biowar agents while undertaking health-related biotech research.

Ron Russell, *A Question of Risk: Plans for a Biodefense "Hot Lab" at Lawrence Livermore Have Ecologists, Disarmament Advocates, and Mainstream Scientists Up in Arms*, SF Weekly (January 28, 2004).

45. Most biodefense research within HHS is performed by the National Institute of Allergy and Infectious Diseases (NIAID), whose biodefense budget has skyrocketed from roughly $17 million in fiscal 1998 to a requested $1.5 billion for fiscal 2005. NIAID's mission, explained in February 2002, is "to carry out the research needed to understand the pathogenesis of [agents of bioterrorism] . . . and the host response to them, and to translate this knowledge into useful interventions and diagnostic tools for an effective response." To pursue research on highly dangerous organisms, last year NIAID launched two Biosafety Level 4 national centers and nine Biosafety Level 3 regional centers, in addition to several Level 4 and many Level 3 facilities under construction elsewhere.

    Susan Wright, *Taking Biodefense Too Far: The United States is Developing a Costly Bioumbrella to Protect its Citizens Against Biothreats that Do Not Now – and May Never – Exist*, BULLETIN OF THE ATOMIC SCIENTISTS, Vol. 60, No. 6, p. 58 (November 1, 2004), *citing* Judith Miller, *New Biolabs Stir a Debate Over Secrecy and Safety*, NEW YORK TIMES, pp. D1, 4 (February 20, 2004).

46. For a more detailed discussion of such measures, *see generally*, Statement of The Honorable Hans Mark, Director, Defense Research and Engineering, before the House Armed Service Committee, (October 20, 1999), *available at* www.globalsecurity.org/wmd/library/congress/1999_h/99-10-20mark.htm.

47. Judith Miller reported: Dr. Anthony S. Fauci, director of the National Institute of Allergy and Infectious Diseases, announced that the institutes would grant $240 million to build two Level 4 National Biocontainment Laboratories at the University of Texas Medical Branch at Galveston and Boston University. Weeks later, the infectious diseases agency issued an additional $120 million in grants ranging from $7 million to $21 million to nine institutions to build Level 3 space at the Regional Biocontainment Laboratories." Judith Miller, *New Biolabs Stir a Debate Over Secrecy and Safety*, NEW YORK TIMES (February 10, 2004). *See also*, Extramural Construction of Biosafety Laboratories. Website of the National Institute of Allergy and Infectious Diseases at http://www3.niaid.nih.gov/Biodefense/Research/rbl.htm.

48. Statement of William F. Raub Ph.D., Deputy Assistant Secretary of Science and Policy for the Department of Health and Human Services. Hearings on National Defense Authorization Act for Fiscal Year 2000 – H.R. 1401 and Oversight of Previously Authorized Programs before the Committee on National Security, House of Representatives, 106th Congress, 1st Session (March 11, 1999), *available at* http://commdocs.house.gov/committees/security/has070010.000/has070010_0.HTM.

49. Testimony, Dr. Penrose C. Albright, Assistant Secretary for Science and Technology, Department of Homeland Security, before The House of Representatives Committee on Select Homeland Security, (June 3, 2004), *quoted in* Dana Shea, *The National Biodefense Analysis and Countermeasures Center: Issues for Congress*, CRS Report for Congress, (April 25, 2005), *available at* http://www.law.umaryland.edu/marshall/crsreports/crsdocuments/RL32891104252005.pdf.

50. Statement of The Honorable Hans Mark, Director, Defense Research and Engineering, before the House Armed Service Committee, (October 20, 1999), *available at* www.globalsecurity.org/wmd/library/congress/1999_h/99-10-20mark.htm.

51. Statement of Dr. Ken Alibek, *quoted in Secret Biodefense Activities Are Undermining the Norm Against Biological Weapons*, Working Group on Biological Weapons, Position Paper, FEDERATION OF AMERICAN SCIENTISTS (January 2003).

52. *See* Annex on the Protection of Confidential Information, *General Principles for the Handling of Confidential Information*, attached to the *Convention on the Prohibition of the Development, Production, Stockpiling, and Use of Chemical Weapons and*

on Their Destruction, (May 16, 1997), *available at* http://www.opcw.org/docs/cwc_eng.pdf (hereinafter cited as "Confidentiality Annex").

53. These principles have been further explained in the *Guidelines for Procedures on the Release of Classified Information by the OPCW*, OPCW C-I/Dec. 13, Part 1, paragraph 2 (May 16, 1997) *available at* http://www.opcw.org/html/global/c_series/csp1/CI_DEC13.html. (hereinafter "Guidelines").

54. *See* Guidelines, Part V, paragraph 3.1.

55. Confidentiality Annex A.2; Guidelines, Part IV. 1.3.2(f).

56. *See* Guidelines, Part IX; *See also*, Confidentiality Annex, paragraph 23.

57. Judith Miller et al., GERMS: BIOLOGICAL WEAPONS AND AMERICA'S SECRET WAR, p. 166 (2001).

58. *Biological Science and Biotechnology in Russia: Controlling Diseases and Enhancing Security*, Committee on Future Contributions of the Biosciences to Public Health, Agriculture, Basic Research, Counterterrorism, and Non-Proliferation Activities in Russia, NATIONAL RESEARCH COUNCIL OF THE NATIONAL ACADEMIES p. 36 (2005).

59. Lauren Arestie, *Issue Brief: The Russian Biological Weapons Complex*, Russian American Nuclear Security Advisory Council (March 2003) *available at* http://www.ransac.org/Publications/Reports%20and%20Publications/Other%20RANSAC%20Papers/index.asp. For an overview of the U.S. and West's efforts to eliminate the Soviet infrastructure of biological WMD, *see* Kenneth N. Luongo et al., *Building a Forward Line of Defense Securing Former Soviet Biological Weapons*, ARMS CONTROL TODAY (July/August 2004), *available at* http://www.armscontrol.org/act/2004_07-08/Luongo.asp#notes2.

60. John V. Parachini et al., DIVERSION OF NUCLEAR, BIOLOGICAL, AND CHEMICAL WEAPONS EXPERTISE FROM THE FORMER SOVIET UNION UNDERSTANDING AN EVOLVING PROBLEM, RAND CORPORATION, p. 26 (2005).

61. *Weapons of Mass Destruction: Additional Russian Cooperation Needed to Facilitate U.S. Efforts to Improve Security at Russian Sites*, GAO Report GAO-03-482 (March 24, 2003), *available at* http://www.gao.gov/htext/d03482.html.

62. *See generally, Advancing International Cooperation on Bio-Initiatives in Russia and the CIS*, Findings and Report from an International Conference April 26–27, 2005 (Spring 2006), available from the author.

63. Craig Thompson, *Missing Links . . . Genetically Altered Biological Weaponry: A Gift from the Biopreparat to the World Part One*, JOURNAL OF COUNTERTERRORISM & HOMELAND SECURITY INTERNATIONAL, (Spring 2003).

64. Lauren Arestie, *Issue Brief: The Russian Biological Weapons Complex*, Russian American Nuclear Security Advisory Council (March 2003), *available at* http://www.ransac.org/Publications/Reports%20and%20Publications/Other%20RANSAC%20Papers/index.asp.

65. *See* Jonathan B. Tucker, *Strengthening the BWC: A Way Forward*, DISARMAMENT DIPLOMACY, Issue No. 78 (July/August 2004); *See also*, BWC Article 10.

66. According to Dr. Milton Leitenberg: On July 7, 1997, the Cuban government filed an official request with the Russian government, in the latter's role as one of the original treaty depositories of the BTWC, requesting that consultation procedures be initiated to examine Cuba's charge that the United States had used biological weapons against it, in the form of a crop destroying insect, Thrips Palmi. Cuba had made roughly a dozen previous charges alleging U.S. bioweapons use involving pathogens against humans, domestic animals, and crop plants since the early 1970s, and had in earlier years addressed summaries of these to the United Nations

Secretary General. This was the first occasion, however, in which Cuba requested consultation under Article V of the BTWC, and it was also the very first time that any nation had requested that the procedures appearing in Article V should be carried out. However, Article VI of the BTWC affords the means for any state party to the BTWC to file a complaint with the UN Security Council if it believes that it is the victim of bioweapons use, and the UN Security Council may then carry out an investigation. On no previous occasion had Cuba ever filed a complaint with the UN Security Council under Article VI and requested an investigation, and it did not do so in this case either.

Milton Leitenberg, *Biological Weapons in the Twentieth Century: A Review and Analysis*, Report prepared for the 7th International Symposium on Protection against Chemical and Biological Warfare, Stockholm, Sweden, June 2001, CRITICAL REVIEWS IN MICROBIOLOGY, Chapter 9 (2001), *available at* http://www.fas.org/bwc/papers/bw20th.htm; *See also, America Accused of Violating the Biological and Toxins Weapons Convention*, CBW CHRONICLE, Vol. II, No. 3 (October 1997), *available at* http://www.stimson.org/cbw/?sn=cb20020113282; *See also, Country Overviews: Cuba: Biological Overview*, NUCLEAR THREAT INITIATIVE, *available at* http://www.nti.org/e_research/profiles/Cuba/Biological/index.html#fnB34.

Chapter 9. The Challenge of Global Governance

1. *Poverty, Infectious Disease, and Environmental Degradation as Threats to Collective Security: A UN Panel Report*; POPULATION AND DEVELOPMENT REVIEW, Vol. 31, No. 3, p. 595(6) (September 1, 2005).

2. Abdullah S. Daar & Peter A. Singer, *Biotechnology and Human Security*, HELSINKI PROCESS PAPERS ON HUMAN SECURITY (2005).

3. The term was coined by Hiroshi Nakajima, former World Health Organization (WHO) Director-General.

4. Calestous Juma, *Biotechnology in a Globalizing World: The Coevolution of Technology and Social Institutions*, BIOSCIENCE, Vol. 55, No. 3 (March 1, 2005).

5. *Science and Technology for Development*, United Nations General Assembly, Resolution 58/200 (January 30, 2004), *available at* http://www.unctad.org/en/docs/ares58200_en.pdf.

6. *Genomics and World Health*, Report of the World Health Organization (2002).

7. *Science and Technology for Development*, United Nations General Assembly, Resolution 58/200 (January 30, 2004), *available at* http://www.unctad.org/en/docs/ares58200_en.pdf. *See also, Globalization and Interdependence: Implementation of General Assembly Resolution 58/200 Science and Technology for Development*, Report by the Secretary-General, United Nations A/60/184 (August 2, 2005).

8. *Biotechnology for Sustainable Growth and Development*, ORGANISATION FOR ECONOMIC CO-OPERATION AND DEVELOPMENT (2004), *available at* http://www.presidencia.pt/docs/ficheiros/Relatorio_Biotechnology_for_sustainable_groth,_OCDE_2004.pdf.

9. *A More Secure World: Our Shared Responsibility*, Report of the High-level Panel on Threats, Challenges, and Change, United Nations General Assembly, 59th Session, UN Doc. A/59/565 (December 2, 2004).

10. *United Nations Millennium Declaration* (also known as the "United Nations Millennium Development Goals"), Resolution adopted by the General Assembly, UN Doc. A/RES/55/2 (September 18, 2000), *available at* http://www.un.org/millenniumgoals/.

11. *Uniting Against Terrorism: Recommendations for a Global Counterterrorism Strategy*, Report of the Secretary-General, UN Doc. A/60/825 (April 27, 2006), *available at* http://www.un.org/unitingagainstterrorism/sg-terrorism-2may06.pdf.

12. *Convention on Access to Information, Public Participation in Decision Making and Access to Justice in Environmental Matters*, 2161 U.N.T.S. 447 (June 25, 1998).

13. *Regulations for Expert Advisory Panels and Committees*, *in* WORLD HEALTH ORGANIZATION: BASIC DOCUMENTS, 45th ed., p. 105 (2005).

14. *See* Jim Whitman, *Disseminative Systems and Global Governance*, GLOBAL GOVERNANCE, Vol. 11, No. 1, p. 85 (January 1, 2005).

15. Ambuj D. Sagar & Stacy D. VanDeveer, *Capacity Development for the Environment: Broadening the Scope*, GLOBAL ENVIRONMENTAL POLITICS, Vol. 5, No. 3 (August 2005).

16. *The Biotechnology Promise: Capacity-building for Participation of Developing Countries in the Bioeconomy*, United Nations Conference on Trade and Development, UNCTAD/ITE/IPC/2004/2 (2004).

17. For example, *see Guinean Institute for Research and Applied Biology, cited in*, Daniel Bausch, *The Ebola-virus:...and the Challenges to Health Research in Africa*, UN CHRONICLE, Vol. 38, No. 2, p. 6 (June 1, 2001); *See also, The Biotechnology Promise: Capacity-building for Participation of Developing Countries in the Bioeconomy*, UNITED NATIONS CONFERENCE ON TRADE AND DEVELOPMENT (2004); *See also*, Calestous Juma, *Biotechnology in a Globalizing World: the Coevolution of Technology and Social Institutions*, BIOSCIENCE, Vol. 55, No. 3, pp. 265–272 (March 1, 2005); *See also*, Peter A. Singer et al., *Harnessing Nanotechnology to Improve Global Equity: The Less Industrialized Countries are Eager to Play an Early Role in Developing This Technology; The Global Community Should Help Them*. ISSUES IN SCIENCE AND TECHNOLOGY, Vol. 21, No. 4, p. 75 (June 22, 2005).

18. Remigius N. Nwabueze, *What Can Genomics and Health Biotechnology Do for Developing Countries?*, 15 ALB. L.J. SCI. & TECH. 369 (2005).

19. Andrew S. Natsios, *The Nine Principles of Reconstruction and Development*, PARAMETERS, Vol. 35, No. 3, p. 4(17) (September 22, 2005).

20. More information on UNAIDS *available at* http://www.unaids.org/en/.

21. More information on the UNDG *available at* http://www.undg.org.

22. *See* the website of the UN Office of Outerspace Affairs, *available at* http://www.unoosa.org/oosa/en/SORegister/index.html.

23. *See* Annex on the Protection of Confidential Information to the Chemical Weapons Convention. *See also*, Operating Procedures of the Confidentiality Commission, OPCW Doc. C-III/Dec. 10 Annex (November 27, 1998). *See also*, Barry Kellman et al., *Disarmament and Disclosure: How Arms Control Verification Can Proceed Without Threatening Confidential Business Information*, 36 HARV. INT'L L.J. 71 (1995); *See also*, Alison Van Lear, *Loud Talk about a Quiet Issue: The International Atomic Energy Agency's Struggle to Maintain the Confidentiality of Information Gained in Nuclear Facility, Inspections*, 28 GA. J. INT'L & COMP. L. 349 (2000).

24. Daniel C. Esty, *Good Governance at the Supranational Scale: Globalizing Administrative Law*, 115 YALE L. J. 1490 (2006).

25. The International Union for the Conservation of Nature and Natural Resources (IUCN) is a quasi-official collection of governments, nongovernmental organizations, and experts that advances international environmental standards. The IUCN has actively supplemented bourgeoning international agreements. Although the IUCN has no political authority to pass such conventions, it tries to motivate key players who do have that authority to implement particular standards. *See* Nicholas

A. Robinson, *IUCN as Catalyst for a Law of the Biosphere: Acting Globally and Locally*, 35 Envtl. L. J. 249 (2005).

26. *The World Bank and Biosafety: Questions and Answers*, The World Bank, *available at* http://web.worldbank.org/WBSITE/EXTERNAL/TOPICS/ENVIRONMENT/ EXTBIODIVERSITY/0,,contentMDK:21009141~menuPK:2794906~pagePK:210058 ~piPK:210062~theSitePK:400953,00.html.

27. *American Interests and UN Reform*, Report on the Task Force on the United Nations, United States Institute of Peace, p. 3 (June 15, 2005).

28. *American Interests and UN Reform*, Report of the Task Force on the United Nations, United States Institute of Peace, p. 70 (June 15, 2005).

29. *See* Thomas M. Franck, The Power of Legitimacy Among Nations, pp. 16, 21–25, 47 (1990); *See also*, Jose E. Alvarez, *The Quest for Legitimacy*, 24 N.Y.U. J. Int'l L. & Pol. 199–255 (1991); *See also*, Dencho Georgiev, *Politics or Rule of Law: Deconstruction and Legitimacy in International Law*, 4 Eur. J. Int'l L. 1, 8 (1993); *See also*, David D. Caron, *The Legitimacy of the Collective Authority of the Security Council*, 87 AJIL 552, 577–88 (1993); *See also*, Allen Buchanan & Robert O. Keohane, *The Legitimacy of Global Governance Institutions*, Ethics & International Affairs, p. 405 (December 1, 2006).

30. Robert McMahon, *Remembering Unmovic*, 30 WTR Fletcher F. World Aff. 93, *at* 96 (2006) *quoting* UNMOVIC, *Twenty-first Quarterly Report of the Activities of UNMOVIC*, (May 27, 2005), *available at* http://www.un.org/Depts/unmovic/new/ documents/quarterly_reports/s-2005-351.pdf.

31. *See* David M. Malone, The International Struggle Over Iraq, (2006).

32. *Organizational Plan for the United Nations Monitoring, Verification, and Inspection Commission*, prepared by the Executive Chairman. UN Doc. S/2000/292. (April 6, 2000).

33. Nahal Kazemi, *Ill at Ease: The Precarious State of the Biological Weapons Convention's Proposed Enforcement Regime*, 17 Fla. J. Int'l L. 137 (March, 2005).

34. *American Interests and UN Reform*, Report on the Task Force on the United Nations. United States Institute of Peace, pp. 70–71 (June 15, 2005).

35. Statement of Hans Blix, *quoted in* David M. Malone, The International Struggle Over Iraq, p. 172–73 (2006).

Bibliography

Introduction

Bombs, Gas, and Microbes: The Desperate Efforts to Block the Road to Doomsday, ECONOMIST (June 6, 1998).

Bausch, Daniel. *The Ebola Virus: . . . and the Challenges to Health Research in Africa,* UN CHRONICLE (June 1, 2001).

Brundtland, Gro Harlem, *Global Health and International Security; Global Insights,* GLOBAL GOVERNANCE (October 1, 2003).

Coghlan, Andy, Rowan Hooper, Ehsan Masood, Fred Pearce, & Curtis Abraham, *Foundations for a Prosperous Future,* NEW SCIENTIST (July 2, 2005).

Cole, Leonard A., THE ELEVENTH PLAGUE: THE POLITICS OF BIOLOGICAL AND CHEMICAL WARFARE, W.H. Freeman and Company (1997).

Ikenberry, G. John, & Anne-Marie Slaughter, FORGING A WORLD OF LIBERTY UNDER LAW: NATIONAL SECURITY IN THE 21ST CENTURY, The Princeton Project Papers, The Woodrow Wilson School of Public and International Affairs (September 27, 2006).

Kellman, Barry, *An International Criminal Law Approach to BioTerrorism,* 25 HARV. J. L. & PUB. POL'Y 721 (2002).

Kellman, Barry, *International Terrorism and International Human Rights,* 17 INT'L ENFORCEMENT L. REP. 263 (2001).

Kellman, Barry, *The Legality of the Use or Possession of Weapons of Mass Destruction,* in INTERNATIONAL CRIMINAL LAW 2d. ed. (M. C. Bassiouni, ed., 1997).

Lederberg, Joshua (ed.), BIOLOGICAL WEAPONS: LIMITING THE THREAT, MIT Press (1999).

Leitenberg, Milton, *Biological Weapons: A Reawakened Concern,* THE WORLD & I (January 1999).

Solomon, Brian (ed.), CHEMICAL AND BIOLOGICAL WARFARE, H. W. Wilson (1999).

Thacker, Eugene, THE GLOBAL GENOME – BIOTECHNOLOGY, POLITICS, AND CULTURE, MIT Press (2005).

Venter, Al J., *Biological Warfare: The Poor Man's Atomic Bomb,* JANE'S INTELLIGENCE REVIEW (March 1999).

Wolf, William T., *Domestic Biological Counter-Terrorism Policy: Are We Doing Enough?,* U. S. Army War College (1999).

Chapter 1

America the Unready. ECONOMIST (January 22, 2000).

Anthrax as a Biological Weapon: Medical and Public Health Management, JOURNAL OF THE AMERICAN MEDICAL ASSOCIATION, Vol. 281, No. 18 (May 12, 1999).

Atlas, Ronald M., *Combating the Threat of Biowarfare and Bioterrorism,* BIOSCIENCE, Vol. 49 (June 1999).

Barnaby, Wendy, *Biological Weapons: An Increasing Threat,* MEDICINE, CONFLICT, AND SURVIVAL (October–December 1997).

Bassiouni, M. Cherif, *War Crimes Research Symposium: "Terrorism on Trial": Terrorism: The Persistent Dilemma of Legitimacy,* 37 CASE W. RES. J. INT'L L. 299 (2005).

Beal, Clifford, *Biological Warfare Defence: Facing the Invisible Enemy.* JANE'S DEFENCE WEEKLY (November 4, 1998).

Cilluffo, Frank J., et al., *Combating Chemical, Biological, Radiological, and Nuclear Terrorism: A Comprehensive Strategy,* A Report of the CSIS Homeland Defense Project (May 2001).

Clevenger, Greg, *And You Thought Getting the Flu Was Bad: Working to Prevent Germ Warfare,* 12 TRANSNAT'L L. & CONTEMP. PROBS. 195 (Spring 2002).

Cohen, William S., *WMD (Weapons of Mass Destruction) Poses Top-Priority Threat to America,* DEFENSE ISSUES, Vol. 13, No. 16 (1998).

Diggs, D. G., WEAPONS OF MASS DESTRUCTION A NETWORK-CENTERED THREAT, Naval War College (1998).

Draft Code of Crimes Against the Peace and Security of Mankind, (1996).

Fidler, David P., *Public Health and National Security in the Global Age: Infectious Diseases, Bioterrorism, and Realpolitik,* 35 GEO. WASH. INT'L L. REV. 787 (2003).

Hearing before the Senate Health, Education, Labor, and Pension Committee, Subcommittee on Bioterrorism and Public Health Preparedness, on *Biological Threats,* (May 11, 2005), Testimony of Dr. Harvey V. Fineberg.

Henderson, D. A., *Bioterrorism as a Public Health Threat,* EMERGING INFECTIOUS DISEASES, Vol. 4, No. 3 (July–September 1998).

Kellman, Barry, *Catastrophic Terrorism – Thinking Fearfully, Acting Legally,* 20 MICH. J. INT.'L L. 537 (1999).

Kellman, Barry, MANAGING TERRORISM'S CONSEQUENCES – LEGAL ISSUES, Memorial Institute for the Prevention of Terrorism (2003).

Kokjohn, Tyler A., & Kimbal E. Cooper, *In the Shadow of Pandemic: Influenza is a Highly Adaptable Virus. Minimizing the Impact of a Global Influenza Outbreak will Require People to be Adaptable as Well,* FUTURIST, Vol. 40, No. 5 (September 1, 2006).

Larsen, Randall J., & Robert P. Kadlec, *Biological Warfare: A Silent Threat to America's Defense Transportation System,* STRATEGIC REVIEW (Spring 1998).

Mackby, Jennifer, *Strategic Study on Bioterrorism,* CENTER FOR STRATEGIC & INTERNATIONAL STUDIES (October 16, 2006).

Miller, Judith, et al., GERMS: BIOLOGICAL WEAPONS AND AMERICA'S SECRET WAR, Simon & Schuster (2001).

New U.S. Rules Set the Stage for Tighter Security, Oversight, SCIENCE (December 20, 2002).

Powers, Mary Buckner, & Nadine Post, *Chemical, Biological Threats Pose New Design Challenges*, ENGINEERING NEWS-RECORD – BUILDING FOR A SECURE FUTURE, Vol. 248, No. 11 (March 25, 2002).

Proliferation of Weapons of Mass Destruction, Office of Technology Assessment, U.S. Congress, OTA-ISC-559 (1993).

Roberts, Brad, & Graham S. Pearson, *Bursting the Biological Bubble: How Prepared Are We For Biowar?*, JANE'S INTERNATIONAL DEFENSE REVIEW (April 1998).

Schulte, Paul. *Chemical and Biological Weapons: Issues and Alternatives*, COMPARATIVE STRATEGY, No. 4 (1999).

Walker, Clive, *Biological Attack, Terrorism, and the Law*, TERRORISM AND POLITICAL VIOLENCE, Vol. 17 (2005).

Yount, Lisa, (ed.), FIGHTING BIOTERRORISM, Greenhaven Press (2004).

Chapter 2

Alibek, Ken, *Behind the Mask: Biological Warfare*, PERSPECTIVE, Vol. IX, No. 1 (September–October, 1998).

Ames, Ben, *Nanotechnology Delivers Military Power: Scientists Are Using Nanotechnology to Create Materials with Properties that Will Revolutionize Military Technology, from Processors to Display Screens and Body Armor to Air Filters; Technology Focus*, MILITARY & AEROSPACE ELECTRONICS, Vol. 16, No. 5. (May 1, 2005).

Anbarasan, Ethirajan, *Genetic Weapons: A 21st-Century Nightmare? Includes Related Article on the Hopes and Dilemmas of Genome Research; Foray into Biological Weapon Research*, UNESCO Courier (March 1, 1999).

ANIMAL HEALTH AT THE CROSSROADS: PREVENTING, DETECTING, AND DIAGNOSING ANIMAL DISEASES, Board on Agriculture and Natural Resources, The National Academies Press (2005).

Anthrax as a Biological Weapon, 2002: Updated Recommendations for Management, JOURNAL OF THE AMERICAN MEDICAL ASSOCIATION, Vol. 287, No.17 (May 2002).

Ashford, David A., et al., *Biological Terrorism and Veterinary Medicine in the U.S.* JOURNAL FOR THE AMERICAN VETERINARY ASSOCIATION, Vol. 217, No. 5 (September 1, 2000).

Atlas, Ronald M., *National Security and the Biological Research Community; Policy Forum: Public Health*, SCIENCE (October 25, 2002).

Ballester, Ferran, & Jordi Sunyer, *Drinking Water and Gastrointestinal Disease: Need of Better Understanding and an Improvement in Public Health Surveillance*, J EPIDEMIOL COMMUNITY HEALTH (2000).

Balter, Michael, *Prions, A Lone Killer or a Vital Accomplise? Creutzfeldt-Jakob Disease; Bovine Spongirm Encephalopathy*, SCIENCE, Vol. 286, p. 660 (October 22, 1999).

Beecher, Douglas, *Forensic Application of Microbiological Culture Analysis to Identify Mail Intentionally Contaminated with Bacillus Anthracis Spores*, APPLIED AND ENVIRONMENTAL MICROBIOLOGY, Vol. 72, No. 8, (August 2006).

Begley, Sharon, *Unmasking Bioterror*, NEWSWEEK (October 8, 2001).

Biek, Roman, et al., *Recent Common Ancestry of Ebola Zaire Virus Found in a Bat Reservoir*, PLoS PATHOGENS, Vol. 2, No. 10 (October, 2006).

Biological Warfare Agents as Potable Water Threats, U.S. Army Center for Health Promotion and Preventive Medicine (1998).

Bioterrorism Agents/Diseases, THE CENTERS FOR DISEASE CONTROL AND PREVENTION, *available at*: http://www.bt.cdc.gov/agent/agentlist-category.asp#adef.

Birenzvige, Amnon, *Acquisition of Chemical and Biological Equipment*, ARMY RD & A (March–April 1998).

Botulinum Toxin as a Biological Weapon: Medical and Public Health Management, JOURNAL OF THE AMERICAN MEDICAL ASSOCIATION, Vol. 285, No. 8 (February 28, 2001).

Carlson, Robert, *The Pace and Proliferation of Biological Technologies*, BIOSECURITY & BIOTERRORISM, Vol. 1, No. 3 (2003).

Casagrande, Rocco, *Biological Warfare Targeted at Livestock*, BIOSCIENCE. Vol. 52, No. 7 (July 1, 2002).

CDC Marburg Hemorrhagic Fever Fact Sheet. Available at http://www.cdc.gov/ncidod/dvrd/spb/mnpages/dispages/fact_sheets/Marburg%20hemmorhagic%Fever%20Fact%20Sheet.pdf.

Cello, Jeronimo, Aniko V. Paul, & Eckhard Wimmer, *Chemical Synthesis of Poliovirus cDNA: Generation of Infectious Virus in the Absence of Natural Template*, SCIENCE (August 9, 2002).

Center for Disease Control and the World Health Organization. *Infection Control for Viral Hemorrhagic Fevers in the African Healthcare Setting*. Atlanta, CENTERS FOR DISEASE CONTROL AND PREVENTION (1998).

Check, Erika, *Synthetic Biologists Face Up to Security Issues*, NATURE (August 18, 2005).

Chelvi, K. T., *The Pox May Be on You*, NEW STRAITS TIMES (April 4, 2005).

Chittaranjan, Kalpana, *Biological Weapons: An Insidious WMD (weapon of mass destruction)*, STRATEGIC ANALYSIS (December 1998).

Cordesman, Anthony H., *The Challenge of Biological Terrorism*, CENTER FOR STRATEGIC AND INTERNATIONAL STUDIES (2005).

COUNTERING AGRICULTURAL BIOTERRORISM, National Academies Press (2002).

Coxiella burnetii, EVANSTON NORTHWESTERN HEALTHCARE, available at http://www.enh.org/healthandwellness/bioterrorism/bi001000.aspx?lid=1093.

Dando, Malcolm, *The Impact of the Development of Modern Biology and Medicine on the Evolution of Offensive Biological Warfare Programs in the Twentieth Century*, DEFENSE ANALYSIS, Vol.15, No. 1 (1999).

Dempsey, Judy, Geoff Dyer, Stephen Fidler, & Alexander Nicoll, *Death Out of Life: Just as Physics Dominated Weapons in the 20th Century, so Biology will Dominate Weapons in the 21st*, FINANCIAL TIMES, London Edition (July 10, 2002).

Dudley, William, (ed.), BIOLOGICAL WARFARE: OPPOSING VIEWPOINTS, Greenhaven Press (2004).

Emerging Infections: What Have We Learned from SARS? EMERGING INFECTIOUS DISEASES, Vol. 10, No. 7 (July 2004).

Emerging Technologies: Genetic Engineering and Biological Weapons, THE SUNSHINE PROJECT, Background Paper, No. 12 (November 2003).

Falcon, Walter P., & Rosamond L. Naylor, *Rethinking Food Security for the Twenty-first Century*, AMERICAN JOURNAL OF AGRICULTURAL ECONOMICS, Vol. 87, No. 5 (December 1, 2005).

Feeney, Michael A., *The Plague – Its History as an Infectious Disease and Its Unlikely Use as a Weapon of Mass Destruction*, JOURNAL OF COUNTERTERRORISM & SECURITY INTERNATIONAL, Vol. 7, No. 4 (Summer 2001).

Flu Bioweapon Fears, BBC NEWS (July 1, 2003).

Fraser, Claire M., & Malcolm R. Dando, *Genomics and Future Biological Weapons: The Need for Preventive Action by the Biomedical Community*, NATURE GENETICS, Vol. 29 (2001).

Garrett, Laurie, *The Next Pandemic?* FOREIGN AFFAIRS (July/August 2005).

Gellman, Barton, *4 Nations Thought to Possess Smallpox; Iraq, N. Korea named, Two Officials Say*, WASHINGTON POST (November 5, 2002).

Gips, Michael, *The First Link in the Food Chain*, SECURITY MANAGEMENT ONLINE (February 2003).

GLOBALIZATION, BIOSECURITY, AND THE FUTURE OF THE LIFE SCIENCES, Committee on Advances in Technology and the Prevention of Their Application to Next Generation Biowarfare Threats, NATIONAL RESEARCH COUNCIL OF THE NATIONAL ACADEMIES (2006).

Gostin, Lawrence O., *When Terrorism Threatens Health: How Far Are Limitations on Personal and Economic Liberties Justified?* 55 FLORIDA LAW REVIEW 5 (December 2003).

Gursky, Elin, Thomas V. Inglesby, & Tara O'Toole, *Anthrax 2001: Observations on the Medical and Public Health Response*, BIOSECURITY AND BIOTERRORISM, Vol. 1, No. 2 (2003).

Hearing before the Committee on International Relations, House of Representatives, on *Russia, Iraq, and other Potential Sources of Anthrax, Smallpox and other Bioterrorist Weapons*, 107th Congress, 1st Session (December 5, 2001), Testimonies of Dr. Kenneth Alibek and Elisa D. Harris.

Hearing before the House Armed Services Committee, Military Procurement and Military Research and Development Subcommittees, (October 20, 1999), Testimony of Hans Mark.

Hearing before the House Intelligence Committee, (March 3, 1999), Testimony of Dr. Kenneth Alibek.

Hearing before the Permanent Subcommittee on Investigations, Staff Statement, U.S. Senate Permanent Subcommittee on Investigations (Minority Staff), on *Global Proliferation of Weapons of Mass Destruction, A Case Study on the Aum Shinrikyo*, 104th Congress, 1st Session (October 31, 1995).

Hearing before the Senate Agriculture Committee, on *Agro-Terrorism Preparedness*, (July 20, 2005), Testimonies of James A. Roth and James Sherwood.

Hearing before the Senate Appropriations Committee, Labor, HHS, Education, and Related Agencies Subcommittee, on *Bioterrorism*, (November 29, 2001), Testimony of Dr. Kenneth Alibek.

Hearing before the Senate Committee on Health Education, Labor, and Pensions, *Biodefense: Next Steps*, (February 8, 2005), Testimony of Dr. George Painter.

Hearing before the Senate Health Education, Labor, and Pension Committee, Bioterrorism and Public Health Preparedness Subcommittee (May 11, 2005), Testimony of Dr. Craig Venter.

Hearing before the Senate Health, Education, Labor, and Pensions Committee, Public Health Subcommittee (June 9, 2005), Testimony of John Vitko.

Hearing before the United States Senate Committee on Agriculture, Nutrition, and Forestry (July 20, 2005).

Heine, Henry S., et al., *Determination of Antibiotic Efficacy Against Bacillus Anthracis in a Mouse Aerosol Challenge Model*, Report prepared for the United States Army Medical Research Institute of Infectious Diseases, Division of Bacteriology, ANTIMICROBIAL AGENTS AND CHEMOTHERAPY (2007).

Hemorrhagic Fever Viruses as Biological Weapons: Medical and Public Health Management, JOURNAL OF THE AMERICAN MEDICAL ASSOCIATION, Vol. 287, No. 18 (May 8, 2002).

Hitchcock, Penny, *Improving Performance of HVAC Systems to Reduce Exposure to Aerosolized Infectious Agents in Buildings; Recommendations to Reduce Risks Posed by Biological Agents*, BIOSECURITY AND BIOTERRORISM: BIODEFENSE STRATEGY, PRACTICE, AND SCIENCE, Vol. 4, No. 1 (2006).

HIV/AIDS at a Glance, THE WORLD BANK (October 2003).

Howe, David, *Planning Scenarios, Executive Summaries*, The Homeland Security Council (July 2004).

IBEA Researchers Make Significant Advance in Methodology Toward Goal of a Synthetic Genome, Press Release issued by the Institute for Biological Energy Alternatives (November 13, 2003).

Influenza (Flu) Questions and Answers: Reconstruction of the 1918 Influenza Pandemic Virus, CENTERS FOR DISEASE CONTROL AND PREVENTION, available at http://www.bt.cdc.gov/scripts/emailprint/print.asp.

Interim Report of the Select Committee to Study Governmental Operations with Respect to Intelligence Activities on the Alleged Assassination Plots Involving Foreign Leaders. Senate Report No. 94-465; 94th Congress, 1st Session (November 20, 1975).

International Plant Protection Convention, TIAS 7465, (December 6, 1951), (Entered into force April 3, 1952).

Johnson, Barbara (Ph.D.), *ABSA Comments on CDC Select Agent Rule*, American Biological Safety Association (February 5, 2003).

Joy, Bill, *Why the Future Doesn't Need Us*, WIRED, Issue 8.04 (April 2000).

Kaiser, J., *ScienceScope*, SCIENCE, Vol. 309 (July 1, 2005).

Kellman, Barry, EMERGING DISEASES OF ANIMALS, Michigan State University Press (2000).

Koplow, David, SMALLPOX – THE FIGHT TO ERADICATE A GLOBAL SCOURGE, University of California Press (2003).

Kornfeld, Itzchak E., *Combating Terrorism in the Environmental Trenches: Responding to Terrorism: Terror in the Water: Threats to Drinking Water and Infrastructure*, WIDENER LAW SYMPOSIUM (2003).

Krug, Robert M., *The Potential Use of Influenza Virus as an Agent for Bioterrorism*, ANTIVIRAL RESEARCH, Vol. 57, No. 1–2 (January 2003).

Kwik, Gigi, et al., *Biosecurity: Responsible Stewardship of Bioscience*, BIOSECURITY AND BIOTERRORISM: BIODEFENSE STRATEGY, PRACTICE, AND SCIENCE, Vol. 1, No. 1 (2003).

Kwik Gronvall, Gigi, & Luciana L. Borio, *Removing Barriers to Global Pandemic Influenza Vaccination*, BIOSECURITY AND BIOTERRORISM: BIODEFENSE STRATEGY, PRACTICE, AND SCIENCE, Vol. 4, No. 2 (2006).

Landrieu, Mary (Senator, D-LA, Chair), *Hearing of the Emerging Threats and Capabilities Subcommittee of the Senate Armed Services Committee* (April 10, 2002).

Laver, Graeme, & Elspeth Garman, *The Origin and Control of Pandemic Influenza*, SCIENCE, Vol. 293, No. 5536 (September 7, 2001).

Levitt, Joseph A., *FDA's Plate Remains Full; Counterterrorism, Nutrition, Safety, and Dietary Regulation will Stay the Focus of Food Regulation*, LEGAL TIMES (March 1, 2004).

Lipshutz, Rob, *Using Microarrays to Detect Disease and Tailor Therapy*, PHARMACEUTICAL DISCOVERY, Vol. 5, No. 7 (September 1, 2005).

Lloyd, Jane, *The Bird Flu: Are We Ready for a Pandemic?*, UN CHRONICLE, Vol. 42, No. 4 (December 1, 2005).

Longini, I. M., et al., *Containing Pandemic Influenza with Antiviral Agents*, AMERICAN JOURNAL OF EPIDEMIOLOGY, Vol. 159, No. 7 (April 1, 2004).

MacAskill, Ewen, et al., *Threat of War: Powell's Evidence Against Saddam: Does It Add Up? Guardian* (London) (February 6, 2003).

MacDonald, Elizabeth, & Robert Langreth, *Spore Wars*, FORBES, Vol. 175, No. 12 (June 6, 2005).

Mad Cow Watch Goes Blind, USA TODAY (August 4, 2006).

Madjid, Mohamad, et al., *Influenza as a Bioweapon*, JOURNAL OF THE ROYAL SOCIETY OF MEDICINE, Vol. 96 (July 2003).

Maier, Thomas, *Anthrax Vaccine; The Debate*, NEWSDAY (November 20, 2005).

Malaria at a Glance, THE WORLD BANK (March, 2001).

Marburg Haemorrhagic Fever: Fact Sheet, WORLD HEALTH ORGANIZATION (March, 2005).

Marburg Hemorrhagic Fever Fact Sheet, THE CENTERS FOR DISEASE CONTROL AND PREVENTION, *available at* http://www.cdc.gov/ncidod/dvrd/spb/mnpages/dispages/Fact_Sheets/Marburg%20Hemmorhagic%20Fever%20Fact%20Sheet.pdf.

Matsumoto, Gary, *Anthrax Powder – State of the Art?* SCIENCE, Vol. 302, No. 5650 (November 28, 2003).

McCook, Alison, *PNAS Publishes Bioterror Paper, After All*, THE SCIENTIST (June 29, 2005).

Miller, Sonia E., *Converging Technologies: Regulating Nanotechnology; The FDA and the EPA Are Likely Federal Watchdogs*, NEW YORK LAW JOURNAL (April 5, 2005).

Montague, Peter, *Welcome to Nanoworld: Nanotechnology and the Precautionary Principle Imperative; The Precautionary Principle*, MULTINATIONAL MONITOR (September 1, 2004).

Mulhall, Douglas, *Reassessing Risk Assessment: The Question of Whether to Pursue the Development of Nanomaterials Isn't Just About Weighing the Pros Wondrous New Technologies and the Cons Environmental Catastrophe*, FUTURIST, Vol. 38, No. 1 (January 1, 2004).

Munro, Neil, *Issues & Ideas – Creating Life to Order* (June 10, 2006).

National Research Council, COUNTERING AGRICULTURAL TERRORISM (2003).

O'Toole, Tara, *Smallpox: An Attack Scenario, available at* http://www.cdc.gov/ncidod/EID/vol5no4/otoole.htm.

Osterholm, Michael T., *Preparing for the Next Pandemic*, FOREIGN AFFAIRS (July–August, 2005).

Parker, Henry S., *Agricultural Bioterrorism: A Federal Strategy to Meet the Threat*, POLICY PAPERS (March 2002).

Perpich, Joseph G., *The Recombinant-DNA Debate and Bioterrorism*, CHRONICLE OF HIGHER EDUCATION (March 15, 2002).

Pierce, Julia, *Nanotechnology – Particles of Hope*, ENGINEER (May 8, 2006).

Pinson, Robert D., *Is Nanotechnology Prohibited by the Biological and Chemical Weapons Conventions?*, 22 BERKELEY J. INT'L L 279 (2004).

Plague as a Biological Weapon: Medical and Public Health Management: Consensus Statement, JOURNAL OF THE AMERICAN MEDICAL ASSOCIATION, Vol. 283, No. 17 (May 3, 2002).

Possession, Use, and Transfer of Select Agents and Toxins; Interim Final Rule, 42 CFR Part 1003, FEDERAL REGISTER, Vol. 240, No. 67 (December 13, 2002).

Poste, George, *Special Report: Biotechnology and Terrorism*, PROSPECT (April 25, 2002).

Q Fever Caused by Coxiella Burnetii, CENTERS FOR DISEASE CONTROL AND PREVENTION, *available at* http://www.cdc.gov/ncidod/dvrd/qfever/index.htm.

Randerson, James, *Synthetic Biology: Lax Laws, Virus DNA, and Potential for Error: Loopholes Mean Anyone can Order Gene Sequences: Scientists Back Voluntary Regulation as First Step*, GUARDIAN (London) (June 14, 2006).

Rappert, Brian, & Malcolm Dando, *Accountability and the Governance of Expertise: Anticipating Genetic Bioweapons*, Full Report of Research Activities and Results, States News Service, *Committee Statement: Preparing a National Bio-Defense* (July 21, 2005).

Rappert, Brian, *Biological Weapons, Genetics and Social Analysis: Emerging Responses, Emerging Issues*, NEW GENETICS AND SOCIETY, Vol. 22, No. 2 (August 2003).

Relman, David A., *Bioterrorism – Preparing to Fight the Next War*, NEW ENGLAND JOURNAL OF MEDICINE (January 12, 2006).

Report on Strategies to Improve Africa's Agriculture, Food Security Presented at UN Headquarters, M2 PRESSWIRE (June 28, 2004).

Researchers Reconstruct 1918 Pandemic Influenza Virus; Effort Designed to Advance Preparedness, CENTERS FOR DISEASE CONTROL AND PREVENTION, Press Release (October 5, 2005).

Ricin and the Umbrella Murder, CNN.COM (October 23, 2003).

Rodier, Guenael, *Confronting a World of Infectious Diseases*, PUBLIC HEALTH REPORTS (March/April 2001).

Rosegrant, Mark W., & Sarah A. Cline, *Global Food Security: Challenges and Policies; Viewpoint*, SCIENCE, Vol. 302, No. 5652 (December 12, 2003).

Rotz, Lisa D., et al., *Public Health Assessment of Potential Biological Terrorism Agents; Report Summary*, EMERGING INFECTIOUS DISEASES, Vol. 8, No. 2 (February 1, 2002).

Russell, Sabin, *Deadliest Flu Bug Given New Life in U.S. Laboratory; Some Applaud Scientific Feat, but Others Decry Move as Reckless*, SAN FRANCISCO CHRONICLE (October 6, 2005).

Schoch-Spana, Monica, *Implications of Pandemic Influenza for Bioterrorism Response*, CLINICAL INFECTIOUS DISEASES, Vol. 31 (December 2000).

Smallpox as a Biological Weapon: Medical and Public Health Management, JOURNAL OF THE AMERICAN MEDICAL ASSOCIATION, Vol. 281, No. 22 (June 9, 1999).

Srinivasan, Arjun, M. D., et al., *Glanders in a Military Research Microbiologist*, NEW ENGLAND JOURNAL OF MEDICINE, Vol. 345, No. 4 (July 26, 2001).

Steinbruner, John D., *Biological Weapons: A Plague Upon All Houses*, FOREIGN POLICY (Winter 1997–1998).

Steinbruner, John, & Elisa D. Harris, *When Science Breeds Nightmares: Dangerous Research*, INTERNATIONAL HERALD TRIBUNE (December 3, 2003).

Stohr, Klaus, & Marja Esveld, *Will Vaccines be Available for the Next Influenza Pandemic?* SCIENCE, Vol. 306, No. 5705 (December 24, 2004).

The Biological Agents and Toxins Act of 2005, Bill No. 26/2005, (September 19, 2005).

The Ecology of Flu, ZKEA EMERGING DISEASES: BIOLOGICAL TERRORISM: BIOLOGICAL WARFARE, *available at* http://www.zkea.com/articles/flu2.html.

Treder, Mike, *Molecular Nanotech: Benefits and Risks: Welcome to the Nanofactory, a Tiny Plant that Makes Products Atom by Atom*, THE FUTURIST, Vol. 38, No. 1 (January 1, 2004).

Tucker, Jonathan B., & Raymond A. Zilinskas, *The Promise and Perils of Synthetic Biology*, NEW ATLANTIS: No. 12 (Spring 2006).

Tucker, Jonathan B., SCOURGE: THE ONCE AND FUTURE THREAT OF SMALLPOX, Grove Press (2002).

Tularemia as a Biological Weapon, Medical and Public Health Management, Consensus Statement, JOURNAL OF THE AMERICAN MEDICAL ASSOCIATION, Vol. 285, No. 1 (June 6, 2001).

Tumpey, Terrence M., et al., *Characterization of the Reconstructed 1918 Spanish Influenza Virus*, SCIENCE, Vol. 310 (October 7, 2005).

U.S. Scientists Split on Smallpox Decision, NATURE, Vol. 398 (April 29, 1999).

Venter, Al J., *Spectre of Biowar Remains*, JANE'S DEFENCE WEEKLY (April 28, 1999).

Vowinkel, Patricia, *A Plate Full of Headaches: Food for Thought: The Contamination of the U.S. Food Supply, a Serious Public Health Risk, Could Devastate the Economy and the $500 Billion U.S. Food Processing Industry; Industry Risk Report*, RISK & INSURANCE, Vol. 15, No. 5 (April 15, 2004).

Walsh, Nick P., *Markov's Umbrella Assassination Revealed*, GUARDIAN (June 6, 2005).

Wannet, W., *Spread of an MRSA Clone with Heteroresistance to Oxacillin in the Netherlands*, EuroSURVEILLANCE, Vol. 7, No. 5 (May 2002).

Warrick, Joby, *Custom-built Pathogens Raise Bioterror Fears*, WASHINGTON POST (July 31, 2006).

Watanabe, Myrna, *The Bioterror Error*, HARTFORD COURANT (September 5, 2004).

Webby, R. J., & R. G. Webster, *Are We Ready for Pandemic Influenza?* SCIENCE, Vol. 302, No. 5650 (November 28, 2003).

Wein, Lawrence M., & Yifan Liu, *Analyzing a Bioterror Attack on the Food Supply: The Case of Botulinum Toxin in Milk*, PROCEEDINGS OF THE NATIONAL ACADEMY OF SCIENCES OF THE UNITED STATES OF AMERICA, Vol. 102 (July 12, 2005).

Weiss, Rick, *A Terrorist's Fragile Footprint; Letter's Anthrax Spores Pose Many Obstacles to Analysis*, WASHINGTON POST (November 29, 2001).

Weiss, Rick, *Polio-Causing Virus Created in N.Y. Lab: Made-From-Scratch Pathogen Prompts Concerns About Bioethics, Terrorism*, WASHINGTON POST (July 12, 2002).

Wheelis, Mark, & Malcolm Dando, *New Technology and Future Developments in Biological Warfare*, DISARMAMENT FORUM (2000).

Wheelis, Mark, Rocco Casagrande, & Laurence V. Madden, *Biological Attack on Agriculture: Low-Tech, High-Impact Bioterrorism*, BIOSCIENCE, Vol. 52, No. 7 (July 2002).

Wheelis, Mark, *Will the New Biology Lead to New Weapons?* ARMS CONTROL TODAY (July 2004).

WHO – Marburg Hemorrhagic Fever Fact Sheet (March 2005).

WMD 411 Chronology – 2002, NUCLEAR THREAT INITIATIVE, *available at* http://www.nti.org/f_wmd411/2002.html.

Wright, Oliver, *Scientists' Bid to Combat TB Made It More Virulent*, LONDON TIMES (December 27, 2003).

Yuen, K. Y., & S. S. Y. Wong, *Human Infection by Avian Influenza A H5N1*, HONG KONG MEDICAL JOURNAL, Vol. 11, No. 3 (June 2005).

Zoon, Kathryn C., *Vaccines, Pharmaceutical Products, and Bioterrorism: Challenges for the U.S. Food and Drug Administration*. Available at http://www.cdc.gov/ncidod/EID/vol5no4/zoon.htm.

Chapter 3

"Dr. Death" To Be Retried, NEW YORK TIMES (September 10, 2005).

Adherence and Compliance with Arms Control, Nonproliferation, and Disarmament Agreements, U.S. Department of State (August 2005).

Adherence to and Compliance with Arms Control Agreements, Defense Treaty Inspection Readiness Program, ARMS CONTROL AND DISARMAMENT AGENCY (1993).

Al Qaeda Tested Germ Weapons, REUTERS (January 1, 2002).

Allen-Mills, Tony, & Uzi Mahnaimi Tel Aviv, *Al-Qaeda Seeks Toxins for Biowarfare Attack*, SUNDAY TIMES (London) (January 2, 2005).

Al-Qa'ida's WMD Activities, Chart prepared by the Weapons of Mass Destruction Terrorism Research Program, CENTER FOR NONPROLIFERATION STUDIES, *available at* http://cns.miis.edu/pubs/other/sjm_cht.htm.

Al-Qaeda Leader Calls for Scientists to Join Cause, WCBS (September 28, 2006).

Al-Qaeda: Anthrax Found in al-Qaeda Home, GLOBAL SECURITY NEWSWIRE (December 10, 2001).

Baker, Peter, *Pakistani Scientist Who Met Bin Laden Failed Polygraphs, Renewing Suspicions*, WASHINGTON POST (March 3, 2002).

Baldwin, Ira, *Special BW Operations*, Memorandum for Executive Secretary, Research and Development Board, Unclassified, THE NATIONAL MILITARY ESTABLISHMENT RESEARCH AND DEVELOPMENT BOARD (October 5, 1948).

Bale, Jeffrey, Anjali Bhattacharjee, Eric Croddy, & Richard Pilch, *Ricin Found in London: An al-Qa'ida Connection*, CENTER FOR NONPROLIFERATION STUDIES (January 23, 2002).

Ball, Deborah Yarsike, & Theodore P. Gerber, *Russian Scientists and Rogue States: Does Western Assistance Reduce the Proliferation Threat?*, INTERNATIONAL SECURITY (Spring 2005).

Balmer, Brian, *The Drift of Biological Weapons Policy in the UK 1945–1965*, JOURNAL OF STRATEGIC STUDIES (December 1997).

Bartholet, Jeffrey, *Terrorist Sleeper Cells*, NEWSWEEK (December 9, 2001).

Bellamy, R. J. & A. R. Freedman, *Bioterrorism*, QUEENS JOURNAL OF MEDICINE (2001).

Bermudez, Joseph S. Jr., *Exposing the North Korean BW (Biological Warfare) Arsenal*, JANE'S INTELLIGENCE REVIEW (August 1998).

Beyond Anthrax: Extremism and the Bioterrorism Threat, ANTI-DEFAMATION LEAGUE (2001).

Bin Laden's Biological Threat, BBC (October 28, 2001).

Biological Weapons Program – Egypt, FEDERATION OF AMERICAN SCIENTISTS, *available at* http://www.fas.org/nuke/guide/egypt/bw/index.html.

Biological Weapons, FEDERATION OF AMERICAN SCIENTISTS, *available at* http://fas.org/nuke/guide/usa/cbw/bw.htm.

Biological Weapons: Attacking the Food Chain, HOMELAND SECURITY & RESILIENCE MONITOR, Vol. 6, No. 1 (February 2007).

Bodansky, Yossef, BIN LADEN: THE MAN WHO DECLARED WAR ON AMERICA, Random House Inc. (2001).

Bolton, John, *Beyond the Axis of Evil: Additional Threats from Weapons of Mass Destruction*, Remarks to the Heritage Foundation, HERITAGE LECTURES, No. 743 (May 6, 2002).

Bowman, Steve, IRAQI CHEMICAL & BIOLOGICAL WEAPONS (CBW) CAPABILITIES, Library of Congress, Congressional Research Service (1998).

Broad, William J., & Judith Miller, *Live Ammo; The Threat of Germ Weapons Is Rising. Fear, Too*, NEW YORK TIMES (December 27, 1998).

Burgess, Stephen, & Helen Purkitt, *The Rollback of South Africa's Biological Warfare Program*, INNS Occasional Paper 37, THE INSTITUTE FOR NATIONAL SECURITY STUDIES (February 2001).

Carrell, Severin, & Raymond Whitaker, *Special Report: Terror in the UK – Ricin the Plot that Never was; A Deadly Poison Said to be at the Heart of a Terrorist Conspiracy*, INDEPENDENT ON SUNDAY (London) (April 17, 2005).

Carus, W. Seth, *Bioterrorism and Biocrimes: Illicit Use of Biological Agents since 1900*, Working Paper, CENTER FOR NONPROLIFERATION RESEARCH (August 1998).

Carus, W. Seth, *Bioterrorism and Biocrimes: Illicit Use of Biological Agents in the 20th Century*, Working Paper, CENTER FOR NONPROLIFERATION RESEARCH (July 1999).

Cohen, Avner, *Israel and Chemical/Biological Weapons: History, Deterrence, and Arms Control*, NONPROLIFERATION REVIEW (Fall/Winter 2001).

Cole, Leonard A. THE ANTHRAX LETTERS: A MEDICAL DETECTIVE STORY, Joseph Henry Press (2003).

Cole, Leonard A. CLOUDS OF SECRECY: THE ARMY'S GERM WARFARE TESTS OVER POPULATED AREAS, Rowman & Littlefield (1990).

Conversation with Terror, TIME MAGAZINE (January 11, 1999).

Cordesman, Anthony, & Khalid R. Al-Rodhan, IRAN'S WEAPONS OF MASS DESTRUCTION, Center for Strategic and International Studies (2006).

Cornish, Paul, *The CBRN System: Assessing the Threat of Terrorist Use of Chemical, Biological, Radiological and Nuclear Weapons in the United Kingdom*, An International Security Programme Report, CHATHAM HOUSE (February 2007).

Country Overviews: Egypt: Biological Chronology, NUCLEAR THREAT INITIATIVE, *available at* http://www.nti.org/e_research/profiles/Egypt/3456.html.

Country Overviews: Iran: Biological Overview, NUCLEAR THREAT INITIATIVE, *available at* http://www.nti.org/e_research/profiles/Iran/Biological/2299.html.

Country Overviews: Israel: Biological Overview, NUCLEAR THREAT INITIATIVE, *available at* http://www.nti.org/e_research/profiles/Israel/Biological/index.html.

Country Overviews: North Korea: Biological Overview, NUCLEAR THREAT INITIATIVE, http://www.nti.org/e_research/profiles/NK/Biological/index.html.

Country Overviews: Syria: Biological Overview, NUCLEAR THREAT INITIATIVE, *available at* http://www.nti.org/e_research/profiles/Syria/Biological/3338.html.

Country Reports: Egypt, MIDDLE EAST DEFENSE NEWS, Vol. 6, No. 13 (April 5, 1993).

Croddy, Eric, CHEMICAL AND BIOLOGICAL WARFARE: A COMPREHENSIVE SURVEY FOR THE CONCERNED CITIZEN, Springer-Verlag New York, Inc. (2002).

Cruickshank, Paul, & Mohanad Hage Ali, *Jihadist of Mass Destruction*, WASHINGTON POST (June 11, 2006).

Cruickshank, Paul, & Mohanad Hage Ali, *Abu Musab Al-Suri: Architect of the New Al Qaeda*, STUDIES IN CONFLICT & TERRORISM, Vol. 30 (2007).

Cullison, Alan, & Andrew Higgins, *Computer in Kabul Holds Chilling Memos*, WALL STREET JOURNAL (December 31, 2001).

Cullison, Alan, & Andrew Higgins, *Files Found: A Computer in Kabul Yields a Chilling Array of al Qaeda Memos*, WALL STREET JOURNAL (December 31, 2001).

Daley, Paul, *Report Says UBL-linked Terrorist Groups Possess 'Deadly' Anthrax, Plague Viruses*, MELBOURNE AGE (June 4, 2000).

Dando, Malcolm, BIOLOGICAL WARFARE IN THE 21ST CENTURY: BIOTECHNOLOGY AND THE PROLIFERATION OF BIOLOGICAL WEAPONS, Brasey's Publishing (1994).

Dao, James, *Muslim Cleric Found Guilty in the 'Virginia Jihad' Case*, NEW YORK TIMES (April 27, 2005).

Davis, Jim A., & Barry R. Schneider (eds.), THE GATHERING BIOLOGICAL WARFARE STORM, Praeger (2004).

Diab, M. Zuhair, *Syria's Chemical and Biological Weapons: Assessing Capabilities and Motivations*, NONPROLIFERATION REVIEW (Fall 1997).

Dudley, William (ed.), BIOLOGICAL WARFARE: OPPOSING VIEWPOINTS, Greenhaven Press (2004).

Dwyer, Timothy, *Prosecution Called 'Overzealous' Guilty Verdict in Terror Case Angers Muslims Who Know Lecturer*, WASHINGTON POST (April 27, 2005).

Eisler, Peter, *U.S., Russia Tussle Over Deadly Anthrax Sample*, USA TODAY (August 19, 2002).

Evans, Dominic, *U.S. Troops Found Afghan Biological Lab*, REUTERS (March 22, 2002).

Fighting Anthrax: A Cold Warrior's Confession, WASHINGTON QUARTERLY, Vol. 25, No. 2 (Spring 2002).

Franz, David R., et al., *The U.S. Biological Warfare and Biological Defense Programs*, *in* MEDICAL ASPECTS OF CHEMICAL AND BIOLOGICAL WARFARE, Textbook of Military Medicine (1997).

Friedman, Gregory H., *Report on Inspection of Department of Energy Activities Involving Biological Select Agents*, Memorandum for the Secretary, DOE/IG-0492, U.S. Department of Energy (February 2, 2001).

Gellman, Barton, *Al-Qaida Near Biological, Chemical Arms Production*, WASHINGTON POST (March 23, 2003).

Getman, Ross E., VANGUARDS OF CONQUEST: AL QAEDA, ANTHRAX AND AYMAN ZAWAHIRI, *available at* http://members.bellatlantic.net/~vze43v8m/alqaedaan-thraxay.html#RequirementofWarning.

Giles, Gregory F., *The Islamic Republic of Iran and Nuclear, Biological, and Chemical Weapons* in PLANNING THE UNTHINKABLE, (Peter Lavoy, Scott Sagan, and James Wirtz, eds.) Cornell University Press, (2000)

Glasser, Susan B., & Kamran Khan, *Pakistan Continues Probe of Nuclear Scientists*, WASHINGTON POST (November 14, 2001).

Goldberg, Jeff, & Tom Mangold, PLAGUE WARS: THE TERRIFYING REALITY OF BIOLOGICAL WARFARE, Macmillan Publishers, Ltd. (1999).

Goldenberg, Suzanne, & Nick Hopkins, *MI5 Says Dirty Bomb Attack Is Inevitable*, GUARDIAN (June 18, 2003).

Gomer, Robert, et al., JAPAN'S BIOLOGICAL WEAPONS: 1930–1945: A HIDDEN CHAPTER IN HISTORY, The Bulletin of the Atomic Scientists (October 1981).

Gordon, Michael R., *U.S. Says it Found Qaeda Lab Being Built to Produce Anthrax*, NEW YORK TIMES (March 23, 2002).

Gould, Chandre, & Peter Folb, PROJECT COAST: APARTHEID'S CHEMICAL AND BIOLOGICAL WARFARE PROGRAMME, United Nations Institute for Disarmament Research (2002).

Guillemin, Jeanne, BIOLOGICAL WEAPONS: FROM THE INVENTION OF STATE-SPONSORED PROGRAMS TO CONTEMPORARY BIOTERRORISM, Columbia University Press (2005).

Gunning For Saddam: Saddam Hussein's Weapons of Mass Destruction, PBS Frontline Special (November 8, 2001).

Harnden, Toby, *Rogue Scientists Gave bin Laden Nuclear Secrets*, DAILY TELEGRAPH(London) (December 13, 2001).

Hays, Kathleen, Gerri Willis, & Valerie Morris, with Dr. Bob Brooks & Dr. Les Beitsch, *Are We Losing the War Against Bio-Terrorism?* Show, The Flipside, CNNfn (February 5, 2004).

Hearing before the Committee on International Relations, House of Representatives, on *Russia, Iraq, and Other Potential Sources of Anthrax, Smallpox, and other Bioterrorist Weapons*, 107th Congress, 1st Session (December 5, 2001).

Hearing before the Joint Economic Committee, United States Congress, *Terrorist and Intelligence Operations: Potential Impact on the U.S. Economy*, (May 20, 1998), Testimony by Dr. Ken Alibek.

Hearing before the Senate Select Committee on Intelligence, on *Current and Projected National Security Threats to the United States and its Interests Abroad* (February 22, 1996).

Hearing before the Senate Armed Services Committee, *Current and Projected National Security Threats to the United States*, (February 28, 2006), Statement of Michael D. Maples.

Hearing before the Senate Foreign Relations Committee, (March 19, 2002), Testimony of Dr. Amy Sands.

Hearing before the Senate Health, Education, Labor, and Pension Committee, Subcommittee on Bioterrorism and Public Health Preparedness, on *Biological Threats*, (May 11, 2005), Testimony by Dr. Harvey V. Fineberg.

Hearing before the Senate Select Committee on Intelligence, on *Global Intelligence Challenges 2005: Meeting Long-Term Challenges with a Long-Term Strategy* (February 16, 2005), Testimony of Director of Central Intelligence Porter J. Goss.

Hearing before the U.S. Senate Permanent Subcommittee on Investigations (Minority Staff), on *Global Proliferation of Weapons of Mass Destruction, A Case Study on the Aum Shinrikyo*, 104th Congress, 1st Session, (October 31, 1995).

Hearing before the U.S.-Israeli Joint Parliamentary Committee, on *Iranian WMD and Support of Terrorism* (September 13, 2003), Testimony of Paula A. DeSutter.

Hoge, Warren, *British Officer Slain, 4 Hurt as Terror Suspects are Seized*, NEW YORK TIMES (January 15, 2003).

Huizenga, Thomas D., BIOLOGICAL WEAPONS: IMPLICATIONS FOR THE OPERATIONAL COMMANDER, Naval War College (1998).

Inspection of Department of Energy Activities Involving Biological Select Agents, U.S. DEPARTMENT OF ENERGY (February 2001).

Iraqi Authorities Announce that Abu Musab al-Zarqawi, Head of Al-Qaeda Branch in Iraq, was Killed in an Air Strike, INTELLIGENCE AND TERRORISM INFORMATION CENTER AT THE CENTER FOR SPECIAL STUDIES (June 8, 2006).

Jacquard, Roland, & Atmane Tazaghart, BENLADEN, LA DESTRUCTION PROGRAMMÉE DE L'OCCIDENT, Picollec (December 2004).

Karmon, Ely, *Hisballah and the War on Terror* (August 1, 2002).

Kelley, Marylia, & Jay Coghlan, *Mixing Bugs and Bombs*, BULLETIN OF THE ATOMIC SCIENTISTS, Vol. 59, No. 5 (September/October 2003).

Kellman, Barry, *Elements of a Middle East Weapons of Mass Destruction Free Zone*, prepared for the Group of Experts on Arms Control and Regional Security in the Middle East, (1995).

Kellman, Barry, *Establishing MEDACO (Middle East Disarmament and Arms Control Organization) – Conception and Supporting Activities*, prepared for the Group of Experts on Arms Control and Regional Security in the Middle East (1995).

Kennedy, Harold, *Military Officials Warn Al Qaeda to Attack with WMD*, NATIONAL DEFENSE (February 2005).

Keren, Michael, *Ben-Gurion and the Intellectuals*, Sdeh Boker: The Ben-Gurion Research Center Press (1988).

Khalid Sharaf al-Din, *Bin Ladin Men Reportedly Possess Biological Weapons*, AL-SHARQ AL-AWSAT (March 6, 1999).

Khripunov, Igor, & Derek Averre, *Russia's CBW Closet Poses Ongoing Threat*, JANE'S INTELLIGENCE REVIEW (May 1999).

Klemick, Michael T., CAN IRAQ BE DETERRED FROM USING WEAPONS OF MASS DESTRUCTION?, Naval Postgraduate School (1997).

Kumaraswamy, P. R., *Has Israel Kept Its BW Options Open?* JANE'S INTELLIGENCE REVIEW (March 1998).

Lavoy, Peter R., et al., (eds.), PLANNING THE UNTHINKABLE: HOW NEW POWERS WILL USE NUCLEAR, BIOLOGICAL, AND CHEMICAL WEAPONS, Ithaca: Cornell University Press (2000).

Lehrman, Thomas D., *Enhancing the Proliferation Security Initiative: The Case for a Decentralized Nonproliferation Architecture*, 45 VA. J. INT'L L. 223 (Fall 2004).

Leibstone, Marvin, & Ezio Bonsignore, *U.S. Military vs. Iraq: The "New Warfare,"* MILITARY TECHNOLOGY (March 1998).

Leitenberg, Milton, *Assessing the Biological Weapons and Bioterrorism Threat*, U.S. Army War College Strategic Studies Institute (December, 2005).

Leitenberg, Milton, *Biological Weapons and "Bioterrorism" in the First Years of the 21st Century*, paper prepared for conference on *"The Possible Use of Biological Weapons by Terrorists Groups: Scientific, Legal, and International Implications,"* ICGEB, Landau Network, Ministry of Foreign Affairs, Italy (April 16, 2002).

Leitenberg, Milton, THE PROBLEM OF BIOLOGICAL WEAPONS, Swedish National Defense College (2004).

Lewis, James H. III., HANDSHAKE WITH THE DRAGON: ENGAGING CHINA IN THE BIOLOGICAL WEAPONS CONVENTION, Naval Post Graduate School (1998).

Lugar, Richard G., *Symposium on Security and Liberty: Essay: Nunn-Lugar in the Second Term*, NOTRE DAME JOURNAL LAW, ETHICS & PUB. POLICY, Vol. 19 (2005).

Mangold, Tom, & Jeff Goldberg, PLAGUE WARS: A TRUE STORY OF BIOLOGICAL WARFARE, Macmillan Publishers Ltd. (1999).

Manier, Jeremy, & Jeff Long, *State Tackles Readiness for Biochemical Attack*, CHICAGO TRIBUNE (October 7, 2001).

Markon, Jerry, *Va. Terror Case Sent Back to Lower Court; Appeals Panel Cites Eavesdropping Program*, WASHINGTON POST (April 26, 2006).

Martinez, Ian, *Rhodesian Anthrax: The Use of Bacteriological & Chemical Agents During the Liberation War of 1965–80*, 13 IND. INT'L & COMP. L. REV. 447 (2003).

McWethy, John, *Bin Laden Set to Strike Again?*, ABC NEWS (June 16, 1999).

Miller, Judith, et al., GERMS: BIOLOGICAL WEAPONS AND AMERICA'S SECRET WAR, Simon & Schuster (2001).

Miller, Judith, *Lab Suggests Qaeda Planned to Build Arms, Officials Say*, NEW YORK TIMES (September 14, 2002).

Miller, Judith, *U.S. Has New Concerns About Anthrax Readiness*, NEW YORK TIMES (December 28, 2003).

Moodie, Michael, *Weapons of Mass Destruction and the Proliferation Dilemma*, 28 FLETCHER F. WORLD AFF. 43 (Winter 2004).

Murphy, Caryle, *Muslim Lecturer Fits Easily in Two Worlds*, WASHINGTON POST (August 8, 2003).

Nasir Bin Hamd Al-Fahd, A TREATISE ON THE LEGAL STATUS OF USING WEAPONS OF MASS DESTRUCTION AGAINST INFIDELS (May 2003).

Nevin v. United States, 696 F.2d 1229 (1983).

Olimpio, Guido, *Islamic Group Said Preparing Chemical Warfare on the West*, CORRIERE DELLA SERA (July 8, 1998).

Office of the White House Press Secretary, *Statement by the President* (November 25, 1969).

Pearson, Graham, *The Importance of On-Site Investigations*, BRIEFING PAPER NO. 1, Department of Peace Studies, University of Bradford, (July 1997).

Perspectives, A Canadian Security Intelligence Service Publication, Report # 2000/05 Biological Weapons Proliferation (June 9, 2000).

Post, George, *Biotechnology and Terrorism*, PROSPECT MAGAZINE (April 25, 2002).

Ray, Ellen, & William H. Schaap, BIOTERROR: MANUFACTURING WARS THE AMERICAN WAY, Ocean Press (2003).

Recognizing Iran as a Strategic Threat: An Intelligence Challenge for the United States, U.S. House of Representatives, Permanent Select Committee on Intelligence (August 23, 2006).

Reichart, John F., *Adversarial Use of Chemical and Biological Weapons*, JOINT FORCES QUARTERLY (Spring 1998).

Report on Status of Disarmament and Monitoring, Letter Dated 27 January 1999 from the Permanent Representatives of the Netherlands and Slovenia to the United Nations Addressed to the President of the Security Council, UNITED NATIONS SPECIAL COMMISSION, UN Doc. S/1999/94 (January 29, 1999).

Ressa, Maria, *Reports: Al Qaeda Operative Sought Anthrax, CNN* (October 10, 2003).

Rimmington, Anthony, *Fragmentation and Proliferation? The Fate of the Soviet Union's Offensive Biological Weapons Programme*, CONTEMPORARY SECURITY POLICY (April 1999).

Salama, Sammy, & Lydia Hansell, *Does Intent Equal Capability?: Al-Qaeda and Weapons of Mass Destruction*, NONPROLIFERATION REVIEW, Vol. 12, No.3 (November 2005).

Scheuer, Michael, IMPERIAL HUBRIS: WHY THE WEST IS LOSING THE WAR ON TERROR (2004).

Shane, Scott, *Buried Secrets of Biowarfare*, BALTIMORE SUN (August 1, 2004).

Shoham, Danny, *Chemical and Biological Weapons in Egypt*, THE NONPROLIFERATION REVIEW (Spring/Summer 1998).

Simon, Jeffrey D., *Terrorists and Biological Weapons*, DEFENSE ANALYSIS (December 1998).

Sketches of Anthrax Bomb Found in Pakistani Scientist's Office, REDIFF.COM (November 28, 2001).

Speech by Interpol Secretary General Ronald K. Noble, *Interpol Asian Bioterrorism Workshop*, Singapore (March 27, 2006).

Spyer, Jonathan, *The Al-Qa'ida Network and Weapons of Mass Destruction*, MIDDLE EAST REVIEW OF INTERNATIONAL AFFAIRS, Vol. 8, No. 3 (September 2004).

State Department Officials Speak at Release of 'Country Reports on Terrorism' for 2004, U.S. FED NEWS (April 27, 2005).

Steele, John, & Sandra Laville, *Six Arrested in Poison Terror Alert*, DAILY TELEGRAPH (January 8, 2003).

Sufaat, Yazid, THE OPEN SOURCE THREAT NETWORK DATABASE (January 26, 2004).

Swibel, Matthew, *Trading With the Enemy*, FORBES, Vol. 173, No. 7 (April 12, 2004).

Terrorism: Terror Organizations, BASICS PROJECT WEBSITE, *available at* http://www.basicsproject.org/terrorism/terror_organizations.htm.

Terrorist Attacks in Iraq, program transcript, NBC Nightly News (March 2, 2004).

Testimony of Gordon C. Oehler, *The Continuing Threat from Weapons of Mass Destruction* (March 27, 1996).

THE 9/11 COMMISSION REPORT, Final Report of the National Commission on Terrorist Attacks Upon the United States (2004).

The Darker Bioweapons Future, Unclassified CIA Report (November 3, 2003).

The Rapport presente a la Conference des Preliminaires de Paix par la Commission des Responsabilites des Auteurs de la Guerre et Sanctions, cited in, The Problem of Chemical and Biological Warfare, Volume I: The Rise of CB Weapons, STOCKHOLM INTERNATIONAL PEACE RESEARCH INSTITUTE (1971).

Tucker, Jonathan B. (ed.), TOXIC TERROR: ASSESSING TERRORIST USE OF CHEMICAL AND BIOLOGCIAL WEAPONS, MIT Press (2000).

Tucker, Jonathan B., *A Farewell to Germs: The U.S. Renunciation of Biological and Toxin Warfare*, 1969–1970, INTERNATIONAL SECURITY (Summer 2002).

Unclassified Report to Congress on the Acquisition of Technology Relating to Weapons of Mass Destruction and Advanced Conventional Munitions, (1 January – 30 June 2003).

U.S. Knew of Bioterror Tests in Iraq, BBC NEWS (August 20, 2002).

U.S. Monitors Kurdish Extremists, FOX NEWS (August 21, 2002).

Venter, Al J., *Elements Loyal to Bin Laden Acquire Biological Agents 'Through the Mail,'* JANE'S INTELLIGENCE REVIEW (August 1999).

Venter, Al J., *Invisible Threat: What Does Russia Have Up Its Biological Warfare Sleeve?*, JANE'S INTERNATIONAL DEFENCE REVIEW (September 1998).

Venter, Al J., *Missing in Iraq: The UN Charts Saddam's Lethal Inventory*, JANE'S INTERNATIONAL DEFENCE REVIEW (May 1999).

Venter, Al J., *UNSCOM (United Nations Special Commission) Odyssey: The Search for Saddam's Biological Arsenal*, JANE'S INTELLIGENCE REVIEW (March 1998).

Warrick, Joby, & John Mintz, *Lethal Legacy: Bioweapons for Sale: U.S. Declined South African Scientist's Offer on Man-Made Pathogens*, WASHINGTON POST (April 20, 2003).

Warrick, Joby, *An Al Qaeda 'Chemist' and the Quest for Ricin*, WASHINGTON POST (May 5, 2004).

Warrick, Joby, *Soviet Germ Factories Pose New Threat*, NEWSBYTES (August 20, 2005).

Weapons of Mass Destruction (WMD) – Biological Weapons – Iran, GLOBALSECURITY.ORG, *available at* http://www.globalsecurity.org/wmd/world/iran/bw .htm.

Weapons of Mass Destruction in the Middle East, CRS REPORT FOR CONGRESS (January 14, 2000).

Wheelis, Mark, *Biological Warfare at the 1346 Siege of Caffa*, CENTERS FOR DISEASE CONTROL AND PREVENTION (September 2002).

Whitfield, Fredricka, et al., *Operation Spear in Iraq; Trial of Former Klan Member; Hijacker Strikes Credit Card Processor; Fort Detrick to House Bioterrorism Response Facility*, Show, CNN Live (June 18, 2005).

Wolfowitz, Paul, *Paul Wolfowitz Announces a Presidential Directive to Strengthen Biodefenses*, FDCH Political Transcripts (April 28, 2004).

Zilinskas, Raymond A., BIOLOGICAL WARFARE: MODERN OFFENSE AND DEFENSE, Lynne Rienner Publishers (2000).

Chapter 4

A Secure Europe in a Better World, EUROPEAN SECURITY STRATEGY (December 12, 2003).

Africa: Creating Sustainable Health Systems: Round-Table Supplement, NEW STATESMAN (July 11, 2005).

Barnes, Scottie, & Frank Sietzen Jr., *GeoIntelligence: A Foundation for Security? Capitol Outlook*, GEOSPATIAL SOLUTIONS (November 1, 2003).

Bassiouni, M. Cherif, CRIMES AGAINST HUMANITY IN INTERNATIONAL CRIMINAL LAW, Springer (1992).

Bassiouni, M. Cherif, *Terrorism: The Persistent Dilemma of Legitimacy*, 37 CASE W. RES. J. INT'L L. 299 (2005).

Bicknell, William J. (M. D.), & Kenneth D. Bloem, *Smallpox and Bioterrorism: Why the Plan to Protect the Nation Is Stalled and What to Do*, CATO INSTITUTE BRIEFING PAPERS No. 85 (September 5, 2003).

Bobbitt, Philip, DEMOCRACY AND DETERRENCE: THE HISTORY AND FUTURE OF NUCLEAR STRATEGY, St. Martin's Press (1988).

Brewer, Timothy F., & S. Jody Heymann, *The Long Journey to Health Equity*, JOURNAL OF THE AMERICAN MEDICAL ASSOCIATION, Vol. 292, No. 2 (July 14, 2004).

Carr, Dana, *Improving the Health of the World's Poorest People*, HEALTH BULLETIN, No. 1 (February 2004).

Chyba, Christopher F., *Toward Biological Security*, FOREIGN AFFAIRS (May/June 2002).

Fenrick, W. J., *Crimes in Combat: The Relationship Between Crimes Against Humanity and War Crimes*, THE HAGUE (March 5, 2004).

Frulli, Micaela, *Are Crimes against Humanity More Serious than War Crimes?*, 12 *EJL* 2 (July 2001).

Gips, Michael A., *Shared Intelligence Makes Everyone Smarter; Information-Sharing Initiatives are Critical to Homeland Security Efforts*, SECURITY MANAGEMENT (January 1, 2004).

Godlee, Fiona, et al., *Can We Achieve Health Information for All by 2015?*, LANCET ONLINE (July 9, 2004).

Gorman, Siobhan, *Second-Class Security*, NATIONAL JOURNAL, Vol. 36, No. 18 (May 1, 2004).

Gwatkin, Davidson R., *Reducing Health Inequalities in Developing Countries*, OXFORD TEXTBOOK OF PUBLIC HEALTH (2002).

Gwatkin, Davidson R., *The Need for Equity-Oriented Health Sector Reforms*, INTERNATIONAL JOURNAL OF EPIDEMIOLOGY, Vol. 30 (2001).

Handl, Elisabeth, *Introductory Note to the German Act to Introduce the Code of Crimes Against International Law*, 42 *ILM* 995 (2003).

Hearing before the Bioterrorism and Public Health Preparedness Subcommittee, on *Preparing a National Biodefense*, STATES NEWS SERVICE (July 21, 2005), Statement of Senator Orrin G. Hatch.

Hearing before the House Homeland Security Committee, Subcommittee on Emergency Preparedness, Science, and Technology, on *Linking Bioterrorism Threats and Countermeasures Procurement* (July 12, 2005), Testimonies by Karen T. Morr and Steward Stimson.

Hearing before the House Homeland Security Committtee, Prevention of Nuclear and Biological Attack Subcommittee, on *National Biodefense Strategy* (July 28, 2005).

Hearing before the House Judiciary Committee, Subcommittee on Crime, Terrorism, and Homeland Security, on *Anti-Terrorism Intelligence Tools Improvement Act*, (May 18, 2004), Testimony by Daniel J. Bryant.

Hearing before the Senate Foreign Relations Committee, on *Threat Reduction of Chemical and Biological Weapons*, (March 19, 2002), Testimony of Michael Moodie.

Houweling, Tanja A. J., Anton E. Kunst, & Johan P. Mackenbach, *Measuring Health Inequality among Children in Developing Countries: Does the Choice of the Indicator of Economic Status Matter?*, INTERNATIONAL JOURNAL FOR EQUITY IN HEALTH (October 9, 2003).

International School for Holocaust Studies, *Crimes Against Humanity*, Shoah Resource Center: The International School for Holocaust Studies.

Kellman, Barry, *Biological Terrorism: Legal Measures for Preventing Catastrophe*, 24 HARVARD JOURNAL OF LAW & PUBLIC POLICY 2 (Spring 2001).

Kellman, Barry, NATIONAL LAWS AND MEASURES FOR COUNTER-TERRORISM AND REGULATION OF BIOLOGY, International Human Rights Law Institute (2003).

Mallat, Chibli, *The Original Sin: "Terrorism" or "Crime Against Humanity"?*, 248 CASE W. RES. J. INT'L L. 34, 245 (2003). 34 CASE W. RES. J. INT'L L. 245, 248

Mena, Jesus, *Homeland Security as Catalyst – New Technology for Intelligent Analysis*, INTELLIGENT ENTERPRISE (July 10, 2004).

Miano, Timothy J., *Understanding and Applying International Infectious Disease Law: UN Regulations During an H5N1 Avian Flu Epidemic*, JOURNAL OF INTERNATIONAL AND COMPARATIVE LAW (Spring 2006).

Nwabueze, Remigius N., *What Can Genomics and Health Biotechnology Do for Developing Countries?*, 15 ALBANY LAW JOURNAL OF SCIENCE & TECHNOLOGY (2005).

Pillar, Paul R., *Counterterrorism after Al Qaeda*, THE WASHINGTON QUARTERLY (Summer 2004).

Pimentel, David, & Marcia Pimentel, *Bioweapon Impacts on Public Health and the Environment*, 30 WM. & MARY ENVTL. L. & POL'Y REV. 625 (Spring 2006).

Princen, Sebastiaan, & Mark Rhinard, *Crashing and Creeping: Agenda-Setting Dynamics in the European Union*, JOURNAL OF EUROPEAN PUBLIC POLICY, Vol. 13, No. 7 (September 2006).

Proposal for a Regulation of the European Parliament and of the Council, Establishing a European Centre for Disease Prevention and Control, Commission of the European Communities 441 final/2, (September 16, 2003).

Rappert, Brian, *Biological Weapons, Genetics, and Social Analysis: Emerging Responses, Emerging Issues – II*, NEW GENETICS AND SOCIETY, Vol. 22, No. 3 (December 2003).

Rappert, Brian, *Biological Weapons, Genetics, and Social Analysis: Emerging Responses, Emerging Issues – I*, NEW GENETICS AND SOCIETY, Vol. 22, No. 2 (August 2003).

Rome Statute of the International Criminal Court, U.N. Doc. A/CONF.183/9 (July 17, 1998).

SMALLPOX BIOSECURITY: PREVENTING THE UNTHINKABLE, Conference, Geneva (October 21–22, 2003).

Statement on Science and Security in an Age of Terrorism, PRESIDENTS OF THE NATIONAL ACADEMIES (October 18, 2002).

Sundelius, Bengt, & Jesper Gronvall, *Strategic Dilemmas of Biosecurity in the European Union*, BIOSECURITY AND BIOTERRORISM: BIODEFENSE STRATEGY, PRACTICE, AND SCIENCE, Vol. 2, No. 1 (2004).

The Kampala Compact: The Global Bargain for Biosecurity and Bioscience, INTERNATIONAL COUNCIL FOR SCIENCE (October 1, 2005).

UN Secretary-General's Message to Parties to Biological Weapons Convention, United Nations Office at Geneva (Nov. 20, 2006), *available at* http://www.unog.ch/80256EDD006B9C2E/(httpNewsByYear_en)/246D92BF4061C961C12-5722C0037EA12?OpenDocument.

War Crimes and Crimes Against Humanity, Canada's War Crimes Program, ENF 18 (December 15, 2005).

Wilson, Rachel, *Empowering Communities to Reduce the Impact of Infectious Diseases*, POPULATION REFERENCE BUREAU (2004).

Yang, Lijun, *Some Critical Remarks on the Rome Statute of the International Criminal Court*, 2 CHINESE J. INT'L L. 599 (2003).

Yearbook of International Law Commission, *Draft Code of Crimes Against the Peace and Security of Mankind*, International Law Commission, Vol. I (1996).

Yoo, John, *Using Force*, 71 U. CHI. L. REV. 729 (Summer 2004).

Chapter 5

ACE: Modernization Information Systems, U.S. CUSTOMS AND BORDER PROTECTION, *available at* http://www.cbp.gov/xp/cgov/toolbox/about/modernization/.

Ackleson, Jason, *Border Security Technologies: Local and Regional Implications*, THE REVIEW OF POLICY RESEARCH Vol. 22, No. 2 (March 1, 2005).

Addressing the Threat of Biological Weapons, Leading Experts' Views, CENTER FOR ARMS CONTROL AND NON-PROLIFERATION (March 2004).

Aichimayr, Mary, *Mission Critical: Closing Security Gaps*, TRANSPORTATION & DISTRIBUTION Vol. 43, No. 5 (May 2002).

Anthony, Ian, Aline Dewaele, Rory Keane, & Anna Wetter, *Strengthening WMD-Related Border Security Management Assistance*, STOCKHOLM INTERNATIONAL PEACE RESEARCH INSTITUTE (September 2005).

Atlas, Robert M., & Judith Rippy, *Globalizing Biosecurity*, BIOSECURITY AND BIOTERRORISM: BIODEFENSE STRATEGY, PRACTICE, AND SCIENCE. Vol. 3, No. 1 (2005).

Avasthi, Amitabh, *Containing Terror*, TECHNOLOGY REVIEW, Vol. 106, No. 7 (September 2003).

Baker, Michael G., & David P. Fidler, *Global Public Health Surveillance Under New International Health Regulations*, EMERGING INFECTIOUS DISEASES, Vol. 12, No. 7 (July 1, 2006).

Basel Convention on the Control of Transboundary Movements of Hazardous Wastes and their Disposal (March 22, 1989; entered into force May 1992).

Bender, Bryan, *DARPA (Defense Advanced Research Projects Agency) Seeks Radical Bacteria Detectors*, JANE'S DEFENCE WEEKLY (August 26, 1998).

Berinato, Scott, *The Short Life, Public Execution, and (Secret) Resurrection of Total Information Awareness*, CSO MAGAZINE (August 1, 2004).

Bower, Jennifer L., *The Terrorist Threat and its Implications for Sensor Technologies, available at* http://www.nato-asi.org/sensors2005/papers/brower.pdf.

Calderwood, James, *More Reporting Could Slow Commerce*, TRANSPORTATION & DISTRIBUTION, Vol. 44, No. 4 (April 2003).

Cavanaugh, Bonnie Brewer, *Keeping Cargo Safe*, BEST'S REVIEW (December 1, 2005).

Choffnes, Eileen, *Bioweapons: New Labs, More Terror?*, BULLETIN OF THE ATOMIC SCIENTISTS (September/October 2002).

Chyba, Christopher F., *Toward Biological Security*, FOREIGN AFFAIRS (May/June 2002).

Commission Directive 2003/29/EC on the Approximation of the Laws of the Member States with Regard to the Transport of Dangerous Goods by Rail (April 7, 2003).

Containing Terror: Electronic Seals and Tracking Efforts Boost Cargo Security, TECHNOLOGY REVIEW (September 2003).

Convention on Civil Aviation, INTERNATIONAL CIVIL AVIATION ORGANIZATION (9th ed. 2006).

Convention on Facilitation of International Maritime Traffic (1965).

Council Directive 96/49/EC on the Approximation of the Laws of the Member States with Regard to the Transport of Dangerous Goods by Rail (July 23, 1996).

Council Regulation (EC) No 1334/2000 Setting Up a Community Regime for the Control of Exports of Dual-use Items and Technology (June 22, 2000).

Crime; Plague Trial Ends in Mixed Verdict; Other Developments, Facts on File, WORLD NEWS DIGEST (December 31, 2003).

CSI in Brief, U.S. CUSTOMS & BORDER PROTECTION (February 15, 2006).

CSI: Container Security Initiative, U.S. CUSTOMS AND BORDER PROTECTION, *available at* http://www.cbp.gov/xp/cgov/border_security/international_activities/csi/.

C-TPAT: Customs-Trade Partnership Against Terrorism, U.S. CUSTOMS AND BORDER PROTECTION, *available at* http://www.cbp.gov/xp/cgov/import/commercial_enforcement/ctpat/.

Culture Collection Organization Statements on Biological Warfare, WORLD FEDERATION FOR CULTURE COLLECTIONS (April 24, 2002).

Data Mining: An Overview, CONGRESSIONAL RESEARCH SERVICE, THE LIBRARY OF CONGRESS (December 16, 2004).

Data Mining: Federal Efforts Cover a Wide Range of Uses, United States General Accounting Office (May 2004).

Day, Graham, & Christopher Freeman, *Operationalizing the Responsibility to Protect – the Policekeeping Approach; Global Insights*, GLOBAL GOVERNANCE, Vol. 11, No. 2 (April 1, 2005).

Deflem, Mathieu, *Global Rule of Law or Global Rule of Law Enforcement? International Police Cooperation and Counterterrorism*, 603 ANNALS 240 (January 2006).

Department of Health and Human Services, *Summary Report on Select Agent Security at Universities* (March 2004).

DeRosa, Mary, DATA MINING AND DATA ANALYSIS FOR COUNTERTERRORISM, CSIS Report (2004).

Dewaal, Caroline Smith, *Rising Imports, Bioterrorism, and the Food Supply*, 59 FOOD DRUG L.J. 433 (2004).

Dille, Donald L., Assistant Inspector General for Grants and Internal Activities, *Summary Report on Select Agent Security at Universities*, Department of Health and Human Services, Office of Inspector General (March 2004).

Directive 2000/54/EC of the European Parliament and of the Council on the Protection of Workers from Risks Related to Exposure to Biological Agents at Work (September 18, 2000).

Durstenfeld, Bob et al., *Cargo Container Security*, OCCUPATIONAL HEALTH & SAFETY, Vol. 72, No. 8 (August 2003).

European Agreement concerning the International Carriage of Dangerous Goods by Road, UNITED NATIONS ECONOMIC COMMISSION FOR EUROPE (4th ed. 2007).

Field, Kelly, *Biosafety Committees Come Under Scrutiny*, THE CHRONICLE OF HIGHER EDUCATION (April 29, 2005).

Flynn, Stephen, *How Vulnerable is the Cargo Shipping System to Attack*, TECHNOLOGY REVIEW (June 2004).

Fulda, Joseph F., *Data Mining and Privacy*, 11 ALB. L.J. SCI. & TECH.105 (2000).

Gaudioso, Jennifer, *A Survey of Asian Life Scientists: The State of Biosciences, Laboratory Biosecurity, and Biosafety in Asia*, BIOLOGICAL WEAPONS NONPROLIFERATION DEPARTMENT, SANDIA NATIONAL LABORATORIES, Report SAND2006–0842 (February 2006).

Gaudioso, Jennifer, & R. M. Salerno, *A Conceptual Framework for Biosecurity Levels*, Paper presented at *BTR 2004: Unified Science and Technology for Reducing Biological Threats and Countering Terrorism*, Proceedings, (March 18–19, 2004).

Gilman, Johnny, *Carnivore: The Uneasy Relationship Between the Fourth Amendment and Electronic Surveillance of Internet Communications*, 9 COMMLAW CONSPECTUS 111 (2001).

Gilman, Timothy K., *Search, Sentence, and (Don't) Sell: Combating the Threat of Biological Weapons Through Inspections, Criminalization, and Restrictions on Equipment*, 12 J. TRANSNAT'L L. & POL'Y 217 (Spring 2003).

Gluodenis, Thomas, & Scott Harrison, *Homeland Security and Bioterrorism Applications: Detection of Bioweapon Pathogens by Micro-fluidic Based Electrophoretic DNA Analysis; Lab Management*, MEDICAL LABORATORY OBSERVER (February 1, 2004).

Gooley, Toby B., *Customs Casts a Wider Security Net*, LOGISTICS MANAGEMENT, (August 2003).

Gostin, Lawrence O., *Dunwody Distinguished Lecture in Law, When Terrorism Threatens Health: How Far are Limitations on Personal and Economic Liberties Justified?*, 55 FLA. L. REV. 1105 (December 2003).

Guidelines for the Establishment and Operation of Collections of Cultures of Microorganisms, WORLD DATA CENTRE FOR MICROORGANISMS (WDCM), 2nd edition (1999).

Gulisano, Vin, *You Can't Outsource Responsibility: A 3PL's View on Security*, PURCHASING, Vol. 132, No. 5 (March 20, 2003).

Hammond, Edward, *Averting Bioterrorism Begins with U.S. Reforms*, THE SUNSHINE PROJECT (2001).

Health Ministers Take Action to Improve Health Security Globally, Ministerial Statements, Ottawa (November 1, 2001).

Hearing before the Committee on Senate Governmental Affairs, *Smuggling of Weapons of Mass Destruction* (June 23, 2004), Testimony of Michael Moodie.

Hearing before the House Committee on International Relations, on *U.S. Efforts To Stop the Spread of Weapons of Mass Destruction*, 108TH CONGRESS (2003), Testimony of John R. Bolton.

Hearing before the House Government Reform Committee, National Security, Emerging Threats, and International Relations Subcommittee, on *Combating Weapons of Mass Destruction* (June 14, 2005), Testimony of Dr. James H. Davis.

Hearing before the House Government Reform Committee, National Security, Emerging Threats, and International Relations Subcommittee, *Control of Surplus Chemical and Biological Lab Equipment* (October 7, 2003), Testimony of Shelton Young.

Hearing before the House Homeland Security Committee, Prevention of Nuclear and Biological Attack Subcommittee, on *Biosecurity and the Intelligence Community* (November 3, 2005), Testimony of David Franz.

Hearing before the House Homeland Security Committee, Prevention of Nuclear and Biological Attack Subcommittee (July 13, 2005), Testimony of Michael V. Callahan.

Hearing before the House Select Homeland Security Committee, on *National Biodefense Strategy* (June 3, 2004), Testimony of Anna Johnson-Winegar.

Hearing before the National Security, Emerging Threats, and International Relations Subcommittee of the House Government Reform Committee (October 7, 2003), Testimony of Shelton Young.

Hearing before the Senate Appropriations Committee, Homeland Security Subcommittee, on *Bioterrorism and BioShield* (April 28, 2005).

Hearing before the Senate Commerce, Science, and Transportation Committee, on *Border Security Measures* (June 17, 2004), Testimony of George Happ.

Hearing before the Senate Foreign Relations Committee, on *Global Partnership Against Weapons of Mass Destruction* (June 15, 2004), Testimony of John R. Bolton.

Hearing before the Senate Governmental Affairs Committee, Financial Management, the Budget, and International Security Subcommittee, on *Smuggling of Weapons of Mass Destruction* (June 23, 2004), Testimonies of Baker Spring and Michael Moodie.

Hearing before the Senate Judiciary Committee, on *Bioterrorism Detection and Response* (May 11, 2004), Testimony of David Relman.

Hearing before the Senate Judiciary Committee, on *Material Aid for Terrorists* (May 5, 2004), Testimony of Daniel Bryant.

Henderson, Diedtra, *New Rules Dictate Lab Safety, Fort Collins Research Facility Among Those Handling Infectious Agents*, Denver Post (November 27, 2003).

Hewish, Mark, *On Alert Against the Bio Agents: Tactical Biological-Agent Detection Approaches Reality*, Jane's International Defence Review (November 1998).

Hoyt, Kendall, & Brooks, Stephen G., *A Double-Edged Sword; Globalization and Biosecurity*, The Center for Strategic and International Studies and the Massachusetts Institute of Technology (Winter 2004).

Hu, Albert G. Z., Gary H. Jefferson, & Qian Jinchang, *R&D and Technology Transfer: Firm-Level Evidence from Chinese Industry*, Review of Economics & Statistics (November 2005).

International Biosecurity Symposium: Securing High Consequence Pathogens and Toxins, Sandia National Laboratories (June 2004).

International Health Regulations, 48th World Health Assembly (May 23, 2005).

International Ship and Port Facility Security Code, SOLAS/CONF.5/34 (December 12, 2002).

Interstate Shipment of Etiologic Agents, 42 CFR PART 72 APPENDIX A, 61 FR 55190, 55199 (October 24, 1996).

Johnston, Van R., & Amala Nath, *Introduction: Terrorism and Transportation Security*, The Review of Policy Research, Vol. 21, No. 3 (May 1, 2004).

Karas, Stan, *Privacy, Identity, Databases*, 52 Am. U.L. Rev. 393 (December 2002).

Kellman, Barry, *Barricading the Nuclear Window: A Legal Regime to Curtail Nuclear Smuggling*, 1996 U. Ill. L. Rev. 667 (co-authored, 1996).

Kellman, Barry, *Biological Terrorism: Legal Measures for Preventing Catastrophe*, 24 Harvard J. Law & Public Pol'y 2 (Spring 2001).

Kellman, Barry, *Bridling the International Trade of Catastrophic Weaponry*, 43 American University Law Review 3 (Spring 1994).

Laboratory Biosafety Manual, World Health Organization, 3rd ed., Ch. 15 (2004).

Laboratory Security and Emergency Response Guidance for Laboratories Working with Select Agents, Centers for Disease Control and Prevention, Morbidity and Mortality Weekly Report, Vol. 51 (2002).

Lane, Michael H., Customs Modernization and the International Trade Superhighway, Quorum Books (1998).

Lee, Jaemin, *Juggling Counter-Terrorism and Trade, the APEC Way: APEC's Leadership in Devising Counter-Terrorism Measures in Compliance with International Trade Norms*, 12 U.C. Davis J. Int'l L. & Pol'y 257 (Spring 2006).

Lee, W. Dean, *Risk Assessments and Future Challenges*, FBI Law Enforcement Bulletin, Vol. 74, No. 7 (July 1, 2005).

Li, Yougen, Yen Thi Hong Cu, & Dan Luo, *Multiplexed Detection of Pathogen DNA with DNA-based Fluorescence Nanobarcodes*, Nature Biotechnology, Vol. 23, No. 7 (July 2005).

Lok, Corie, *Cargo Security*, Technology Review (June 2004).

Mackenzie, Debora, *How the U.S. Crackdown on Terrorism is Backfiring; Vital Collections are Being Destroyed and Scientists are Abandoning Research, Leaving the*

World more Vulnerable to Natural Disease Outbreaks and Deliberate Attacks, New Scientist (November 8, 2003).

Malinowski, Michael J., Biotechnology: Law, Business and Regulation Aspen Publishers (1999).

Mandate of the Commission, Weapons of Mass Destruction Commission (January 28, 2004).

Mangels, John, *Plagued by Fear*, Plain Dealer (March 26, 2006).

Mangels, John, *Vials Reported Missing and Feds Swarm In*, Plain Dealer (March 27, 2006).

Maritime Transportation Security Act of 2002, 46 *U.S.C.S.* §§ 70101–117.

McCue, Colleen, Emily S. Stone, & Teresa P. Gooch, *Data Mining and Value-added Analysis*, FBI Law Enforcement Bulletin (November 1, 2003).

Melselson, Matthew, *"Law Enforcement" and the CWC*, CBW Conventions Bulletin, Vol. 58 (December 2002).

Meyerson, Laura A., & Jamie K. Reaser, *Biosecurity: Moving Toward a Comprehensive Approach*, Bioscience, Vol. 52, No. 7 (July 1, 2002).

Miller, Judith, *New Biolabs Stir a Debate Over Secrecy and Safety*, New York Times (February 10, 2004).

Neil Monro, *Securing Science*, The National Journal (September 6, 2003).

New Proposals to Reduce Threats by Weapons of Mass Destruction, Weapons of Mass Destruction Commission Press Release (June 1, 2006).

Office of Inspector General, *Audit Report – Adequacy of Controls to Prevent the Improper Transfer of Sensitive Technology*, USDA, Report No. 02601–1-Ch (September 2005).

Office of Inspector General, *Inspection Report – Coordination of Biological Select Agent Activities at Department of Energy Facilities*, Department of Energy, DOE/IG-0695 (July 2005).

Paarlberg, Robert L., *Knowledge as Power; Science, Military Dominance, and U.S. Security*, International Security (Summer 2004).

Phillips, James D., *Improving Border Management*, International Journal, Vol. 60, No. 2 (April 1, 2005).

Piller, Charles, *A Trying Time for Science; Bioterrorism-related Charges are Sending a Noted Researcher into Court for his Handling of Plague Vials. In U.S. Labs, the Case Elicits an Outcry*, Los Angeles Times (October 28, 2003).

Piller, Charles, *Biodefense Lab on Defensive; Calls for More Funds to Fight Bioterrorism are Met with Cries for Greater Scrutiny at the United States' Lead Research Facility*, Los Angeles Times (February 12, 2003).

Possession, Use, and Transfer of Select Agents and Toxins; Interim, Final Rule, 42 CFR Part 1003, Federal Register, Vol. 240, No. 67 (December 13, 2002).

Price, Willard, *Reducing the Risk of Terror Events at Seaports*, 21 Review of Policy Research (May 1, 2004).

Proliferation Security Initiative, U.S. Department of State, available at http://www.state.gov/t/np/c10390.htm.

Public Health Response to Biological and Chemical Weapons: WHO Guidance, Second Edition of Health Aspects of Chemical and Biological Weapons: Report of a WHO Group of Consultants, WORLD HEALTH ORGANIZATION (2004).

Purkitt, Helen E., *Biowarfare Lessons, Emerging Biosecurity Issues, and Ways to Monitor Dual-Use Biotechnology Trends in the Future,* INSTITUTE FOR NATIONAL SECURITY STUDIES, Occasional Paper 61 (September 2005).

Ramasastry, Anita, *Lost in Translation? Data Mining, National Security and the "Adverse Inference" Problem,* 22 SANTA CLARA COMPUTER & HIGH TECH L.J. 757 (2006).

Randerson, James, *Synthetic Biology: Lax Laws, Virus DNA and Potential for Terror: Loopholes Mean Anyone can Order Gene Sequences: Scientists Back Voluntary Regulation as First Step,* GUARDIAN (June 14, 2006).

Renke, Wayne N., *Who Controls the Past Controls the Future: Counterterrorism, Data Mining, and Privacy,* 43 ALBERTA L. REV. 779 (2006).

Rivera, Susan B., Jennifer Gaudioso, Natalie Barnett, & Reynolds M. Salerno, *Letters: A Bioterror Risk-Assessment Methodology,* SCIENTIST, Vol. 18 (July 5, 2004).

Roach, Ashley, *Container and Port Security: A Bilateral Perspective,* 18 INTERNATIONAL JOURNAL OF MARINE & COASTAL LAW 3 (September 2003).

Salerno, Reynolds M., *The U.S. Select Agent Rule and an International Opportunity to Achieve Defensible Biosecurity Guidelines,* SANDIA NATIONAL LABORATORIES (April 27, 2004).

Salerno, Reynolds M., & Daniel P. Estes, *Biosecurity: Protecting High Consequence Pathogens and Toxins Against Theft and Diversion,* SANDIA NATIONAL LABORATORIES (October 2003).

Salerno, Reynolds M., & Jennifer G. Koelm, *Biological Laboratory and Transportation Security and the Biological Weapons Convention,* Prepared for National Nuclear Security Administration, OFFICE OF NONPROLIFERATION POLICY (February 2002).

Salerno, Reynolds M., *A Possible Approach to Biosecurity for the BMBL,* SANDIA NATIONAL LABORATORIES (April 12, 2004).

Salerno, Reynolds M., *Biosecurity Methodology,* BIOSAFETY AND SECURITY INTERNATIONAL PROGRAM REVIEW (March 31, 2004).

Salerno, Reynolds M., *Defining Biosecurity in Theory and Practice,* SANDIA NATIONAL LABORATORIES (April 14, 2004).

Salerno, Reynolds M., *Improving the Security of High-Consequence Microbial Agents and Toxins,* SANDIA NATIONAL LABORATORIES (March 14, 2002).

Salerno, Reynolds M., *Secure Transfer of Select Agents,* Presented at BWC Experts Group Meeting (August 2003).

Salerno, Reynolds M., *U.S. Laboratory Biosecurity Policy Paper,* SANDIA NATIONAL LABORATORIES (February 2002).

Shipping and Importing Biological Materials: Guidelines and Regulations, MOUNT SINAI SCHOOL OF MEDICINE (2002).

Shulman, Mark R., *The Proliferation Security Initiative and the Evolution of the Law on the Use of Force*, 28 HOUSTON JOURNAL OF INTERNATIONAL LAW 3 (September 22, 2006).

Sprinkle, Robert H., *The Biosecurity Trust*, BIOSCIENCE, Vol. 53, No. 3 (March 2003).

Steele, Bill, *Researchers Make Synthetic DNA 'Barcodes' to Tag Pathogens, Providing an Inexpensive, Off-the-Shelf Monitoring System* eBIOLOGY NEWS (June 13, 2005).

Steinbock, Daniel J., *Data Matching, Data Mining, and Due Process*, 40 GA. L. REV. 1 (2005).

Sutton, Victoria, *Dual Purpose Bioterrorism Investigations in Law Enforcement and Public Health Protection: How to Make Them Work Consistent with the Rule of Law*, 6 HOUS. J. HEALTH L. & POL'Y 151 (Fall 2005).

Szyliowicz, Joseph S., *International Transportation Security*, REVIEW OF POLICY RESEARCH, Vol. 21, No. 3 (May 1, 2004).

Treadwell, Tracee A., et al., *Epidemiologic Clues to Bioterrorism*, PUBLIC HEALTH REPORTS, Vol. 118 (March–April 2003).

Tucker, Jonathan B., *Biosecurity: Limiting Terrorist Access to Deadly Pathogens*, UNITED STATES INSTITUTE OF PEACE (November 2003).

Tzannatos, E. S., *A Decision Support System for the Promotion of Security in Shipping*, DISASTER PREVENTION AND MANAGEMENT: AN INTERNATIONAL JOURNAL, Vol. 12, No. 3 (2003).

UN Model Regulations on the Transport of Dangerous Goods, Committee of Experts on the Transport of Dangerous Goods, UNITED NATIONS ECONOMIC AND SOCIAL COUNCIL, 14TH REV. ed., (2005).

Van de Voort, Martin, et al., *"Seacurity," Improving the Security of the Global Sea-Container Shipping System*, RAND CORPORATION (2004).

Watanabe, Myrna E., *Bioterror Error*, HARTFORD COURANT (September 5, 2004).

Watson, Samuel, Joe Suyama, Stefanie Fiddner Junker, & Michael Allswede, *Connecting the Dots: Characterizing Preparations for a Bio Attack*, Unpublished Paper – Final Document (February 21, 2006).

Weaver, Jefferson Hane, *Lessons in Multilateral Negotiations: Creating a Remote Sensing Regime*, 7 TEMP. INT'L & COMP. L.J. 29 (Spring 1993).

White House, *G-8 Action Plan on Proliferation*, Federal Document Clearing House, Inc. (June 9, 2004).

WHO Laboratory Biosafety Manual, INTERIM GUIDELINES 2nd ed. (2003).

Winner, Andrew C., *The Proliferation Security Initiative: The New Face of Interdiction*, WASHINGTON QUARTERLY, Vol. 28, No. 2 (Spring 2005).

Wolfowitz, Paul, *Paul Wolfowitz Announces a Presidential Directive to Strengthen Biodefenses*, FDCH Political Transcripts (April 28, 2004).

Yagupsky, Pablo, & Ellen Jo Baron, *Laboratory Exposures to Brucellae and Implications for Bioterrorism; Perspective*, EMERGING INFECTIOUS DISEASES, Vol. 11, No. 8 (August 1, 2005).

Zanders, Jeal Pascal, *A Verification and Transparency Concept for Technology Transfers under the BWC*, The Weapons of Mass Destruction Commission (December 17, 2004).

Chapter 6

2003 Biotech's 2nd Best Year and 2004 Looks Better, BIOTECH FINANCIAL REPORTS (February 2004).

A Survey of the Use of Biotechnology in U.S. Industry, U.S. DEPARTMENT OF COMMERCE (November 2003).

Abott, Frederick M., *The WTO Medicines Decision: World Pharmaceutical Trade and the Protection of Public Health*, 99 A.J.I.L. 317 (2005).

Achievements in Public Health, 1900–1999 Impact of Vaccines Universally Recommended for Children – United States, 1990–1998, CENTERS FOR DISEASE CONTROL AND PREVENTION, MORBIDITY AND MORTALITY WEEKLY REPORT, Vol. 48, No. 12 (April 2, 1999).

Ad Hoc Group of the States Parties to the Convention on the Prohibition of the Development, Production, and Stockpiling of Bacteriological (Biological) and Toxin Weapons and on Their Destruction, *Fulfilling the Objectives of the Biological and Toxin Weapons Convention: Resolving the Issue of Trade and Exchange of Technology*, BWC/AD HOC GROUP/WP.424 (July 20, 2000).

Aggarwal, Raj, *Technology and Globalization as Mutual Reinforcers in Business: Reorienting Strategic Thinking for the New Millennium*; MANAGEMENT INTERNATIONAL REVIEW (July 15, 1999).

Aginam, Obijiofor, *Between Life and Profit: Global Governance and the Trilogy of Human Rights, Public Health and Pharmaceutical Patents*, 31 N.C.J. INT'L L. & COM. REG. 901 (Summer 2006).

Agreement on Trade-Related Aspects of Intellectual Property Rights, Marrakesh Agreement Establishing the World Trade Organization (April 15, 1994).

AIDS Drugs; U.S. Offers to Help South Africa Obtain Affordable Medicines, CHICAGO TRIBUNE (August 2, 1999).

Aldhous, Peter, & Michael Reilly, *Friend or Foe?; Efforts to Combat Killer Pathogens with New Vaccines and Drugs Could Be Inadvertently Writing a Handbook for Biowarfare*, NEW SCIENTIST (October 14, 2006).

Aldhous, Peter, *The Accidental Terrorists; Too Many Biologists Remain Blind to the Danger that They Could Be Aiding the Spread of Terrorism*, NEW SCIENTIST (June 10, 2006).

An Introduction to Biological Weapons, their Prohibition, and the Relationship to Biosafety, THE SUNSHINE PROJECT, Backgrounder Series, No. 10 (April 2002).

Andrawiss, Mariam, *Plant-Made Pharmaceuticals; Biopharming Might Be as Easy as Literally Growing Drugs on Trees, if It Wasn't for the International Regulations, Technical Challenges, and Safety Issues*, DRUG DISCOVERY AND DEVELOPMENT (March 1, 2006).

Anex, Robert, *Growing the Future*, BioScience, Vol. 55, No. 10 (October 1, 2005).

Anthrax Vaccine Immunization Program (AVIP), Information Statement and Acknowledgment, U.S. Department of Defense, available at http://www .seafarers.org/members/Anthraxack.pdf.

Anthrax: Replacement for VaxGen Vaccine Likely 'Years Away, American Health Line (December 22, 2006).

Arnold, Wayne, *Luring Top Stem Cell Researchers with Financing and Freedom*, New York Times (August 17, 2006).

Atlas, Ronald M., *National Security and the Biological Research Community; Policy Forum: Public Health*, Science (October 25, 2002).

Attaran, Amir, *How Do Patents and Economic Policies Affect Access to Essential Medicines in Developing Countries?; Poverty, not Patent Policies, More Often Inhibits Access to Essential Medicines in the Developing World*, Health Affairs, (May–June 2004).

Barker, Brent, *Technology and the Quest for Sustainability*, EPRI Journal (June 22, 2000).

Behreandt, Dennis, *Future Tech: 8 Amazing Scientific and Technological Advances on the Horizon – Made by Mixing Hefty Parts of Human Ingenuity with the Freedom to Employ It*, New American, Vol. 22, No. 8 (April 17, 2006).

Bell, James John, *Exploring the "Singularity,"* Futurist, Vol. 37, No. 3 (May 1, 2003).

Bhutkar, Arjun, *Synthetic Biology: Navigating the Challenges Ahead*, 8 J. Biolaw & Bus. 2 (2005).

Biotechnology for Sustainable Growth and Development, Meeting of the OECD Committee for Scientific and Technological Policy at Ministerial Level (January 29–30, 2004).

Biotechnology Industry Code of Conduct, AusBiotech: Australia's Biotechnology Organisation (March 2005).

Biotechnology Industry Statement of Ethical Principles, BIOTECanada: Canada's Voice for Biotechnology, available online at http://www.biotech.ca/ content.php?doc=19.

Biotechnology Research in an Age of Terrorism, Confronting the "Dual Use" Dilemma, National Research Council of the National Academies (2003).

Black, Julia, *Regulation as Facilitation: Negotiating the Genetic Revolution*, 61 Mod. L. Rev. 621 (1998).

Boerma, J. Ties; Holt, Elizabeth; & Black, Robert, *Measurement of Biomarkers in Surveys in Developing Countries: Opportunities and Problems*, Population and Development Review, Vol. 27, No. 2 (June 1, 2001).

Boyle, Francis A., Biowarfare and Terrorism, Clarity Press, Inc., (2005).

Braach-Maksvytis, Vijoleta, & Biesenbach, Reinie, *The Global Research Alliance: A Knowledge Pool for Global Good*, UN Chronicle, Vol. 42, No. 1 (March 1, 2005).

Brainard, Jeffrey, *Scientists Question Buildup in Biodefense Spending*, Chronicle of Higher Education (March 25, 2005).

Brickner, Philip W. et al., *The Application of Ultraviolet Germicidal Irradiation to Control Transmission of Airborne Disease: Bioterrorism Countermeasure; Practice Articles*, PUBLIC HEALTH REPORTS, Vol. 118, No. 2 (March 1, 2003).

Brignati, Michael J., *Access to the Safe Harbor: Bioterrorism, Influenza, and the Supreme Court's Interpretation of the Research Exemption from Patent Infringement*, 13 J. INTELL. PROP. L. 375 (Spring 2006).

Broad, William J., & Judith Miller, *A Nation Challenged: The Investigation; U.S. Recently Produced Anthrax in a Highly Lethal Powder Form*, NEW YORK TIMES (December 13, 2001).

Bruntland, Gro Harlem, *Global Health and International Security; Global Insights*, GLOBAL GOVERNANCE (October 1, 2003).

Buckland, Barry C., *The Process Development Challenge for a New Vaccine*, NATURE MEDICINE, Vol. 11 (April 2005).

Campaign for the Peaceful Development of the Biological Sciences, COUNCIL FOR RESPONSIBLE GENETICS, (June 30, 2004).

Cardiac Deaths After a Mass Smallpox Vaccination Campaign – New York City, 1947, CENTERS FOR DISEASE CONTROL AND PREVENTION, MORBIDITY AND MORTALITY WEEKLY REPORT, Vol. 52 (October 3, 2003).

Carr, Kathleen, et al., *Implementation of Biosurety Systems in a Department of Defense Medical Research Laboratory*, BIOSECURITY AND BIOTERRORISM: BIODEFENSE STRATEGY, PRACTICE, AND SCIENCE, Vol. 2, No. 1 (2004).

Cello, Jeronimo, et al., *Chemical Synthesis of Poliovirus cDNA: Generation of Infectious Virus in the Absence of Natural Template*, SCIENCEXPRESS (July 11, 2002).

Chiarello, Kaylynn, *New Vaccine Technologies Carry and Deliver*, PHARMACEUTICAL TECHNOLOGY, Vol. 29, No. 5 (May 1, 2005).

Clarke, Victoria, *Defense Department Regular Briefing*, FEDERAL NEWS SERVICE (September 4, 2001).

Code of Conduct for Life Science Professionals, UNIVERSITY OF SOUTHERN CALIFORNIA GLOBAL BUSINESS INITIATIVE, http://www.globalbiobusiness.org/bioethics.html.

Code of Ethics, AMERICAN SOCIETY FOR MICROBIOLOGY (2005).

Collard-Wexler, Simon, *Comparative Review of Biosecurity-Related Legislation*, CENTER FOR NONPROLIFERATION STUDIES, MONTEREY INSTITUTE OF INTERNATIONAL STUDIES (September 2002).

Commission Directive 2003/63/EC on the Community Code Relating to Medicinal Products for Human Use (June 25, 2003).

Committee on Advances in Technology and the Prevention of Their Application to Next Generation Biowarfare Threats, GLOBALIZATION, BIOSECURITY, AND THE FUTURE OF THE LIFE SCIENCE, The National Academies Press (2006).

Conference of the Parties to the Convention on Biological Diversity Serving as the Meeting of the Parties to the Cartagena Protocol on Biosafety, UNEP/CBD/BS/COP-MOP/1/8. 23–27 (February 2004).

Conference on Ethical Implications of Scientific Research on Bioweapons and Prevention of Bioterrorism, EUROPEAN COMMISSION, DG RESEARCH DIRECTORATE

E: BIOTECHNOLOGY, AGRICULTURE AND FOOD RESEARCH (February 3–4, 2004).

Cookson, Clive, *Eastern Rebirth of the Life Sciences* RESEARCH AND DEVELOPMENT IN ASIA, FINANCIAL TIMES (June 10, 2005).

Cox, George, et al., *Driving Innovation Forward: A Round-Table Discussion*, NEW STATESMAN (January 16, 2006).

Declaration on Science and the Use of Scientific Knowledge, UNESCO, WORLD CONFERENCE ON SCIENCE (July 1, 1999).

Declaration on the TRIPS Agreement and Public Health, WORLD TRADE ORGANIZATION, Ministerial Conference, 4th Session, WT/MIN(01)/DEC/W/2 (November 14, 2001).

Definitions and Regulations Involved in the Classified-Sensitive Information-Unclassified Debate, ASSOCIATION OF AMERICAN UNIVERSITIES (March 3, 2003).

Derek, Ellison, *Accelerating European Biomanufacturing*, PHARMACEUTICAL TECHNOLOGY EUROPE, Vol. 16, No. 9 (September 1, 2004).

Donohue, Laura K., *Censoring Science Won't Make Us any Safer*, WASHINGTON POST (June 26, 2005).

Draft Recommendations for a Code of Conduct for Biodefense Programs, FEDERATION OF AMERICAN SCIENTISTS (November 2002).

Dreyfuss, Barbara, *Patents Pending*, NATIONAL LEGISLATIVE ASSOCIATION ON PRESCRIPTION DRUG PRICES (February 23, 2005).

Dyer, Geoff, et al., *U.S. Climbs Down Over Brazil's Patent Law*, FINANCIAL TIMES (London) (June 26, 2001).

Elhefnawy, Nader, *Societal Complexity and Diminishing Returns in Security*, INTERNATIONAL SECURITY (Summer 2004).

Ensirenk, Martin, *Entering the Twilight Zone of What Material to Censor*, SCIENCE (November 22, 2002).

Ethical Aspects of Clinical Research in Developing Countries, Opinion of the European Group on Ethics in Science and New Technologies to the European Commission, No. 17 (February 4, 2003).

EU Draft Proposal for a Compromise Solution, Consumer Project on Technology (2003).

European Commission – Science and Society, *Globalization and New Epidemics: Ethics, Security, and Policy Making*, Bioethical Implications of Globalization Processes (May 2006).

Evans, G., *Vaccine Injury Compensation Programs Worldwide*, HRSA Advisory Commission on Childhood Vaccines Meeting and Conference Call Minutes (March 9, 2006).

Falcon, Walter P., & Rosamond L. Naylor, *Rethinking Food Security for the Twenty-first Century*, AMERICAN JOURNAL OF AGRICULTURAL ECONOMICS, Vol. 87, No. 5 (December 1, 2005).

Farmer, Paul, & Nicole Gastineau Campos, *New Malaise: Bioethics and Human Rights in the Global Era*, JOURNAL OF LAW, MEDICINE & ETHICS (Summer 2004).

Fauci, Anthony S., *Bioterrorism: Defining a Research Agenda*, 57 FOOD DRUG L.J. 413 (2002).

Ferrone, Jason D., *Compulsory Licensing During Public Health Crises: Bioterrorism's Mark on Global Pharmaceutical Patent Protection*, 26 SUFFOLK TRANSNAT'L L. REV. 385 (Summer 2003).

Field, Robert I., et al., *Toward a Policy Agenda on Medical Research Funding: Results of a Symposium; Greater Cooperation among Government, Industry, and Foundations is Vital*, HEALTH AFFAIRS (May–June 2003).

Fonda, Darren, *Inside the Spore Wars*, TIME (January 9, 2006).

Fox, John, *Legislators Propose Measure to Speed Up Biodefense Program*, GLOBAL SECURITY NEWSWIRE (February 22, 2007).

Frazier, Marvin E. et al., *Realizing the Potential of the Genome Revolution: The Genomes to Life Program*, SCIENCE (April 11, 2003).

Fresco, Louise O., *A New Social Contract on Biotechnology*, FAO (2003).

Fukuda-Parr, Sakiko, *Millennium Development Goals: Why They Matter*, GLOBAL GOVERNANCE, (October 1, 2004).

Future Visions; How Will Genetics Change Our Lives? TIME MAGAZINE (February 17, 2003).

Gaudioso, Jennifer, & Reynolds M. Salerno, *BioSecurity and Research: Minimizing Adverse Impacts*, SCIENCE, Vol. 304, No. 5671 (April 30, 2004).

Geissler, Erhard, & John P. Woodall (eds.), *Control of Dual-Threat Agents: The Vaccines for Peace Programme*, STOCKHOLM INTERNATIONAL PEACE RESEARCH INSTITUTE (1994).

Genomics and the Global Health Divide, WORLD HEALTH ORGANIZATION, available at http://who.int/genomics/healthdivide/en/print.html.

Ghanaian Chronicle, *The Day of Scientific Renaissance of Africa*, AFRICA NEWS (June 30, 2005).

Glenn, Jerome C., & Theodore Gordon, *Update on the State of the Future: Environmental Sustainability, Global Partnerships Against Terror, Technology, and Drug Availability Figure in Humanity's Future*, FUTURIST (January 1, 2006).

Goldman, Michael A., *Promises and Perils of Technology's Future; Living with the Genie Essays on Technology and the Quest for Human Mastery*, SCIENCE (January 30, 2004).

Gomez-Pompa, Arturo, *The Role of Biodiversity Scientists in a Troubled World; Plenary*, BIOSCIENCE (March 1, 2004).

Gonzalez, Andres Guandamuz, *Open Science: Open Source Licenses in Scientific Research*, 7 N. C. J. L. & TECH. 321 (Spring 2006).

Gorman, Brian J., *Balancing National Security and Open Science: A Proposal for Due Process Vetting*, 7 YALE JOURNAL OF LAW & TECHNOLOGY 59 (2004–2005).

Gorman, Brian J., *Biosecurity and Secrecy Policy: Problems, Theory, and a Call for Executive Action*, I/S: A JOURNAL OF LAW AND POLICY, Vol. 2.1 (2006).

Gould, Ronald M., & Simon Stern, *Catastrophic Threats and the Fourth Amendment*, 77 S. CAL. L. REV. 777 (May 2004).

Greenberger, Michael, *Choking BioShield: The Department of Homeland Security's Stranglehold on Biodefense Vaccine Development*, MICROBE MAGAZINE (June 2006).

Grobowski, Henry, *Encouraging the Development of New Vaccines*, 24 HEALTH AFFAIRS 697 (2005).

Guidelines to Prevent Malevolent Use of Biomedical Research, AMERICAN MEDICAL ASSOCIATION (June 2004).

Hanney, Stephen R., et al., *The Utilisation of Health Research in Policy-Making: Concepts, Examples, and Methods Assessment*, HEALTH RESEARCH POLICY AND SYSTEMS, Vol. 1, No. 2 (January 13, 2003).

Hawkins, Andrew J., *National Biosecurity Advisory Board Members Stress Balance, International Implications*, RESEARCH POLICY ALERT (July 1, 2005).

Healthy People 2010, Immunizations and Infectious Disease, U.S. DEPARTMENT OF HEALTH AND HUMAN SERVICES, available at http://www.healthypeople.gov/Document/HTML/Volume1/14Immunization.htm.

Hearing before the Bioterrorism and Public Health Preparedness Subcommittee, Committee on Health, Education, Labor, and Pensions, United States Senate, on *Biodefense: Building a Medical Countermeasure Capability* (February 8, 2005), Testimony of Gerald L. Epstein.

Hearing before the House Armed Services Committee, Military Procurement and Military Research and Development Subcommittees (October 20, 1999), Testimony of Hans Mark.

Hearing before the House Armed Services Committee, Terrorism, Unconventional Threats and Capabilities Subcommittee, on *Counterterrorism Technology Sharing* (July 21, 2005), Testimony of Tony Tether.

Hearing before the House Government Reform Committee, on *Bioshield Oversight* (July 14, 2005), Testimonies of John Vitko Jr. and Stewart Simonson.

Hearing before the House Homeland Security Committee, Emergency Preparedness, Science, and Technology Subcommittee, on *Linking Bioterrorism Threats and Countermeasure Procurement* (July 12, 2005), Testimony of Dr. John Vitko.

Hearing before the House Homeland Security Committee, Prevention of Nuclear and Biological Attack Subcommittee, on *Engineering Biological Weapons* (July 13, 2005), Testimonies of Dr. Kenneth Alibek and Michael V. Callahan.

Hearing before the House Science Committee, Research Subcommittee, on *Plant Biotechnology Research in Africa* (June 12, 2003), Testimony of Dr. Rita Colwell.

Hearing before the House Select Homeland Security Committee, on *National Biodefense Strategy* (June 3, 2004), Testimonies of Anna Johnson-Winegar, Anthony S. Fauci, and Shelley Hearne.

Hearing before the Senate Armed Services Committee, Emerging Threats and Capabilities Subcommittee, on *Biological Terrorism: Department of Defense Research and Development* (April 10, 2002), Testimony of Dr. Dale Klein.

Hearing before the Senate Commerce, Science and Transportation Committee, Science, Technology and Space Subcommittee, on *Fighting Terrorism: Using*

America's Scientists and Entrepreneurs to Find Solutions (February 5, 2002), Testimony of Dr. Anna Johnson-Winegar.

Hearing before the Senate Commerce, Science and Transportation Committee, Disaster Prevention and Prediction Subcommittee, on *Research and Development to Protect America's Communities from Disaster* (June 8, 2005), Testimony of Dr. Hratch G. Semerjian.

Hearing before the Senate Committee on Health, Education, Labor, and Pensions, on *The National Immunization Program: Is It Prepared for the Public Health Challenges of the 21st Century?*, 107TH CONGRESS, 1ST SESSION (November 27, 2001), Statement of Dr. John E. Calfee.

Hearing before the Senate Health, Education, Labor, and Pensions Committee, on *Biodefense: Next Steps* (February 8, 2005), Testimony of Dr. George Painter.

Hearing before the Senate Health, Labor, Education, Labor, and Pensions Committee, on *Liability Protection for Makers of Bioshield Drugs* (October 6, 2004), Testimonies of Jeff Kushan, John G. Bartlett, and Joseph Lieberman.

Hearing before the Senate Judiciary Committee, on *Bioterrorism Detection and Response* (May 11, 2004), Testimony of Dr. Harvey Meislin.

Hearing of the House Armed Services Committee, on *Terrorism, Unconventional Threats and Capabilities Subcommittee, on Fiscal Year 2004 Science and Technology Programs* (March 27, 2003).

Hearing of the House Government Reform Committee, on *Project Bioshield Evaluation* (July 14, 2005).

Hearing of the National Security, Veterans Affairs and International Relations Subcommittee of the House Government Reform Committee, on *Biological Weapons Convention* (September 13, 2000).

Hearing of the Senate Appropriations Committee, Homeland Security Subcommittee, on *Bioterrorism and Bioshield* (April 28, 2005).

Heller, Nathan J., *Scientists Balance Research with Security Demands*, HARVARD CRIMSON (May 9, 2003).

Henderson, Diedtra, *New Rules Dictate Lab Safety Fort Collins Research Facility Among Those Handling Infectious Agents*, DENVER POST (November 27, 2003).

Hernandez, Nelson, *Ebola's Dogged Enemies; Team of Fort Detrick Scientists Labored for Years to Develop Vaccine*, WASHINGTON POST (October 2, 2005).

Ho, Cynthia M., *Inoculation Inventions: The Interplay of Infringement and Immunity in the Development of Biodefense Vaccines*, 8 J. HEALTH CARE L. & POL'Y 111 (2005).

Hoen, Ellen F. M., *The Responsibility of Research Universities to Promote Access to Essential Medicines*, 3 YALE J. HEALTH POL'Y L. & ETHICS 293(Summer 2003).

Homeland Security Act of 2002, PUBLIC LAW 107–296, Title VIII, Subtitle G, §§ 862–865, 116 Stat. 2238–2241 (November 25, 2002).

Human Development Report 2001: Making New Technologies Work for Human Development, UNITED NATIONS DEVELOPMENT PROGRAMME (2001).

IAP Statement on Biosecurity, THE INTERACADEMY PANEL ON INTERNATIONAL ISSUES, (November 7, 2005).

Inspection of the FBI's Security Risk Assessment Program for Individuals Requesting Access to Biological Agents and Toxins, U.S. Department of Justice (March 2005).

Integrity and Misconduct in Research, Report of the Commission on Research Integrity, U.S. Department of Health and Human Services, USGPO 19960746–425 (1995).

Integrity in Scientific Research: Creating an Environment that Promotes Responsible Conduct, INSTITUTE OF MEDICINE (2002).

Intentional Biology and Open-Source Biology, THE MOLECULAR SCIENCES INSTITUTE (December 10, 2000).

Is Bioshield Doing the Job? 24 BIOTECHNOLOGY L. REP. 56 (February 2005).

IUMS Code of Ethics Against Misuse of Scientific Knowledge, Research, and Resources, INTERNATIONAL UNION OF MICROBIAL SOCIETIES (April 28, 2006).

Jack, Andrew, *Cut-price HIV Drugs Drive May Spur Patents Clash*, FINANCIAL TIMES (London) (August 11, 2006).

Jackson, Ronald J., et al., *Expression of Mouse Interleukin-4 by a Recombinant Ectromelia Virus Suppresses Cytolytic Lymphocyte Responses and Overcomes Genetic Resistance to Mousepox*, JOURNAL OF VIROLOGY (February 2001).

Jacobi, Paula, *Pharmaceutical Tort Liability: A Justifiable Nemesis to Drug Innovation and Access?*, 38 J. MARSHALL L. REV. 987 (Spring 2005).

Javitt, Gail H., *Drugs and Vaccines for the Common Defense: Refining FDA Regulation to Promote the Availability of Products to Counter Biological Attacks*, 19 J. CONTEMP. HEALTH L. & POL'Y 37 (Winter 2002).

Jenkins, Michael; Scherr, Sara J.; & Inbar, Mira, *Markets for Biodiversity Services: Potential Roles and Challenges*, ENVIRONMENT (July 1, 2004).

Ji-Wei, Guo, & Xue-Sen Yang, *Ultramicro, Nonlethal, and Reversible: Looking Ahead to Military Biotechnology; Transformation*, MILITARY REVIEW, Vol. 85, No. 4 (July 1, 2005).

Johnson, Steve, *U.S. Dumps VaxGen: Brisbane Company Had Won $877.5 Million Contract to Develop Anthrax Vaccine*, MERCURY NEWS (December 19, 2006).

Juma, Calestous, *Biotechnology in a Globalizing World: The Co-Evolution of Technology and Social Institutions*, BIOSCIENCE (March 1, 2005).

Kahn, Laura H., *Biodefense Research: Can Secrecy and Safety Coexist?*, BIOSECURITY AND BIOTERRORISM: BIODEFENSE STRATEGY, PRACTICE, AND SCIENCE,Vol. 2, No. 2 (2004).

Kaiser, Jocelyn et al., *Bioterrorism: Bioshield is Slow to Build U.S. Defenses Against Bioweapons*, SCIENCE, Vol. 313, No. 28 (2006).

Kellman, Barry, *Chemical Weapons Convention Inspections of Private Facilities: Application of United States Environmental and Safety Laws* (DNA-TR-93–70) (1993).

Kellman, Barry, *Legal Implications Special Access Visits under START: Revoking Consent; Visits on Foreign Soil; Gaining Access to Department of Defense Contractor Facilities* (September 1, 1993).

Khan, Michael J., & Daya B. Reddy, *Science and Technology in South Africa: Regional Innovation Hub or Passive Consumer?*, DAEDALUS (January 1, 2001).

Knox, John H., *A New Approach to Compliance with International Environmental Law: The Submissions Procedure of the NAFTA Environmental Commission*, 28 Ecology Law Quarterly 1 (2001).

Koblenz, Gregory, *Countering Dual-use Facilities: Lessons from Iraq and Sudan*, JANE'S INTELLIGENCE REVIEW (March 1999).

Kurzweil, Ray, AN EXPONENTIALLY EXPANDING FUTURE FROM EXPONENTIALLY SHRINKING TECHNOLOGY, Council on Foreign Relations (December 2, 2005).

Kurzweil, Ray, THE SINGULARITY IS NEAR, Penguin Books (2005).

Kwik, Jeanna, *Preventing the Misuse of Biotechnology*, PANEL DISCUSSION OF THE CARNEGIE INTERNATIONAL NON-PROLIFERATION CONFERENCE (November 15, 2002).

Lacayo, Arnoldo, *Seeking a Balance: International Pharmaceutical Patent Protection, Public Health Crises, and the Emerging Threat of BioTerrorism*, 33 U. MIAMI INTER-AM. L. REV. 295 (Summer/Fall 2002).

Lam, Clarence, Crystal Franco, & Ari Schuler, *Billions for Biodefense: Federal Agency Biodefense Funding, FY2006-FY2007*, 4 BIOSECURITY & BIOTERRORISM 113 (2006).

Lavery, James V., *Commentary: Putting International Research Ethics Guidelines to Work for the Benefit of Developing Countries*, 4 YALE J. HEALTH POL'Y L. & ETHICS 319 (Summer 2004).

Lawler, Andrew, *The Unthinkable Becomes Real for a Horrified World; Research and Development to Combat Terrorism; Statistical Data Included*, SCIENCE (September 21, 2001).

Lederberg, Joshua, *The Freedoms and the Control of Science: Notes from the Ivory Tower*, 45 S. CAL. L. REV. 596 (1972).

LeRoy, Michael H., *Pox Americana? Vaccinating More Emergency Doctors for Smallpox: A Law and Economics Approach to Work Conditions*, 54 EMORY LAW JOURNAL (Winter 2005).

Liability Protections for Adult Vaccines, Reports of Board of Trustees, Report 10, AMERICAN MEDICAL ASSOCIATION, RESOLUTION 710-I04 (June 2005).

Lipman, Zada, *Gene Technology Regulation and the Precautionary Principle: How Australia Measures Up*, 8 J. INT'L WILDLIFE LAW & POL'Y 1 (January 1, 2005).

Lipton, Eric, *Bid to Stockpile Bioterror Drugs Stymied by Setbacks*, NEW YORK TIMES (September 18, 2006).

Lohan, Dagmar, *Assessing the Mechanisms for the Input of Scientific Information into the UNFCCC*, 17 COLO. J. INT'L ENVTL. L. & POL'Y 249 (Spring 2006).

Mair, J. S., & M. Mair, *Vaccine Liability in the Era of Bioterrorism*, BIOSECURITY AND BIOTERRORISM: BIODEFENSE STRATEGY, PRACTICE, AND SCIENCE, Vol. 1 (2003).

MAKING THE NATION SAFER: THE ROLE OF SCIENCE AND TECHNOLOGY IN COUNTERING TERRORISM, The National Academies Press (2002).

Marshall, Patricia, & Barbara Koenig, *Accounting for Culture in Globalized Bioethics*, 32 J.L. MED. & ETHICS 252 (Summer 2004).

Maskus, Keith E., *Using the International Trading System to Foster Technology Transfer for Economic Development*, MICH. ST. L. REV. 219 (Spring 2005).

Maurer, Stephen M., Keith V. Lucas, & Starr Terrell, *From Understanding to Action: Community-Based Options for Improving Safety and Security in Synthetic Biology*, UNIVERSITY OF CALIFORNIA AT BERKELEY (April 15, 2006).

McDonald, Barry P., *Government Regulation or other "Abridgements" of Scientific Research: The Proper Scope of Judicial Review Under the First Amendment*, 54 EMORY L.J. 979 (Spring 2005).

McMichael, Anthony J., et al., *Globalization and the Sustainability of Human Health: An Ecological Perspective*, BIOSCIENCE (March 1, 1999).

Mello, Michelle M., & Troyen A. Brennan, *Legal Concerns and the Influenza Vaccine Shortage*, JOURNAL OF THE AMERICAN MEDICAL ASSOCIATION, Vol. 294, No. 14 (2005).

Melson, Ashley R., *Bioterrorism, Biodefense, and Biotechnology in the Military: A Comparative Analysis of Legal and Ethical Issues in the Research, Development, and Use of Biotechnological Products on American and British Soldiers*, 14 ALB. L.J. SCI. & TECH. 497 (2004).

Merle, Renae, *Bioterror Antidote: Unfulfilled Prescription*, WASHINGTON POST (January 16, 2007).

Milstien, Julie B., *Regulation of Vaccines: Strengthening the Science Base*, JOURNAL OF PUBLIC HEALTH POLICY, Vol. 25, No. 2 (2004).

Mitchell, Ronald B., *Sources of Transparency: Information Systems in International Regimes*, INTERNATIONAL STUDIES QUARTERLY, Vol. 42, No. 1 (March 1998).

Mock, William B. T., *An Interdisciplinary Introduction to Legal Transparency: A Tool for Rational Development*, 18 DICK. J. INT'L L. 293 (Winter 2000).

Monge-Najera, Julian, & Vanessa Nielsen, *The Countries and Languages that Dominate Biological Research at the Beginning of the 21st Century*, REVISTA DE BIOLOGÍA TROPICAL, Vol. 53, No. 1–2 (March 1, 2005).

Monshipouri, Mahmood, *Promoting Universal Human Rights: Dilemmas of Integrating Developing Countries*, 4 YALE H.R. & DEV. L.J. 25 (2001).

Mordini, Emilio, *Conclusions of the International Conference on Ethical Implications of Research into the Prevention of Bioterrorism*, BIOETHICAL IMPLICATIONS OF GLOBALIZATION PROCESSES, POLICY PAPER 1 (April 2004).

Moynihan, Mark F., *The Scientific Community and Intelligence Collection*, PHYSICS TODAY, Vol. 53, No. 12 (December 2000).

Mullin, Thomas F., *Aids, Anthrax, and Compulsory Licensing: Has the United States Learned Anything? A Comment on Recent Decisions on the International Intellectual Property Rights of Pharmaceutical Patents*, 9 ILSA J. INT'L & COMP. L. 185 (Fall 2002).

Munro, Neil, *Securing Science*, NATIONAL JOURNAL (September 6, 2003).

Nanda, Ved P., *Sustainable Development, International Trade and the Doha Agenda for Development*, 8 CHAP. L. REV. 53 (Spring 2005).

Nanosignificance, STATESMAN (India) (April 3, 2006).

National Childhood Vaccine Injury Act of 1986, 42 USC §30aa.

National Science Advisory Board for Biosecurity Charter, DEPARTMENT OF HEALTH AND HUMAN SERVICES (March 4, 2004).

Natsios, Andrew S., *The Nine Principles of Reconstruction and Development*, PARAM-ETERS, Vol. 35, No. 3 (September 22, 2005).

Neuman, Victor A., & John P. Martin, *Biosafety Level 4 Labs: Up Close and Personal: More High-containment Biosafety Level 4 Labs are Being Built Today to Address the Twin Threats of Terrorism and Infectious Diseases*, HEATING/PIPING/AIR CON-DITIONING ENGINEERING, No. 3, Vol. 77 (March 1, 2005).

Nonpharmaceutical Interventions for Pandemic Influenza, National and Community Measures, World Health Organization Writing Group, Policy Review, EMERG-ING INFECTIOUS DISEASES, Vol. 12, No. 1 (January 2006).

Notes on the Scope of Diseases to be Covered in the Paragraph Six 'Solution' (December 20, 2002).

Null, Gary, (Ph.D.), GERMS, BIOLOGICAL WARFARE, VACCINATIONS, Seven Stories Press (2003).

Nwabueze, Remigius N., *What Can Genomics and Health Biotechnology Do for Developing Countries?*, 15 ALB. L.J. SCI. & TECH. 369 (2005).

O'Reilly, James T., *Bombing Bureaucratic Complacency: Effects of Counter-Terrorism Pressures upon Medical Product Approvals*, 60 N.Y.U. ANN. SURV. AM. L. 329 (2004).

Paarlberg, Robert L., *The Great Stem Cell Race: Scientists Around the World Are Scrambling to Unlock the Potential of Stem Cells*, FOREIGN POLICY (May 1, 2005).

Palmer, Larry I., *Should Liability Play a Role in Social Control of Biobanks?*, 33 J.L. MED. & ETHICS 70 (Spring 2005).

Pandemic and All-Hazards Preparedness Act, S 3678, PUBLIC LAW 109–417 (December 19, 2006).

Pandemic Flu and Medical Biodefense Countermeasure Liability Legislation, PUBLIC LAW 109–148, Division C (2005).

Parker, Elizabeth Rindskopf, & Leslie Gielow Jacobs, *Government Controls of Information and Scientific Inquiry*, BIOSECURITY AND BIOTERRORISM, Vol. 1, No. 2 (2003).

Parrett, James W. Jr., *A Proactive Solution to the Inherent Dangers of Biotechnology: Using the Invention Secrecy Act to Restrict Disclosure of Threatening Biotechnology Patents*, 26 WM. & MARY ENVTL. L. & POL'Y REV. 145 (Fall 2001).

Pearson, Graham S., *How to Make Microbes Safer*, NATURE, Vol. 394, No. 16 (July 1998).

Peart, Mark, *Business Research Unlocking the Genome and Building a Stronger Economy*, NEW ZEALAND BUSINESS (May 2003).

Petro, James B., Theodore R. Plasse, & Jack A. Mcnulty, *Biotechnology: Impact on Biological Warfare and Biodefense*, BIOSECURITY & BIOTERRORISM, Vol. 1, No. 3 (2003).

Picker, Colin B., *A View From 40,000 Feet: International Law and the Invisible Hand of Technology*, 23 CARDOZO L. REV. 149 (November 2001).

Poverty, Infectious Disease, and Environmental Degradation as Threats to Collective Security: A UN Panel Report, POPULATION AND DEVELOPMENT REVIEW (September 1, 2005).

Preventing Hostile Use of the Life Sciences: From Ethics and Law to Best Practices INTERNATIONAL COMMITTEE OF THE RED CROSS (November 11, 2004).

Public Health Security and Bioterrorism Response Act of 2002, P.L. 107–188.

Public Law No. 97–414, 96 Stat. 2049 (1983) (codified as amended 1988).

Rappaport, Frank, et al., *Project Bioshield Act of 2004: Dawn of a New Industry?* 40-SPG PROCUREMENT LAW 3 (2005).

Rappert, Brian, *Biological Weapons, Genetics and Social Analysis: Emerging Responses, Emerging Issues*, NEW GENETICS AND SOCIETY, Vol. 22, No. 2 (August 2003).

Rappert, Brian, *Responsibility in the Life Sciences: Assessing the Role of Professional Codes*, BIOSECURITY AND BIOTERRORISM: BIODEFENSE STRATEGY, PRACTICE, AND SCIENCE, Vol. 2 (July 2004).

Responsible Science, Volume 1: Ensuring the Integrity of the Research Process, INSTITUTE OF MEDICINE (1992).

Riley, Margaret Foster with Richard A. Merrill, *Regulating Reproductive Genetics: A Review of American Bioethics: Commissions and Comparison to the British Human Fertilisation and Embryology Authority*, 6 COLUM. SCI. & TECH. L. REV. 1 (2005).

Ripandelli, Decio, *Biological Weapons and International Regulations*, INTERACADEMY PANEL ON INTERNATIONAL ISSUES (2004).

Rivera-Monroy, Victor H., et al., *A Conceptual Framework to Develop Long-term Ecological Research and Management Objectives in the Wider Caribbean Region*, BIOSCIENCE (September 1, 2004).

Rosenthal, Elisabeth, *Wealthy Nations Announce Plan to Develop and Pay for Vaccines*, NEW YORK TIMES (February 10, 2007).

Russell, Ron, *A Question of Risk, Plans for a Biodefense "Hot Lab" at Lawrence Livermore Have Ecologists, Disarmament Advocates, and mainstream Scientists Up in Arms*, SF WEEKLY (January 28, 2004).

Russell, Sabin, *Deadliest Flu Bug Given New Life in U.S. Laboratory; Some Applaud Scientific Feat, but Others Decry Move as Reckless*, SAN FRANCISCO CHRONICLE (October 6, 2005).

Safrin, Sabrina, *Hyperownership in a Time of Biotechnological Promise: The International Conflict to Control the Building Blocks of Life*, 98 AM. J. INT'L L. 641 (October 2004).

Salerno, Reynolds M., et al., *Balancing Security and Research at Biomedical and Bioscience Laboratories*, Paper presented at "BTR 2003: Unified Science and Technology for Reducing Biological Threats and Countering Terrorism," University of New Mexico, Albuquerque, NM, SAND No. 2003–0701C (March 2003).

Salyers, Abigail A., *The Implications for Academic Freedom, Innovation, and Competitive Advantage: Microbes and the Law: From Censorship to Forensics*, U. ILL. J.L. TECH. & POL'Y 413 (Fall, 2002).

Sato, Shorge, *Sustainable Development and the Selfish Gene: A Rational Paradigm for Achieving Intergenerational Equity*, 11 N.Y.U. ENVTL. L.J. 503 (2003).

Schaefer, Brett D., *How Economic Freedom Is Central to Development in Sub-Saharan Africa*, Heritage Foundation Reports (February 3, 2006).

Schneider, John, *Bioterrorists Beware: Biotech Is Not Your Friend*, GENOMICS AND PROTEOMICS (January 1, 2006).

SciDev.Net, *Continent Must Engage Directly in Fight Against Malaria*, AFRICA NEWS (December 1, 2005).

Seckinelgin, Hakan, *A Global Disease and Its Governance: HIV/AIDS in Sub-Saharan Africa and the Agency of NGOs*, GLOBAL GOVERNANCE (July 1, 2005).

Security and Development Links Key to UN Reform, IRISH TIMES (September 17, 2005).

Seeking Security: Pathogens, Open Access, and Genome Databases, NATIONAL RESEARCH COUNCIL OF THE NATIONAL ACADEMIES (2004).

Seguin, Beatrice, et al., *Scientific Diasporas as an Option for Brain Drain: Recirculating Knowledge for Development*, 8 INT. J. BIOTECHNOLOGY 78 (2006).

Sell, Susan K., *The Quest for Global Governance in Intellectual Property and Public Health: Structural, Discursive, and Institutional Dimensions*, 77 TEMP. L. REV. 363 (Summer 2004).

Sharing Germ Information Outweighs Risks, Developing Vaccines More Important, Experts Say, ASSOCIATED PRESS (September 9, 2004).

Sharma, Shalendra D., *The Promise of Monterrey: Meeting the Millennium Development Goals*, WORLD POLICY JOURNAL (September 22, 2004).

Sharp, Philip A., *1918 Flu and Responsible Science*, SCIENCE, Vol. 310 (October 7, 2005).

Shea, Dana A., *Balancing Scientific Publication and National Security Concerns: Issues for Congress*, CONGRESSIONAL RESEARCH SERVICE (January 10, 2003).

Shea, Dana A., *Oversight of Dual-Use Biological Research*, The National Science Advisory Board for Biosecurity, CONGRESSIONAL RESEARCH SERVICE REPORT (July 10, 2006).

Shea, David M., *The Project Bioshield Prisoner's Dilemma: An Impetus for the Modernization of Programmatic Environmental Impact Statements*, 33 B. C. ENVTL. AFF. L. REV. 695 (2006).

Sheridan, Cormac, *The Business of Making Vaccines*, NATURE BIOTECHNOLOGY, Vol. 23, No. 11 (November 2005).

Shoemaker, C. J., *Description of Vaccine Litigation: A Call To Arms*, *available at* http://www.attorneyaccess.net/CallToArms.cfm.

Sidawari, Danielle, & Skip Derra, *Proteomics' Growing Role in Biodefense; Fueled by Large Government Grants, Researchers Are Honing Techniques that Will Help Defend Against Bioterror Attacks and the Spread of Infectious Diseases*, R AND D (July 1, 2005).

Sidel, Victor W., *Defense Against Biological Weapons: Can Immunization and Secondary Prevention Succeed?*, *in* Susan Wright, (ed.), BIOLOGICAL WARFARE AND DISARMAMENT, Rowman & Littlefield (2002).

Silverstein, Ken, *Flaws in the BioShield: VaxGen Looks for Another Federal Bailout*, HARPER'S MAGAZINE (December 12, 2006).

Singer, Peter A., et al., *Harnessing Nanotechnology to Improve Global Equity: The Less Industrialized Countries Are Eager to Play an Early Role in Developing this Technology; The Global Community Should Help Them*, ISSUES IN SCIENCE AND TECHNOLOGY, Vol. 21, No. 4 (June 22, 2005).

Smallpox Emergency Personnel Protection Act of 2003, PUBLIC LAW 180–20, 117 Stat. 638 (2003).

Smithson, Amy E., *Compliance Through Science: U.S. Pharmaceutical Industry Experts on a Strengthened Bioweapons Nonproliferation Regime*, THE HENRY STIMSON CENTER, Report #48 (September 2002).

Solomon, Anne G. K., (ed.), TECHNOLOGY FUTURES AND GLOBAL POWER, WEALTH, AND CONFLICT, CSIS Report (2005).

Somerville, Margaret A., & Ronald M. Atlas, *Ethics: A Weapon to Counter Bioterrorism*, SCIENCE, Vol. 307 (March 25, 2005).

Spoth, Richard L., & Mark T. Greenberg, *Toward a Comprehensive Strategy for Effective Practitioner-Scientist Partnerships and Larger-Scale Community Health and Well-Being*, AMERICAN JOURNAL OF COMMUNITY PSYCHOLOGY, Vol. 35, No. 3–4 (June 1, 2005).

Stark, Barbara, *Sustainable Development and Postmodern International Law: Greener Globalization?*, 27 WM. & MARY ENVTL. L. & POL'Y REV. 137 (Fall 2002).

State News Service, *HHS Accomplishment in Biodefense Preparedness*, (January 13, 2006).

State News Service, *NIH Implementation of Project Bioshield in Research and Development of Defense Countermeasures* (July 14, 2005).

State News Service, *The Role of HHS in Development and Acquisition of Medical Countermeasures Under Project Bioshield*, (July 14, 2005).

State News Service, Statement by Anthony S. Fauci on NIH Biomedical Research Response to Threat of Bioterrorism (July 28, 2005).

Statement on Scientific Publication and Security, Journal Editors and Authors Group, SCIENCE (February 21, 2003).

Steinbruner, John, Elisa D. Harris, Nancy Gallagher, & Stacy Okutani, *Controlling Dangerous Pathogens: A Prototype Protective Oversight System*, CENTER FOR INTERNATIONAL AND SECURITY STUDIES(December 2005).

Stone, Christopher D., *Common but Differentiated Responsibilities in International Law*, 98 AM. J. INT'L L. 276 (April 2004).

Sukovski, Katerina, *The Ethical Aspects of Biomedical Research in Developing Countries*, Report of the European Group on Ethics in Science and New Technologies to the European Commission (2003).

Sunstein, Cass R., *A New Progressivism*, 17 STAN. L. & POL'Y REV. 197 (2006).

Swine Flu Act, Public Law 94–380 § 2(k)(2)(A) (1976).

Sylvan, J. C., *The Millennium Development Goals and HIV/AIDS*, 6 SUSTAINABLE DEV. L. & POL'Y 32 (Fall 2005).

Szekiely, Alberto (Amb.), *Symposium: Biotechnology and International Law: Modified Organisms and International Law: An Ethical Perspective*, 14 TRANSNAT'L LAW, 129 (Spring 2001).

Tano, Mervyn L., *Interrelationships Among Native Peoples, Genetic Research, and the Landscape: Need for Further Research into Ethical, Legal, and Social Issues*, 34 J.L. MED. & ETHICS 301 (Summer 2006).

Tansey, Bernadette, *U.S. Requires Scientists to Give FBI Fingerprints: Thousands who use Bioterror Compounds Must Disclose Data for Background Checks*, SAN FRANCISCO GATE (March 12, 2003).

Taylor, Michael R., & Jerry Cayford, *American Patent Policy, Biotechnology, and African Agriculture: The Case for Policy Change*, 17 HARV. J. LAW & TECH.321 (Spring 2004).

Terry, Mark, *Partners in Preparedness Against Disease Weapons*, DRUG DISCOVERY AND DEVELOPMENT (August 1, 2004).

The Art of Foresight: Preparing for a Changing World; A Special Report from the World Future Society, FUTURIST (May 1, 2004).

THE MILITARILY CRITICAL TECHNOLOGIES LIST, United States Department of Defense (1998).

The Need for Biosafety Laboratory Facilities, NATIONAL INSTITUTE OF ALLERGY AND INFECTIOUS DISEASES (February 2004).

Thorsteinsdotir, Halla, et al., *Health Biotechnology Publishing Takes Off in Developing Countries*, 8 INT. J. BIOTECHNOLOGY 23 (2006).

Toh Mei Ling, & Lee Wei Lian, *Net Value: States Hitch On to Biotech*, THE EDGE MALAYSIA (September 12, 2005).

Tordes, Jonathan, et al., *International Health Law*, 40 INT'L LAW 453 (2006).

Tucker, Jonathan B., *Research on Biodefense Can Get Generous Funds, But With Strings Attached*, THE CHRONICLE OF HIGHER EDUCATION (March 5, 2004).

Tumpey, Terrence M. *Characterization of the Reconstructed 1918 Spanish Influenza Virus*, SCIENCE, Vol. 310 (October 7, 2005).

United Nations Report of the International Conference on Financing for Development Monterrey, Mexico, 18–22 March 2002, 10 LAW & BUS. REV. AM. 85 (Winter 2004).

United Nations, *Hunger, Health, Education Closely Linked and Must Be Addressed Together, Economic and Social Council Told, as High-level Session Continues*, M2 PRESSWIRE (July 2, 2002).

United Nations, *General Assembly Endorses Outcome of World Summit for Information Society, Welcomes Digital Solidarity Fund*, U.S. FED NEWS (March 27, 2006).

United Nations, *Implementation of General Assembly Resolution 58/200 Science and Technology for Development*, United Nations General Assembly, A/60/184 (August 2, 2005).

United Nations, *The Biotechnology Promise; Capacity-building for Participation of Developing Countries in the Bioeconomy*, United Nations Conference on Trade and Development (2004).

U.S. Fed News, *General Assembly Endorses Outcome of World Summit for Information Society, Welcomes Digital Solidarity Fund*, U.S. FED NEWS (March 27, 2006).

USA Seeks More Protection Against WMD (Weapons of Mass Destruction), JANE'S DEFENCE WEEKLY (May 27, 1998).

Vaccine Supply and Innovation, INSTITUTE OF MEDICINE, National Academies Press (1985).

Valach, Anthony P. Jr., *Trips: Protecting the Rights of Patent Holders and Addressing Public Health Issues in Developing Countries*, 4 CHI-KENT J. INTELL. PROP. 156 (February 2005).

Varmus, Harold, *Building a Global Culture of Science*, THE LANCET (December 2002).

Venkataraman, Krishnamoorthy, *Looking After India's Biodiversity*, MANAGING INTELLECTUAL PROPERTY, No. 151 (July 1, 2005).

Venter, Al J., *Keeping the Lid on Germ Welfare*, JANE'S INTERNATIONAL DEFENCE REVIEW (May 1998).

Wagner, Cynthia G., *Creating a More Intelligent Future*, FUTURIST (November 1, 2004).

Wagner, Cynthia G., *Partners for Progress: Creating Global Strategies for Humanity's Future*, FUTURIST, Vol. 40, No. 6. (November 1, 2006).

Ward, Amelia K.; White, David S.; & Barrett, Gary W., *The Growing Relevance and Role of the Association of Ecosystem Research Centers*, BIOSCIENCE (July 1, 2004).

Watson, James, *How Will Genetics Change Our Lives*, TIME MAGAZINE (February 17, 2003).

Weatherspoon, Dave; Joyce Cacho, & Ralph Christy, *Linking Globalization, Economic Growth and Poverty: Impacts of Agribusiness Strategies on Sub-Saharan Africa*, AMERICAN JOURNAL OF AGRICULTURAL ECONOMICS, Vol. 83, No. 3 (August 1, 2001).

Wechsler, Jill, *Manufacturers Face New Challenges Battling Global Threats: Efforts to Expand Drug Production Capacity Reflect Fears of a Pandemic Flu Outbreak, Bioterrorism, and New Infectious Diseases*, PHARMACEUTICAL TECHNOLOGY, Vol. 29, No. 8 (August 1, 2005).

Weed, D. L., *Preventing Scientific Misconduct*, AMERICAN JOURNAL OF PUBLIC HEALTH, Vol. 88 (1998).

Whelan, Jo, *My Enemy's Enemy; Injecting People with Live Viruses Sounds Crazy, but They Are the Latest Weapon in the War Against Cancer*, NEW SCIENTIST (November 19, 2005).

Whitesell, Stephen; Robert J. Lilieholm, & Terry L. Sharik, *A Global Survey of Tropical Biological Field Stations*, BIOSCIENCE, Vol. 52, No. 1 (January 1, 2002).

Whitman, Jim, *Disseminative Systems and Global Governance*, GLOBAL GOVERNANCE (January 1, 2005).

With an Additional $1 Billion per Year, Immunization Could Save Ten Million More Lives in a Decade, UNICEF, Joint Press Release (December 9, 2005).

WORLD TRADE ORGANIZATION, THE LEGAL TEXTS: THE RESULTS OF THE URUGUAY ROUND OF MULTILATERAL TRADE NEGOTIATIONS (1999).

Zelicoff, Alan P. & Michael Bellomo, MICROBE, American Management Association (2005).

Zilinskas, Raymond, & Jonathan B. Tucker, *Limiting the Contribution of the Open Scientific Literature to the Biological Weapons Threat*, JOURNAL OF HOMELAND SECURITY (December 2002).

Chapter 7

A Bill to Provide for Global Pathogen Surveillance and Response, S.2487, *107th Congress*, (October 1, 2002).

Ackerman, Bruce, *The Emergency Constitution*, 113 YALE L. J. 5 (March 2004).

Altman, Lawrence K., *Duplicated Efforts Are Hampering AIDS Fight, Conferees Say*, NEW YORK TIMES (July 13, 2004).

Asher, Lauren Z., *Confronting Disease in a Global Arena*, 9 CARDOZO J. INT'L & COMP. 135 (Spring 2001).

Ban, Jonathan, HEALTH, SECURITY, AND U.S. GLOBAL LEADERSHIP, CBACI Special Report (2001).

Barbera, Joseph A., & Anthony G. Macintyre, *The Reality of the Modern Bioterrorism Response*, THE LANCET, Vol. 260, No. 1 (December 21, 2002).

Beaglehole, Robert, & Mario R. Dal Poz, *Public Health Workforce: Challenges and Policy Issues*, HUMAN RESOURCES FOR HEALTH (July 17, 2003).

Bishop, David, *Lessons from SARS: Why the WHO Must Provide Greater Economic Incentives for Countries to Comply with International Health Regulations*, 26 GEORGETOWN J. INT'L LAW (2005).

Blendon, Robert J., et al., *Attitudes Toward the Use of Quarantine in a Public Health Emergency in Four Countries*, HEALTH AFFAIRS, Vol. 25, No. 2 (2006).

Blum, John D., *Balancing Individual Rights versus Collective Good in Public Health Enforcement*, 25 MEDICINE & LAW 1 (2006).

Blyn, Lawrence B., *Biosensors and Food Protection*, FOOD TECHNOLOGY (February 2006).

Bower, Jennifer L., *The Terrorist Threat and its Implications for Sensor Technologies*, presented at Advances in SENSING WITH SECURITY APPLICATIONS (July 2005).

Bradley, Colleen A. et al., *BioSense: Implementation of a National Early Event Detection and Situational Awareness System*, MORBIDITY AND MORTALITY WEEKLY REPORT, Vol. 54, No. 33 (August 26, 2005).

Buckeridge, David L., et al., *Evaluating Detection of an Inhalational Anthrax Outbreak*, EMERGING INFECTIOUS DISEASES (December 1, 2006).

Burkle, Frederick M., *Population-based Triage Management in Response to Surge-capacity Requirements during a Large-scale Bioevent Disaster*, ACADEMIC EMERGENCY MEDICINE, Vol. 13, No. 11 (2006).

Burlke, Frederick M. (M.D.), *Mass Casualty Management of a Large-scale Bioterrorist Event: An Epidemiological Approach that Shapes Triage Decisions*, EMERGENCY MEDICINE CLINICS OF NORTH AMERICA, Vol. 20 (2002).

Bush Issues Medical Emergency Directive, NEW YORK TIMES (February 8, 2007).

Cheng, Cecila, *To Be Paranoid is the Standard? Panic Responses to SARS Outbreak in the Hong Kong Special Administrative Region*, ASIAN PERSPECTIVE, Vol. 28 (2004).

Chilakamarri, Varu, *A New Instrument in National Security: The Legislative Attempt to Combat Terrorism via the Safe Drinking Water Act*, 91 GEORGETOWN LAW J. (April 2003).

Clark, Wayne, et al., *Advanced UV Source for Biological Agent Destruction*, TECHNICAL REPORT. Novatron Inc., (2006).

Cohen, H. W., et al., *Correspondence: Preparedness for Bioterrorism*, NEW ENGLAND JOURNAL OF MEDICINE, Vol. 345, No. 19 (2001).

Cohen, Hillel W., et al., *The Pitfalls of Bioterrorism Preparedness*, AMERICAN JOURNAL OF PUBLIC HEALTH, Vol. 94, No. 10 (2004).

Communication from the Commission to the Council and the European Parliament, on Cooperation in the European Union on Preparedness and Response to Biological and Chemical Agent Attacks (Health Security), COMMISSION OF THE EUROPEAN COMMUNITIES (June 2, 2003).

Constitution of the World Health Organization (July 22, 1946).

Correcting the 10/90 Gap: From the 1990 Commission to the 2004 Mexico Summit, in 10/90 REPORT ON HUMAN RESEARCH 2003–2004, Global Forum for Health Research (May 2004).

Currie, Peter, *How Can Resources be Mobilized to Confront a Global Health Emergency? – An Introduction to the Problem*, 4 YALE J. HEALTH POL'Y L. & ETHICS 125 (Winter 2004).

Darling, Miranda, *The Pandemic Threat; Health*, QUADRANT, Vol. 49, No. 10 (October 1, 2005).

Day, Troy, et al., *When Is Quarantine a Useful Control Strategy for Emerging Infectious Diseases?* AMERICAN JOURNAL OF EPIDEMIOLOGY, Vol. 163 (2006).

Department of Veterans Affairs Emergency Preparedness Act of 2002, PUBLIC LAW 107–287 [H.R. 3253] (November 7, 2002).

Doe v. Rumsfeld, 297 F. Supp. 2d 119 (2003).

Doe v. Rumsfeld, 297 F. Supp. 2d 200 (2004).

Doedert, Joseph, *The Biosurveillance Evolution*, HEALTH DATA MANAGEMENT, Vol. 15, No. 2 (February 2007).

DOMESTIC WMD INCIDENT MANAGEMENT, *Legal Deskbook* (December 2003).

Dvorak, Paul, *Biodefense: The Best Defense After a Biological Attack May Be a Good Filter*, MEDICAL DESIGN, Vol. 6, No. 10 (December 1, 2006).

Early Efforts Initiated But Comprehensive Privacy Approach Needed for National Strategy, GAO REPORT, GAO-07-238 (January 10, 2007).

Esty, Daniel, *Good Governance at the Supranational Scale: Globalizing Administrative Law*, 115 YALE L. J. (2006).

Fedson, David S., *Preparing for Pandemic Vaccination: An International Policy Agenda for Vaccine Development*, JOURNAL OF PUBLIC HEALTH POLICY, Vol. 26, No. 1 (2005).

Fidler, David P., *From International Sanitary Conventions to Global Health Security: The New International Health Regulations*, 4 CHINESE J. INT'L L. (2005).

Fidler, David P., *Public Health and National Security in the Global Age: Infectious Diseases, Bioterrorism, and Realpolitik*, 35 GEO. WASH. INT'L L. REV. 787 (2003).

Fidler, David P., *Symposium: SARS, Public Health, and Global Governance: Article: Constitutional Outlines of Public Health's "New World Order,"* 77 TEMP. L. REV. 247 (Summer 2004).

Fidler, David P., *U.S. Foreign Policy and Human Rights: Article: Fighting the Axis of Illness: HIV/Aids, Human Rights, and U.S. Foreign Policy*, 17 HARV. HUM. RTS. J. 99 (Spring 2004).

Fowler, Robert A., et al., *Cost-Effectiveness of Defending against Bioterrorism*, ANNALS OF INTERNAL MEDICINE, Vol. 142, No. 8 (2005).

Gamble, John King, Charlotte Ku, & Chris Strayer, *Human-Centric International Law: A Model and a Search for Empirical Indicators*, 14 TUL. J. INT'L & COMP. L. 61 (Winter 2005).

Gandhi, Devender, *Securing Urban Water Supply and Treatment Facilities: A Laboratory Information Management System Can Provide Secure Interoperability Between Laboratories and Governing Bodies; LIMS/Laboratory Informatics*, SCIENTIFIC COMPUTING & INSTRUMENTATION, Vol. 22, No. 6 (May 1, 2005).

Garrett, Laurie, *Understanding Media's Response to Epidemics*, PUBLIC HEALTH REPORTS, Vol. 116, p. 87 (2001).

Gentilman, Mark F. (Lieutenant Colonel), *An Analysis to Determine Whether Quarantine is an Effective Response to a Bioterrorist Attack in the United States*, American Academy of Medical Administrators (June 3, 2005).

Glass, Thomas, & Monica Schoch-Spana, *Bioterrorism and the People: How to Vaccinate a City against Panic*, CLINICAL INFECTIOUS DISEASES, Vol. 34 (January 15, 2002).

Gluodenis, Thomas, & Scott Harrison, *Homeland Security and Bioterrorism Applications: Detection of Bioweapon Pathogens by Microfluidic-based Electrophoretic DNA Analysis; Lab Management*, MEDICAL LABORATORY OBSERVER (February 1, 2004).

Goldman, Janlori, *Balancing in Crisis? Bioterrorism, Public Health, and Privacy*, 38 J. HEALTH L. 3 (2005).

Gonzalez Block, Miguel A., & Anne Mills, *Assessing Capacity for Health Policy and Systems Research in Low and Middle Income Countries*, HEALTH RESEARCH POLICY AND SYSTEMS, Vol. 1, No. 1 (2003).

Goodman, Richard A., Judith W. Munson, Kim Dammers, Zita Lazzarini, & John P. Barkley, *Forensic Epidemiology: Law at the Intersection of Public Health and Criminal Investigations*, J. L. MED. & ETHICS (2003).

Gostin, Lawrence O., et al., *Quarantine: Voluntary or Not?*, 32 J. L. MED. & ETHICS (2004).

Gostin, Lawrence O., *How Far are Limitations on Personal and Economic Liberties Justified?*, 55 FLA. L. REV. 1105 (December 2003).

Gostin, Lawrence O., *Revision of the World Health Organization's International Health Regulations*, JOURNAL OF THE AMERICAN MEDICAL ASSOCIATION, Vol. 291, No. 21 (June 2004).

Gostin, Lawrence O., *When Terrorism Threatens Health: How Far Are Limitations on Human Rights Justified?*, 31 J. L., MED. & ETHICS 4 (2003).

Greenberger, Michael, *The 800-Pound Gorilla Sleeps: The Federal Government's Lackadaisical Liability and Compensation Policies in the Context of Pre-Event Vaccine Immunization Programs*, 8 J. HEALTH CARE L. & POL'Y 7 (2005).

Gronvall, Gigi Kwik, & Luciana Borio, *Removing Barriers to Global Pandemic Influenza Vaccination*, BIOSECURITY AND BIOTERRORISM: BIODEFENSE STRATEGY, PRACTICE, AND SCIENCE, Vol. 4 (2006).

Gross, Jane, *A Nation Challenged: The Doctors*, NEW YORK TIMES (October 17, 2001).

Grotto, Andrew J., & Jonathan B. Tucker, *Biosecurity: A Comprehensive Action Plan*, CENTER FOR AMERICAN PROGRESS (June 2006).

Guidance for Protecting Building Environments from Airborne Chemical, Biological, and Radiological Attacks, NATIONAL INSTITUTE FOR OCCUPATION SAFETY AND HEALTH (April 2003).

Guidance on Initial Responses to a Suspicious Letter/Container with a Potential Biological Threat, UNCLASSIFIED COORDINATED DOCUMENT, FEDERAL BUREAU OF INVESTIGATION, DEPARTMENT OF HOMELAND SECURITY, CENTERS FOR DISEASE CONTROL AND PREVENTION (November 2, 2004).

Guidelines for Smallpox Response and Management in the Post-Eradication Era, U.S. DEPARTMENT OF HEALTH (December 15, 2003).

Gursky, Elin, & Avani Parikh, *Some Right Jabs and Back in the Ring: Lessons Learned from the Phase I Civilian Smallpox Program*, 8 J. HEALTH CARE L. & POL'Y 162 (2005).

Hanson, Kara, et al., *The Economics of Malaria Control Interventions*, GLOBAL FORUM FOR HEALTH RESEARCH (January 2004).

Hearing before the Committee on House Government Reform Subcommittee on National Security, Emerging Threats, and International Relations, on *Assessing Anthrax Detection Methods* (April 5, 2005), Testimony by Keith Rhodes.

Hearing before the House Armed Services Committee, Subcommittee on Military Personnel, on *Defense Health Programs Overview* (October 19, 2005), Testimony of George Taylor Jr. and William Winkenwerder, Jr.

Hearing before the House Energy and Commerce Committee, Environment and Hazardous Materials Subcommittee, *Drinking Water Security* (September 30, 2004), Testimony of Benjamin H. Grumbles.

Hearing before the House Government Reform Committee, National Security, Emerging Threats, and International Relations Subcommittee, on *Assessing Anthrax Detection Methods* (April 5, 2005), Testimony of Tanya Popovic.

Hearing before the House Homeland Security Committee, *Prevention of Nuclear and Biological Attack Subcommittee* (July 28, 2005), Testimony of Dr. Julie Gerberding.

Hearing before the House Homeland Security Committee, Subcommittee on Emergency Preparedness, Science, and Technology, on *Linking Bioterrorism Threats and Countermeasure Procurement* (July 12, 2005), Testimonies by Richard Hollis and Eugene Carr.

Hearing before the Senate Commerce, Science, and Transportation Committee, Subcommittee on Science, Technology, and Space, on *Bioterrorism Preparedness* (February 5, 2002), Testimonies by Bruno W.S. Sobral and Richard Klausner.

Hearing before the Senate Foreign Relations Committee, on *Global Partnership Against Weapons of Mass Destruction* (June 15, 2004), Testimony of John R. Bolton.

Hearing before the Senate Judiciary Committee, on *Bioterrorism Detection and Response* (May 11, 2004).

Hearing of the Prevention of Nuclear and Biological Attack, Subcommittee of the House Homeland Security Committee, on *Creating a Nationwide Integrated Biosurveillance System* (May 11, 2006).

Herholz, Cornelia, *EU Extends Salmonella Monitoring*, SFVO MAGAZINE (2004).

Hodge, James G. Jr., *Bioterrorism Law and Policy: Critical Choices in Public Health*, 30 J. L. MED. & ETHICS 254 (Summer 2002).

Hodge, James G., Jr., Lance A. Gable, & Stephanie H. Calves, *The Legal Framework for Meeting Surge Capacity Through the Use of Volunteer Health Professionals During Public Health Emergencies and Other Disasters*, 22 J. CONTEMP. HEALTH L. & POLICY (Fall 2005).

Incentives for the Use of Health Information Technology and Establishing the Position of the National Health Information Technology Coordinator, Executive Order 13335 (April 27, 2004).

Inglesby, T. V., J. B. Nuzzo, T. O'Toole, & D. A. Henderson, *Disease Mitigation Measures in the Control of Pandemic Influenza*, BIOSECURITY AND BIOTERRORISM: BIODEFENSE STRATEGY, PRACTICE, AND SCIENCE, Vol. 4 (2006).

International Health Regulations, 48th World Health Assembly (May 23, 2005).

Javitt, Gail H., *Old Legacies and New Paradigms: Confusing "Research" and "Treatment" and Its Consequences in Responding to Emergent Health Threats*, 8 J. HEALTH CARE L. & POL'Y 38 (2005).

Katz, Rebecca, *Public Health Preparedness: The Best Defense Against Biological Weapons*, WASHINGTON QUARTERLY, Vol. 25, No. 3 (Summer 2002).

Keim, Paul, *Microbial Forensics: A Scientific Approach*, AMERICAN ACADEMY OF MICROBIOLOGY (2003).

Kellman, Barry, *Managing Terrorism's Consequences: Legal Issues*, NATIONAL MEMORIAL INSTITUTE FOR THE PREVENTION OF TERRORISM (2003).

Kent, David M., *Clinical Trials in Sub-Saharan Africa and Established Standards of Care: A Systematic Review of HIV, Tuberculosis, and Malaria Trials*, JOURNAL OF THE AMERICAN MEDICAL ASSOCIATION, Vol. 292, No. 2 (July 14, 2004).

Khan, Ali S., & David A. Ashford, *Ready or Not, Preparedness for Bioterrorism*, NEW ENGLAND JOURNAL OF MEDICINE, Vol. 345, No. 4 (July 26, 2001).

Klein, Jerome O., & Martin G. Myers, *Vaccine Shortages: Why They Occur and What Needs to be Done to Strengthen Vaccine Supply*, PEDIATRICS, Vol. 117, No. 6 (June 2006).

Koblentz, Gregory, *Pathogens as Weapons; The International Security Implications of Biological Warfare*, INTERNATIONAL SECURITY (Winter 2004).

Koplow, David, *Arms Control Inspection: Constitutional Restrictions on Treaty Verification in the United States*, 63 N.Y.U. L. REV. (May 1988).

Kornfeld, Itzchak E., *Combating Terrorism in the Environmental Trenches: Responding to Terrorism: Terror in the Water: Threats to Drinking Water and Infrastructure*, 9 WID. L. SYMP. J. 439 (2003).

Kostyack, Paul T., *The Emergence of the Healthcare Information Trust*, 12 HEALTH MATRIX 393 (Summer 2002).

Krebs, Melisa D., et al., *Detection of Biological and Chemical Agents Using Differential Mobility Spectrometry (DMS) Technology*, IEEE SENSORS JOURNAL, Vol. 5, No. 4 (2005).

Lam, C., R. Waldhorn, E. Toner, T. V. Inglesby, & T. O'Toole, *The Prospect of Using Alternative Medical Care Facilities in an Influenza Pandemic*, BIOSECURITY AND BIOTERRORISM: BIODEFENSE STRATEGY, PRACTICE, AND SCIENCE, Vol. 4 (2006).

Lane, J. Michael, & Joel Goldstein, *Evaluations of 21st-Century Risks of Smallpox Vaccination and Policy Options*, ANNALS OF INTERNAL MEDICINE, Vol. 138 (March 18, 2003).

Ludbroth, J., *International Cooperation and Preparedness in Responding to Accidental or Deliberate Biological Disasters: Lessons and Future Directions*, REV. SCI. TECH. OFF. INT. EPIZ., Vol. 25, No. 1 (2006).

MacLean, J. Dick, et al., *Malaria Epidemics and Surveillance Systems in Canada*, EMERGING INFECTIOUS DISEASE, Vol. 10, No. 7 (July 2004).

Macroeconomics and Health: Investing in Health for Economic Development, Report of the Commission on Macroeconomics and Health, WORLD HEALTH ORGANIZATION (December 20, 2001).

Markovits, Daniel, *Quarantine and Distributive Justice*, J. L., MED. & ETHICS, Vol. 33, No. 2 (2005).

Martin, Robyn, *The Exercise of Public Health Powers in Cases of Infectious Disease: Human Rights Implications*, 14 MED. L. REV. (2006).

May, Thomas, *Political Authority in a Bioterror Emergency*, 32 J.L. MED. & ETHICS 159 (March 22, 2004).

McDonald, Ryan, *Juries and Crime Labs: Correcting the Weak Links in the DNA Chain.* 24 AM. J. L. & MED. 203 (1998).

Meier, Benjamin Mason, & Larisa M. Mori, *The Highest Attainable Standard: Advancing a Collective Human Right to Public Health*, 37 COLUM. HUMAN RIGHTS L. REV. 101 (Fall 2005).

Meinhardt, Patricia L., *Water and Bioterrorism*, 26 ANNUAL REV. OF PUB. HEALTH 213 (April 2005).

Melnick, Alan, et al., *Public Health Ethics in Action: Flu Vaccine and Drug Allocation Strategies*, 33 J. LAW, MED. & ETHICS 4, pp. 102–105 (2005).

Menon, K. U., & K. T. Goh, *Transparency and Trust: Risk Communication and the Singapore Experience in Managing SARS*, JOURNAL OF COMMUNICATION MANAGEMENT, Vol. 9 (2005).

Milstien, Julie B., et al., *The Impact of Globalization on Vaccine Development and Availability*, HEALTH AFFAIRS, Vol. 25, No. 4 (2006).

Molecular Diagnostic Methods for Infectious Diseases; Approved Guideline – Second Edition, CLINICAL AND LABORATORY STANDARDS INSTITUTE, CLSI DOCUMENT MM3-A2 Vol. 26, No. 8 (2006).

Molyneux, David H, *"Neglected" Diseases but Unrecognised Successes – Challenges and Opportunities for Infectious Disease Control*, LANCET ONLINE (July 13, 2004).

National Animal Health Monitoring System, Animal and Plant Health Inspection Service, U.S. DEPARTMENT OF AGRICULTURE, *available at* http://www.aphis.usda.gov/vs/ceah/ncahs/nahms/.

Nauscheutz, William F., *Straight Talk on Bioterror from the Army's LRN Gatekeeper, Laboratory Response Network,* MEDICAL LABORATORY OBSERVER, Vol. 37, No. 6 (June 1, 2005).

New Law to Provide Medical Countermeasures Against WMD Attack; Bush Signed into Law on July 21, State Department Briefing (July 22, 2004).

Nuzzo, Jennifer B., *The Biological Threat to U.S. Water Supplies,* BIOSECURITY AND BIOTERRORISM: BIODEFENSE STRATEGY, PRACTICE, AND SCIENCE, Vol. 4 (2006).

Overview of the Synthesis of Existing Practices, Rules and Standards Relevant to Article 18 of the Cartagena Protocol on Biosafety: Consideration of the Needs and Modalities for Developing Measures for Documentation Accompanying Living Modified Organism, Conference of the Parties to the Convention on Biological Diversity Serving as the Meeting of the Parties to the Cartagena Protocol on Biosafety, UNEP/CBD/BS/TE-HTPI/1/2 (May 10, 2001).

Parmet, Wendy E., *Informed Consent and Public Health: Are They Compatible When It Comes to Vaccines?,* 8 J. HEALTH CARE L. & POL'Y 71 (2005).

Parmet, Wendy E., *Quarantine Redux: Bioterrorism, AIDS and the Curtailment of Individual Liberty in the Name of Public Health,* 13 HEALTH MATRIX 85 (Winter 2003).

Pesik, N., M. E. Keim, & K. V. Iserson, *Terrorism and the Ethics of Emergency Medical Care,* ANNALS OF EMERGENCY MEDICINE, Vol. 37 (2001).

Plant Health: Crop Biosecurity and Emergency Management, Animal and Plant Health Inspection Service, U.S. DEPARTMENT OF AGRICULTURE, *available at* http://www.aphis.usda.gov/plant_health/plant_pest_info/biosecurity/index.shtml.

Plant Protection and Quarantine: Importation of Plants for Planting, Protocols and Critical Issues, USDA Animal and Plant Health Inspection Service, U.S.DEPARTMENT OF AGRICULTURE, *available at* http://www.aphis.usda.gov/ppq/Q37/protocols.html.

Predictions of Chemical, Biological Terror Fuel Military-Civilian Defense Partnership, NATIONAL DEFENSE (September 1998).

Pridan-Frank, Shira, *A Challenge to the Rules of the Game of International Law,* 40 COLUM. J. TRANSNAT'L L. 619 (2002).

Programme for Civil Protection Activities, Dutch Presidency of the European Union, July–December 2004 (June 8, 2004).

Proliferation: Threat and Response, U.S. Secretary of State's Report (1997).

Public Health and World Bank Operations, THE INTERNATIONAL BANK FOR RECONSTRUCTION AND DEVELOPMENT, THE WORLD BANK (2002).

Public Health Guidance for Community-Level Preparedness and Response to Severe Acute Respiratory Syndrome (SARS), Department of Health and Human Services, CENTERS FOR DISEASE CONTROL AND PREVENTION (January 8, 2004).

Public Safety WMD Response – Sampling Techniques and Guidelines (Participant Manual), NATIONAL CENTER OF BIOMEDICAL RESEARCH AND TRAINING, Academy of Counter-Terrorist Education, (on file available with author).

Rappert, Brian, *Biological Weapons, Genetics and Social Analysis: Emerging Responses, Emerging Issues.* NEW GENETICS AND SOCIETY, Vol. 22, No. 2 (August 2003).

Recommendations and Reports, Centers for Disease Control and Prevention, MORBIDITY AND MORTALITY WEEKLY REPORT, Vol. 51, No. 19 (December 6, 2002).

Responding to Bioterrorism: AHRQ Helps Clinicians, Health Systems, and Policymakers, AGENCY FOR HEALTHCARE RESEARCH AND QUALITY (October 2001).

Review of the Centers for Disease Control and Prevention's Smallpox Vaccination Program Implementation. Committee on Smallpox Vaccination Program Implementation, Board on Health Promotion and Disease Prevention, INSTITUTE OF MEDICINE, National Academies Press (2003).

Richards, Edward P., et al., *Quarantine Laws and Public Health Realities*, 33 J. L. MED. & ETH. (2005).

Schutzer, Steven E., Bruce Budowle, & Ronald M. Atlas, *Biocrimes, Microbial Forensics, and the Physician*, PLoS MEDICINE, Vol. 2, No. 12 (December 2005).

Schwartz, John, *The Truth Hurts*, NEW YORK TIMES (October 28, 2001).

Sciarrino, Alfred J., *The Grapes of Wrath & the Speckled Monster (Epidemics, Biological Terrorism, and the Early Legal History of Two Major Defenses – Quarantine and Vaccination)*, 7 MICH. ST. J. MED. & LAW 117 (Spring 2003).

Scutchfield, F. Douglas, Carol Ireson, & Laura Hall, *The Voice of the Public in Public Health Policy and Planning: The Role of Public Judgment*, JOURNAL OF PUBLIC HEALTH POLICY, Vol. 25, No. 2 (2004).

Seckinelgin, Hakan, *A Global Disease and Its Governance: HIV/AIDS in Sub-Saharan Africa and the Agency of NGOs*, GLOBAL GOVERNANCE (July 1, 2005).

Sharpe, Kendra V., *Homeland Security Technology*, ISSUES IN SCIENCE AND TECHNOLOGY (Winter 2001–2002).

Sidel, Victor W., & Barry S. Levy, *Security and Public Health*, SOCIAL JUSTICE (September 22, 2002).

Smith v. State, 677 So. 2d 1240, 1245 (Ala. Crim. App. 1995).

Soelberg, Scott D., et al., *A Portable Surface Plasmon Resonance Sensor System for Real-time Monitoring of Small to Large Analytes*, JOURNAL OF INDUSTRIAL MICROBIAL BIOTECHNOLOGY, Vol. 32, No. 11 (December 2005).

Speakman, Jane, et al., *Quarantine in Severe Acute Respiratory Syndrome (SARS) and Other Emerging Infectious Diseases*, 31 J. L. MED. & ETHICS (2003).

Sprinkle, Robert H., *The Biosecurity Trust; Forum*, BIOSCIENCE (March 1, 2003).

Stolberg, Sheryl Gay, *A Nation Challenged: Steps Against Anthrax*, NEW YORK TIMES (January 8, 2002).

Strategic Medical Intelligence Manual, Guidelines and Practices to Support Forensic Epidemiology Investigations, The Strategic Medical Intelligence (SMI) Study Group, University of Pittsburgh Medical Center (May, 17, 2005).

Sutton, Victoria, *Dual Purpose Bioterrorism Investigations in Law Enforcement and Public Health Protection: How to Make Them Work Consistent with the Rule of Law*, 6 Hous. J. HEALTH L. & POL'Y 151 (Fall 2005).

The Significance of Surveillance to Safeguarding American Animal Health, APHIS FACT SHEET, VETERINARY SERVICES (July 2003).

Treadwell, Tracee A., Denise Koo, Kathleen Kuker, & Ali S. Khan, *Epidemiologic Clues to Bioterrorism; Practice Articles*, PUBLIC HEALTH REPORTS, Vol. 118, No. 2 (March 1, 2003).

United States Food Safety System, U.S. Food and Drug Administration, U.S. Department of Agriculture (March 3, 2000).

Update: Adverse Events Following Civilian Smallpox Vaccination, CENTERS FOR DISEASE CONTROL AND PREVENTION, MORBIDITY AND MORTALITY WEEKLY REPORT, Vol. 53 (2003).

Vartabedian, Ralph, *The Nation; U.S. Funnels Billions to Science to Defend Against Terrorism; Air Monitors, National Sensor Networks and GPS Shipping Containers are Some of the Projects*, LOS ANGELES TIMES (March 7, 2004).

Vasterman, Peter, et al., *The Role of the Media and Media Hypes in the Aftermath of Disasters*, EPIDEMIOLOGICAL REVIEWS, Vol. 27 (2005).

Weaver, Jefferson Hane, *Lessons in Multilateral Negotiations: Creating a Remote Sensing Regime*, 7 TEMP. INT'L & COMP. L.J. 29 (Spring 1993).

Weible, Jack, *States Selected to Host Rapid-Assessment Teams*, AIR FORCE TIMES (June 8, 1998).

White House, *G-8 Action Plan on Proliferation*, Federal Document Clearing House, Inc. (June 9, 2004).

Williamson, Kenny Mallow, *Comment: Proving Causation in Acts of Bioterrorism*, 33 CUMB. L. REV. 709 (2002/2003).

Wilson, J. R., Dawn M. Bolen, Michael Dukes, & Steve Faulisi, *Chem/Bio Attacks; Scope of Threats Precludes Near-term Solutions*, ARMED FORCES JOURNAL (March 1, 2004).

Wong, Weng-Keen et al., *Use of Multiple Data Streams to Conduct Bayesian Biologic Surveillance*, The Centers for Disease Control & Prevention, MORBIDITY AND MORTALITY WEEKLY REPORT, Vol. 54, No. 33 (August 26, 2005).

Woo, Gordon, & Andrew Coburn, *The Deadly Plague Returns to America: The Pandemic Scenario*, RISK & INSURANCE, Vol. 15, No. 5 (April 15, 2004).

Yougen Li, Yen Thi Hong Cu, & Dan Luo, *Multiplexed Detection of Pathogen DNA with DNA-based Fluorescence Nanobarcodes*, NATURE BIOTECHNOLOGY, Vol. 23, No. 7 (July 2005).

Zoon, Kathryn C., *Vaccines, Pharmaceutical Products, and Bioterrorism: Challenges for the U.S.* FOOD AND DRUG ADMINISTRATION, *available at* http://www.cdc.gov/ncidod/EID/vol5no4/zoon.htm.

Chapter 8

Alexander, John B. (Col.), WINNING THE WAR: ADVANCED WEAPONS, STRATEGIES, AND CONCEPTS FOR THE POST-9/11 WORLD, THOMAS DUNNE BOOKS (2003).

Alexander, Lexi R., & Julia L. Klare, *Nonlethal Weapons: New Tools for Peace*, ISSUES IN SCIENCE AND TECHNOLOGY, Vol. 12 (Winter 1995/1996).

Allison, Graham T., Paul X. Kelley, & Richard L. Garwin, *Nonlethal Weapons and Capabilities*, COUNCIL ON FOREIGN RELATIONS (2004).

America Accused of Violating the Biological and Toxins Weapons Convention, CBW CHRONICLE, Vol. II, No. 3 (October 1997).

Ames, Ben, *Nanotechnology Delivers Military Power*, MILITARY & AEROSPACE ELECTRONICS, Vol. 16, No. 5 (May 1, 2005).

Annex on the Protection of Confidential Information, General Principles for the Handling of Confidential Information, attached to the *Convention on the Prohibition of the Development, Production, Stockpiling, and Use of Chemical Weapons and on their Destruction* (May 16, 1997).

Arestie, Lauren, *Issue Brief: The Russian Biological Weapons Complex*, Russian American Nuclear Security Advisory Council (March 2003).

Arms Control: Efforts to Strengthen the Biological Weapons Convention, GAO Report to the Chairman, Subcommittee on National Security, Veterans Affairs, and International Relations, Committee on Government Reform, House of Representatives (September 2002).

Badkhen, Anna, *Fear Follows Plan to Build More Deadly-Disease Labs*, SAN FRANCISCO CHRONICLE (August 22, 2004).

Biden, Joseph (D-DE, Senator, Chairman), *Panel II of a Hearing of the Senate Foreign Relations Committee*, FEDERAL NEWS SERVICE (March 19, 2002).

Biological Science and Biotechnology in Russia: Controlling Diseases and Enhancing Security, Committee on Future Contributions of the Biosciences to Public Health, Agriculture, Basic Research, Counter-Terrorism, and Non-Proliferation Activities in Russia, NATIONAL RESEARCH COUNCIL OF THE NATIONAL ACADEMIES (2005).

Biological Weapons Anti-Terrorism Act of 1989, 18 U.S.C.S. § 175, 178 (1994).

Carafano, James Jay, *Sustaining Military Capabilities in the 21st Century: Rethinking the Utility of the Principles of War*, HERITAGE FOUNDATION REPORTS (September 6, 2005).

Case Study: Yellow Rain. Fact Sheet. BUREAU OF VERIFICATION, COMPLIANCE, AND IMPLEMENTATION (October 1, 2005).

Compliance (Article 34), Procedures and Mechanisms on Compliance under the Cartagena Protocol on Biosafety, Conference of the Parties to the Convention on Biological Diversity Serving as the Meeting of the Parties to the Cartagena Protocol on Biosafety, UNEP/CBD/BS/COP-MOP/1/8 (November 18, 2003).

Coppernoll, Margaret-Anne (Lieutenant Colonel), *The Non-Lethal Weapons Debate*, NAVAL WAR COLLEGE REVIEW, Vol. 52, No. 2 (Spring 1999).

Country Overviews: Cuba: Biological Overview. NUCLEAR THREAT INITIATIVE, *available at* http://www.nti.org/e_research/profiles/Cuba/Biological/index.html#fnB34.

Dando, Malcolm, A NEW FORM OF WARFARE, Potomac Books (1996).

Davison, Neil, & Nick Lewer, *Bradford Non-Lethal Weapons Research Project*, Bradford University (May 2004).

Deller, Nicole, & John Burroughs, *Arms Control Abandoned: The Case of Biological Weapons*, WORLD POLICY INSTITUTE WORLD POLICY JOURNAL, Vol. 20, No 2 (June 22, 2003).

DoD Directive 3000.3, *Policy for Non-Lethal Weapons* (July 9, 1996).

Draft Recommendations for a Code of Conduct for Biodefense Programs, FEDERATION OF AMERICAN SCIENTISTS (FAS) WORKING GROUP ON BW (November 2002).

Duncan, James C. (Lieutenant Colonel), *A Primer on the Employment of Nonlethal Weapons*, XLV NAVAL L. REV. (1998).

Enhanced Degradation of Military Material. Available at http://www.sunshine-project.org/incapacitants/jnlwdpdf/nrlbwp.pdf.

Estabrooks, Sarah, & Robin Collins, *A Step in the Right Direction: The Global Partnership Against the Spread of Weapons and Materials of Mass Destruction*, PLOUGHSHARES MONITOR, Vol. 26, No. 3 (September 22, 2005).

Extramural Construction of Biosafety Laboratories, Website of the NATIONAL INSTITUTE OF ALLERGY AND INFECTIOUS DISEASES, *available at* http://www3.niaid.nih. gov/Biodefense/Research/rbl.htm

Fidler, David P., *The International Legal Implications of Nonlethal Weapons*, 21 MICH. J. INT'L L. 51 (Fall 1999).

Fraser, Claire M., & Malcolm R. Dando, *Genomics and Future Biological Weapons: The Need for Preventative Action by the Biomedical Community*, NATURE GENETICS, Vol. 29 (November 2001).

Fumento, Michael, BIOEVOLUTION – HOW BIOTECHNOLOGY IS CHANGING OUR WORLD, Encounter Books (2003).

G-8 Action Plan on Nonproliferation, REGULATORY INTELLIGENCE DATA (June 9, 2004).

Guidelines for Procedures on the Release of Classified Information by the OPCW, OPCW C-I/DEC. 13 (May 16, 1997).

Hannigan, Timothy, Lori Raff, & Rod Paschall, *Mission Applications of Nonlethal Weapons*, Jaycor Technical Study for The Office of the Assistant Secretary of Defense for Special Operations and Low Intensity Conflict (August 1996).

Hart, John, Frida Kuhlau, & Jacqueline Simon, *Chemical and Biological Weapon Developments and Arms Control*, SIPRI Yearbook 2003: Armaments, Disarmament and International Security, NON-PROLIFERATION, ARMS CONTROL, DISARMAMENT (2002).

Hearing before the House Armed Service Committee, (October 20, 1999), Statement of The Honorable Hans Mark.

Hearing before the House Government Reform Committee, Subcommittee on National Security, Veterans Affairs and International Relations, on *The Biological Weapons Convention Protocol: Status and Implications* (June 5, 2001), Statement of Donald Mahley.

Hearing before the House Homeland Security Committee, Prevention of Nuclear and Biological Attack Subcommittee, on *Engineering Biological Weapons* (July 13, 2005), Testimony of Michael V. Callahan.

Hearing before the House Select Homeland Security Committee, on *National Biodefense Strategy* (June 3, 2004), Testimonies of Anthony S. Fauci and Dr. Penrose C. Albright.

Hearing of the National Security, Veterans Affairs and International Relations Sub-committee of the House Government Reform Committee, on *Biological Weapons Convention* (September 13, 2000).

Hearing of the Western Hemisphere, Peace Corps, and Narcotics Affairs Subcom-mittee of the Senate Foreign Relations Committee, on *Cuba's Pursuit of Biological Weapons: Fact or Fiction?* (June 5, 2002).

Hearings before the Committee on National Security, House of Representatives, on *National Defense Authorization Act for Fiscal Year 2000 – H.R. 1401 and Oversight of Previously Authorized Programs* 106th Congress, 1st Session (March 11, 1999), Statement of William F. Raub Ph.D.

Is Non-Proliferation Policy Heading for Failure?, Conference (February 10–12, 2006).

Ji-Wei, Guo, & Xue-Sen Yang, *Ultramicro, Nonlethal, and Reversible: Looking Ahead to Military Biotechnology; Transformation*, MILITARY REVIEW, Vol. 85, No. 4 (July 1, 2005).

Kahn, Laura H., *Biodefense Research: Can Secrecy and Safety Coexist?* BIOSECURITY AND BIOTERRORISM: BIODEFENSE STRATEGY, PRACTICE, AND SCIENCE, Vol. 2, No. 2 (2004).

Keefer, Scott, *International Control of Biological Weapons*, 6 ILSA J INT'L & COMP L 107 (Fall 1999).

Kellman, Barry, *A Comparative Study of the Legal Implementation of the Chemical Weapons Convention in Foreign Jurisdictions* (DNA-TR-93-59) (1993).

Kellman, Barry, David S. Gualtieri; Kenneth E. Apt; & Edward A. Tanzman, *Advancing the Law of Weapons Control – Comparative Approaches to Strengthen Nuclear Non-Proliferation*, 16 Mich. J. Int'l L. 1029 (1995).

Kellman, Barry, *Applicability of Chemical Weapons Convention Verification Provisions for Strengthening the Nuclear Non-Proliferation Regime*, DRAFT REPORT FOR THE DOE INTERNATIONAL SAFEGUARDS DIVISION (October 1994).

Kellman, Barry, *Ballistic Missile Defense in the Context of Multilateral, Multi-Faceted Security*, 4 NEXUS J. OP. 73 (1999).

Kellman, Barry, *Bridling the International Trade of Catastrophic Weaponry*, 43 AM. U. L. REV. 3 (Spring 1994).

Kellman, Barry, *International Consensus and States Non-Parties*, in FUTURE LEGAL RESTRAINTS ON ARMS PROLIFERATION: ARMS CONTROL & DISARMAMENT LAW, United Nations (Julie Dahlitz, ed., 1996).

Kellman, Barry, MANUAL FOR NATIONAL IMPLEMENTATION OF THE CHEMICAL WEAPONS CONVENTION (2nd edition, February 1998, published in English and Arabic) (1st edition, December 1993).

Kellman, Barry, *National Missile Defense and the ABM Treaty: Considerations of International Security and Law* 5 J. CONFLICT & SECURITY LAW 281 (2000).

Kellman, Barry, *State Responsibility for Preventing Bioterrorism*, INTERNATIONAL LAWYER (2002).

Kellman, Barry, *The Advent of International Chemical Regulation – The Chemical Weapons Convention Implementation Act*, 25 J. LEG.117 (1999).

Kellman, Barry, *The Draft Model Convention on the Prohibition and Prevention of Biological Terrorism*, 14 TERRORISM AND POLITICAL VIOLENCE (2002).

Kellman, Barry, *The Role of Nuclear Weapons in Deterring Chemical/Biological Weapons Attacks: National and Non-national Threats*, 31 CASE W. RES. J. INT'L L. 619 (1999).

Kellman, Barry, *WMD Proliferation – An International Crime?*, NONPROLIFERATION REVIEW (Spring 2001).

Kelly, David C., *The Trilateral Agreement: Lessons for Biological Weapons Verification*, VERIFICATION YEARBOOK 2002 (2002).

Koblentz, Gregory, *Pathogens as Weapons; The International Security Implications of Biological Warfare*, INTERNATIONAL SECURITY (Winter 2004).

Kohler, Michael, & Wolfgang Fritzsche, NANOTECHNOLOGY: AN INTRODUCTION TO NANOSTRUCTURING TECHNIQUES, Wiley VCH (2004).

Koplow, David, NONLETHAL WEAPONS: THE LAW AND POLICY OF REVOLUTIONARY TECHNOLOGIES FOR THE MILITARY AND LAW ENFORCEMENT, Cambridge University Press (2006).

Koplow, David, *Tangled up in Khaki and Blue: Lethal and Non-Lethal Weapons in Recent Confrontations*, 36 GEO. J. INT'L L. 703 (Spring 2005).

Laws and Regulations Governing the Protection of Sensitive but Unclassified Information, A Report prepared by the Federal Research Division, Library of Congress under an Interagency Agreement with the NASA Office of Inspector General (September 2004).

Leitenberg, Milton, *Biological Weapons in the Twentieth Century: A Review and Analysis*, Report prepared for the 7th International Symposium on Protection against Chemical and Biological Warfare, CRITICAL REVIEWS IN MICROBIOLOGY (2001).

Leitenberg, Milton, *Distinguishing Offensive from Defensive Biological Weapons Research*, CRITICAL REVIEWS IN METHODOLOGY, Vol. 29, No. 3 (2003).

Littlewood, Jez, THE BIOLOGICAL WEAPONS CONVENTION: A FAILED REVOLUTION, Ashgate (2005).

Luongo, Kenneth N., et al., *Building a Forward Line of Defense Securing Former Soviet Biological Weapons*, ARMS CONTROL TODAY (July/August 2004).

Media Briefing with Secretary of Homeland Security Tom Ridge; Secretary of Health and Human Services Tommy Thomson; and Deputy Secretary of Defense Paul Wolfowitz, *Biodefense for the 21st Century*, Location: Auditorium, Health and Human Services (April 28, 2004).

Melson, Ashley R., *Bioterrorism, Biodefense, and Biotechnology in the Military: A Comparative Analysis of Legal and Ethical Issues in the Research, Development, and Use of Biotechnological Products on American and British Soldiers*, 14 ALB. L.J. SCI. & TECH. 497 (2004).

Memorandum: Preliminary Legal Review of Proposed Chemical-Based Nonlethal Weapons, Naval Security Law Branch, Department of the Navy, Office of the Judge Advocate General, International and Operational Law Division (November 30, 1997).

Meselson, Matthew, & Julian Robinson, *A Draft Convention to Prohibit Biological and Chemical Weapons Under International Criminal Law*, FLETCHER F. WORLD AFF. 28 (Winter 2004).

Miller, Judith, Stephen Engelberg, & William J. Broad, *U.S. Germ Warfare Research Pushes Treaty Limits*, NEW YORK TIMES (September 4, 2001).

Miller, Judith, *New Biolabs Stir a Debate Over Secrecy and Safety*, NEW YORK TIMES (February 20, 2004).

Monath, Thomas, & Lance Gordon, *Strengthening the Biological Weapons Convention*, SCIENCE, Vol. 282 (November 20, 1998).

Moodie, Michael, *Weapons of Mass Destruction and the Proliferation Dilemma: Confronting the Biological and Chemical Weapons Challenge: The Need for an "Intellectual Infrastructure,"* 28 FLETCHER F. WORLD AFF. 43 (Winter 2004).

Non-Lethal Weapons Research in the U.S.: Genetically Engineered Anti-Material Weapons, THE SUNSHINE PROJECT, Backgrounder Series, Number 9 (March 2002).

Olson, Inga, *Nuclear Labs Move into the "Biodefense" Business; Biodevastation 7*, SYNTHESIS REGENERATION, No. 34 (March 22, 2004).

Ostrander, Jeremy, *Between Empire and Community: The United States and Multilateralism 2001–2003*, 21 BERKELEY J. INT'L L. 495 (2003).

Panofsky, Wolfgang K. H., *Dismantling the Concept of "Weapons of Mass Destruction,"* ARMS CONTROL TODAY (April 1998).

Parachini, John V., et al., DIVERSION OF NUCLEAR, BIOLOGICAL, AND CHEMICAL WEAPONS EXPERTISE FROM THE FORMER SOVIET UNION – UNDERSTANDING AN EVOLVING PROBLEM, RAND Corporation (2005).

Paris, Kristen, *The Expansion of the Biological Weapons Convention: The History and Problems of a Verification Regime*, 24 HOUS. J. INT'L L. 509 (Spring 2002).

Pearson, Graham S., *Scientific and Technical Implications of the Implementation of the BTWC Protocol*, Report of the NATO Advanced Research Workshop Warsaw, Poland (November 2–4, 2000).

Pearson, Graham S., *The Protocol to Strengthen the BTWC: An Integrated Regime*, POLITICS AND THE LIFE SCIENCES, Vol. 17, No. 2 (1998).

Pearson, Graham, *The Biological Weapons Convention Sixth Review Conference*, The CBS Conventions Bulletin, Issue 74 (December 2006).

Pettitt, Leah, *Weapons of Mass Destruction Stockpiled in Russia: Should the United States Continue to Implement Programs Designed to Reduce and Safeguard These Weapons?* 16 TRANSNAT'L LAW 169 (Fall 2002).

Pinson, Robert D., *Is Nanotechnology Prohibited by the Biological and Chemical Weapons Conventions?*, 22 BERKELEY J. INT'L L. 279 (2004).

Posteraro, Christopher Clarke, *Intervention in Iraq: Towards a Doctrine of Anticipatory Counter-Terrorism, Counter-Proliferation Intervention*, 15 FLORIDA J. INT'L LAW (Fall 2002).

Practice Randomly Selected Transparency Visit to a Biodefense Facility, BWC/AD HOC GROUP/WP.437 (December 13, 2000).

Rennack, Dianne E., NUCLEAR, BIOLOGICAL, CHEMICAL, AND MISSILE PROLIFERATION SANCTIONS: SELECTED CURRENT LAW, Library of Congress. Congressional Research Service (1998).

Rissanen, Jenni, *Continued Turbulence Over BWC Verification*, VERIFICATION YEARBOOK 2002 (December 2002).

Roberts, Guy, *Arms Control Without Arms Control: The Failure of the Biological Weapons Convention Protocol and a New Paradigm for Fighting the Threat of Biological Weapons*, INSS Occasional Paper #49, INSTITUTE FOR NATIONAL SECURITY STUDIES (March 2003).

Robinson, Clarence A. Jr., *Missile Technology Access Emboldens Rogue Nations*, SIGNAL (April 1999).

Rosenberg, Barbara Hatch, *Defending Against Biodefense: The Need for Limits*, DISARMAMENT DIPLOMACY, No. 69 (February/March 2003).

Russell, Ron, *A Question of Risk: Plans for a Biodefense "Hot Lab" at Lawrence Livermore Have Ecologists, Disarmament Advocates, and Mainstream Scientists Up in Arms*, SF WEEKLY (January 28, 2004).

Secret Biodefense Activities Are Undermining the Norm Against Biological Weapons, Working Group on Biological Weapons, Position Paper, FEDERATION OF AMERICAN SCIENTISTS (January 2003).

Seven Good Reasons to Stand Up for Information Freedom on Bioweapons Research: And What Agendas May Be at Work to Squelch the Public's Right to Know, THE SUNSHINE PROJECT, News Release (October 30, 2001).

Shea, Dana, *The National Biodefense Analysis and Countermeasures Center: Issues for Congress*, CRS REPORT FOR CONGRESS (April 25, 2005).

Sidawi, Danielle, & Skip Derraf, *Proteomics' Growing Role in Biodefense*, R AND D (July 1, 2005).

Sims, Nicholas A., *The Evolution of Biological Disarmament*, Stockholm International Peace Research Institute (2001).

Sims, Nicholas A., *The New Multilateral Approach for the BTWC: Ambiguities and Opportunities, Briefing Paper No. 2 (Second Series)*, University of Bradford (UK) Department of Peace Studies (January 2003).

Siniscalchi, Joseph, *Non-Lethal Technologies: Implications for Military Strategy*, Occasional Paper No. 3, CENTER FOR STRATEGY AND TECHNOLOGY (March 1998).

Smith, Bradley T.; Thomas V. Inglesby, & Tara O'Toole, *Biodefense R & D: Anticipating Future Threats, Establishing a Strategic Environment*, BIOSECURITY AND BIOTERRORISM: BIODEFENSE STRATEGY, PRACTICE AND SCIENCE, Vol. 1, No. 3 (2003).

State Department, *New Law to Provide Medical Countermeasures Against WMD Attack; Bush Signed Bill to Improve Homeland Security*, Federal Information and News Dispatch (July 22, 2004).

Statement by the International Committee of the Red Cross, Geneva. First Special Session of the Conference of the States Parties to Review the Operation of the Chemical Weapons Convention. First Review Conference, The Hague (April 28– May 9, 2003).

Stern, Jessica, *Dreaded Risks and the Control of Biological Weapons*, INTERNATIONAL SECURITY (Winter 2002/2003).

Stockman, Farah, *Weapons 'Inspectors,' Canadian Activists Plan to Spotlight U.S. Research on Germ, Chemical Warfare*, BOSTON GLOBE (December 30, 2002).

Sutton, Victoria, *Biodefense: Who's In Charge?*, HEALTH MATRIX, Vol. 13, No. 117 (2003).

Technical Justification for Limited Size of the Area of Investigation, BWC/AD HOC GROUP/WP.434 (November 28, 2000).

The Convention on the Prohibition of the Development, Production, and Stockpiling of Bacteriological (Biological) and Toxin Weapons and on their Destruction, 26 U.S.T. 583; T.I.A.S. 8062; 1015 U.N.T.S. 163 (Signed April 10, 1972; entered into force March 26, 1976).

Thompson, Craig, *Missing Links . . . Genetically Altered Biological Weaponry: A Gift from the Biopreparat to the World Part One*, JOURNAL OF COUNTERTERRORISM & HOMELAND SECURITY INTERNATIONAL (Spring 2003).

Thränert, Oliver, *The Compliance Protocol and the Three Depository Powers*, in BIOLOGICAL WARFARE AND DISARMAMENT: NEW PROBLEMS/NEW PERSPECTIVES, Susan Wright (ed.), Rowman & Littlefield Publishers, (2002).

Toje, Asle, *Time to Change the Rules? The EU Response to WMD and Weapons of Minimal Destruction proliferation*, EU POLICY NETWORK *available at* http://www.europeananalysis.com/research/toje1.pdf

Toner, Mike, *World Argues Biological Arms Ban*, ATLANTA JOURNAL-CONSTITUTION (November 10, 2002).

Tornudd, Klaus, *Disarmament Processes for a World at Peace in Twenty Years*, DISARMAMENT(1997).

Trial Inspection of a Biological Production Facility, Working Paper Submitted by Australia, The Ad Hoc Group of the States Parties to the Convention on the Prohibition of the Development, Production, and Stockpiling of Bacteriological and Toxin Weapons and on Their Destruction, BWC/AD HOC GROUP/WP.77 (July 18, 1996).

Tucker, Jonathan B, *A Farewell to Germs; The U.S. Renunciation of Biological and Toxin Warfare, 1969–70*, INTERNATIONAL SECURITY (Summer 2002).

Tucker, Jonathan B., *Strengthening the BWC: A Way Forward*, DISARMAMENT DIPLOMACY, Issue No. 78 (July/August 2004).

U.S. Special Forces Seek Genetically Engineered Bioweapons, THE SUNSHINE PROJECT, News Release (August 12, 2002).

Weapons of Mass Destruction: Additional Russian Cooperation Needed to Facilitate U.S. Efforts to Improve Security at Russian Sites, GAO REPORT GAO-03-482 (March 24, 2003).

Wheelis, Mark, & Malcolm Dando, *Back to Bioweapons?*, BULLETIN OF THE ATOMIC SCIENTISTS, Vol. 59, No. 1 (January/February 2003).

Wheelis, Mark, *"Nonlethal" Chemical Weapons: A Faustian Bargain*, ISSUES IN SCIENCE AND TECHNOLOGY (Spring 2003).

Wheelis, Mark, *Biotechnology and Biochemical Weapons*, NONPROLIFERATION REVIEW, Vol. 9, No. 1 (Spring 2002).

Wheelis, Mark, *Investigating Disease Outbreaks under a Protocol to the Biological and Toxin Weapons Convention*, EMERGING INFECTIOUS DISEASES, Vol. 6, No. 6 (November–December 2000).

Winner, Andrew C., *The Proliferation Security Initiative: The New Face of Interdiction*, WASHINGTON QUARTERLY, Vol. 28, No. 2 (Spring 2005).

Working Paper submitted by China, Cuba, India, Indonesia, the Islamic Republic of Iran, Mexico, and Pakistan, The Ad Hoc Group of the States Parties to the Convention on the Prohibition of the Development, Production, and Stockpiling of Bacteriological and Toxin Weapons and on Their Destruction, BWC/AD HOC GROUP/WP.432 (November 23, 2000).

Working Paper submitted by the Group of NAM and Other Countries, Establishment of a Cooperation Committee, The Ad Hoc Group of the States Parties to the Convention on the Prohibition of the Development, Production, and Stockpiling of Bacteriological and Toxin Weapons and on Their Destruction, BWC/AD HOC GROUP/WP.349 (January 1999).

Working Paper submitted by the Netherlands and New Zealand BWC Article X/Protocol Article VII, The Ad Hoc Group of the States Parties to the Convention on the Prohibition of the Development, Production, and Stockpiling of Bacteriological and Toxin Weapons and on Their Destruction (April 1999).

Wright, Susan, (ed.), BIOLOGICAL WARFARE AND DISARMAMENT: NEW PROBLEMS/NEW PERSPECTIVES, Rowman & Littlefield Publishers (2002).

Wright, Susan, *Taking Biodefense Too Far: The United States is Developing a Costly Bioumbrella to Protect Its Citizens Against Biothreats that Do Not Now – and May Never – Exist*, BULLETIN OF THE ATOMIC SCIENTISTS, Vol. 60, No. 6 (November 1, 2004).

Chapter 9

A More Secure World: Our Shared Responsibility, Report of the High-level Panel on Threats, Challenges, and Change, United Nations General Assembly, 59th Session, UN Doc. A/59/565 (December 2, 2004)

Adams, William. M., et al., *Biodiversity Conservation and the Eradication of Poverty*, SCIENCE (November 12, 2004).

Aginam, Obijiofor, GLOBAL HEALTH GOVERNANCE: INTERNATIONAL LAW AND PUBLIC HEALTH IN A DIVIDED WORLD, University of Toronto Press (2005).

Alexander, David, *Globalization of Disaster: Trends, Problems and Dilemmas*, JOURNAL OF INTERNATIONAL AFFAIRS, Vol. 59, No. 2 (March 22, 2006).

Alvarez, Jose E., *The Quest for Legitimacy*, 24 N.Y.U. J. INT'L L. & POL. 199 (1991).

American Interests and UN Reform, Report on the Task Force on the United Nations, UNITED STATES INSTITUTE OF PEACE (June 15, 2005).

Annex on the Protection of Confidential Information to the Chemical Weapons Convention, ORGANIZATION FOR THE PROHIBITION OF CHEMICAL WEAPONS (2005).

Arzberger, Peter, et al., *An International Framework to Promote Access to Data; Science and Government*, SCIENCE (March 19, 2004).

Badar, Mohamed Elewa, *From the Nuremberg Charter to the Rome Statute: Defining the Elements of Crimes Against Humanity*, 5 SAN DIEGO INT'L L.J. 73 (2004).

Banerjee, Subhabrata Bobby, *Who Sustains Whose Development? Sustainable Development and the Reinvention of Nature*, ORGANIZATION STUDIES (January 1, 2003).

Barnett, Michael N., & Martha Finnermore, *The Politics, Power, and Pathologies of International Organizations*, INTERNATIONAL ORGANIZATION, Vol. 53, No. 4 (Autumn 1999).

Batson, Amie, & Matthias M. Bekier, *Vaccines Where They're Needed; Financing Research*, MCKINSEY QUARTERLY (September 22, 2001).

Bausch, Daniel, *The Ebola-virus:...and the Challenges to Health Research in Africa*, UN CHRONICLE, Vol. 38, No. 2 (June 1, 2001).

Biermann, Frank., & Steffen Bauer, A WORLD ENVIRONMENT ORGANIZATION, Ashgate (2006).

Biotechnology for Sustainable Growth and Development, ORGANISATION FOR ECONOMIC CO-OPERATION AND DEVELOPMENT (2004).

Biotechnology Sparks an Industrial Revolution; Pulping, BIOTECHNOLOGY INDUSTRY ORGANIZATION (October 1, 2004).

Bishop, David, *Lessons from SARS: Why the WHO Must Provide Greater Economic Incentives for Countries to Comply with International Health Regulations; Severe Acute Respiratory Syndrome*, GEO. J. INT'L L. (June 22, 2005).

Blix, Dr. Hans, *Freidman Award Address: Developing International Law and Inducing Compliance*, 41 COLUM. J. TRANSNAT'L L. 1 (2002).

Bluemel, Erik B., *Separating Instrumental from Intrinsic Rights: Toward an Understanding of Indigenous Participation in International Rule-Making*, 30 AM. INDIAN L. REV. 55 (2005/2006).

Bone, Paula F., & Karen Russo France, *International Harmonization of Food and Nutrition Regulation: The Good and the Bad*, JOURNAL OF PUBLIC POLICY & MARKETING, Vol. 22, No. 1 (Spring 2003).

Bradford, William, *International Legal Compliance: Surveying the Field*, 36 GEO. J. INT'L L. 495 (Winter 2005).

Brunnee, Jutta, *A Fine Balance: Facilitation and Enforcement in the Design of a Compliance Regime for the Kyoto Protocol*, 13 TUL. ENVTL. L.J. 223 (Summer 2000).

Buchanan, Allen, & Robert O. Keohane, *The Legitimacy of Global Governance Institutions*, ETHICS & INTERNATIONAL AFFAIRS (December 1, 2006).

Burris, Scott, *Governance, Microgovernance, and Health*, 77 TEMP. L. REV. 335 (Summer 2004).

Busch, Per-Olof; Helge Jorgens; & Kerstin Tews, *The Rise of Regulatory Capitalism: The Global Diffusion of a New Order: Special Editors: David Levi-Faur, Jacint Jordana: Section Three: The Diffusion of Social Regulations: The Global Diffusion of Regulatory Instruments: The Making of a New International Environmental Regime*, 598 ANNALS 146 (March 2005).

Capacity-Building for Implementation of the Cartagena Protocol on Biosafety, United Nations Environment Programme Convention on Biological Diversity, UNEP/CBD/BS/COP-MOP/MISC/2004/2 (October 31, 2003).

Caron, David D., *The Legitimacy of the Collective Authority of the Security Council*, 87 A.J.I.L. 552 (1993).

Cassese, Sabino, *Global Standards for National Administrative Procedure*, 68 L. & CONTEMP. PROBS. 109 (October 12, 2005).

Charnovitz, Steve, *The Boundaries of the WTO: Triangulating the WTO*, 96 AM. J. INT'L L. 28 (2002).

Charnovitz, Steve, *Triangulating the World Trade Organization*, 96 AM. J. INT'L L. (January 2002).

Chichilnisky, Graciela, *What is Sustainable Development? Special Issue: Defining Sustainability*, LAND ECONOMICS, Vol. 73, No. 4 (November, 1997).

Cissé, M. K., Sokona, Y., & Thomas, J-Philippe, *Capacity Building: Lessons from Sub-Saharan Africa*, ENVIRONNEMENT ET DÉVELOPPEMENT DU TIERS-MONDE (ENDA-TM) (1999).

Cohen, William S., *NATO at 50: New Challenges in a New Age*, DEFENSE ISSUES, Vol. 13, No. 17 (1998).

Convention on Access to Information, Public Participation in Decision-Making and Access to Justice in Environmental Matters, 2161 *U.N.T.S.* 447 (June 25, 1998).

Cornish, Edward et al., *The Opportunity Century; Forecasting the Future*, FUTURIST, Vol. 34, No. 1 (January 1, 2000).

Council on Foreign Relations Meeting, *The Nexus of Science and Foreign Policy: U.S. Biotechnology and Global Competitiveness*, FEDERAL NEWS SERVICE (November 23, 2005).

Crossen, Teall, *Multilateral Environmental Agreements and the Compliance Continuum*, 16 GEO. INT'L ENVT'L. L. REV. 473 (Spring 2004).

Crow, Melissa E., *Smokescreens and State Responsibility: Using Human Rights Strategies to Promote Global Tobacco Control*, 29 YALE J. INT'L L. 209 (Winter 2004).

Daar, Abdullah S., & Peter A. Singer, *Biotechnology and Human Security*, HELSINKI PROCESS PAPERS ON HUMAN SECURITY (2005).

Davis, Stan, *Beyond the Information Age – Biotech and nanotech Could Become the Basis of the Next Economic Shift; It's Time to Begin Thinking About Aligning IT and Business Strategies to the New Model*, OPTIMIZE (December 1, 2002).

Dempsey, Paul Stephen, *Compliance and Enforcement in International Law: Achieving Global Uniformity in Aviation Safety*, 30 N.C.J. INT'L L. & COM. REG. 1 (Fall 2004).

Dennis, Michael J., & David P. Stewart, *Justiciability of Economic, Social, and Cultural Rights: Should There be an International Complaints Mechanism to Adjudicate the Rights to Food, Water, Housing, and Health?*, 98 AM. J. INT'L L. 462 (July 2004).

Downs, George W. et al., *The Transformational Model of International Regime Design: Triumph of Hope or Experience?*, 38 COLUM. J. TRANSNAT'L L. 465 (2000).

Duffey, William S., Jr., *Public Health and Law Enforcement: Intersecting Interests, Collegiality, and Cooperation*, 32 J. L. MED. & ETHICS (Winter 2004).

Eckert, Amy E., & Manooher Mofidi, *Doctrine or Doctrinaire – The First Strike Doctrine and Preemptive Self-Defense Under International Law*, 12 TUL. J. INT'L & COMP. L. 117 (Spring 2004).

Ehrmann, Markus, *Procedures of Compliance Control in International Environmental Treaties*, 13 COLO. J. INT'L ENVTL. L. & POL'Y 377 (Summer 2002).

Esty, Daniel C., *Good Governance at the Supranational Scale: Globalizing Administrative Law*, 115 YALE L. J. 1490 (2006).

Etzioni, Amitai, *Commentary on the Need for More Transnational Capacity*, 56 FLA. L. REV. 921 (December 2004).

Ferrone, Jason D., *Compulsory Licensing During Public Health Crises: Bioterrorism's Mark on Global Pharmaceutical Patent Protection*, 26 SUFFOLK TRANSNAT'L L. REV. 385 (Summer 2003).

Fidler, David P., *Caught Between Paradise and Power: Public Health, Pathogenic Threats, and the Axis of Illness*, 35 MCGEORGE L. REV. 45 (2004).

Fischer-Lescano, Andreas, & Gunther Teubner, (translated by Michelle Everson), *Diversity or Cacophony?: New Sources of Norms in International Law Symposium: Article: Regime-Collisions: The Vain Search for Legal Unity in the Fragmentation of Global Law*, 25 MICH. J. INT'L L. 999 (Summer 2004).

Franck, Thomas M., THE POWER OF LEGITIMACY AMONG NATIONS, Oxford University Press (1990).

Frischmann, Brett, *A Dynamic Institutional Theory of International Law*, 51 BUFFALO L. REV. 679 (Summer 2003).

Gamble, John King, Charlotte Ku, & Chris Strayer, *Human-Centric International Law: A Model and a Search for Empirical Indicators*, 14 TUL. J. INT'L & COMP. L. 61 (Winter 2005).

Genomics and World Health, Report of the World Health Organization (2002).

Georgiev, Dencho, *Politics or Rule of Law: Deconstruction and Legitimacy in International Law*, 4 EUR. J. INT'L L. 1 (1993).

Gilbert, Tal, & Leah Gilbert, *Globalisation and Local Power: Influences on Health Matters in South Africa*, HEALTH POLICY, Vol. 67 (2004).

Global Funding for HIV/AIDS in Resource Poor Settings, THE HENRY J. KAISER FAMILY FOUNDATION (December 2003).

Globalization and Interdependence: Implementation of General Assembly Resolution 58/200 Science and Technology for Development, Report by the Secretary-General, United Nations A/60/184 (August 2, 2005).

Globalization and New Epidemics: Ethics, Security and Policy Making, BIOETHICAL IMPLICATIONS OF GLOBALIZATION PROCESSES (May 23, 2006).

Gostin, Lawrence O., THE AIDS PANDEMIC: COMPLACENCY, INJUSTICE, AND UNFULFILLED EXPECTATIONS, University of North Carolina Press (2004).

Gostin, Lawrence O., *World Health Law: Toward a New Conception of Global Health Governance for the 21st Century*, 5 YALE J. HEALTH POL'Y L. & ETHICS 413 (Winter 2005).

GOVERNANCE AND PUBLIC SECURITY, Campbell Public Affairs Institute (January 2002).

Gruskin, Sofia, *Is there a Government in the Cockpit: A Passenger's Perspective or Global Public Health: The Role of Human Rights*, 77 TEMP. L. REV. (Summer 2004).

Guzman, Andrew T., *A Compliance-Based Theory of International Law*, 90 CALIF. L. REV. 1823 (December 2002).

Hall, Jonathan, et al., *Forging Community Legal Partnerships, Public Health and Law Enforcement: Future Directions*, 32 J. L., MED. & ETHICS (Winter 2004).

Hasenclever, Andreas; Peter Mayer; & Volker Rittberger, *Interests, Power, Knowledge: The Study of International Regimes*, MERSHON INTERNATIONAL STUDIES REVIEW, Vol. 40, No. 2 (October 1996).

Hathaway, Oona A., *The Cost of Commitment*, 55 STAN. L. REV. 1821 (May 2003).

Helfer, Laurence R., *Understanding Change in International Organizations: Globalization and Innovation in the ILO*, 59 VAND. L. REV. 649 (April 2006).

Henisz, Witold J., Zelner, Bennet A., & Guillen, Mauro F., *International Coercion, Emulation and Policy Diffusion: Market-Oriented Infrastructure Reforms, 1977–1999*, REGINALD H. JONES CENTER FOR MANAGEMENT POLICY, STRATEGY AND ORGANIZATION AT THE WHARTON SCHOOL (June 17, 2004).

Hockett, Robert, *From Macro to Micro to "Mission-Creep": Defending the IMF's Emerging Concern with the Infrastructural Prerequisites to Global Financial Stability*, 41 COLUM. J. TRANSNAT'L L. 153 (2002).

Jackson, Robert, THE GLOBAL COVENANT – HUMAN CONDUCT IN A WORLD OF STATES, Oxford University Press (2000).

Jagers, Sverker C., & Johannes Stripple, *Climate Governance Beyond the State*, GLOBAL GOVERNANCE (July 1, 2003).

Jinks, Derek, *September 11 and the Laws of War*, 28 YALE J. INT'L L. 1 (Winter 2003).

Juma, Calestous, *Biotechnology in a Globalizing World: the Coevolution of Technology and Social Institutions*, BIOSCIENCE, Vol. 55, No. 3 (March 1, 2005).

Kahn, Paul W., *Balance of Power: Redefining Sovereignty in Contemporary International Law: Article: The Question of Sovereignty*, 40 SAN. J. INT'L L. 259 (Summer 2004).

Kazemi, Nahal, *Ill At Ease: The Precarious State of the Biological Weapons Convention's Proposed Enforcement Regime*, 17 FLA. J. INT'L L. 137 (March 2005).

Kellman, Barry, *Elements of a Prospective Regional Security Regime in the Middle East*, prepared for the Group of Experts on Arms Control and Regional Security in the Middle East (2000).

Kellman, Barry, et al., *Disarmament and Disclosure: How Arms Control Verification Can Proceed Without Threatening Confidential Business Information*, 36 HARV. INT'L L.J. 71 (1995).

Kellman, Barry, *Harmonizing the Chemical Weapons Convention with the United States Constitution* (DNA-TR-91-216) (1992).

Kellman, Barry, MANUAL ON THE INTERNATIONAL CONTROL AND ELIMINATION OF WEAPONS OF MASS DESTRUCTION (prepared for the Group of Experts on Arms Control and Regional Security in the Middle East, (published in English and Arabic, 1998).

Kellman, Barry, *The Soft Law of Nuclear Materials Protection*, in COMMITMENT AND COMPLIANCE: THE ROLE OF NON-BINDING NORMS IN THE INTERNATIONAL LEGAL SYSTEM, Oxford University Press (D. Shelton, ed., 1998).

Kelly, Claire R., *Enmeshment as a Theory of Compliance*, 37 N.Y.U. J. INT'L L. & POL. 303 (Winter 2005).

Kelly, Claire R., *Power, Linkage, and Accommodation: The WTO as an International Actor and Its Influence on Other Actors and Regimes*, 24 BERKELEY J. INT'L L. 79 (2006).

Knox, John H., *A New Approach to Compliance with International Environmental Law: The Submissions Procedure of the NAFTA Environmental Commission*, 28 ECOLOGY L.Q. 1 (2001).

Konde, Victor, *The Biotechnology Promise: Capacity-building for Participation of Developing Countries in the Bioeconomy*, United Nations Conference on Trade and Development. UNCTAD/ITE/IPC/MISC/2004/2 (2004).

Koven Levit, Janet, *A Bottom-Up Approach to International Lawmaking: The Tale of Three Trade Finance Instruments*, 30 YALE J. INT'L L. 125 (Winter 2005).

Kreps, Sarah Elizabeth, & Anthony Clark Arend, *Why States Follow the Rules: Toward a Positional Theory of Adherence to International Legal Regimes*, 16 DUKE J. COMP. & INT'L L. 331 (Spring 2006).

Krishna-Hensel, Sai Felicia, GLOBAL COOPERATION – CHALLENGES AND OPPORTUNITES IN THE TWENTY-FIRST CENTURY, Ashgate (2006).

Krizner, Ken, *Collaborative Efforts Help Spur Growth in Biotech Industry: Companies in the U.S. and Canada Use Public-Private Partnerships and Access to Academia to Develop Products, Expand Operations; Biotechnology; Quebec Biotechnology Innovation Centre; Cover Story*, EXPANSION MANAGEMENT (May 1, 2004).

Leahy, Stephen, *Medicine: Biotech Would Save Many Lives in Poor Nations, U.N. Says*, IPS – INTER-PRESS SERVICE (October 21, 2004).

Lee, Jaemin, *Juggling Counter-Terrorism and Trade, the APEC Way: APEC's Leadership in Devising Counter-Terrorism Measures in Compliance with International Trade Norms*, 12 U.C. DAVIS J. INT'L L. & POL'Y 257 (Spring 2006).

Lele, Uma, *Biotechnology: Opportunities and Challenges for Developing Countries*, AMERICAN JOURNAL OF AGRICULTURAL ECONOMICS, Vol. 85, No. 5 (December 1, 2003).

Levit, Janet Koven, *A Bottom-Up Approach to International Lawmaking: The Tale of Three Trade Finance Instruments*, 30 YALE J. INT'L L. 125 (Winter 2005).

Lobel, Orly, *The Renew Deal: The Fall of Regulation and the Rise of Governance in Contemporary Legal Thought*, 89 MINN. L. REV. 342 (December 2004).

Lohan, Dagmar, *A Framework for Assessing the Input of Scientific Information Into Global Decision-Making*, 17 COLO. J. INT'L ENVTL. L. & POL'Y 1 (Winter 2006).

Lohan, Dagmar, *Assessing the Mechanisms for the Input of Scientific Information into the UNFCCC*, 17 COLO. J. INT'L ENV'TL. L. & POL'Y 249 (Spring 2006).

Malone, David M., THE INTERNATIONAL STRUGGLE OVER IRAQ, Oxford University Press (2006).

McMahon, Robert, *Remembering Unmovic*, 30-WTR FLETCHER F. WORLD AFF. 93 (2006).

Mitchell, Ronald B., *Sources of Transparency: Information Systems in International Regimes*, INTERNATIONAL STUDIES QUARTERLY, Vol. 42, No. 1 (March 1998).

Moore, Spencer, *Aid Coordination in the Health Sector: Examining Country Participation in Sector-Wide Approaches*, JOURNAL OF HEALTH & POPULATION IN DEVELOPING COUNTRIES (July 1, 2003).

Morris, Herbert V., *Symposium: Globalization and Sovereignty: The Quest for International Standards: Global Governance vs. Sovereignty*, 50 KAN. L. REV. 779 (May 2002).

Nanda, Ved P., *Section Three: International Processes: The "Good Governance" Concept Revisited*, 603 ANNALS 269 (January 2006).

Narula, Smita, *The Right to Food: Holding Global Actors Accountable Under International Law*, 44 COLUM. J. TRANSNAT'L L. 691 (2006).

NATO's Contribution to the Fight Against Terrorism, 5TH HIGH LEVEL MEETING BETWEEN UN AND REGIONAL ORGANIZATIONS (July 30, 2003).

Natsios, Andrew S., *The Nine Principles of Reconstruction and Development*, PARAMETERS, Vol. 35, No. 3 (September 22, 2005).

Nicolaidis, Kalypso, & Gregory Shaffer, *Transnational Mutual Recognition Regimes: Governance Without Global Government*, L. & CONTEMP. PROB. (June 22, 2005).

Noortmann, Math, ENFORCING INTERNATIONAL LAW, Ashgate (2005).

Nwabueze, Remigius N., *What Can Genomics and Health Biotechnology Do for Developing Countries?*, 15 ALB. L.J. SCI. & TECH. 369 (2005).

Onzivu, William, *Globalism, Regionalism, or Both: Health Policy and Regional Economic Integration in Developing Countries, an Evolution of a Legal Regime?* 15 MINNESOTA J. INT'L LAW (Winter 2006).

Onzivu, William, *International Environmental Law, the Public's Health, and Domestic Environmental Governance in Developing Countries*, 21 AM. U. INT'L L. REV. 597 (2006).

Operating Procedures of the Confidentiality Commission, OPCW DOC. C-III/DEC. 10 ANNEX (November 27, 1998).

Organizational Plan for the United Nations Monitoring, Verification, and Inspection Commission, prepared by the Executive Chairman, UN Doc. S/2000/292 (April 6, 2000).

Partnership Action Plan against Terrorism, NATO (November 22, 2002).

Pearson, Graham S., & Malcolm Dando, *Visits: An Essential and Effective Pillar*, BRIEFING PAPER NO. 18, Department of Peace Studies, University of Bradford (January 1999).

Pearson, Graham S., *The Necessity for Non-Challenge Visits*, Briefing Paper #2, Bradford: Department of Peace Studies, University of Bradford (September 1997).

Perkovich, George, *How to be a Nuclear Watchdog*, FOREIGN POLICY (January/February 2005).

Picker, Colin B., *A View from 40,000 Feet: International Law and the Invisible Hand of Technology*, 23 CARDOZO L. REV. 149 (November 2001).

Poverty, Infectious Disease, and Environmental Degradation as Threats to Collective Security: A UN Panel Report, POPULATION AND DEVELOPMENT REVIEW, Vol. 31, No. 3 (September 1, 2005).

Pridan-Frank, Shira, *Human-Genomics: A Challenge to the Rules of the Game of International Law*, 40 COLUM. J. TRANSNAT'L L. 619 (2002).

Qaim, Matin, *Agricultural Biotechnology Adoption in Developing Countries*, AMERICAN JOURNAL OF AGRICULTURAL ECONOMICS, Vol. 87, No. 5 (December 1, 2005).

Rappert, Brian, *Biological Weapons and the Life Sciences: The Potential for Professional Codes*, SCIENCE, TECHNOLOGY AND THE CBW REGIMES (2005).

Raustiala, Kal, *Compliance and Effectiveness in International Regulatory Cooperation*, 32 CASE W. RES. J. INT'L. 387 (Summer 2000).

Regulations for Expert Advisory Panels and Committees, in WORLD HEALTH ORGANIZATION: BASIC DOCUMENTS, 45th ed. World Health Organization (2005).

Reich, Arie, *The WTO as a Law-Harmonizing Institution*, 25 U. PA. J. INT'L ECON. L. 321 (Spring 2004).

Retzlaff-Roberts, Donna, et al., *Technical Efficiency in the Use of Health Care Resources: A Comparison of OECD Countries*, HEALTH POLICY, Vol. 69 (2004).

Robinson, Nicholas A., *IUCN as Catalyst for a Law of the Biosphere: Acting Globally and Locally*, 35 ENVTL. L. 249 (Spring 2005).

Rosenberg, Jonathan, & Linus Spencer Thomas, *Participating or Just Talking? Sustainable Development Councils and the Implementation of Agenda 21*, GLOBAL ENVIRONMENTAL POLITICS, MIT Press (May 2005).

Ruger, Jennifer Prah, *Toward a Theory of a Right to Health: Capability and Incompletely Theorized Agreements*, 18 YALE J.L. & HUMAN. 273 (Summer 2006).

Sagar, Ambuj D., & Stacy D. VanDeveer, *Capacity Development for the Environment: Broadening the Scope*, GLOBAL ENVIRONMENTAL POLITICS (August 2005).

Sarooshi, Dan, *Diversity or Cacophony?: New Sources of Norms in International Law Symposium: Article: The Essentially Contested Nature of the Concept of Sovereignty: Implications for the Exercise by International Organizations of Delegated Powers of Government*, 25 MICH. J. INT'L L. 1107 (Summer 2004).

Sassen, Saskia, *Symposium: Globalization and Governance: The Prospects for Democracy: Part I: Transnational and Supranational Democracy: The Participation of States and Citizens in Global Governance*, 10 IND. J. GLOBAL LEG. STUD. 5 (Winter 2003).

Science and Technology for Development, United Nations General Assembly, Resolution 58/200 (January 30, 2004).

Sell, Susan K., *Symposium: SARS, Public Health, and Global Governance: Article: The Quest for Global Governance in Intellectual Property and Public Health: Structural, Discursive, and Institutional Dimensions*, 77 TEMP. L. REV. 363 (Summer 2004).

Shaffer, Gregory, *Can WTO Technical Assistance and Capacity-Building Serve Developing Countries?*, 23 Wis. Int'l L.J. 643 (Fall 2005).

Singer, Peter A., et al., *Harnessing Nanotechnology to Improve Global Equity: The Less Industrialized Countries Are Eager to Play an Early Role in Developing this Technology; The Global Community Should Help Them*, Issues in Science and Technology, Vol. 21, No. 4 (June 22, 2005).

Slaughter, Anne-Marie, *Note and Comment: Security, Solidarity, and Sovereignty: The Grand Themes of UN Reform*, 99 A.J.I.L. 619 (July 2005).

Sokonu, M. K. Cissé, & J-Philippe Thomas, *Capacity Building: Lessons from Sub-Saharan Africa*, Environnement et Développement du Tiers-Monde. (1998).

Steinberg, Paul F., *Understanding Policy Change in Developing Countries: The Spheres of Influence Framework*, Global Environmental Politics (February 2003).

Stephan, Paul B., *Symposium – Institutions for International Economic Integration: Accountability and International Lawmaking: Rules, Rents, and Legitimacy*, 17 NW J. Int'l L. & Bus. 681 (Winter 1996/Spring 1997).

Stone, Christopher D., *Common but Differentiated Responsibilities in International Law*, 98 A.J.I.L. 276 (April 2004).

Stroud, Alice, *A Review of the Role of the CITES Secretariat in the Implementation of the Non-Detriment Funding Requirement*, 30 Wm. & Mary Envt'l. L. & Pol'y Rev. 661 (Spring 2006).

Swepston, Lee, *Human Rights Law and Freedom of Association: Development Through ILO Supervision*, International Labour Review, Vol. 137, No. 2 (1998).

Swope, Christopher, *The Biotech Bet*, Governing Magazine (March 1999).

Sylvan, J. C., *The Millennium Development Goals and HIV/AIDS*, Sustainable Development Law & Policy (Fall 2005).

Tan, David, *Towards a New Regime for the Protection of Outer Space as the "Province of All Mankind,"* 25 Yale J. Int'l L. 145 (Winter 2000).

Tannenwald, Nina, *Law versus Power on the High Frontier: The Case for a Rule-Based Regime for Outer Space*, 29 Yale J. Int'l L. 363 (Summer 2004).

Tarullo, Daniel K., *The Limits of Institutional Design: Implementing the OECD Anti-Bribery Convention*, 44 Va. J. Int'l L. 665 (Spring 2004).

Taylor, Allyn L., *Governing the Globalization of Public Health*, 32 J.L. Med. & Ethics 500 (Fall 2004).

The Biotechnology Promise: Capacity-building for Participation of Developing Countries in the Bioeconomy, United Nations Conference on Trade and Development, UNCTAD/ITE/IPC/2004/2 (2004).

The Fundamental Role of Science and Technology in International Development: An Imperative for the U.S. Agency for International Development, National Academies Press (2006).

The World Bank and Biosafety: Questions and Answers, The World Bank, *available at* http://web.worldbank.org/WBSITE/EXTERNAL/TOPICS/ENVIRONMENT/

EXTBIODIVERSITY/0,,contentMDK:21009141~menuPK:2794906~pagePK:2100 58~piPK:210062~theSitePK:400953,00.html.

Theisen, Christine, & Stacye Bruckbauer, *Defining Global Health: Who Is Responsible for the World's Burden of Disease?*, JOURNAL OF THE NATIONAL CANCER INSTITUTE (November 5, 2003).

Tucker, Jonathan B., *Updating the International Health Regulations*, BIOSECURITY AND BIOTERRORISM: BIODEFENSE STRATEGY, PRACTICE, AND SCIENCE, Vol. 3, No. 4 (2005).

Twenty-first Quarterly Report of the Activities of UNMOVIC (May 27, 2005).

United Nations Millennium Declaration (also known as the "United Nations Millennium Development Goals"), Resolution adopted by the General Assembly, UN DOC. A/RES/55/2 (September 18, 2000).

Uniting Against Terrorism: Recommendations for a Global Counter-Terrorism Strategy, Report of the Secretary-General, UN DOC. A/60/825 (April 27, 2006).

Using Outer Space for Peaceful Purposes, M2 PRESSWIRE, (October 18, 2005).

Van Lear, Alison, *Loud Talk about a Quiet Issue: The International Atomic Energy Agency's Struggle to Maintain the Confidentiality of Information Gained in Nuclear Facility, Inspections*, 28 GA. J. INT'L & COMP. L. 349 (2000).

Varmus, H. et al., *Grand Challenges in Global Health; Public Health*, SCIENCE (October 17, 2003).

Wagner, Cynthia G., *Partners for Progress: Creating Global Strategies for Humanity's Future*, FUTURIST (November 1, 2006).

Wallach, Lori M., *Symposium: Globalization and Sovereignty: Accountable Governance in the Era of Globalization: The WTO, NAFTA, and International Harmonization of Standards*, 50 KAN. L. REV. 823 (May 2002).

Walser, Bryan L., *Shared Technical Decision-making and the Disaggregation of Sovereignty: International Regulatory Police, Expert Communities, and the Multinational Pharmaceutical Industry*, 72 TUL. L. REV. 1597 (May 1998).

Whitman, Jim, *Disseminative Systems and Global Governance*, GLOBAL GOVERNANCE, Vol. 11, No. 1 (January 1, 2005).

Whitman, Jim, *Human Systems and Global Governance*, SYSTEMS RESEARCH AND BEHAVIORAL SCIENCE (July 1, 2005).

Wong, Jacky, *Database Centre for Life Sciences*, SOUTH CHINA MORNING POST (Hong Kong) (March 5, 1998).

Yamin, Alicia Ely, *Not Just a Tragedy: Access to Medications as a Right Under International Law*, 21 B.U. INT'L L.J. 325 (Fall 2003).

Index

Africa, 31, 156, 158, 237
agro-violence
  availability and feasibility, 41–42
  crop diseases, 43–44
  economic devastation, 40–41
  International Plant Protection
    Convention, 44
  livestock diseases, 42–43
airports, 17, 164, 165, 168, 189
Al Qaeda
  acquisition of bioagents, expertise,
    77–79
  bioviolence preparations, plots,
    78–80
  Encyclopedia of Jihad, 72
  legality of bioviolence, 74–77
  motivation for bioviolence, 73–78
  principle of reciprocity, 75
American Medical Association, 141
American Type Culture Collection
  (ATCC), 62, 82
Animal Health Organization (OIE), 41, 44,
  110, 113
anthrax
  2001 attacks, 14, 34, 94, 108, 150, 157,
    176
  Al Qaeda interest in, 77–80
  Aum Shinrikyo interest in, 81
  availability, 34–35
  characteristics and symptoms, 22,
    33–34
  dissemination methods, 12, 33–38
  extremist group interest in, 82

historical use and development as a
    bioweapon, 56, 57–58, 60–63, 64, 69,
    70
  modification of, 49, 63, 69, 133, 134
  Sverdlovsk accident, 60
  vaccine, 34–35, 94, 150, 151, 155, 176,
    179
  weaponization challenges, 35–36
arms control, 65, 69, 70, 93, 194, 234, 239

biochemical weapons, 200
biodefense
  classification issues, 143, 209–211
  funding, 150
  overview, 207–209
  projects of concern, 211–213
  strengthening confidence, 194, 213–215
  vaccine development, 154
Biological Weapons Convention
  Article I – general purpose criterion,
    196–197
  Article IV – national legislation
    requirement, 117, 125
  Article X – protection of biotechnology
    exchange, 220
  compliance and verification, 125, 205
  condemned agents, 110
  confidence building measures, 206
  defining biological weapons, 193,
    195–196
  governance structure and the lack
    thereof, 98, 125, 205, 220–221
  Implementation Support Unit, 193

Biological Weapons Convention (*cont.*)
nonlethal bioagents, 197–198
nonproliferation, 98
normative prohibition of biological
weapons, 192
ratification of, 59, 65, 71
Review Conferences, 125, 192–195
strengthening the BWC, 125, 194
bio-offender, defined, 6
bioregulators and inhibitors, 52–53
biosafety, 113, 114, 125, 237
bioscience
anxieties, 105–108
bioscience defined, 1
bioscience paradox, 92, 132, 134, 135
bioviolence risks, 19, 20
codes of conduct, ethics, 88, 114,
139–142, 195, 228
constraining development, 136–139
criminal bioscience, 103, 105, 109, 142,
143
dangerous research, 18, 140, 144
disease construction, 51–52
dual-use research, 133–134
emerging advances, 47–54, 93, 224, 226
free trade concerns, 220
molecular biology, 49
oversight, 134–136, 142, 146
policy discussions, 91, 92–94, 136
professional education, certification,
144–146
research of concern, 138
right to bioscience, 228
scientific freedom, 103, 136
sythetic viruses, 52
transformative phenomena, 3, 4
whistleblowers, 146–147
Bioshield. *See* United States programs
and initiatives
biosurveillance
clues of a bioviolence attack, 170
databases, potential utility, 111, 115,
121, 123
national health security information
infrastructure, 172
overview, 172
pathogen marking, 111–112
bioviolence
clues of preparations, 120

commission of, 11–12
criminalization of, 95
delayed effects, 12–15
distinguished from bioterrorism, 5–6
evaluating risks, 18–19
methods of attack, 20–24, 33–36, 38
policy failure, 2–3
potential for devastation, 15
self-infection scenarios, 27, 31, 32, 33,
35, 120
tactics behind an attack, 14–15
BioWatch, 167, 168
bioweapons
agents historically used, 45–47
alleged bioweapons programs, 66,
68–71
compared to nuclear weapons, 16–17
ethnic-specific bioweapons, 51
international nonproliferation,
192–195
military efficacy, 67–68
modification of, 49–50
offensive programs, 56–66
technical hurdles, 35–36, 109, 116
terminology, 6
the right to bioweapons, 193
botulinum
Al Qaeda interest in, 77, 79
assassination attempts, 39
characteristics and symptoms, 22,
38–39
dissemination methods, 39
extremist group interest in, 81
historical use and development as a
bioweapon, 58, 61–63, 64
Iraqi weaponization, 39, 62
milk supply contamination, 40
overview, 38–40
brucellosis, 62
historical use, 57, 58

capacity building, 231–233, 237
Cartegena Protocol on Biosafety, 237
Chemical Weapons Convention, 217, 221
cholera, 22
historical use, 57, 69
civil liberties and privacy, 118, 119, 122,
123, 143, 144, 160, 173, 182, 185, 190,
235

contagion
  panic, 1, 13, 14, 18, 19, 21, 38, 163, 179, 184–185
  preventing spread, 173–184
Council for Responsible Genetics, 141
crimes against humanity, 94

detecting criminal preparations
  clues and patters, 119–121
  databases. *See* biosurveillance: databases, potential utility of
  detecting and analyzing attacks, 169–171
  pattern recognition, 121–122

Egypt bioweapons program
  historical overview, 64–65
  Military Plant 801, 65, 193
extremist groups linked to bioviolence
  Aum Shinrikyo, 31, 37, 81, 120
  Benchellali network, 81
  collectively, 71–72
  Dark Harvest Commandos, 83
  Hamas, 70
  Islamic fundamentalists. *See* Al Qaeda
  Islamic Jihad, 70
  Jemaah Islamiyah, 78
  Minnesota Patriots Council, 82, 83
  Rajneeshee Cult, 81
  Republic of Texas, 82
  World Islamic Front Against Jews and Crusaders, 79

French Naval Chemical Research Laboratory, 56

Geneva Protocol, 56–57, 193, 238
German bioweapons program, 56

hardening targets
  against attacks, generally, 164
  air circulation systems, 37, 38, 58, 165, 166
  building security, 11, 16, 38, 164, 165, 166, 170
  entertainment venues, 17, 38, 164, 165
  office buildings, 34, 38, 166
  sensors, 164, 166–168

transportation hubs, 164
  water supply and filtration systems, 58, 65, 165–166, 218
hemorrhagic fever viruses
  Al Qaeda interest in, 77
  availability, 31–32
  characteristics, 31
  disadvantages of use as a weapon, 33
  dissemination of, 32–33
  ebola, 22, 26, 31, 33, 52, 59, 94, 133, 150
  historical use and development as a bioweapon, 57, 59, 60, 70
  marburg, 22, 31, 33, 60
  modification of, 26, 32, 133
  transmissibility, 32
  vaccine development, 152
  weaponization, 31
HIV/AIDS, 3, 14, 25, 157–158, 223, 231, 234

influenza
  Avian Flu, 3, 29, 40, 50
  characteristics and symptoms, 22, 28
  genetic code publication, 29, 137–138
  lethality, 28–29
  modification of, 28, 50
  Spanish Flu (1918), 28–29, 30, 101, 109, 139
  Spanish Flu, reconstruction of, 52
  United States preparations against, 29
  vaccines and antivirals, 29–30
Institute for Viral Preparations, 25
Interacademy Panel on International Issues, 141
International Atomic Energy Agency, 217, 221
International Civil Aviation Organization, 127
International Committee of the Red Cross, 197
International Maritime Organization, 128
International Science and Technology Center, 216
International Union of Microbiological Scientists, 141

Interpol
   assessing risks, 18–19
   Bioterrorism Prevention Program, 111,
      174
   harmonizing standards, 226
   improvement of law enforcement
      authority, 101
   police training programs, 2, 116, 171,
      174
   Preventing BioTerrorism Office, 116
Iran's bioweapons program
   historical overview, 70–71
   Soviet scientific training, 61
Iraq's bioweapons program
   Al-Hakam Facility (Project 324), 62
   anti-crop agents, 40
   history of, 61–63, 66
   Military Industrial Commission, 62
   UNSCOM & UNMOVIC inspections,
      63, 239, 240
Israel's bioweapons program, 64–66

Japan's bioweapons program – Unit 731,
   57, 59, 182

laboratory security, 35, 51, 88, 102,
   112–114, 134
law enforcement
   cooperation with public health, 171
   denial tactics, 109
   due process concerns, 118–119
   interdiction, 116–124
   investigations, 124
   legal gaps, 102–103, 117–118
   regulation and oversight of bioscience.
      See bioscience: anxieties
   responsibilities, 101–102
   tracking critical items. *See* movement
      of critical items

medical counter-measures
   civil liberties protections, 182, 190
   compulsory and voluntary
      vaccinations, 175–178, 181–184
   effective communication, 184–185
   mitigating an attack, 13, 163, 173–185
   placement of victims, 178–179
   protective equipment, 36, 164–168

reasons for refusal, 181, 182
microbial forensics
   chain of custody, 173
   distinguishing between background
      pathogens, 167, 172
   epidemiology, 173
   rights of victims, 173
   sampling, 173, 239
molecular biology. *See* bioscience
mousepox, 59, 137
movement of critical items
   equipment tracking, 114–116, 124
   pathogen transfers, 109–112, 124
   tracking location, 121
   transport security, 124–131
   triple packaging system, 126

nanotechnology, 6, 47, 53–54, 224
National Academies of Science
   case studies, 40, 53
   National Research Council, 44, 218
   panel discussions, 50, 108
   Panel on Scientific Responsibility and
      the Conduct of Research, 144
   research of concern, 138
national legislation, 103, 116, 125, 195
nonlethal bioagents
   biochemical weapons, 200
   bioremediation, 200
   genetically altered microbial agents
      (GAMA), 201, 203
   Operation United Shield, 199
   overview, 197–200
   prohibition under the Biological
      Weapons Convention, 204–205
   terminator technology, 201
   types of nonlethal bioagents, 200–
      202
   U.S. nonlethal military programs,
      202–204
nonproliferation
   Biological Weapons Convention. *See*
      Biological Weapons Convention:
      nonproliferation
   prevention. *See* prevention strategies
North Korea's bioweapons program, 69
   Biopreparat scientific training, 61
Nuclear Nonproliferation Treaty, 220

nuclear weapons, 16–17, 61, 66, 67, 73, 93, 94, 142

Operation United Shield, 199
Organization for Economic Cooperation and Development, 224
Organization for the Prohibition of Chemical Weapons, 217, 221

panic. *See* contagion: panic
pathogens
    accounting for dangerous pathogens, 111
    agents used as bioweapons. *See* bioweapons
    marking pathogens, 111–112
    pathogen defined, 6
    pathogen registry, 108–109
pharmaceuticals
    commercial facilities, 59, 194
    industry, 19, 70, 71, 106, 107, 148, 151
    intellectual property, 194
    licensing, 155–157, 159
plague
    Al Qaeda interest in, 77
    characteristics and symptoms, 45
    historical use and development as a bioweapon, 45–46, 57, 60, 62, 63, 64, 69, 70
    Soviet weaponization, 46
    vaccine and treatment, 45
port security, 127–129
prevention strategies
    complication, 96
    denial measures, 104–105
    nonproliferation, 98
    overview, 100
    preparedness, 97–98
    pre-planning, 169
    principals, 99
    resistance, 96–97
    terminology, 7
Proliferation Security Initiative. *See* United States programs and initiatives
public health
    communication networks, 172, 189, 190, 222
    concept of herd immunity, 181
    coordination with law enforcement, 2, 107, 120, 121, 161, 170, 171
    early warning surveillance, 125, 161
    emergencies, 110, 122, 154, 156, 158, 182, 188, 189
    infrastructure, 175, 236
    lack of resources, 48, 142, 149, 171, 174, 223
    maintaining public confidence, 184–185, 188, 190
    preparedness, 160–164, 173, 177, 181, 190
    resource management, 13, 107, 161, 175, 180, 184

Q fever
    characteristics, 23, 47
    extremist group interest in, 81
    historical use and development as a bioweapon, 58, 59
quarantines
    authorization of use for influenza, 29
    legal standard, 183
    need for command authority, 186–187
    need for public support, 187
    need for redress and accountability, 187–188
    overview, 185–191
    SARS, 186, 187
    World Health Organization authority, 188–191

reciprocity, principle of, 75
ricin
    Al Qaeda interest in, 79
    as a chemical weapon, 12
    assassination and biomurder methods, 47
    characteristics, 23, 47
    extremist group interest in, 81, 82
    historical use and development as a bioweapon, 62, 70

SARS, 3, 185, 186, 187, 188
Science and Technology Center, 216
select agent list, 109, 110

smallpox
  aerosolization, 26
  availability, 25–27
  bioengineering potential, 27
  characteristics, 24
  eradication, 24–25
  historical use and development as a
    bioweapon, 59, 60, 70
  immunization of armed forces, 69
  ring vaccination, 24, 27
  Soviet weapons program, 59–60
  vaccine, 26, 27, 94, 152
South Africa's bioweapons program-
  Project Coast, 63–64, 68
sovereignty, 4, 5, 58, 89, 126
Soviet bioweapons program
  Biopreparat, 59–61
  Ecology program, 40
  historical overview, 59–61
  Ministry of Defense, 59
  Obolensk, 215
  official end of, 60
  Scientific Field Testing Laboratories,
    59
  Stepnogorsk, 215
  stockpile disarmament, 215–219
  Sverdlovsk anthrax accident, 60
  Vektor, 25, 215
Sunshine Project, 202
synthetic genomics, 51
Syria's bioweapons program
  historical overview, 71

terrorist attacks
  2001 anthrax attacks. *See* anthrax: 2001
    attack
  9/11 attacks, 11, 73, 74
  London subways, 11
  Madrid bombings, 11
  Oregon salmonella contamination, 81
  Tokyo subway attack, 82, 120
toxins
  botulinum. *See* botulinum
  ricin. *See* ricin
  use as a contaminant, 39
translucency
  distinguished from classified research,
    143–144

distinguished from transparency,
    142–143, 214
  principle of, 142–144, 213
tularemia
  characteristics, 23, 46
  historical use and development as a
    bioweapon, 46, 58, 59, 60, 62, 70
  modification of, 46, 49, 50
  vaccine development, 152

United Nations
  Commission on Macroeconomics and
    Health, 232
  Committee of Experts on the Transport
    of Dangerous Goods (UNCETDG),
    127
  Development Programme (UNDP),
    231
  Food and Agriculture Organization
    (FAO), 44
  Global Environment Facility (GEF), 231
  Global Health Research Fund, 233
  High-level Panel on Threats,
    Challenges and Change, 227
  Millennium Development Goals, 227,
    234
  Monitoring, Verification and
    Inspection Commission, 125, 239
  Security Council Resolutions, 239, 240
  Special Commission (UNSCOM), 63
  UNAIDS, 234
  UNESCO, 230
  UNICEF, 149
  Weapons of Mass Destruction
    Commission, 124
United States agencies and departments
  Arms Control and Disarmament
    Agency, 65
  Centers for Disease Control and
    Prevention (CDC), 25, 34, 109–110,
    168, 177
  Coast Guard, 129
  Commission on Research Integrity, 145,
    146
  Defense Advanced Research Projects
    Agency, 123, 203
  Defense Intelligence Agency, 70, 71
  Department of Agriculture (USDA), 174

Department of Defense Joint Nonlethal Directorate, 197
Federal Bureau of Investigation (FBI), 64, 71, 78, 145
Food and Drug Administration (FDA), 151, 180
Health and Human Services, 151, 172
Interagency Weapons of Mass Destruction (WMD) Counter Measures Working Group, 42
National Committee on Clinical Laboratory Standards (NCCLS), 174
National Institutes of Health (NIH), 150, 152, 168
United States bioweapons program
Army Medical Research Institute of Infectious Disease (USAMRIID), 59
cancellation of, 59, 67
Chemical Warfare Service, 56, 57
Committee on Biological Warfare, 58
experimentation and testing, 33, 57, 58–59
facilities and sites, 57, 203–204
funding, 211–212
historical overview, 57–59
Lawrence Livermore National Laboratory, 204
nonlethal bioagents. *See* nonlethal bioagents: U.S. nonlethal military programs
Oak Ridge National Laboratory, 204
Operation Whitecoat, 58
United States laws and directives
National Childhood Vaccine Injury Act, 154
National Security Decision Directive, 210–211
Orphan Drug Act (ODA), 150
Pandemic and All-Hazards Preparedness Act, 152
Public Readiness and Emergency Preparedness Act (PREP), 154
Smallpox Emergency Personnel Protection Act of 2003, 155
Support Anti-terrorism by Fostering Effective Technologies Act (SAFETY), 154

United States programs and initiatives
Biological Weapons Proliferation Prevention Program, 216
Bioshield, 150, 151–152
Container Security Initiative (CSI), 123, 129
Joint Nonlethal Weapons Program, 203
Microbial Genome Program, 203
National Biodefense Analysis and Countermeasure Center (NBACC), 213
National Swine Flu Immunization Program, 153
National Vaccine Injury Compensation Program, 154, 155
Operation Safe Commerce (OSC), 123
Proliferation Security Initiative (PSI), 129–131
Scientists Helping America, 203
Security Risk Assessment (SRA), 145
Student and Exchange Visitor Information System (SEVIS), 145
US Research and Development Program, 58

vaccinations
anthrax. *See* anthrax: vaccine
child vaccinations, 153
compulsory licensing, 157–158
development of, 147–149
emergency vaccinations, 25
eradication strategy, 45
financial barriers to, 149–152
for first responders, 175–178
for the general public, 181–184
global distribution and stockpiling challenges, 148, 149, 176, 179–181
influenza. *See* vaccines and antivirals
liability issues, 152–155
mass vaccination, 24, 25, 27, 186
patent issues, 155–156
plague. *See* plague: vaccine and treatment
Q fever, 47
smallpox. *See* smallpox: vaccine
vaccination rates in underdeveloped countries, 149

water distribution systems. *See* hardening targets: water supply
World Bank, 225, 230, 231, 236, 237
World Customs Organization, 44, 128
World Data Centre for Microorganisms (WDCM), 111
World Federation for Culture Collections, 111, 235
World Health Organization (WHO)
  coordination of response activities, 241
  Global Immunization Vision and Strategy, 149
  guidance on packaging and labeling, 126, 127
  harmonizing standards, 226
  influenza vaccines, 30
  international authority and the lack thereof, 110, 188
  International Health Regulations, 110, 125, 189

  Laboratory Biosafety Manual, 113
  Participation of Representatives of Associate Members and of Intergovermental and Nongovernmental Organizations and of Observers of Non-Member States, 229
  reference and collaborating facilities, 113
  SARS, experience with, 185, 188
  smallpox, experience with, 24–27
  smallpox, opposition to mass vaccination, 177
  threat assessment, 34, 45, 46
  Weapons of Mass Destruction Commission recommendations, 125
World Trade Organization (WTO)
  Doha Declaration, 156, 158
  Trade Related Aspects of Intellectual Property Rights, 155